INFORMIX–OnLine Dynamic Server Handbook

BI-TECH Software
890 Fortress St.
Chico, CA 95973

PRENTICE HALL PTR INFORMIX SERIES

ADVANCED INFORMIX-4GL PROGRAMMING
  Art Taylor

EVOLUTION OF THE HIGH PERFORMANCE DATABASE
  Informix Software, Inc.

INFORMIX DATABASE ADMINISTRATOR'S SURVIVAL GUIDE
  Joe Lumbley

INFORMIX–NEW ERA: A GUIDE FOR APPLICATION DEVELOPERS   Art Taylor & Tony Lacy-Thompson

INFORMIX-ONLINE DYNAMIC SERVER HANDBOOK
  Carlton Doe

INFORMIX PERFORMANCE TUNING, SECOND EDITION
  Elizabeth Suto

INFORMIX STORED PROCEDURE PROGRAMMING
  Michael L. Gonzales

OPTIMIZING INFORMIX APPLICATIONS   Robert D. Schneider

PROGRAMMING INFORMIX SQL/4GL: A STEP-BY-STEP APPROACH   Cathy Kipp

To see a complete list of Informix Press titles, point to
http://www.prenhall.com/~informix

INFORMIX-OnLine Dynamic Server Handbook

Carlton Doe

To join a Prentice Hall PTR Internet mailing List, point to
http://www.prenhall.com/mail_lists/

Prentice Hall PTR
Upper Saddle River, New Jersey 07458
http://www.prenhall.com

Library of Congress Cataloging-in-Publication Date
Doe, Carlton,
   INFORMIX-OnLine Dynamic Server Handbook / Carlton Doe.
     p. cm.
   Includes index.
   ISBN 0-13-605296-7
   1. Database management. 2. INFORMIX-OnLine Dynamic Server
3. Client/server computing I. Title.
QA76.9.D3D59   1997
005.75'65--dc21   97-12291
                                                 CIP

Editorial/Production Supervision: Joanne Anzalone
Acquisitions Editor: Mark L. Taub
Editorial Assistant: Tara Ruggiero
Buyer: Alexis Heydt
Cover Design: Anthony Gemmellaro
Cover Design Direction: Jerry Votta
Art Director: Gail Cocker-Bogusz
Series Design: Claudia Durrell Design
Marketing Manager: Dan Rush
Manager, Informix Press: Sandy Emerson

 © 1997 Prentice Hall PTR    Informix Press
       Prentice-Hall, Inc.   Informix Software, Inc.
       A Simon & Schuster Company   4100 Bohannon Drive
       Upper Saddle River, NJ 07458   Menlo Park, CA 94025

The following are worldwide trademarks of Informix Software, Inc., or its subsidiaries, registered in the United States of America as indicated by ®, and in numerous other countries worldwide:
INFORMIX®, Informix DataBlade® Module, Informix Dynamic Scalable Architecture™, Informix Illustra™ Server, InformixLink®, INFORMIX®-4GL, INFORMIX®-4GL Compiled, INFORMIX®-CLI, INFORMIX®-Connect, INFORMIX®-ESQL/C, INFORMIX®-MetaCube™, INFORMIX®-Mobile, INFORMIX®-NET, INFORMIX®-NewEra™, INFORMIX®-NewEra™ Viewpoint™, INFORMIX®-NewEra™ Viewpoint™ Pro, INFORMIX®-OnLine, INFORMIX®-OnLine Dynamic Server™, INFORMIX®-OnLine Workgroup Server, INFORMIX®-OnLine Workstation, INFORMIX®-SE, INFORMIX®-SQL, INFORMIX-Superview™, INFORMIX®-Universal Server

The publisher offers discounts on this book when ordered in bulk quantities.
For more information, contact
Corporate Sales Department,
Prentice Hall PTR
One Lake Street
Upper Saddle River, NJ 07458
Phone: 800-382-3419; FAX: 201-236-7141
E-mail (Internet): corpsales@prenhall.com

All rights reserved. No part of this book may be
reproduced, in any form or by any means, without
permission in writing from the publisher.
Printed in the United States of America
10 9 8 7 6 5 4 3 2 1

ISBN 0-13-605296-7

Prentice-Hall International (UK) Limited, *London*
Prentice-Hall of Australia Pty. Limited, *Sydney*
Prentice-Hall Canada Inc., *Toronto*
Prentice-Hall Hispanoamericana, S.A., *Mexico*
Prentice-Hall of India Private Limited, *New Delhi*
Prentice-Hall of Japan, Inc., *Tokyo*
Simon & Schuster Asia Pte. Ltd., *Singapore*
Editora Prentice-Hall do Brasil, Ltda., *Rio de Janeiro*

To my wife, Catherine;
for her unwavering love, tremendous support, and
(almost) infinite patience.

To my children,
Whitney, Cameron, Mikhael, and Ethan;
for your love, understanding, worrying, patience,
and prayers during this whole process.
Yes! It's now your turn to use the computer!

Contents

Foreword xvi

Preface xviii

About This Book xxii
   Book Structure   xxiii
   Intended Audience   xxiii
   Book Summary   xxiv
      Chapter 1—Introduction to OnLine Dynamic Server   xxiv
      Chapter 2—Preparing for Initialization   xxiv
      Chapter 3—Initializing an OnLine Dynamic Server Instance   xxiv
      Chapter 4—Basic Administrative Tasks   xxiv
      Chapter 5—Building a Database Environment   xxv
      Chapter 6—Archiving and Restoring   xxv
      Chapter 7—Monitoring the Instance   xxv
      Chapter 8—Enhancing Performance   xxv
      Chapter 9—Providing High Availability and Reliability   xxvi
      Chapter 10—Recovering from a Crash   xxvi
      Chapter 11—Distributed Transactions   xxvi
      Chapter 12—Scripts to Help Get the Job Done   xxvii
   Conventions Used in This Book   xxvii

PART 1 • Preparing to Use the Engine 2

Chapter 1 Introduction to OnLine Dynamic Server 4
What Is OnLine Dynamic Server? 5
The OnLine Dynamic Server Architecture Model 8
   The Process Component 9
   The Shared Memory Component 11
      The Resident Portion 12
      The Virtual Portion 13
      The Message Portion 14
   The Disk Component 15
Definition of Terms 16
   Physical Elements 16
   Instance Elements 18
   Database Terms 18
   Types of Database Environments 21
   Transactions 21
   Checkpoints 22
Summary 22
Coming Up 23

Chapter 2 Preparing for Initialization 24
Logical Database Design 25
Calculating Table Sizes 28
Disk Drive Issues 32
   Mirroring 33
   RAID 34
      Level 0 35
      Level 1 36
      Level 0+1 37
      Levels 5 and 6 37
   Software-Based Disk Management 38
   Which to Choose? 39
   Using Symbolic Links 39
   Using "Cooked" Files for dbspaces 41
Dbspace Design Issues 43
Kernel Tuning 45
Archiving Strategies 46
Setting Up the Environment 47

Required files 48
　The Onconfig File 48
　The sqlhosts file 49
　　Field 1—Instance Name 50
　　Field 2—Nettype "Word" 50
　　Field 3—Hostname 52
　　Field 4—Network Service Name 52
　　Field 5—Connection Options 53
　　The Keep-Alive Option 54
　　The Security Options 54
　　Communication Buffer Size Option 56
　　Examples 57
Environment Variables 59
　Required Variables 59
　　INFORMIXDIR 59
　　ONCONFIG 60
　　INFORMIXSERVER 60
　　INFORMIXSQLHOSTS 61
　　DBEDIT 61
　Other Variables 61
Multiple Residency Issues 61
Summary 62
Coming Up 63

PART 2 • Initializing, Configuring, and Operating the Engine 64

Chapter 3 Initializing an OnLine Dynamic Server Instance 66

The Onmonitor Utility 67
Stepping Through the Initialization Process 70
　Initial Device Configuration 71
　Shared Memory Configuration 76
　VP and Performance Configuration 86
　Data Replication 93
　Diagnostics 95
　Parallel Data Query (PDQ) 98
The Sysmaster Database and the SMI Interface 103
Summary 104
Coming Up 105

Chapter 4 Basic Administrative Tasks 106
Changing Operating Modes 107
Changing Database Logging Modes 111
Managing Dbspaces and BLOBspaces 114
   Offsets 114
   Partitions 115
   Temporary Dbspaces 116
   Creating a Dbspace or BLOBspace 118
   Adding a Disk Chunk 122
   Dropping a Disk Chunk 123
   Dropping a Dbspace or BLOBspace 124
   Adding or Dropping a Mirror 125
   Changing the Status of a Chunk 126
   Setting or Changing DATASKIP 127
Creating, Moving, and Resizing Logs 127
   The Physical Log 128
   The Logical Log 130
Killing a User Thread 134
Starting and Stopping OnLine Dynamic Server
   Automatically 135
Summary 136
Coming Up 137

Chapter 5 Building a Database Environment 138
Logging Modes 139
Creating the Database 142
Table and Index Creation and Fragmentation 144
   Creating Tables and Indexes 144
   Fragmenting Tables 145
      Round-Robin Fragmentation 146
      "By Expression" Fragmentation 147
      Evaluating the Expression 149
   Fragmenting Indexes 151
   Altering Fragments 152
      Initializing, Adding, or Modifying Fragments 152
      Dropping Fragments 154
      Attaching Tables 154
      Detaching Fragments 155
Constraints, Referential Integrity, and Indexes 156
   Stored Procedures 157
   Constraints and Indexes 158
   Fragmenting Constraints 161

Populating the Database   162
  Dbimport   162
  The SQL "load" Statement   163
  The Dbload Utility   164
  The OnLoad Utility   165
  The High-Performance Parallel Loader   165
  Flat File Loads Through 4GL Applications   166
Concurrency and Isolation Levels   168
  Lock Types and Modes   169
  Understanding and Setting Isolation Levels   170
OnLine-Specific SQL Statements   172
  Violations and Diagnostics, Constraint and Index Enabling,
    and Filtering   172
  Roles   174
  Session Authorization   175
  Rename Database   175
Summary   176
Coming Up   177

PART 3 • Planning for Database Recovery and Performance Tuning   178

Chapter 6 Archiving and Restoring   180
Archiving Strategies   181
  The Focused Approach   183
  The "Whole-istic" Approach   184
Logical Logs   187
Tape Devices   189
Understanding the Archiving Process   193
Using the Ontape Utility   195
  Creating Archives   196
  Restoring from Archives   197
Summary   198
Coming Up   199

Chapter 7 Monitoring the Instance   200
Command Line Utilities   201
  Engine Status Reports: The Onstat Utility   202
    Looking at User Threads   205

Disk and Chunk Information   207
General Instance Monitoring   211
Database Integrity Reports: The Oncheck Utility   213
Instance Reserved Pages   216
System Catalog Tables   220
Tablespace Report   222
Chunk Free List and Tablespace Interleaving   225
Verifying Data and Index Consistency and Integrity   227
Graphical Utilities   228
D/B Cockpit   228
Onperf   238
Using the Sysmaster Database   243
Summary   244
Coming Up   245

Chapter 8 Enhancing Performance   246

Tuning Virtual Processors   247
What Are Virtual Processors?   248
VP Classes   250
Monitoring and Tuning Virtual Processors   252
Adding or Removing Virtual Processors   254
Adding VPs   254
Dropping VPs   256
Update Statistics and Data Distributions   256
Modes and Distributions   257
Distributions and Resolution   257
Data Distributions   258
Data Resolutions   259
Update Statistics Modes   259
Usage Recommendations   261
The OnLine Query Optimizer   263
Factors Affecting Optimization   263
OPTCOMPIND and Joins   267
PDQ and MGM   269
PDQ   270
MGM   271
Summary   276
Coming Up   277

PART 4 • Expanding Your Horizons, Additional Topics and Technologies 278

Chapter 9 Providing High Availability and Reliability 280
What Is High-Availability Data Replication? 281
How Does HADR Work? 283
    Logical Log Transfer Modes 283
        Synchronous Transfer Mode 283
        Asynchronous Transfer Mode 284
    Server Actions When a Failure Occurs 285
        What Is a Failure? 286
        What Happens in a Failure Condition? 287
Initializing HADR 288
    Server and Software Conditions 289
    OnLine Dynamic Server Conditions 289
    Network Conditions 291
    A Step-by-Step Approach to Initializing HADR 292
Recovering After a HADR Failure 297
    Effect of the DRAUTO Parameter on the Recovery Process 298
    A Step-by-Step Approach to Recovering from HADR Failure Conditions 300
        Restarting HADR After a Scheduled Maintenance Period 301
        Recovering from a Physical Failure 301
            Primary Server Failure with DRAUTO = 0 or 1 302
            Primary Server Failure with DRAUTO = 2 302
        Recovering from a Logical Failure 304
HADR and Applications 305
Summary 306
Coming Up 307

Chapter 10 Recovering from a Crash 308
How Does the Engine Protect Itself? 309
    Physical Mechanisms 309
    Logical Mechanisms 311
The Fast Recovery Process 314
    What Is a Checkpoint? 315

What Is the Fast Recovery Process?   319
  The First Phase—Verifying the Physical Integrity of the Instance   319
  The Second Phase—Verifying the Logical Integrity of the Data   320
Informix Technical Support Options   323
  The Informix Support Organization   328
    The Front Line Group   328
    The Advanced Support Group   329
    The International Support Group   330
  How You Can Help Informix's Technical Support Group   331
Responsibilities of the Administrator Following a Crash   332
Summary   334
Coming Up   335

Chapter 11 Distributed Transactions   336
Introduction to Distributed Transactions   337
Distributed Transaction Commit Protocols   341
  The Heterogeneous Commit Protocol   342
  The Two-Phase Commit Protocol   343
    Terminology and Technology   343
Case Study #1—Successful Commit   347
Case Study #2—Coordinator Failure   348
  Failure in the Precommit Phase   348
  Failure in the Postdecision Phase   349
Case Study #3—Participant Failure   351
What Is an Independent Action?   352
Case Study #4—Heuristic Rollback Condition   354
Case Study #5—Heuristic End Transaction Condition   356
Recovering from a Heuristic Failure   357
Summary   358
Coming Up   359

Chapter 12 Scripts to Help Get the Job Done   360
Archiving Scripts   363
  archive_db   363
  chk_archiving   365
  do_archive   366
Automating Administrative Tasks   367
  Starting and Stopping the Instance   368

Instance Log Maintenance   369
Monitoring the Instance   370
　checkon   371
　chk_chunks   371
　chk_dbspaces   371
　chk_ckpoint   373
　control_chkpt_intervals   375
　chk_logging   375
Database Monitoring and Schema Modification   377
　chk_table_size   377
　where_are_tables   377
　find_db_names   380
　transaction_size   380
　strip_index   380
　dbdiff2.shr   385
　Miscellaneous   392
　　datadctnry.4gl   393
　　dbpriv.uue   393
　　html_ec.shr and systabs.shr   394
　　The Informix FAQ and misql.shr   394
　　uninstall.shr   395
　　upd_stat.4gl   396

Appendix A Other Informix Resources   398
Publications   399
　Hard-Copy and Web-Based Publications   399
　Web-Based-Only Publications   401
　Miscellaneous Publications   402
International and Local User Groups   403
The Informix Worldwide User Conference   406
Using the Internet to Access Informix-Oriented Resources   409
　Accessing the Internet   410
　　On-Line Services   410
　　Internet Service Providers (ISPs)   411
　Understanding Internet Addresses   411
　Internet Information Services   412
　　Usenet News   412
　　The World Wide Web (WWW)   413
　　Anonymous ftp   413
　　Electronic Mail   414
　　　E-Mail Lists   414
　　　informix-list   415

　　　　Telnet　416
　　　　Archie　416
　　　Where to Find Informix-Oriented Information　417

Appendix B Table Sizing Worksheets 418
　Using the Table Sizing Worksheet for OnLine Versions 5.x and Earlier　419
　　Initial Extent Size　419
　　Next Extent Size　420
　Using the Table Sizing Worksheet for OnLine Dynamic Server　421
　　Section 1—Calculating the Data Portion　421
　　　Row Length Smaller than Page Size　422
　　　Row Length Greater than Page Size　422
　　　Remainder Portion Greater than the Remainder Page Size　423
　　　Remainder Portion Less than the Remainder Page Size　423
　　Section 2—Calculating the Index Portion　424

Appendix C An Interview with Gary Kelley 426

Index 448

Foreword

Over the last few years we have seen explosive growth in new OnLine Dynamic Server installations. Most of these installations are business-critical, supporting OLTP, application packages, data warehousing, and exciting new Web applications. No matter how expert its users, every OnLine Dynamic Server installation will have one or more administrators who have the ultimate responsibility for keeping the system up and running, and the data safe from harm.

Even after administration becomes a matter of routine maintenance, OnLine Dynamic Server's workload grows and changes over time. The server is flexible and expandable, but it must be configured and tuned to give its best to your business. Your administrators need inside information from people who have used OnLine Dynamic Server over time in real-world, production environments.

As General Manager of Enterprise Products for Informix Software, Inc., I welcome the appearance of this book written especially for OnLine administrators. One of the few books available that takes a comprehensive view of our core OnLine Dynamic Server technology, the Handbook pulls together basic information that every OnLine Dynamic Server administrator needs. The information is presented in a logical, approachable way by Carlton Doe, who knows and loves Informix and has worked with its products for more than eight years.

Carlton, the current president of the International Informix User Group, heads an organization of those interested in improving their proficiency with Informix's products. In addition, the IIUG provides valuable feedback to us on our products and strategies. The IIUG hosts web pages on their own Web site, maintains an archive of the Informix news group, and sponsors a definitive collection of "frequently asked questions" and Informix-oriented, user-contributed software.

The *INFORMIX-OnLine Dynamic Server Handbook* guides OnLine administrators through all the aspects of their work, beginning with "Preparing to Use the Engine"—system architecture and definition of terms—and extending through archiving, performance monitoring and tuning, and setting up a distributed system. The author even provides a CD with runnable scripts the administrator can use to automate administrative tasks. With OnLine Dynamic Server in use worldwide by an amazingly diverse customer base, this book can help administrators quickly become self-sufficient and productive, and able to grow with their Informix-supported enterprises.

—Brett Bachman
General Manager, Enterprise Products, Informix Software

Preface

First of all, I want to thank you for purchasing this book. I know you didn't have to, but I hope you'll find in it answers to questions you might have, as well as comments that will lead you to a better understanding of this product and how to use it in your environment.

I've been using Informix products for close to ten years and during that amount of time I've seen the good, the bad, and the ugly as far as their products and services are concerned. I can honestly say that things have never been better for Informix, their product lines, and services. Sure, I wish they hadn't shelved the 4GL product, and I would have really liked to see NewEra achieve its potential; but 4GL is still a useful, viable product and there are a number of choices for PC- or web-based application tools you can use and connect to a database instance. The engines though are another story. They have never been better, or more fun to use. No other competitor has better technology to handle any need you might have in a database environment. Whether you consider OnLine Dynamic Server, OnLine Extended Parallel Server, or the newly released Informix-Universal Server—you'll have the right tool to get the job done. Each one uses, at its core, the same powerful multithreaded libraries and other technologies that lead the industry not only in terms of raw performance, but also in flexibility, stability, scalability, and extensibility. It's actually fun to know I've got a *big* hammer to bring to bear.

Although it may not look like it, this book is the result of just over a year's worth of 3 AM mornings. I am amazed that it's actually being published because so many times I just wanted to chuck the whole thing. Now that's it's almost done, it really feels good.

I have a great deal more respect for those whose books I've read in the past—especially from Informix Press. Their efforts established the publishing process I benefited from when writing this book.

I didn't write this book alone though; many others made significant contributions or provided support. Cathy Kipp originally got me into this with a couple of strategic phone calls and the reassurance that I might actually make minimum wage for my efforts. Mark Taub, the Acquisitions Editor at Prentice Hall, exhibited a tremendous amount of faith in leaving me alone for the better part of the project when I know he probably wanted to find out if I was even remotely close to being on schedule. My thanks to Cathy, the-copy-editor-with-no-last-name, for taking what I thought was a pretty good manuscript and cleaning it up to make it more readable. Finally, sincere appreciation to Joanne Anzalone, my Production Editor at Prentice Hall. She was very patient as well as firm, but willing to help a first-time author understand what was happening. Throughout the whole preproduction process, she made me feel as though what I had submitted was important and deserved to be handled well. Thank you to all.

On the Informix Press side, Sandy Emerson was tremendous. She helped refine the manuscript and advocated on my behalf inside Informix for material included in the book as well as on the disc. She too wanted to make sure this book was handled well, and that I felt it was worthwhile to have written it. Future Informix Press authors will undoubtedly have a good experience working with her.

Special mention and appreciation also needs to be made to Nancy Twomey of Informix Software. That the interview with Gary Kelley ever occurred, and then could be published, is, in no small way, due to her efforts. She opened the door for me to talk with him and provided the administrative support after the interview to prepare the transcript. After Gary left Informix, there were many inside Informix who wanted the interview removed from the book, but she was an effective and fair advocate of both sides of the issue. Nancy's "good people," as she would say; she's honest, fair, calls them as she sees 'em, and always willing to help out any way she can.

There are many others who had an impact on this project. Byron Goodwin, my boss at Associated Food Stores, has been very supportive and understanding as I've come stumbling into work at various hours, and needed time off for this, or IIUG business. Gary Kelley spent a good deal of time talking with me about a wide range of issues concerning Informix's technology although he had no clue who I was or if I would treat the conversation fairly. John Lengyel provided some excellent technical detail on several topics. Brett Backman was kind enough to write the Foreword. Angela Sanchez allowed me to include several *TechNotes* articles, in html, on the cd-rom. Chris Williams and Lester Knutsen reviewed much of the early version of the manuscript for technical accuracy. Any mistakes in the book though, are mine and mine alone. Lester, Gavin Nour, Kerry Sainsbury, Tim Schaefer, Jack Parker, Valentin Carciu, and Jonathan Leffler provided tools and utilities. Christine Shannon, the Informix User Group Liaison, and the members of the IIUG Board of Directors were patient and understanding when I dragged my feet dealing with their issues while I paid more attention to writing this book. There were others who simply offered encouragement; it was always appreciated even if they initially reacted with surprise and amazement. Thanks to one and all.

In closing, to my parents who taught me to love learning and always strive to do my best, even if "you're just digging a ditch!" My wife, Catherine, who has put up with more than any wife should have to, and this book is only the latest "chapter." Thanks for loving, and living with a tired grouch "who has no life." Finally, I don't think my kids really understood, until the end, what was involved in writing this book. Nonetheless, they let me hog the computer, they chewed me out for staying up "way past your bedtime, Dad," they worried and fretted about the deadlines as much as I did, and, as only a child can do, they prayed for me and my success. My love to all of you.

Carlton Doe
April, 1997

About This Book

Since you are reading this book, you are either a database administrator (DBA) or responsible for maintaining one or more OnLine Dynamic Server database environments—what I call an OnLine administrator (OLA). What I don't know is whether you are new to Informix database engines or, if not, how much experience you have with them.

If you are like me, opening the box containing the software distribution and documentation was both exciting and a little daunting. I was excited to get my hands on what is widely regarded as the fastest and best-architected general-purpose relational database engine on the market today. I wanted to try it out, kick the tires a little bit, see how well it performed. At the same time I was intimidated at the amount of documentation that came with it; a quick count totaled about 1800 pages. Was the engine so complicated that it required this much explanation?

The answer to that question is both a yes and a no. Yes, OnLine Dynamic Server is more sophisticated than previous versions of Informix engines and, as a result, more complicated to maintain and tune. You do not, on the other hand, have to ingest the documentation to run or tune the engine. The documentation is there to explain, often down to the bit and byte level, what the engine does so that you can be a better OLA or DBA. To their credit, Informix's documentation is fairly complete, easy to understand, and more or less extensive with regards to explaining and illustrating the concepts.

Book Structure

In this book, I try to take the dry technical details in the documentation and put them in the context of daily life. I cover topics in what I think are their logical order of occurrence when working with a database environment. First you design the environment, then build and populate it. You create archives on a regular basis as well as monitor and tune as necessary. There are other responsibilities and functions, but these are the most important. I used this approach to build the subjects covered in each chapter.

This book is not intended to cover every single feature or mechanism of the OnLine Dynamic Server engine. Instead, it was designed to help you through the process of starting up and running database environments. You'll find that I cover all of the important and most commonly used features of the engine, as well as some others I think you should know about and be able to use.

Intended Audience

This book was written at a high to medium level in terms of technical detail, and is focused toward those either new to OnLine Dynamic Server or converting from earlier versions of the OnLine engine. I have purposely avoided the bits and bytes stuff as much as possible. For that level of understanding, consult the *Informix-OnLine Dynamic Server Administrator's Guide* and the other reference material that comes with the software.

Because much of what is covered in this book is explained somewhere in the documentation which came with the software, do not assume that this book is intended to replace Informix's documentation. Nor should you assume that this book is simply an overview of what Informix provides. Recommendations and guidance is given here that is the result of a number of years of personal experience with Informix engines in general, and the OnLine Dynamic Server engine in specific. This hands-on experience is not reflected in Informix's documentation.

I do make one major assumption in writing this; that you have a good understanding of the relational database model and the concepts of tables, columns, and other components of a relational database.

Book Summary

Chapter 1—Introduction to OnLine Dynamic Server

This chapter covers the general design of the OnLine Dynamic Server engine. Terms and key words that will be used extensively throughout the rest of the book are introduced and defined.

Chapter 2—Preparing for Initialization

In this chapter, I cover many of the topics that need to be addressed from a design perspective when planning for the implementation of an OnLine Dynamic Server environment. For the most part, it is very general in scope because there are very few hard and fast rules to follow when building a database environment. Where rules do exist, they are stated. At the close of the chapter, all the required environment variables or files are explained in detail, as well as how to set them up.

Chapter 3—Initializing an OnLine Dynamic Server Instance

In this chapter, I cover all the steps and configuration parameters for creating an OnLine Dynamic Server database environment or instance. Specific recommendations are given on most, if not all, the parameters discussed. This chapter is very detail-oriented, as opposed to the first two chapters.

Chapter 4—Basic Administrative Tasks

In this chapter, most of the general day-to-day, or occasional, instance-oriented administrative tasks are explained. This includes adding or dropping disk space, starting up or shutting down the instance, and killing user threads in the instance.

Chapter 5—Building a Database Environment

In this chapter, I trade my OLA's hat for that of a DBA, and cover building and populating databases in OnLine Dynamic Server instances. Covered in this chapter are new database features that were unavailable in previous versions. These features include fragmented tables, partitioned indexes, and OnLine Dynamic Server-specific SQL statements such as roles and a type of database "superuser" command.

Chapter 6—Archiving and Restoring

One of the least glamorous but still important functions of operating a database engine is archiving out to tape what's on disk. In this chapter, I cover a couple of approaches to the archiving process as well as the `ontape` archiving utility. I also explain how moment-in-time archives and restores are accomplished.

Chapter 7—Monitoring the Instance

Throughout the book I will make reference to, and include illustrations of, output generated by the various OnLine Dynamic Server monitoring commands. In this chapter I focus exclusively on those commands and some of the more commonly monitored activities of a database environment. In addition to the command line utilities, I also cover the `Onperf` and `D/B Cockpit` graphical utilities.

Chapter 8—Enhancing Performance

This is the last chapter in the more or less linear process of building and maintaining an OnLine Dynamic Server environment. The remaining chapters cover other important features or mechanisms of the database engine. Many of you reading this book will probably turn straight to this chapter because performance is not something you can ever have too much of. I cover the key components related to overall environment performance such as the query optimizer, virtual processors, and the Parallel Data Query (PDQ) functionality of the engine. I do not, however, provide a specific "do this/don't do that" section. That information is covered throughout the book in the section to which it best applies. I believe this will help you understand the recommendations better as they will be given in their proper context. In addition, the effect of the recommendation can be used to better explain the concept itself.

Chapter 9—Providing High Availability and Reliability

In this chapter I cover the High-Availability Data Replication (HADR) utility. HADR configuration parameters, initialization, and the various recovery processes are explained in some detail.

Chapter 10—Recovering from a Crash

There comes a time when, regardless of what you try to do to prevent it, the database environment, or the server it resides on, falls over and fails. In this chapter I explain some of the safeguards built into the engine to prevent data corruption from occurring as well as what the engine does to recover from a failure situation. I also touch on the technical support services Informix provides and the responsibilities you have as a database or OnLine Dynamic Server administrator.

Chapter 11—Distributed Transactions

While not necessarily new to OnLine Dynamic Server, data from separate database environments can be used by a single application. In this chapter I cover, from the database perspective, the issues you need to address to ensure a successful implementation of what are called "global transactions."

Chapter 12—Scripts to Help Get the Job Done

This chapter contains documentation on a collection of software I have either created or borrowed from others that I have found to be helpful in administering either an OnLine Dynamic Server instance or a database. The software itself is included on the accompanying media.

Conventions Used in This Book

I used the following conventions when preparing this book:

- Each chapter begins with a general list of topics to be covered.
- Each chapter ends with a brief summary of the most important points you should remember as well as an introduction to the topics to be covered in the following chapter.
- Reserved words in source code examples are *not* capitalized. I find source code loaded with capitalized words makes it more difficult to read and find important points of interest the developer might have wanted me to see easily. Personally, I only use capitalized words in source code comments to call attention to an important word or instruction. This is an easy and less time-consuming way to highlight this information than building some sort of window-box.
- Flags for command line utilities are most often listed in a bulleted list.
- Examples of commands and the output they generate are shown in a fixed-width font, for example, `onstat -s -L 0 -U ar_system`.
- Warnings or other important messages are called out by using the following notation:

Sidebar comments or additional notes are called out through the following notation:

INFORMIX–OnLine Dynamic Server Handbook

Part 1

Preparing to Use the Engine

When I laid out the design of this book, I wanted to take you through a natural progression of events that began with an explanation of the "what's this" in the engine, and culminate in having a somewhat efficiently tuned database environment you could work with. In addition, there were elements of this engine's technology that were important to cover yet did not occur naturally as part of a functional evolution. This progression, and the additional elements are divided into the sections this book contains.

In this section, I'll cover thse basics of the engine's architecture as well as your need to understand the scope, breadth, and depth of any database project. I'll introduce the terminology I'll use for the remainder of the book and walk you through a simplified database and database environment design process. I'll discuss some of the hardware and software issues you'll need to deal with and the impact these decisions will have on your design and implementation. I'll close by explaining what the various preconfiguration files and environment variables are, and how to set them up.

When you've completed this section, you should be, as some call it—"intimate with your data" and be able to sketch out on paper the physical implementation of the logical plans.

Introduction to OnLine Dynamic Server

- *Understanding the engine's architecture*
- *Definition of terms*

By virtue of the fact that you're reading this book, you are either new to Informix's database products in general and the OnLine Dynamic Server engine in specific, or you need to upgrade your current engine to OnLine Dynamic Server. In either case, you're in for a good learning experience. There's no sarcasm intended in that statement; your experience will be a positive one. That's not to say there won't be some speed bumps along the way in understanding how this engine operates and how to make it perform in your particular environment.

The intent of this book is to make this entire learning process easier by distilling for you the information you really *need* to know in order to configure, run, and tune a database environment using this engine. While at first glance OnLine Dynamic Server seems to be similar to the 5.x version of the Informix OnLine engine—they share the same types of interfaces and end user access, monitoring, and tuning utilities—the two engines are radically different. All it takes to really understand the differences is to work with an OnLine version 5.x engine after coming to understand and using OnLine Dynamic Server.

While I will assume some level of familiarity with the SQL language and relational database concepts, I will not engage in a bits-and-bytes discussion. If you need that level of detail, it can be found in the documentation that accompanied your port of the software. This initial chapter will introduce and explain the architecture of the engine and its three main components. I will define a number of terms or key words that are either unique to OnLine Dynamic Server, or have a new or different meaning when used in conjunction with this product. By the end of this chapter you should understand why the product has the name it does, what a thread is, and what the three fundamental components of the engine are.

What Is OnLine Dynamic Server?

OnLine Dynamic Server is a database engine, or, to use a marketing buzzword, a relational database management system (RDBMS). Its job is to provide an environment whereby data can be stored, retrieved, altered, and deleted in such a way that the data itself is neither lost, compromised, nor altered outside the rules established by the database or database engine administrator. There are both logical and physical mechanisms within the database engine to accomplish these tasks.

From a logical point of view, there is the ability to set rules and conditions governing not only what range of values is acceptable for a column in a table, but where a row will be stored on disk and the conditions which must exist for data elements in that row to be modified or deleted. You can set up procedures to be invoked automatically and to execute specific database actions to enforce still other rules when data in a table or column is added, modified, or deleted.

From a physical point of view, a series of logs records changes made to data as they occur as well as a locking mechanism which can ensure that data requested by one application cannot be changed or deleted by a second application. The database engine has the ability to create copies of database environments either within the same physical server or on a separate server in order to minimize the impact of a physical server failure. Finally, there is the ability to create archives of database environments and use these archives to restore back to a specific moment in time should a catastrophic failure occur.

While from a marketing perspective this product appears to be just another point release of the OnLine engine, nothing could be further from the truth. Unlike the Informix Standard Engine or OnLine versions 5.x and earlier, which are medium-speed or low-maintenance database engines, OnLine Dynamic Server represents a complete and total rearchitecture of the product to enhance performance and increase or improve administrative tools and functionality. It was designed to run on, and take advantage of, today's computer systems with multiple physical CPUs and larger memory stores. In fact, field studies have shown that as more physical resources, such as CPUs, are added to the system, linear increases in performance occur. It was also designed to reduce the amount of downtime required to administer and tune database environments. Most of the configuration parameters can be reconfigured while the engine is online and functioning. In addition, the engine itself will allocate and release some resources dynamically. These two features account for the word "dynamic" in the product's name.

note

I would draw your attention to a discussion I was able to have with Gary Kelley, the general architect of the OnLine Dynamic Server database engine. An edited transcript of that conversation is included at the end of this book in Appendix C.

During our conversation, he discussed the architectural goals and technological products that drove the creation of this product. He also discusses what he believes the database engine will become over time.

Working from the assumption that this product would be run on multiple processor systems, the designers incorporated into the overall functionality of the engine a concept called "process parallelization" or the processing of tasks in parallel. They rewrote a number of administrative actions as well as the general query processing mechanisms of the engine to work in smaller discrete steps. These discrete steps are then allocated across the physical CPUs, through a process I'll cover in the next section of this chapter, so that they occur more or less simultaneously. Figure 1-1 illustrates how this process works from a conceptual point of view.

Figure 1-1 illustrates how a query might be executed in parallel. At the beginning of the process, a series of disk reads occur. The results from this step, and every other in the process, are passed up the processing ladder of functional operations. At each level of the process there are fewer rows to work with, and the results generated by each operation are joined together with the results of the other operations at the same level. Eventually the final result is returned to the application in what amounts to significantly less time than if the query process executed each step serially and with larger amounts of data as happened in OnLine version 5.x and earlier.

In addition to processing queries faster, some administrative functions such as index building, the updating of database statistical information, and the checking and repairing of the database system after a failure were rewritten to execute in parallel. With this type of functionality, though, comes the responsibility of monitoring and tuning for it. As the database engine administrator, you need to set the resource limitations within which parallel processing of queries and other activities must occur. The process of turning on, monitoring, and tuning parallel processing are covered in Chapter , Enhancing Performance.

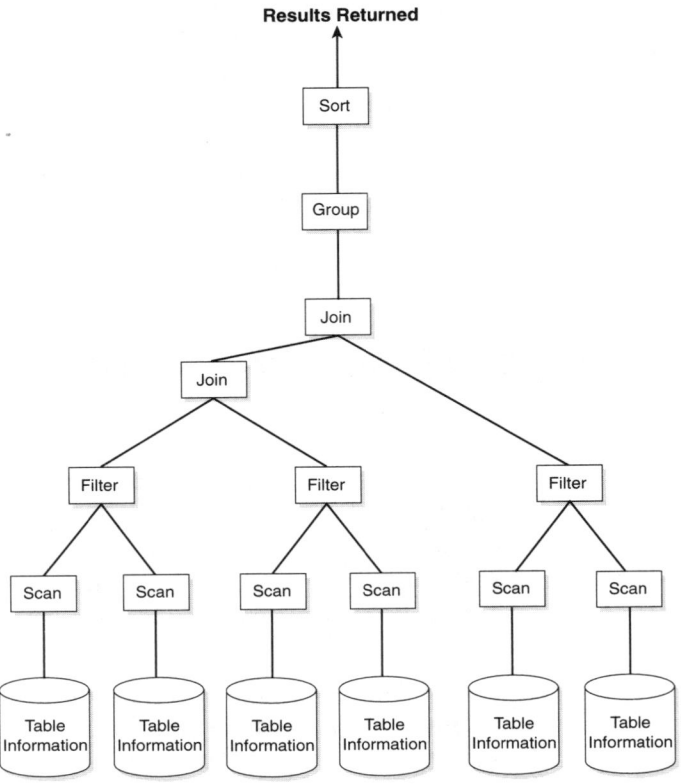

Figure 1-1 *Conceptual view of parallel task processing.*

In the next section, let's look at the major functional components that were combined to create OnLine Dynamic Server.

The OnLine Dynamic Server Architecture Model

As I mentioned in the previous section, OnLine Dynamic Server was designed to work with multiple physical CPUs and larger memory stores to create an operating environment with greater engine performance and improved stability. There are three major functional components that make up the architectural model for OnLine Dynamic Server. They are

- The process component
- The shared memory component
- The disk component

Each one was redesigned and, in many cases, rewritten to take advantage of today's hardware processing horsepower and the promises tomorrow's systems will bring. Let's look at each one of these components individually.

The Process Component

As explained in Appendix C, this component underwent the greatest amount of change from previous versions of the engine. It is the key to the performance and scalability of the engine. In earlier versions of the OnLine engine, every database process, whether it was engine overhead or end user access, was a separate UNIX process owned by whoever started the process. As such, each process had to have its own data stack, instruction cache, and other operating system overhead. There were elements of this overhead that were stored in shared memory managed by the engine, but in many ways these processes were independent of each other. Each of these processes had to queue and wait for their turn on the physical CPUs. This resulted in only average performance since each process was held "in state" for its allotted timeslice on the CPU, whether it needed that amount of time or not. Since each process was owned by the user id that created it, end users could, if they had sufficient access to the server, kill their own engine processes from the command line. This often resulted in crashed database environments and administrators trying to verify whether or not data had been corrupted. Finally, since each user's connection to the database was a separate UNIX process, there was almost nothing in terms of administrative tools to monitor what a specific user connection was actually doing.

OnLine Dynamic Server's foundation was created atop what Informix called "virtual processors," or vps for short. Just as UNIX is a multitasking, multi-user operating system, vps are multi-threaded UNIX processes. Exactly how they work is explained in greater detail in the "What Are Virtual Processors?" section of Chapter 8, Enhancing Performance. For the purposes of discussion at this point in the book, all of the overhead- and end user-oriented tasks the database engine needs to process are grouped together, broken down into discrete tasks called *threads*, and executed by vps that were written and optimized to perform those specific tasks.

From an operating system perspective, the database engine requires fewer UNIX processes; but each process actually does more work during its allotment of CPU time. Each vp will only perform the amount of work needed for any given thread at any moment in time. If a vp determines that nothing more can be done for its active thread, the vp will work on tasks for one or more other threads for the remainder of its CPU time. Performance increases significantly because every moment of CPU time each vp receives is being used to process work, not just sit there, as was the case in OnLine version 5.x and earlier single-threaded engines. In addition, the tasks themselves execute quicker because each task does not need to carry with it as much processing overhead—just the data stack that needs to be processed. Because there is less overhead to load, the vp can get to work on a thread's tasks much quicker, wasting fewer CPU clock cycles.

Vps can only be started or stopped by the root or informix user id, which makes them much less vulnerable to being killed by end users. Their design also included administrative access, resulting in the ability to look at, and analyze, engine- or user-requested activity. The `onstat` and `oncheck` administrative utilities have expanded significantly because of the monitoring functionality built into vps.

> **note**
>
> *While it has no real impact on performance or functionality, Informix chose with this release to rename almost all of the administrative utilities. Rather than starting with a prefix of "tb," a holdover from the precursor of the OnLine engine called Informix Turbo, administration utility names now use an "on" prefix. So* `tbstat` *is now* `onstat`; `tbmonitor` *was changed to* `onmonitor`. *The names of some utilities such as* `dbaccess` *or* `dbimport` *were not changed.*
>
> *A careful look in the $INFORMIXDIR/bin subdirectory will show that executables with the old names still exist for backward compatibility. These executables provide the same level of functionality as their "new name" counterparts. If you are converting from earlier versions of OnLine to OnLine Dynamic Server, I recommend that you modify all*

shell scripts and other applications to use the new names as soon as possible after you finish the conversion process. Informix has not yet said how long they will continue to include these "old name" executables.

From an end user's perspective, no more work is required to attach to and use this new multithreaded engine then older versions of OnLine. To the user, it still behaves like the OnLine version 5.x database server—only it performs much faster. Users will be completely oblivious to the vp scheduling and task switching that is occurring behind the scenes, as well they should be.

The Shared Memory Component

With the consolidation of tasks and processes into vps, all the memory used by the engine for a database environment was consolidated as well. This large single block of shared memory enables data to be easily transferred among the vps. It also allows other user connections to determine if the data they need has already been queried by another user request and can be used for their request, rather than having to go out to disk to get it. The memory inside this block is used and reused as needed to process user connections. Because the environment requires more memory to process its workload, the engine will allocate large blocks of memory dynamically until it reaches a limit set during configuration. When the need for the additional memory is gone, the additional segments of memory are released. This helps eliminate downtime to retune the amount of shared memory allocated to the environment as the workload increases and decreases. Released memory is returned to the general O/S pool for use by other processes, further enhancing the efficiency of the engine's use of shared memory.

There are three "portions" to OnLine Dynamic Server's shared memory component: resident, virtual, and message. When you start up a database environment, all three portions are allocated according to the shared memory configuration parameters set during the initialization process. See the "Shared Memory" section of Chapter 3, Initializing an OnLine Dynamic Server Instance, for more information on the shared memory configuration parameters. The following sections will briefly describe each portion of the shared memory component of the OnLine Dynamic Server engine.

The Resident Portion

The resident portion contains, among other things, general environment information and the buffer pool that holds data queried for use by user or environment processes. Normally, when the UNIX O/S stops working on a process and "swaps" its environmental information out to disk, all of the information is swapped. This portion of the engine's memory can be designated to remain "resident" in the O/S's main memory stack if the O/S provides this functionality and the RESIDENT configuration parameter has been turned on. See the "Shared Memory" section of Chapter 3 for information on this parameter. Setting this portion to remain "resident" is strongly recommended provided you have enough physical memory on the system to support the memory needs for the O/S and other processes running on the system.

There are a number of systemwide structures maintained in this portion of shared memory. The logical and physical log buffer caches are here, as well as what are referred to as the "system tables." System tables maintain information on chunks, dbspaces, locks, user connections, transactions, and mirrors. These system tables are accessible to queries through the SMI interface explained in the section on "The Sysmaster Database and the SMI Interface" in Chapter 3. If high-availability data replication (HADR) is enabled, the replication buffer is stored in this portion as well. See Chapter 9, Providing High Availability and Reliability, for more information on this mechanism.

The biggest part of the resident portion of shared memory in terms of size are the data buffers used to store queried or modified data for user applications. These buffers can help eliminate a lot of disk I/O depending on the types of queries run. The number of buffers and how they are used are determined by the BUFFERS and LRU (least recently used) configuration parameters. These two parameters are explained in the "Shared Memory" and "VP and Performance Configuration" sections of Chapter 3. When people speak of a table (or portion of a table or index) used so frequently that it's "cached," the data to which they are referring is actually stored in these data buffers. The LRU queues are used to maintain only those data elements that have been recently requested or used. It keeps those elements in the buffer pool and flushes the rest. In a situation where the same data elements are constantly being requested, the LRU queues will keep those elements in the buffer pool, thereby "caching" them.

The Virtual Portion

Unlike the resident portion of shared memory, the virtual portion is not affected by the RESIDENT configuration parameter and is swapped out to disk when requested by the operating system. The virtual portion contains "thread stacks," or thread-specific instructions for the processing of each thread. Along with the thread stacks, pointers are maintained to the data being used by the thread in the buffer pool of the resident portion. This portion of shared memory contains pools of memory for sorting data, caching database dictionaries that contain information about the tables and indexes in the environment's databases, the big buffer pools for the AIO vps, the storage of compiled versions of stored procedures, and what is called the "global" pool to handle network protocol-based application communication.

Depending on the amount of memory required to accomplish its tasks, the virtual portion of shared memory will expand and contract as needed. This is the dynamic portion of shared memory I spoke of earlier in this chapter. You set the initial size of this portion through the SHMVIRTSIZE parameter. The size of the additional segments added to this portion of shared memory is controlled by the SHMADD parameter. The total amount of shared memory that the environment can allocate (which includes all three portions) is controlled by the SHMTOTAL parameter.

One of the more interesting pools in this portion of shared memory is the big buffer pool. In OnLine versions 5.x and earlier, there were two types of buffers, regular and big buffers. The regular buffers acted much like the buffers stored in the resident portion of OnLine Dynamic Server do now; but for every 100 regular buffers, OnLine version 5.x and earlier engines would allocate a single big buffer. It was eight data pages in size and was used to buffer large sequential reads or large writes such as a BLOB write. In OnLine Dynamic Server, a big buffer is allocated for each AIO vp. At 32 pages in size, the big buffer is significantly larger than in earlier versions of the engine enabling it to more efficiently service the sorting of writes during a checkpoint or the reading in of larger amounts of data for complicated analytical queries. Once data is read into the big buffer, it is reallocated to the regular buffer pool in the resident portion of shared memory for actual use. Because of the potential size of a BLOB, the reading or writing of a BLOB is handled through the big buffer rather than through the regular buffer pool. See the "Definition of Terms" section later in this chapter for an explanation of what a data page, checkpoint, or BLOB is.

The Message Portion

This portion is sometimes referred to as the "communication portion" because it contains the buffers for exchanging information to and from local client applications running on the same physical server and connecting to the database engine via a shared memory connection.

In earlier versions of the OnLine engine, there were two connection methods:

- Remote—Communication between the database server and the application occurred across the network and was filtered through an additional Informix product layer, called I-Star on the server and I-Net on the client.
- Local—In cases where the database server and application were local to the same physical server, communication between the two occurred through direct shared memory calls.

With OnLine Dynamic Server, all connections to the database server are treated as though they are remote; the only difference is whether the connection protocol is network or IPC (inter-process communication, or, in other words, shared memory) based. In either case, the communication layers for each connection protocol are now bundled as part of OnLine Dynamic Server as well as the Informix application tool. See the information on the NETTYPE configuration parameter in the "VP and Performance Configuration" section of Chapter 3 to set up and enable these connection protocols.

Every connection protocol you want to use to connect with databases managed by OnLine Dynamic Server must be defined. If a shared memory connection protocol is enabled, local applications connecting to the database server through shared memory leave messages requesting data or other actions, and retrieve data or confirmation messages from previous requests in the messages portion of shared memory. This same type of communication process occurs for network-protocol-based application connections, although not through this portion of shared memory, as explained in conjunction with the NETTYPE configuration parameter in Chapter 3. With network-protocol-based connections, messages and data are passed to and from the global pool in the virtual portion of shared memory by the listen thread.

The Disk Component

In most installations of OnLine Dynamic Server, the OnLine engine itself, rather than the UNIX O/S, manages all interactions between the disks storing data and the database environment. As will be discussed in much greater detail in the next chapter, database environments can be built on disk drives devoid of UNIX filesystems. The engine reads from, and writes to, these disks through DMA (direct memory access) calls and RSAM (raw sequential access method) mechanisms similar to OnLine versions 5.x and earlier. The actual RSAM mechanisms have not changed from OnLine version 5.x; they're just more efficiently implemented, resulting in greater I/O performance. Because RSAM mechanisms are so much better suited to database-oriented disk activity than the UNIX file system and its series of write buffers, there is significantly better performance in letting the engine manage the disks instead of the UNIX O/S.

There are a number of physical and logical divisions that occur with disk drives to actually make up this component of the engine. In order to put them in their proper context, some additional key words need to be introduced and explained. In the next section, I will explain these key words as well as some others that you need to know to understand this component of the engine. In the "Disk Drive Issues" section of Chapter 2, Preparing for Initialization, there is an in-depth discussion of this component as well.

Definition of Terms

As I have already done in this chapter, and will continue to do so throughout the book, I will be using key words or phrases that are either unique to OnLine Dynamic Server, or have a new or different meaning as far as this product is concerned. Before I go too much further, let me define some of the more common key words that I have not used as yet and how they apply to this product. As you read this book, it might appear as though many of these key words have, or could be, used interchangeably. This is not the case. I will be very cautious to use the proper term in the proper context to avoid ambiguity as far as scope or precision are concerned. I will also refrain from using computational slang, which can be misleading, especially to those who are new to using this product.

Throughout the book I will be referring to **instances** and occasionally to **engines**. An **engine** is the compiled source code you purchased from Informix and loaded on your physical server; it is OnLine Dynamic Server. The engine contains all the utilities and programs to create, secure, administer, and connect database services to end user applications. You do very little, if anything, with the engine itself in terms of administration and tuning. An **instance**, on the other hand, is a unique working environment that *you create* to host a collection of databases to which end users may or may not have access, depending on the instance rules or database-level security enabled. Up to this point in the book, I've been using the term "database environment" in place of the instance key word. Instances, and databases for that matter, *are* tuned for performance and throughput. Any changes made to the general operating environment of a database are made at the instance level. The engine provides the operational code and maintains the general overhead as defined by the instance's configuration parameters.

Physical Elements

The basic physical element of an instance is called a **data page**—sometimes referred to as the **page size,** or simply a **page**. This is the smallest amount of data read or written from or to disk. The page size for your port of OnLine Dynamic Server will most likely be 2 KB, though this is highly O/S-dependent; some ports of the engine use a 4 KB page size. Most of the monitoring and reporting utilities covered in the "Command Line Utilities" section of Chapter 7, Monitoring the Instance, that display disk space usage will list the space in pages rather than in KB or MB. When converting to "real" numbers, you can simply multiply the number of pages by 2 or 4, depending on whether you have a 2 KB or 4 KB page size, to get a very accurate size in MB.

While data is read and written in pages, the smallest piece of disk you can work with from an administrative point of view is called a **chunk**. From a physical point of view, a chunk is usually an entire disk partition, though it can be a smaller but contiguous portion of a single disk partition, as explained in the "Offsets" section of Chapter 4, Basic Administrative Tasks. From a logical point of view, a chunk is a collection of data pages and is the basic building block for creating, or adding to, **dbspaces**.

A **dbspace** is a logical collection of one or more chunks created from one or more physical disks. It is in a dbspace that databases and their data, arranged in tables and columns, are created and stored. As explained in the "Temporary Dbspaces" section of Chapter 4, dbspaces can also be used to sort or order queried data before passing the final query results to end users. Dbspaces cannot be shared between instances, though the physical disk from which a chunk was used to create, or add to (also known as "expend"), a dbspace can contain chunks used by other dbspaces in the same or other instances on the same physical server.

When a dbspace is initially created, the first chunk of disk space allocated to the dbspace is addressed directly from within the dbspace creation process. Once created, if a dbspace needs more or less disk space, you accomplish this by adding or dropping additional chunks, as explained in the sections on adding and dropping chunks in Chapter 4. You can never drop the initial chunk allocated to a dbspace. The dbspace itself must be dropped in order to reuse the initial disk chunk.

So an **instance** is a completely standalone data processing environment with a collection of dbspaces containing temporary work areas to sort and order data, databases that store data in a relational order of tables and columns, and precompiled functions called **stored procedures**. As you will see in the chapters that follow, an instance has its own logical name by which it is known on the network and its own configuration parameters which determine, to a certain degree, how the instance will operate.

Instance Elements

Inside an instance there are a couple of structures that are critical to the overall health and stability of the instance itself. The **rootdbs** is the core **dbspace** for the instance. This dbspace contains all the instance wide overhead information and can be used to sort and order queried data if temporary dbspaces are not defined. Corruption in the **rootdbs** will render the entire instance inaccessible; likewise for the **physical** and **logical logs**. The **physical log** is used to hold the "before image" of data before it is changed. If the engine needs to reverse a change made to data by an application, it uses the information stored in the physical log. The **logical log** is used to store the same "before image" of the data, but it also records what changes were made to the data and whether those changes were actually written to disk. Without these two types of logs, the instance cannot function.

Database Terms

I assume you already have a good idea of what a "relational database" is, and how they are structured from a conceptual point of view. You understand that data elements are stored in **columns** and that a series of one or more columns creates a **row**. Rows of data are grouped together in **tables**, and important, or **key**, columns can be used to create fast access paths into the data called **indexes**.

In addition to the character and numeric data types common to all relational databases, Informix has a special, proprietary data type called a **BLOB**. **BLOB**s, or binary large objects, are black-box data types as far as the engine is concerned. At a table level there are references to where the BLOB is stored on disk, but there is no inherent definition of or interface into the BLOB other than the descriptive information you choose to add in regular character columns for that row of data. The advantage of BLOBs is that a large amount of contiguous information or nonstandard data can be stored together rather than broken up into fixed-length amounts, as is required with standard data types. BLOBs can be handled differently than regular data types when storing them on disk as well. You can create a specially tuned dbspace called a **BLOBspace** to store BLOBs. See "Creating a Dbspace or BLOBspace" in Chapter 4 for more information about creating BLOBspaces.

BLOBs can be of two types, **Text** or **Binary**. Text BLOBs, as the name implies, are mainly character in nature. I've worked with instances where WordPerfect documents, with all their control codes, were stored as a single row in a table in a Text BLOB datatype column. When a row was selected out of the table, the BLOB column was passed as a parameter to a shell script that invoked the WordPerfect program. To save the document inside the database, the user invoked a macro that passed the document back to the database for storage with an insert or update SQL command.

The same type of interaction could also be used with BLOBs that are binary in nature. A Binary BLOB is any other piece of nonstandard data to be stored in the database. This could be a digitized sound sample, digitized images or video, or anything else digitally created outside of the database environment that needs to be stored. Similar to the WordPerfect documents I stored as Text BLOBs, the application would be completely responsible for receiving and manipulating the Binary BLOB data stream as it comes out of the table.

Tables to store data within an OnLine Dynamic Server instance reside in **dbspaces** created with **chunks** that can have two different disk formats, **raw** or **cooked**. When a disk is partitioned, you have to decide whether the disk space that will be used to make up the instance's chunks will have a file system created in it or not. A chunk created with disk space having a file system is referred to as **cooked**. Tables and indexes created inside dbspaces created by using cooked chunks will appear, and act, as regular UNIX files. As explained in the "Using 'Cooked' Files for Dbspaces" section of Chapter 2, Preparing for Initialization, most OnLine administrators do not use cooked space when creating chunks.

A chunk created with disk space that *does not* have a file system on it is said to be **raw**. As I explained in the "Disk Component" section of this chapter, OnLine Dynamic Server does most of the management of disk I/O to raw disk space, resulting in much better throughput and scalability than when using cooked space. When using raw space, the engine writes directly to the disk via **DMA**, or direct memory access, calls. The data goes straight from the shared memory the engine maintains to disk. With cooked space, the data must first pass through the UNIX O/S buffer system and is then flushed to disk whenever the kernel flushes its buffers. Another reason raw space is a faster environment to work in is the disk and table management the engine is able to do with raw space that cannot be done with standard file system space. A file managed by the UNIX O/S, which in our case could be a table or an index, will be spread out all over the disk with inodes pointing backward and forward to the rest of the file, not unlike a DOS F.A.T. system file. In order to read the file, the disk heads have to move around to find all the parts. This brings into play the "seek time" and "latency" factors of the disk and affect how fast the data is returned. When chunks are created using raw space, OnLine Dynamic Server will group a table's rows adjacent to each other. Disk heads do not have to thrash all over the place to read the table since one row leads to the next within a fixed amount of disk space.

This grouping together of a table's rows is called a **table extent**. In the "Calculating Table Sizes" section of Chapter 2, you'll see that, based on the number of rows you anticipate a table will need to hold, you can create an **extent** large enough to hold all those rows contiguous to one another. If the table extent fills up with data and more disk space is required, the table will add another extent, though it may not be contiguous to the initial extent if there are other tables in the same dbspace. When additional extents are not contiguous but are separated by extents of other tables, this is called **interleaving**. Too many noncontiguous extents will cause a thrashing condition to occur when reading data, not unlike what occurs when tables are stored in cooked space. Commands can be run to show how much interleaving is occurring in an instance so that you can take steps to reduce it.

In OnLine Dynamic Server, when a table is created, it can either reside completely in one dbspace or be split it up into different dbspaces, depending on rules you set up. This process is called **fragmentation** or **fragmenting a table**. In the past, **indexes** were always stored with the tables to which they referred. Indexes can also be **fragmented** or **partitioned** into different dbspaces. This process will be explained in much greater detail in Chapter 5, Building a Database Environment.

Types of Database Environments

Database environments themselves fall into two broad categories to which I will refer frequently in this book. These categories are called **OLTP** and **OLAP**. **OLTP**, or on-line transaction processing, is usually a very disk read and write intensive environment. There are usually a large number of users executing limited and focused database activities and, depending on the processing environment, requiring almost instantaneous response times. Most general business workflow applications are OLTP oriented; for example, order taking and processing, payroll modifications, and shipping and receiving functions. **OLAP**, or on-line analytical processing, environments are characterized as having fewer total users but much larger data stores, more complex queries covering longer time periods, and less stringent response times. These environments are sometimes referred to as **DSS**s or decision support systems.

Transactions

Sometimes several database activities have to occur in unison, or all changes have to be reversed. This is called a **transaction**. A commonly used example of a transaction is the transfer of money in a bank. You need to transfer money from your savings account to your checking account. For the transfer to be successfully completed, the sum of money to be transferred needs to be debited from the balance of the savings account and credited to the checking account. This balances the transaction financially. Should the debit or credit action fail, both actions must be reversed and the balances restored to their original values.

In OnLine Dynamic Server, changes made to data as part of a transaction are tracked in two components saved to disk—the **physical** and **logical logs**. The **physical log** keeps the original values of the data about to change. This information, along with the changes made, are copied out to the **logical logs** on a regular basis. Using our banking example, when both changes of the transaction complete, the transaction is said to be **committed**. The original values and the changes made are written to the logical logs and marked as completed. If one part fails the transaction is **rolled back,** and the original values stored in the physical log are used to return the data to its original state.

Checkpoints

Periodically information stored in shared memory must be written to disk. In some cases this automatically occurs at the end of a task; in others, the writes occur as part of a **checkpoint**. During a checkpoint, data on disk is updated to reflect what is in shared memory. During a checkpoint all other database activity is suspended in order to prevent any changes from occurring during the write to disk. At the end of the checkpoint, the instance is said to be in a **consistent** state: the data stored on disk accurately reflects what its true value should be.

Summary

In this chapter I reviewed the general architecture of the OnLine Dynamic Server engine. Some of the basic terms and key words were explained in the context in which they are used with this engine. You should understand what the three basic components of the engine are, what the three portions of its shared memory are, and the structures each portion contains. You should understand the basic terminology and key words including, the difference between an engine and an instance, what a chunk or dbspace is, and the difference between cooked and raw disk space. You should understand the basic differences between an OLTP and OLAP environment, what a BLOB and a transaction are, as well as what a checkpoint does.

Coming Up

With the terminology defined, you are now ready to look in greater detail at what's involved in setting and running an OnLine Dynamic Server instance. We'll begin in Chapter 2 by looking at what's involved in planning for the initialization of an instance. This discussion will be somewhat general in nature because there are very few solid rules from which to work. Each OnLine Dynamic Server instance created will have its own unique conditions and requirements that will affect where and how the instance is created and managed.

Chapter 2

Preparing for Initialization

- *General Database Design Issues*
- *Disk Drive Configuration Issues*
- *Introduction to Archiving Strategies*
- *Setting the Required Environment Variables*
- *Setting Up Multiple Residency*

This chapter will cover a broad range of topics, all related to general design considerations and decisions that need to be made prior to initializing an OnLine Dynamic Server instance and creating a database. While much of what is covered is factual in nature, there are areas that are purely subjective. I have tried to make a clear distinction between fact and opinion, but it is up to you, the DBA, to decide what will work best in your individual environments.

In this chapter I'll be discussing database design issues, my approach to proper table sizing within a database, the various options regarding disk drive subsystems, how to approach the archiving of an instance, and what files and environment variables need to be created, or set, to begin creating an instance. By the end of the chapter, you should have a good understanding of most of the important database and instance design issues and be able to set up the environment in order to create a new instance of OnLine Dynamic Server.

For some of the issues that will be discussed, there are no definitive rules to look to for guidance. Your application and data needs will be unique to your environment. What might be appropriate for one environment will not be appropriate in another. Administering database engines such as OnLine Dynamic Server is as much an art as it is a science. With the flexibility and "configurability" of the Dynamic Server engine, performance is highly dependent on the ability of the administrator to tune the engine in response to the types of applications run against it.

Logical Database Design

In preparing for a new or additional OnLine Dynamic Server instance, as much time as possible should be spent in the design phase of both the instance and the databases it will contain. Taking the time to identify factors such as overall performance requirements, general database and table sizes, table interdependencies, frequency of access or update, the required granularity of a restore, and other elements will help ensure that the performance, security, manageability, and cost of implementation will meet expectations.

In my experience, you should never create a design for the stated overall length of the project. The instance and databases will invariably exist for significantly longer. The ability in terms of access and capacity to manage and modify the instance, databases, and tables should reflect this longer-term thinking. That said, we all have to work with the amount of money allocated for the project. Depending on how your company works, you'll either have to limit your design to the budget allocated, or help sell a budget to satisfy the design, and ultimately work with the approved budget. In any case, when considering the factors that will have an impact on the instance or the databases it contains, you cannot ask too many questions nor seek to understand too much the application processes that will be run against the instance.

Considering the database portion for a moment, you'll need to know not only how many tables there are but how the data elements are interrelated. You also need to have a pretty good idea of how much growth is anticipated in individual tables over a given period of time. You need to forecast the impact this growth will have in terms of disk space. This will determine how tables will be created and affect their dbspace placement and fragmentation. In turn, this will have an influence on the number and size of the dbspaces created, the disks that will hold the dbspaces, as well as how the dbspaces will be protected against media failure.

Other factors affecting table design, placement, and fragmentation include the types of applications that will be run against the database. Will they be read or update intensive? What are the types and scope of the common queries that will be run? Will end users be allowed direct query access into the engine with SQL query tools? If so, what protection must be placed on tables or columns?

The best way to discover the various factors and conditions that will affect the database is to create a good functional design of the entire application process. This involves analyzing general performance requirements and availability constraints. To begin, ask the following types of questions:

- What information does the end user need to see, and how will it be displayed?
- What types of data are going to be stored to provide this information?
- How will the application query the data?
- How will data be entered, modified, or deleted? When and how will this occur?
- What is the acceptable length of time for a database operation to complete?

- How much data will be used to populate the tables to get started?
- What is the anticipated growth pattern each table will experience? Under what conditions?

I've heard some people call this process "getting intimate with your data." As a DBA, you need to have this level of understanding to assist the application development process.

If you buy application software from an outside source, the same level of understanding can, in fact, be more critical. Like any other developer, the vendor will have weaknesses and strengths that are reflected in the product delivered. One of the vendor's obvious strengths will be the functionality of the application—otherwise you wouldn't have purchased it. The vendor might not be as good at creating, or take the time to properly create, the database environment that will best support the application. You can have a direct positive impact on the speed of the application by getting as much information as possible from the vendor on their database design and how the application works against it.

When the application is installed, look at the size, placement, and population of the dbspaces. Depending on your hardware resources, you might be able to use suggestions from this book, and other sources regarding table placement and fragmentation, to alter their default installation and achieve better performance.

In addition, you should monitor the types and sizes of database operations performed, and tune the instance's shared memory or query optimizer to enhance concurrency and performance. Do not simply take the vendor's word on how to set up or tune the instance. Remember though, that you might be able to learn something from the vendor, so keep your eyes and ears open to the ideas and approaches the vendor uses for any given condition.

Based on performance requirements and an understanding of table relationships, sizes, and growth patterns, decisions can be made on the amount of disk space needed to implement the design. The logical design of the database should be the guide to building the database at the physical level. It will dictate whether or not to fragment tables and indexes, as well as how the fragmentation expressions should be written. Table and index fragmentation will be discussed in greater detail in Chapter 5, Building a Database Environment.

Taking this design process one step further and considering the impact on the design of the instance, the number, type, size, and placement of dbspaces within the disk spindles will become obvious when the type of data each table will store and the expected usage pattern for each table are understood.

Understanding how the application works will enable you to determine the logging mode for the database and will influence the decisions regarding the archiving of the logical logs. Preliminary values for shared memory and other Dynamic Server tunable parameters may also be derived for use when initializing the instance.

Calculating Table Sizes

Informix OnLine Dynamic Server engines allocate disk space for tables by creating contiguous reserved sections within dbspaces of a size set by the DBA. This is done to eliminate disk head movement as the table is read. Rather than skip around all over the disk, the head can move through contiguous allocations of disk space. The end result is a significant increase in performance.

Whenever a table needs more space, the engine will attempt to allocate the space next to another section of the same table and join them together. This preserves the efficiency of the read process. In dbspaces with more than one table growing, the new addition of any table cannot always be attached to existing table allocations. This creates a condition called "interleaving" that looks very much like it sounds. An allocation for table A follows an allocation for table B. This, in turn, is followed by an allocation for table C, but is followed by another allocation for table A. After a while, you can have any number of allocations, or "table extents," scattered all over the dbspace.

Severe interleaving defeats the purpose of reserving a given amount of disk space for a table because the disk head starts flying all over the place trying to read the table. Interleaving can be controlled somewhat by calculating, in advance, how much disk space a table will need at creation time and over a given amount of time.

When I worked in an Informix OnLine 5.x environment, I used the following general rules when calculating table sizes:

- Start with the original row count for the table and add to it the anticipated number of new rows that will be added to the table over the next six months.
- Use that number of rows to calculate the initial extent size.
- Use that same six-month growth number to calculate the next extent size.

When calculating the next extent size, I divided by 6 rather than by 7 as Informix recommends. Dividing by 6 yielded a slightly larger next extent size, but the desired end result was fewer additional table extents overall. I recommend using a six-month growth rate to allow sufficient time to roll out the application and see how the database actually grows. You can track usage and growth patterns more accurately over this longer period.

Another benefit of using a six-month window is that if some tables grow faster than anticipated, there should be sufficient time to review and revise the database design because the original table size is larger. As a result, the table will not begin allocating additional extents as quickly. The new design can then be tested and installed as part of the overall development process instead of just resorting to allocating more chunks to dbspaces or moving the table into other, larger dbspaces in a moment of crisis.

A worksheet for sizing tables for both the OnLine version 5.x and OnLine Dynamic Server engines can be found in Appendix B.

I use the same general philosophy when calculating table sizes for Dynamic Server engines. However, with OnLine Dynamic Server you now have the ability to fragment tables across dbspaces and fragment indexes away from the table into different dbspaces. This can make the table sizing and placement process more complicated.

To calculate table sizes for nonfragmented tables, use the OnLine D.S.A. worksheet provided in Appendix B. The six-month anticipated growth figure is used, but it can be adjusted up or down depending on your confidence in understanding the growth that will take place in any given table. Should you decide to fragment a table, or indexes away from a table, a different approach to table sizing is needed.

First, let's have an introduction to fragmentation. Table fragmentation is the ability to place parts of tables in any number of dbspaces based on logical conditions you create. There are two options for table fragmentation: round-robin and "by expression." Using a round-robin fragmentation strategy creates an even distribution of rows across all the table fragments based on row count alone. "By expression" fragmentation allows you to explicitly state conditions that determine the specific dbspace in which a row will be stored. How the expression can and should be written will be covered in greater detail in the "Fragmenting Tables" section of Chapter 5.

If the columnar data for any given row is modified, and the column (or columns) are part of the fragmentation expression, the row will automatically be moved into the appropriate dbspace. This is one of the reasons why "rowid" is no longer a valid structure in OnLine Dynamic Server—it will vary depending on which dbspace the row is in.

One of the biggest performance benefits you can realize in your database environment can come from fragmenting tables by expression. The engine will, where possible, use the expression statement to determine the table fragments to include and exclude when processing a data request. This can eliminate a significant amount of I/O overhead when processing a query or update statement.

The ability to fragment indexes means an index can either be left in the same dbspace (or dbspaces) as the table ("in table"), or be "partitioned off" into one or more dbspaces using a logical statement similar to that used to fragment tables. In writing the index fragmentation expression, you select combinations and values of the index keys. However, you cannot specify extent sizes for indexes as you can for tables.

When trying to calculate extent sizes for fragmented tables, you need to be aware that you can only specify one set of extent sizes for the entire table. The initial extent size of all the table's fragments will be the same size regardless of the logic in the fragmentation expression that will determine fragment population.

Much like a nonfragmented table, when a fragment needs more space the engine attempts to allocate to it the amount specified in the "next size" phrase of the extent sizing statement. If you fragment a table using round-robin fragmentation, the table's fragments will all take additional disk space at about the same time. This makes sense, because the fragments are holding about the same amount of data at any given moment in time. In trying to calculate extent sizing for a table fragmented with round-robin fragmentation, use the normal table sizing worksheet. When completed, take the initial and next extent sizes and divide them by the number of table fragments you plan on using.

If you fragment a table using round-robin fragmentation, be sure to partition off any indexes into another dbspace. See the "Fragmenting Indexes" section of Chapter 5 for a more detailed explanation of the reasons why this is so important.

If you are using "by expression" fragmentation, a fragment will only take additional space when it fills. In sizing tables that will be fragmented using the "by-expression" method, balance the amount of data you anticipate will be stored in the various fragments with the sizes of the dbspaces in which they'll be created. Try to load balance the disks as evenly as possible without sacrificing the advantages gained by fragmentation. Be aware that unless the data can, from a logical point of view, be fairly evenly distributed, there will be wasted disk space.

In deciding on a next extent size, you might be tempted to make it fairly large if all you're considering is the largest or most active fragments of the table. However, a large extent allocation could swamp a dbspace if a small, little-used fragment of the table finally filled up and needed more space. This fragment would be allocated a large amount of disk space that would be wasted.

For this reason, it's preferable to place larger, more active table fragments in their own dbspaces and use a rather small next size value regardless of the initial extent size. The little-used fragments will allocate a small amount of disk space when they need it. The larger or more active fragments will allocate more extents, but these extents will be concatenated together to form one large extent because there's nothing else in the dbspace to cause an interleave condition.

So how do you calculate extent sizes on fragmented tables? Place larger, more active fragments in their own dbspaces; smaller fragments can be put in dbspaces with other tables. Use the table sizing worksheet in Appendix B, and calculate the initial and next size values using the projected row count for one of the smaller fragments you expect to have based on the fragmentation expression.

Calculating Table Sizes   31

One final note on "by expression" fragmentation—you need to balance the constraints of the total amount of disk space available with the business or system logic driving the decision to fragment. The amount of disk available will determine whether or not the cost of the wasted disk from fragmentation can be justified vis-à-vis the benefit gained through faster performance.

The decision to partition indexes off from the table should be driven by the general operational environment of the database. OLAP queries are more sequential in nature and will see less of a performance gain than OLTP queries, which are heavily index-driven. Should you partition off and fragment indexes across dbspaces, the sizing of the index extents is done for you automatically. The index extents are created based on the extent size given in the table creation statement as well as the size of the index keys. If disk space is at a premium in your environment, be aware that the total size of an index row grows by 4 bytes *per key value* if the index is fragmented.

Disk Drive Issues

Whenever I work with people to set up a new OnLine system, or to make modifications to an existing system, one of the first questions I ask is how they're "running" their database drives. Are the drives mirrored, in a RAID array, in a disk farm, or just sitting on SCSI controllers and treated independently as JABOD (Just A Bunch Of Disks)? The question isn't really as pointless as it may appear. Disk farms can be configured with or without simple hardware-based mirroring, memory caches, and hardware-based RAID controllers. To further complicate the picture, you can implement simple mirroring or RAID functionality from a software level and, in some cases, as a function of the operating system itself. Each of these options has implications to the OnLine Dynamic Server environment in terms of performance, reliability, and availability.

Depending on what your performance requirements are—or what your level of paranoia is—you'll probably have a mixture of these disk drive environments to deal with. While there might not be one definitive answer for any given environment, there are some guidelines that should be followed.

There is one statement which can be made categorically about drives that will be used in any OnLine Dynamic Server instance: **Regardless of what you do with the other drives in the instance, the drives in which the rootdbs, the logical logs, and the physical log reside MUST be protected in some fashion.** Whether you choose to use controller or software-based mirroring or a RAID array, these instance structures are too important to the operation of the instance to be subject to mechanical disk failure without immediate failover protection. The following sections address each of the disk drive options mentioned earlier and the trade-offs you must accept in using each.

Mirroring

Looking first at software-based mirroring, your first choice is what is provided by Informix within the OnLine Dynamic Server engine itself. You set up mirrors of whole dbspaces within instances, and the OnLine engine handles the maintenance of the mirrors. While the mirrors operate asynchronously, performance is affected because the engine must wait for the completion signal to come back from the mirror as well as the primary disk before a disk write is considered complete.

There are two disadvantages to using Informix's mirroring. The first is speed. The writes to the mirror are controlled by the CPU and AIO virtual processors. These tasks must be coordinated with all the other service requests these vps are processing. While it may generally be true that hardware-based mirroring is faster than software-based, it is heavily dependent on the controller managing the mirroring process.

The second disadvantage is that whole dbspaces must be mirrored; there are no options for mirroring just one section of a dbspace. Not too many years ago the price of disk storage made purchasing an extra complement of disk space to act as mirrors an expensive proposition. Nowadays the cost of purchasing a second set of storage has decreased significantly. It's still not cheap, but it's better than it used to be.

On the flip side of this issue, the argument can be made that the engine itself should be monitoring the drives for sanity because it's the process directing the write operations. The logic within the engine dictates what conditions constitute a disk failure. These conditions might or might not constitute a failure condition to an outside layer of software or a hardware controller.

Another advantage in using Informix's mirroring is an increase in query performance. The OnLine Dynamic Server engine will use the mirrors as well as the primary disks for data reads under certain conditions. This technology did not exist in earlier versions of the OnLine engine. Reading from the mirrors can free up the primary disks to satisfy other query operations or to accept and process write operations, further boosting throughput.

In an environment that is more OLAP-oriented, queries will complete faster because twice as many disks are available for the query to be "parallelized" over. It should also be noted that, while not the fastest in terms of I/O throughput, mirroring is the best option to ensure data availability.

The second option for software-based mirroring is from within the operating system itself. Almost all the popular UNIX operating systems now provide some way of mirroring disks or portions thereof with operating-system-based utilities. Sometimes, this functionality must be purchased separately.

The nice thing about operating system (or O/S) mirroring is that it is faster than Informix's mirroring and can be more flexible in the granularity of what is mirrored and what is not. You could, for example, build a dbspace out of multiple chunks on the same disk (or other disks for that matter) and only mirror certain chunks.

A disadvantage of using O/S-based mirroring is that it is unknown to the OnLine Dynamic Server engine. The mirror disks cannot be leveraged for better query performance. It's possible, however, that the O/S *may* try to optimize the read process by reading from whichever disk in the mirror pair has its arm closest to the block of data to be read.

RAID

In the last few years RAID technology, originally developed for the PC fileserver market, has been ported into the UNIX environment. This technology is now mature enough that you can feel pretty safe using almost any vendor's products for your mission-critical database needs. That said, features and performance do vary from one vendor to another.

RAID-level specifications are slightly vague, so you will find some differences in how any given RAID level is implemented from vendor to vendor. Although seven RAID levels exist, most vendors have products in levels 0, 1, 2, 3, 5, and 6. Some vendors also have a pseudolevel called 0+1, which is a combination of levels 0 and 1.

For most database applications, levels 0 and 1 (and the hybrid) are the most appropriate to use because of their relative speed when compared to the other RAID levels. If disk performance is not an issue but total disk usage is, you should consider implementing RAID level 5. Let's look at each of the more common RAID levels in greater detail.

Level 0

In a level 0 RAID set, data is stripped across two or more drives, somewhat akin to round-robin fragmentation. The primary advantage gained from using RAID level 0 is access speed when processing large blocks of data.

When a call is made for a row of data, all the drives on the RAID set initiate a search for the row or components thereof. Because each drive has a smaller subset of the rows to parse, the row in question should be found more quickly than by searching through one larger drive.

Unlike with Informix's fragmentation, you cannot be assured that a single record will be completely stored on any one disk volume. Its components could be spread across more than one disk, which could cause problems should a drive fail and there isn't any other protection scheme, other than archives, in place. There would be orphaned components of rows out on the surviving disks that could never be cleaned up or completely restored short of dropping the table, recreating it, and reloading the data.

Unlike fragmentation by expression, logic cannot be applied to how the data is spread on the disks either. A query request activates all disks rather than just those containing fragments determined to possibly contain the requested data based on the expression statement. Because all drives are handled synchronously, this could have a significant impact on performance in high-volume OLTP environments. For any given query, all the drives would be busy searching for a small number of rows that might not even exist on their media. Reads and writes would be delayed while all disks report back to the controller the status of each individual read or write request.

In OLAP environments, you should see a general increase in performance using this RAID level since larger blocks of data are usually being processed.

The decision to choose between RAID level 0 and round-robin fragmentation would have to be based on real-world tests of performance to see which runs faster in your environment. Speed of access should not be the sole criterion when deciding which technology to use. You should also be aware that a disk environment using RAID level 0, while potentially providing faster response time, has no failure protection incorporated into it.

Level 1

A level 1 RAID set is simply hardware-based mirroring. This level provides the highest level of data availability, although it is the most costly to implement of all the RAID levels because of the disk space requirements.

The RAID controllers monitor the result codes returning from the drives as well as any diagnostics the controller might run. If the controller detects what it determines to be a failure, the primary drive will be removed from service and the mirror activated.

In choosing a vendor for a level 1 RAID set, check to see if the mirror drive is handled synchronously or asynchronously, since it will have an impact on performance. Some vendors have not only the 1:1 mirroring, but also a mirror "spare" that is part of the RAID set. This "spare" becomes a surrogate mirror for any surviving disk in a disk pair that experiences a failure. This provides comprehensive and continuous mirroring even in the event of a drive failure.

You would have to test to see if any particular level 1 RAID set was faster or slower than Informix's mirroring utility. The one advantage most level 1 RAID sets provide, along with other higher-level RAID sets, is the ability to hot swap drives. Whether or not it works as advertised and won't crash the RAID array, and your instance with it, is another matter and should be tested in a controlled situation. If your level of paranoia is such that you'll shut the instance down as well as the RAID set to swap out a failed drive, unless there is a significant performance boost from using RAID mirroring, save your money and use Informix's mirroring.

Level 0+1

There are now quite a few vendors who have, within their products, a pseudolevel called 0+1. As the name implies, this is a mirrored stripe set. This enables you to take advantage of the speed RAID level 0 striping can offer in the correct environment, and the security and availability RAID level 1 mirroring provides. Because this is not an official RAID level, vendors' implementations of this will vary more than other RAID levels.

Levels 5 and 6

RAID levels 5 and 6 are the slowest of all the RAID levels. You should only implement this level if access speed is not an issue or you're running Windows NT, which in itself precludes high performance.

Levels 5 and 6 are almost identical in that data is stored in up to 75 percent of the disk space. The remaining 25 percent of the disk is used to store what are called "parity bits." These parity bits are the result of work done by a special Hamming Error Correction Code algorithm. These code bits allow for the reconstruction of data on other drives should the data become unavailable on the primary disk.

In RAID level 5, each disk holds its own parity bits, while in level 6 each disk stores parity information for other disks. The I/O throughput for these levels is very low because of the disk contention involved in trying to write not only the original data to the target disk, but the parity information as well to one or more other disks. In the event of a disk failure, reading from parity information is pathetically slow.

The one advantage these two RAID levels have is that they provide a decent degree of data availability at about half the disk cost of implementing a RAID level 1 mirror set. The only way to successfully implement a level 5 or 6 RAID set is to have a large write memory cache on the controller. This will have an impact on the hardware costs and should be factored into the evaluation of using this RAID level in conjunction with performance.

Software-Based Disk Management

Some of the functionality hardware-based RAID sets provide can also be had through the use of utilities called "logical storage" or "volume managers" that come with the O/S. Using this type of disk management software, you can build "logical disks" by taking all or part of the available space on any number of physical disks on the system. From an engine perspective, these logical disks have unique device names and are treated as though they were actual physical disks.

The disk management software can set up a logical disk to mirror another logical disk. You can build logical stripe sets by taking sections of a number of different disks. These logical stripe sets differ from other logical disk sets because the O/S will preserve the logical separation between the physical disks. Data will be striped across the stripe set, not just written anywhere as occurs with other logical disk sets.

Operating-system-based disk management software can only imitate RAID levels 0, 1, and 0+1. You can purchase software-based RAID products, but there is a significant performance penalty when compared to hardware-based RAID. Therefore, it will not be discussed.

While disk management software can make all the tasks involved with disk management easier to accomplish, you do lose the ability to control where on a disk a partition (either logical or physical) is created. You do not necessarily know if the first partition created on the disk is closest to the center of the spindle. Likewise, you have no way of knowing where data is actually being stored on logical disks created with pieces from more than one physical disk. It is more difficult to manage spindle contention if more than one logical disk or dbspace is created using the same group of physical disks. Please see the "Disk and Chunk Information" section of Chapter 7, Monitoring the Instance, for information about commands that can be run to monitor disk usage and possibly contention.

Unlike hardware-based solutions, these logical managers usually do not provide the ability to hot swap failed drives. This requires shutting down the system to deal with drive failures. In very advanced, high-end hardware platforms such as the Digital Alpha 8400 series server running Digital UNIX 4.0, there is some RAID functionality built into the CPU hardware system itself which interfaces with the storage manager software and allows you to hot swap drives without having a separate RAID controller.

Which to Choose?

Which of all these possible disk solutions should you choose? It depends on what's important to you and your site, and on any budgetary constraints. If high availability is important, then use Informix's mirroring or RAID level 1. Use RAID level 0 for higher query performance with large block transfers, such as in an OLAP environment. If cost is a greater factor than performance, use RAID level 5 or 6, depending on the level of availability you want to achieve.

If you really want to have some fun, build your tables using fragmentation by expression. Fragment your indexes by expression as well. Create the dbspaces that will contain the table and index fragments by using disk chunks that are actually logical devices created by either a software-based management system or a RAID controller out of space from multiple drives. Mirror the logical disk sets using the same mechanism you used to create the logical disk sets. The physical implementation and documentation will drive you nuts, but, provided there's a decent CPU driving the whole system, disk I/O should absolutely scream.

Using Symbolic Links

However you choose to run your disks, when it comes time to enter device names for disk and tape drives on configuration screens or as parameters to command line utilities, you need to use symbolic links that point to these devices rather than the actual device name. There are a number of reasons for using symbolic links. The two most important are disk/tape device management and the ability to migrate the environment to another server or to another set of disks on the same server. By way of personal experience, let me illustrate why using symbolic links should be used.

I once worked in an environment where the chunks used to create the dbspaces were referenced by using the actual device names returned from the disk partitioning process. One day, a drive failed and I replaced it with another. Even though the drives were the same model, the replacement disk ended up having 30 MB less usable space after the disk analysis phase completed.

Because the environment was using actual device names, and there wasn't another replacement drive available, I had no choice but to use that one physical disk. Luckily for me, even though the disk had less usable storage space, the last partition of the drive had not been used to create a chunk that was used within the instance so I was able to continue the disk swap.

Had symbolic links been used to reference the disk partitions, and I had needed that last 30 MB, I could have grabbed the total amount of space I needed from another drive or created a logical drive with segments from two or more other drives. Then I could have pointed the original symbolic link to wherever I created the new space. There would not have been an impact on the instance.

Should you ever need to move your database system from one part of a disk farm to another or change the underlying disk formats (e.g. nonstriped to striped), having symbolic links for chunk identifiers makes the process significantly easier—especially if you're using Informix mirroring.

This process involves the following steps:

- Configure the new physical disks as well as any new logical disks.
- Take the mirrors off-line.
- Drop and recreate the mirror disk's symbolic links so they point to the new disks.
- Bring the mirrors back up and allow them to fully recover.
- Once the mirrors have recovered, repeat the steps for the primary chunks.

If you need to move to a new machine, and the new machine and software are compatible enough for a database restore to work, the use of symbolic links for chunk and tape identifiers will enable you to avoid almost all the problems or issues related to disk media in the move. Simply create the new disk partitions or logical disks, recreate the symbolic links in the same directory structures as on the original machine, and execute a restore from archive.

Another advantage to using symbolic links is the ability to use naming conventions that make sense for your environment. It could also make it easier to trace the physical implementation of the logical design. Because the device name used to build the chunk is what is returned from the `onstat -d` command, you should use names that make sense to you and help you administer the system rather than something like /dev/rdsk/c0b0t2d0s5.

Creating symbolic links is fairly easy to do. When I set up a new instance, I create a subdirectory under $INFORMIXDIR called "disk". Under the "disk" directory, I create another directory using the instance name for each OnLine instance which will be running on that machine. I create all the symbolic links to the chunks I'll be using for an instance in the appropriate subdirectory using the "link" command. Check your O/S manual for the correct syntax for the link command. It is generally called "`ln`" and, for symbolic links, uses the following format:

```
ln -s actual_device_name symbolic_name_you_want
```

For example, to create a symbolic link called "styx_chnk_1" in the $INFORMIXDIR/disk/styx directory, you would type:

```
ln -s /dev/rdsk/c3b0t4d0s3 styx_chnk_1
```

Although symbolic links have their own unchangeable permissions, the ownership and permissions of the original devices file to which they point need to be set correctly in order for the device to be usable by the instance. Use the "`chown`" and "`chgrp`" commands to set ownership and group membership of disk and tape devices to be used by an OnLine Dynamic Server instance to "informix"; the file permissions should be 660 or rw-rw----.

Using "Cooked" Files for dbspaces

With very few exceptions, OnLine Dynamic Server dbspaces are usually created using "raw" or unformatted disk space. You can use regular UNIX file system space, or "cooked" files, to create dbspaces as well. If you're running the OnLine Dynamic Server product family in a Windows NT environment, you can only use cooked files to create chunks or dbspaces.

Using cooked files for dbspaces introduces a significant performance penalty when compared with raw space performance. You lose the DMA, or direct memory access, transfer of data directly out of shared memory to disk when using cooked files. In addition, you are constrained by factors within the operating system regarding file sizes, filesystem limits, and so on. The one advantage to using cooked files is that you can quickly create a chunk or dbspace without having to invoke a number of system administrative commands.

The process of creating and then using cooked files in an instance is not difficult. First, select a directory and file name to create. Second, use the "`touch`" command to create the file in the chosen directory. Finally, set the permission, ownership and group membership of the file as explained at the end of the section on symbolic links.

Figure 2-1 illustrates the creation of a couple of cooked files that will be used for dbspaces in an instance.

```
#
# cd /home2/inf_disk
# touch r_dbs
# touch chnk1
# chmod 660 r_dbs
# chown informix r_dbs
# chgrp informix r_dbs
# chmod 660 chnk1
# chown informix chnk1
# chgrp informix chnk1
# ls -l
rw-rw--- informix informix 18:34 0 r_dbs
rw-rw--- informix informix 18:34 0 chnk1
#
```

Figure 2-1 *Creating cooked files for use by an OnLine instance.*

When you actually use the cooked file to create the dbspace or chunk, the engine will expand the file created by the `touch` command to whatever size was specified for the dbspace or chunk. Remember that the system `ulimit` and other file-oriented kernel parameters will have an impact on the successful expansion of the file. Be sure to check the operating system documentation for the names and acceptable values of these parameters and tune the kernel as needed.

While you can create chunks and dbspaces using both raw and cooked files within an instance, I would not recommend creating an individual dbspace with chunks created out of both raw and cooked space. You still can, and should, create symbolic links to cooked files for the same reasons you would create them for raw space.

Dbspace Design Issues

The process of taking disk drives, dividing them into chunks, and then creating dbspaces populated with tables is two parts science and three parts trial and error. I touched on this at the beginning of the chapter when I said that you need to know as much as possible about the logical design of the database. The types and frequency of DML statements that will occur in the database, the number and size of the most active tables, whether they are reference tables or "active" tables receiving new data or updates and deletes, and the desired granularity in a restore will have an impact on how many dbspaces to create and where, physically, they are created.

The overall goal in moving from the logical design to the physical installation through the placement and creation of dbspaces is to balance I/O across the drive spindles. At the same time, you also want to set up your physical installation, or model, to maximize the effect of your decision regarding the mechanism to protect your data and enhance throughput—be it Informix mirroring, RAID level 0, or anything else.

I don't need to say how important it is in an OLTP environment to put the most active tables into dbspaces isolated to their own disks or with other dbspaces containing little used reference tables. In addition, you want to put the most active dbspaces in chunks created as close to the center of the drive spindle as possible to minimize actuator movement. If you use mirroring, be it Informix or one of the other suggested approaches, not only should the mirror devices be created on different disks but the disks containing the mirrors should be attached to a different controller than the primary disk devices. That's the science part.

Once the instance, database, and application is implemented and running, you'll see how close the theory was to actual use and make any adjustments needed to increase performance or enhance security—the three parts trial and error. The flexibility OnLine Dynamic Server has designed into it makes this part of your job much easier to accomplish. Gone are the OnLine 5.x limitations where table management was limited to a single dbspace. Using table fragmentation by expression, you can rather painlessly divide tables across dbspaces to balance I/O and maximize the efficiency of both the table and the dbspaces in which the table is built.

Informix recommends a 1:1 correspondence of disk chunks to dbspaces. Some engineers even go so far as to say that rather than loading up a dbspace with a bunch of tables or fragments of tables, you should only put a couple of smaller whole tables or a fragment of one larger table in a dbspace. At first look this might appear a bit absurd, but if you take into account the added flexibility of the archive/restore process as well as the DATASKIP parameter, this makes sense.

The DATASKIP parameter allows the instance to continue operating even if dbspaces are completely off-line, provided the down dbspace does not contain the rootdbs, or the physical or any of the logical logs. A table that might have some but not all of its fragments in dbspaces which are off-line will still respond to queries provided the data required is not on the down fragments. An error is returned as well to the application indicating part of the table is unavailable.

Because OnLine Dynamic Server now provides the ability to execute a "warm restore" of noncritical dbspaces, you can restore any dbspace that is off-line while the instance is up and running. See Chapter 6, Archiving and Restoring, for more information on the archive and restoration process.

If you follow the 1:1 chunk to dbspace recommendation as well as guidelines regarding table population within a dbspace, should a dbspace completely fail, only one part of a table or a couple of small tables will be affected. These can be restored from tape in a relatively short amount of time.

A closing thought on dbspaces: Just as you should calculate your table sizes with an element of fudge for unexpected growth, don't skimp on the size of your dbspaces. As you begin to work in your new environment, you will invariably see unexpected growth in tables or the sudden need to maintain new data elements. I've seen too many companies try to keep expenses down by buying just enough disk space to keep the project going at what was perceived as current needs. It usually didn't take too long before they were facing an expensive investment in time and material to either purge data they would rather have kept available or buy more hardware and bring in additional resources to meet new demands or relieve disk performance bottlenecks. It is always more expensive in the long run not to plan for growth.

Kernel Tuning

One significant difference between OnLine 5.x and OnLine Dynamic Server, from a management perspective, is that OnLine Dynamic Server requires more system resources to run well. As was covered in Chapter 1, overhead and resource demands from an OnLine 5.x server were distributed over more actual UNIX processes—the sqlturbo process. In this environment, a single database server process was not going to require a disproportionate amount of kernel resources. You tuned the kernel of your database server machine to reflect a more general multi-user environment.

With OnLine Dynamic Server, all the engine and end user overhead is absorbed by the virtual processors—the CPU and AIO vps, in particular. These virtual processors are separate UNIX processes. Given that these processes are multithreaded, they will demand far more operating system resources than other processes. If all you intend to run on your physical server is one or more instances of OnLine Dynamic Server, you need to tune the server to support a power-user environment.

You will specifically need to look at shared memory and process parameters. Each instance will need a semaphore for each vp and shared memory connection. You'll also need to tune for semaphore "sets" because a set is needed for every 100 shared memory user sessions. Another set is needed for each group of 100 or less vps that initialize whenever the instance is brought from off-line mode to on-line mode. Another set of semaphores is needed whenever a vp is added dynamically while the instance is in operation.

On a machine running one instance of OnLine Dynamic Server, be sure to verify that the SHMMAX kernel parameter is set to a value large enough so that the amount of shared memory the instance will require can be allocated in one block. On a server supporting multiple instances of OnLine Dynamic Server, SHMMAX needs to be set to a value big enough to support the total amount of shared memory all the instances will require.

If you're using cooked files for dbspaces you might need to look at the `ulimit`, I/O buffers, and other filesystem parameters.

When the Informix product set is installed, there is a "release" subdirectory under $INFORMIXDIR that is populated with a number of files. The files put there include last-minute documentation updates, product bug information, and so on. There are two files created by the installation of OnLine Dynamic Server that are important to review. These documents, and others that are installed as part of the OnLine Dynamic Server load, are located in subdirectories beneath $INFORMIXDIR/release directory.

ONLINEDOC_7.x contains documentation errata and updates. ONLINE_7.x contains kernel tuning parameters for the particular computer, operating system, and port of the product installed as well as technical specifications for the SQLHOSTS file, O/S patches that were used by Informix when creating the port of the product, and other related items.

You should evaluate the kernel tuning parameters as a baseline for proper operation of the OnLine Dynamic Server database engine on your machine. Informix makes these recommendations based on how they configured their test machines as far as RAM, number of CPUs, and so on, are concerned. The proper use of system performance monitoring tools will allow you to see how well the baseline parameters are actually working in your system. You'll find that adjustments will probably have to be made to optimize performance on your machine. This too is part of the trial-and-error process of operating OnLine Dynamic Server.

Archiving Strategies

One of the more important decisions to make in the overall instance design process is how and when OnLine Dynamic Server instances will be archived. This includes the logical logs as well. As far as OnLine Dynamic Server version 7.2 or lower is concerned there is, in my opinion, only one choice for an archiving tool: the `ontape` utility. See Chapter 6 for the reasons supporting that statement as well as an introduction to the `onbar` API which is available in later releases of the 7.2 version of OnLine Dynamic Server.

The functionality of the `ontape` utility was expanded in OnLine Dynamic Server. `Ontape` still only archives an entire instance, but it now contains the ability to restore to the dbspace level. Provided the dbspace does not contain critical elements like the rootdbs, or the physical or logical logs, the restore can occur while the engine is on-line and functioning.

Some general factors to take into consideration when putting your archive strategy together:

1. How critical is the data? Granted, all the data in the database is important or you wouldn't be saving it, but how much can you afford to lose? How long could your business operate while you recreate the data?
2. Can you recreate the data? What would the manpower, equipment, processing, and other costs be to recover and/or rebuild the lost data?
3. What is an acceptable length of time to complete a full restore of the database? What is an acceptable length of time for a warm restore of a down dbspace containing part of a critical table or a collection of static reference tables?
4. How important is it that you can recover to an approximate moment in time?

The answers to these questions will determine whether or not the logical logs are archived to tape, how often the instance is archived, and what archive level is used. Please refer to Chapter 6 for a more in-depth discussion of these topics. These decisions will have an impact on the dbspace design as the number, size, and placement of tables within dbspaces is considered against the functionality of an `ontape` restore.

Setting Up the Environment

In preparation for actually invoking the `onmonitor` utility to initialize an OnLine Dynamic Server instance, there are some files that need to be created or modified, and some global environment variables that need to be set. For the purposes of this chapter, I will limit my scope to those items that are required on the UNIX server for the instance to function or a UNIX-based database application to run.

The non-UNIX client environment is changing too quickly, and the effort required to get it to connect to the database varies too drastically depending on the hardware platform, operating system, network topology, network protocol, and actual end user interface for more than a cursory comment. For non-UNIX clients to connect to the database, a data-access driver such as ODBC will need to be correctly configured on the client. Correctly configuring the driver and any other software or hardware on the client side of the connection is left to the reader as an exercise.

Required files

If we exclude the symbolic links created to point to disk chunks or tape devices as explained earlier in this chapter, there are three files you need to work with before attempting to initialize an instance of OnLine Dynamic Server. The first two, $INFORMIXDIR/etc/sqlhosts and /etc/services, require adding to or modifying what's already there. The third file, $INFORMIXDIR/etc/onconfig.std, needs to be copied to another unique name for modification by the `onmonitor` utility.

The Onconfig File

The file that acts as the onconfig file contains all the raw information for the OnLine Dynamic Server process to create the basic shared memory structures for the instance. It also holds directions to, and information about, the most crucial physical devices the database server process needs to contact in order to complete instance initialization, or initiate a restore.

A template of this file called "onconfig.std" is installed in the $INFORMIXDIR/etc directory when OnLine Dynamic Server is properly installed. It needs to be copied using a unique name within the same directory for use by an instance of the engine.

In the current release of OnLine Dynamic Server, the onconfig file used by an instance must be located in the $INFORMIXDIR/etc subdirectory. In later releases of the 7.2 version, the location and name of this file can vary and is defined by the $ONCONFIGLOCATION environment variable.

While you can use almost any name you want for this file, if only one OnLine instance will be created on the physical server, it is a common practice to name the copied file "onconfig." If more than one instance will be created, each instance needs its own onconfig file, obviously with its own unique name.

When I create the onconfig files on a physical server that will be supporting more than one instance (called "multiple residency"), the file name for each instance's onconfig file includes an abbreviation of the instance name as well as the word "onconfig." For example, the reference system I'm using to write this book has instances named after rivers—kern, columbia, styx, and amazon. The onconfig files supporting those instances are called "onconfig.ker," "onconfig.col," and so on. In Chapter 3, each entry in the onconfig file will be explained in much greater detail.

It is crucial that the file permissions of the ONCONFIG file copy not be altered from those of the onconfig.std template when the copy is created or altered. Also, do NOT delete or change the original onconfig.std file. Should the file be writable by others and be altered by someone other than the DBA, it is possible the instance will be destroyed the next time it is restarted from an off-line mode.

I also do not recommend hand-editing the onconfig file, especially once the instance is built and running. There will always be rare cases when hand editing will be required, but it is better to use the `onmonitor` utility and have it perform the field-level validation it does. One small typo in this file can destroy the instance.

The sqlhosts file

The $INFORMIXDIR/etc/sqlhosts file acts as a connectivity guide to instances created on any physical server anywhere on the network. A template called "sqlhosts" is provided when OnLine Dynamic Server is installed. By setting the $INFORMIXSQLHOSTS environment variable, you can change the location and/or name of the file that will act as the "sqlhosts" file.

Unlike the onconfig.std template, which must be preserved in its original form, I use the sqlhosts file that is installed when the OnLine Dynamic Server product was loaded and modify it as necessary to support the instances I need.

The format of the file is quite simple. It is a five-field row, with each field separated by a tab or white space. One row is required for each instance or instance alias on the network to which you want to connect from the server on which you're modifying the $INFORMIXSQLHOSTS file. (This includes instances on the same physical server.)

The format of the row is shown in Table 2-1.

Table 2–1   The format of a row in the $INFORMIXSQLHOSTS file.

Field Number	Description
1	The instance name or alias, 18 characters maximum
2	The nettype "word" for the instance
3	The hostname of the physical server on which the instance resides, 64 characters maximum
4	The network service name to be used by the local machine to connect to the instance, 128 characters maximum
5	Options to be used when connecting to the instance

Field 1—Instance Name   As the field name implies, this is the name entered in either the server name field or server alias field during instance initialization. This name needs to be unique among all OnLine Dynamic Server instances across the network.

Field 2—Nettype "Word"   This field describes what network protocol and type of interface need to be used to connect to the instance. The contents of this field consist of an eight-character "word" organized into three components, as illustrated in Table 2-2.

Table 2–2   The three components of the nettype word.

Component Number	Description
1	Type of database engine
2	Network interface
3	Network protocol

The nettype word components are divided and organized as shown in Table 2-3.

Table 2–3 Possible values for each component of the nettype word.

Character Positions	Possible Values	Description
1, 2	on	OnLine, generally used
	ol	OnLine, allowed but not the generally accepted standard
	se	Informix Standard Engine
	dr	Informix Gateway product—with DRDA
3–5	ipc	Interprocess communication interface, for shared memory connections
	tli	Transport-level interface
	soc	Socket interface
6–8	tcp	The TCP/IP protocol
	spx	The Novell IPX/SPX protocol
	shm	Shared memory communication, for applications running on the same server

The first two characters of the nettype word represent the database engine.

Characters three through five indicate the network interface to use to establish a connection between the instance and the client application. Note that there is a separate entry for shared memory connections. This is reserved for applications running on the same physical machine as the database engine.

The fact that there is a separate interface for shared memory connections implies that all connections to the database engine operate from a client/server model regardless of where the application is running. All applications can, and should, be developed to take advantage of this model.

Characters six through eight of the nettype word specify the network protocol to use in order to connect to the instance.

There are only a few valid combinations of nettype words that can be used. Using an OnLine Dynamic Server instance as an example server, they are listed in Table 2-4.

Table 2–4   Valid nettype words for an OnLine Dynamic Server instance.

Nettype Word	Description
ontlispx	An SPX/IPX connection across the TLI interface
ontlitcp	A TCP/IP connection across the TLI interface
onipcshm	A shared memory connection
onsoctcp	A TCP/IP connection using sockets

Check the machine-specific notes in the ONLINE_7.x file to see which words are valid for your port of the engine.

Field 3—Hostname   This field contains the name of the physical server hosting the instance. This hostname needs to be resolvable either through /etc/hosts or a DNS (domain name service) lookup.

Field 4—Network Service Name   The value of this field will vary depending on the nettype word used for the instance. Depending on the interface and network protocol specified in the nettype word, this field may or may not have a real value in the connection process. However, in no case should it be left empty.

If the nettype word defines a local shared memory connection (e.g., onipcshm), this field of the $INFORMIXSQLHOSTS row is not used. It functions simply as a placeholder—any character value can be entered in this field.

For all other connections, the value entered here must correspond to a "service name" entry in the /etc/services file. This service name is used as a cross-reference to the network port number and protocol through which the network-based database connection will be established. The network service names for each instance on a physical server must be unique since the service name entries in the /etc/services file must be unique. Network service names do *not* need to be unique across the network since their scope is physical-server-specific. Nevertheless, it is a good idea to make them unique where possible.

To modify the /etc/services file to include the necessary services for an OnLine Dynamic Server instance, add an entry similar in format to those already in the file. Use the network service name from the $INFORMIXSQLHOSTS file as the service name in this file, choose a port number that has not already been used, and indicate the network protocol to use.

The port number chosen for a database service number must be unique across the network for database access to occur from remote clients or servers. All other physical servers hosting instances that need to connect to this instance will need to use the same port number in their /etc/services file. The service name used in their /etc/services file does not have to match the service name entered in this copy of the file.

You are generally safe in choosing a port number above 1500; however, please refer to the documentation that came with your operating system for any restrictions or suggestions.

Field 5—Connection Options This fifth field is a new addition to the $INFORMIXSQLHOSTS file with the release of version 7.1.UC1. Unlike the previous four fields in the $INFORMIXSQLHOSTS file, you are not required to enter any values into this field. This field's function is to allow you to set specific operational states for connections to the database server. As I will explain in a moment, I feel that it should be mandatory to set one of the states.

The syntax for setting values in this field is as follows:

```
option_letter=value
```

where *option_letter* is replaced by a letter to indicate an entry for one of the following operational states:

- The connection buffer size
- Connection security options
- The keep-alive mode

Multiple options can be set for any one instance defined in the $INFORMIXSQLHOSTS file. These options must be comma delimited with no white space in the option itself or between options.

Table 2-5 shows the operational states that can be set with the available options in this field. The following text describes them in greater detail.

The Keep-Alive Option Of the three states that can be affected through this field, I strongly suggest leaving the keep-alive option enabled. Only affecting TCP/IP and IPX/SPX connections to the instance, this option periodically checks the connections between each user thread in the instance and the client application. If the client does not respond within a given amount of time, the user thread is terminated, and all engine resources associated with it are released.

If the keep-alive option is disabled, the detection of a broken network connection will cause the engine to immediately terminate the threads and resources associated with that connection. Be aware, however, that in the event of temporary network saturation, the server could interpret a blocked connection as a dropped connection and kill off threads that should be kept alive.

In the absence of the k=0 parameter for an instance definition in the $INFORMIXSQLHOSTS file, the keep-alive option is enabled by default.

The Security Options The security options allow you to control how a request for a connection to an instance and database is verified. When a request is made to connect to an instance for database services, the engine verifies that the userid making the request as well as the machine from which the request is originating are "known and trusted" within the network. In the absence of a userid, as can be the case in a PC-based client connection, the network identity of the PC must be "known and trusted," and the userid is verified by the "connect" SQL statement.

Table 2–5 Database connection options that can be set in the $INFORMIXSQLHOSTS file.

Operational State	Possible Values	Description
Keep-Alive	k=1	Enables the TCP/IP & IPX/SPX keep-alive feature
	k=0	Disables the TCP/IP & IPX/SPX keep-alive feature
Security	s=3	Enables /etc/hosts.equiv and ~/.rhosts server side lookup
	s=2	Enables only ~/.rhosts server side lookup
	s=1	Enables only /etc/hosts.equiv server side lookup
	s=0	Disables /etc/hosts.equiv and ~/.rhosts server side lookup
	r=1	Enables ~/.netrc client side lookup
	r=0	Disables ~/.netrc client side lookup
Buffer Size	b=buffer_value	TCP/IP communication buffer size in bytes

This verification process occurs in several steps:

1. The user-id is verified by checking in the server's /etc/passwd file. If the userid making the request also exists on the server, the userid is assumed to be known and trusted.
2. The client machine from which the request is originating is verified. The client's hostname must be resolvable either through the server's /etc/hosts file or via a DNS lookup.
3. After resolving the client's hostname, a check is made to see if the client machine is to be trusted or not by the server. For the purposes of discussion here, suffice it to say that if a remote machine is trusted, services will be extended to the remote machine for userids existing on both machines without requiring a password.

4. If an entry exists for the remote machine in the /etc/hosts.equiv file, the instance and database connection is made. If no entry exists in the /etc/hosts.equiv fmile for the remote machine, the ~/.rhosts file is checked to see if an entry exists there for the userid and remote machine name combination. If it exists, the connection is made; otherwise, the connection request is rejected.

The ~/.rhosts file allows a user who has an account on both the database server machine and an *untrusted* client machine to establish an instance and database connection without having to enter a password. This file is created in the user's home directory on the server machine. Consult the documentation that came with your operating system for the format of this file. The general format is as follows:

```
user_id@remote_host_name
```

The .netrc file also exists in the user's home directory and permits connections from network-based clients where the userid for the individual differs from that on the database server.

tip

When advising a user on the creation of an .rhosts or .netrc file in an environment using DNS, be sure to have the user create an entry with just the remote host name as well as an entry with the remote host name and the domain suffix.

The security option that can be set as part of this field in the $INFORMIXSQLHOSTS file determines to what level the server should search to verify that the connection is "known and trusted." The "s=3" option is the default. The "s=0" option prevents any remote access to the server while "s=2" only allows specific remote userid connections. The "s=1" option prevents all access from non-trusted hosts by preventing .rhosts lookups from occurring.

Communication Buffer Size Option   The last option that can be set in this field of the $INFORMIXSQLHOSTS file, the communication buffer size, allows you to tune the TCP/IP communication buffer to more efficiently handle the amount of data commonly transmitted.

Check the documentation that came with your O/S to see what the default buffer size is and the maximum size allowed. If you find that the server is consistently handling data transfers that are larger than the current buffer size (e.g., BLOBs), use this option to specify, in bytes, how large the buffer should be.

Be aware that each client connection allocates its own communication buffer. When setting the size of this buffer, make sure you have sufficient physical memory on the machine to service all the concurrent users and their buffers in addition to the OnLine Dynamic Server instances, and any other applications running on the server.

Informix recommends that the communication buffers be sized identically on both the server machine and client machines for the most efficient network throughput and least amount of network-related overhead on either machine.

Options that affect client connections, such as the keep-alive option and client-side .netrc lookups, can be changed at will and become effective for client connections established after the change is made. Server-oriented parameters, such as the server-specific security options or communication buffer size, can be set at will but will not become effective until the instance is shut down and restarted.

Examples By way of example, Figure 2-2 shows how to properly configure an $INFORMIXSQLHOSTS file to recognize and route instance and database access to two separate servers. The host called "cadmus" is the local machine and supports several instances; "epaphus" is the remote server.

Notice that for the instances supported by the local machine, there are both shared memory and TCP/IP-based connections defined. For the "amazon" instance on epaphus, the remote server, only a TCP/IP-based connection is defined in cadmus' $INFORMIXSQLHOSTS file because a shared memory connection is not possible from cadmus.

For consistency and manageability, a single universal $INFORMIXSQLHOSTS file with all possible connections defined can be used on all servers. Access security can be enforced through the fifth field of the file.

Note that in Figure 2-2 access definition statements for the `onprobe` and `D/B Cockpit` monitoring utilities are defined. These utilities will be explained in greater detail in the "Graphical Utilities" section of Chapter 7, Monitoring the Instance.

```
columbia         onipcshm    cadmus     local_col
columbia_tcp     onsoctcp    cadmus     col_tcp
columbia_pit     onsoctcp    cadmus     col_cockpit

styx             onipcshm    cadmus     local_sty
styx_tcp         onsoctcp    cadmus     sty_tcp
styx_pit         onsoctcp    cadmus     sty_cockpit

kern             onipcshm    cadmus     local_ker
kern_tcp         onsoctcp    cadmus     ker_tcp     k=1,s=1
kern_pit         onsoctcp    cadmus     ker_cockpit    s=1

amazon_tcp       onsoctcp    epaphus    ama_tcp
amazon_pit       onsoctcp    epaphus    ama_cockpit
```

Figure 2–2 *$INFORMIXSQLHOSTS file setup to communicate with a remote instance.*

Figure 2-3 shows the appropriate network service port entries in the /etc/services file of *both* servers. In order for cross-instance communication to occur, the network service port number defined for any given instance service must be the same on all servers attempting to connect to the instance.

```
## INFORMIX RELATED SERVICES
col_tcp          1500/tcp    ## columbia tcp/ip connection service
col_cockpit      1531/tcp    ## oncockpit service -- columbia

sty_tcp          1501/tcp    ## styx tcp/ip connection service
sty_cockpit      1530/tcp    ## oncockpit service -- styx

ker_tcp          1502/tcp    ## kern tcp/ip connection service
ker_cockpit      1532/tcp    ## oncockpit service -- kern

ama_tcp          1503/tcp    ## amazon tcp/ip connection service
ama_cockpit      1533/tcp    ## oncockpit service -- amazon
```

Figure 2–3 */etc/services network port definitions to support cross-instance communication.*

Notice several things in this figure. First, the value entered in the fourth field of the $INFORMIXSQLHOSTS file is used in the /etc/services file as the service name cross-reference. Second, there is no entry in this file for the shared memory connections defined in the $INFORMIXSQLHOSTS file. Although a "network service name" is required for each row in the sqlhosts file, since shared memory connections do not involve network services, that field's value functions as a placeholder and is not used anywhere else. Finally, the use of network service port numbers was defined in advance. General instance connectivity uses port numbers 1500 through 1530; `onprobe` and `D/B Cockpit` connections use port numbers 1531 through 1561. Every effort you make to set up a clearly defined set of parameters to govern the installation and administration of OnLine Dynamic Server instances will pay off in ease of use and the ability to troubleshoot problems later in the life of the instance.

Environment Variables

There are a number of environment variables that can be set to influence how OnLine Dynamic Server functions. A few are required; others are optional and should be set if the working environment differs from the Informix defaults. These variables can be set globally for all users in either the /etc/profile or $INFORMIXDIR/etc/informix.rc files, superseded at an individual user level by the ".informix" file in a user's home directory, or set within an application for the purposes and duration of the application.

Required Variables

The INFORMIXDIR, ONCONFIG, and INFORMIXSERVER environment variables are required to be set for instance initialization or access. In addition, I also recommend setting the DBEDIT environment variable as well. Let's look at each one of these variables in greater detail.

INFORMIXDIR INFORMIXDIR represents the full path name to the directory where Informix products such as OnLine Dynamic Server are installed. This variable must be set and exported into the user's environment before any of the variables that follow.

Although commonly done, there is no rule that states Informix products have to be installed in the /usr directory or that the directory itself be called "informix." In fact you can have multiple directories containing different release levels of Informix products (e.g., informix_711, informix_713). By simply resetting the $INFORMIXDIR, $ONCONFIG, $INFORMIXSERVER, and $INFORMIXSQLHOSTS environment variables, as well as $PATH, you can easily switch between release levels of product to test functionality or support third-party applications using different versions.

In order for users to be able to run Informix executables, "$INFORMIXDIR/bin" needs to be added to each user's PATH statement after INFORMIXDIR has been exported into the environment.

If you are developing applications to sell to others, **NEVER** *hard code a path for the Informix product directory or assume that it will be called "informix." Always read the $INFORMIXDIR environment variable from the working environment. Shell scripts should be written to read these environmental settings in as well.*

ONCONFIG ONCONFIG represents the name of the file, originally located in the $INFORMIXDIR/etc directory, containing the active instance's configuration parameters. It is automatically pathed to $INFORMIXDIR/etc, so the correct syntax, in a Bourne or Korn shell environment, would look like

```
ONCONFIG=onconfig.sty; export ONCONFIG
```

INFORMIXSERVER This is the name of the default OnLine Dynamic Server instance to which connections will be made. When setting up your environment to initialize a new instance, this is the name you'll enter in the "server name" field of the shared memory screen in onmonitor.

One note of caution; from a technical point of view, this variable does not *have* to be set before initializing the instance. However, if it is not set, the sysmaster database will not be created in the instance during the initialization process. The sysmaster database is vitally important to the reporting and overall maintenance functions of OnLine Dynamic Server. I will briefly introduce the sysmaster database in the last section of Chapter 3, Initializing an OnLine Dynamic Server Instance. I recommend setting this variable prior to initializing an instance.

INFORMIXSQLHOSTS This variable is not required unless you are going to use a file name other than "sqlhosts" to define database connectivity, or the "sqlhosts" file will be located somewhere other than in the $INFORMIXDIR/etc directory. The file specified by this variable must have the same format as the standard "sqlhosts" file provided as part of the OnLine Dynamic Server product distribution. If this variable is set, the $INFORMIXDIR/etc/sqlhosts file is never used for database connectivity.

DBEDIT You are not required to set this variable prior to initialization, but I recommend doing it to eliminate having to choose an editor every time you use dbaccess or I-SQL. My preference is to set this to "vi."

Other Variables

There are a number of other variables, such as $DBCENTURY, $DBMONEY, or $DBDATE, that can be set to affect how the Informix products either operate, manipulate data, or display it to the user. They are explained in greater detail in the *Informix Guide to SQL: Reference*, which accompanied your distribution of the software.

Multiple Residency Issues

Multiple residency is just a fancy way of saying "supporting more than one instance of OnLine Dynamic Server at a time on a physical server." This is accomplished not by reinstalling the OnLine Dynamic Server product into another directory, but by creating unique copies of a couple of files and properly setting the required environment variables, covered in the previous section of this chapter.

The $INFORMIXDIR environment variable will not change unless you want to run a different version of the engine and have it installed in another directory. You can add all instance connection information for all the engine versions to one "sqlhosts" file if you want. If you need to support different versions of the engine, installed in separate directories, setting the $INFORMIXSQLHOSTS environment variable will allow all instances of any version on the server to reference this single "sqlhosts" file. Otherwise, all the instances can use the "sqlhosts" file in their $INFORMIXDIR/etc directory.

A unique $ONCONFIG file will need to be created for each instance as well as a MSGPATH file. The server name, server aliases, and server number need to be unique for all the instances on each physical server.

Obviously, the $ONCONFIG and $INFORMIXSERVER variables will be different for each instance. It also goes without saying that instances cannot share disk chunks in any way. The MSGPATH file and server number will be explained in the next chapter when a step-by-step process to initialize an OnLine Dynamic Server instance will be presented.

Beyond these changes, there isn't anything very difficult about supporting several instances of OnLine Dynamic Server on the same physical server. The same questions need to be asked and answered for each additional instance as for the first.

Of primary concern is the amount of CPU, memory, and I/O resources that will be available to support the operation of all the instances. The varying demands each instance will make on the server need to be carefully considered to not overwhelm one or more elements of the system resources. This is particularly important for tuning shared memory within the kernel and setting the "forced resident" flag in the $ONCONFIG file. The RESIDENT configuration parameter will be discussed in the "Shared Memory" section of the next chapter.

Finally, depending on the number of tape drives available to the system, the archiving of logical logs or the instances themselves may require some coordination.

Summary

It should be clear that careful planning is necessary when creating any new system, and OnLine Dynamic Server is no exception. When preparing to initialize your instance, you must remember that decisions on certain issues will be influenced largely by your own specific situation, and that there are no hard-and-fast rules to guide you through this process. Your own skill, intuition, and previous experiences will be your only guides.

When planning for a new OnLine Dynamic Server instance, keep the following points in mind:

- During the design phase, identify as many of the performance requirements, general database sizes, table interdependencies, and other elements of the working environment as you can.
- Regarding your disk drive options, regardless of what you do with the other drives in the instance, the drives that contain the rootdbs, the logical logs, and the physical log MUST be protected in some fashion against media failure. Know the pros and cons of each option before you decide which is best for you.
- Always use symbolic links rather than actual device names when referring to disk and tape devices.
- When estimating table and dbspace sizes, don't skimp just to save a few bucks. It's always more expensive in the long run not to plan for growth.
- The $INFORMIXDIR, $ONCONFIG, $INFORMIXSERVER, and, in some cases, the $INFORMIXSQLHOSTS environment variables must be set prior to initializing an instance or connecting to one.
- When creating applications for resale, or for greater portability, NEVER assume that the location of $INFORMIXDIR is fixed to an arbitrary standard (which doesn't really exist) or that you can dictate where it should be and hard code it into your applications. Always use the environment variable from the working environment to determine the location of the Informix-installed binaries.

Coming Up

With the ambiguities involved in preparing for a new OnLine Dynamic Server instance safely behind us, the next chapter will get into the nuts and bolts of actually initializing an OnLine Dynamic Server instance. I'll be using the `onmonitor` utility to walk through this process, and by the end of Chapter 3 you will have a good understanding of each instance configuration parameter as well as a basic idea of how you can tune the instance for better performance.

Part 2

Initializing, Configuring, and Operating the Engine

Okay, let's get into the good stuff! Having looked at, and resolved, all the major design issues and set the various performance and reliability standards and expectations, it's now time to fire up the engine, build an instance and a database, and put theory into practice to see what happens.

I'll walk you through initializing an instance and, in the process, explain what each of the configuration parameters is and the impact each has to instance or database operations. I'll cover the basic tasks that an OnLine or database administrator would be expected to know and perform. These include log maintenance, chunk and dbspace management, mirroring, creating databases and altering their logging modes, table and/or index creation and fragmentation, constraints, and concurrency issues.

At the end of this section, you should be able to create and manage instances and databases. Though there is still more you need to understand about the engine and how it operates, if you're a "cut to the chase" type of person just looking to turn the engine on and use it, the information is here.

Chapter 3

Initializing an OnLine Dynamic Server Instance

- *How is an instance initialized?*
- *What does each configuration parameter affect? What values should I use?*
- *What is the sysmaster database and how can I query it?*

The previous chapter was pretty light in that the topics covered there received only a superficial discussion. This couldn't be helped, given that each administrator and project will have unique biases and requirements. Few definitive statements could be made because of the interrelationship of so many factors and the differing degree of importance they can have in the overall design of the database environment.

From this chapter forward, the nuts and bolts of initializing, administering, and tuning an OnLine Dynamic Server will be exposed. In this chapter, I'll walk you through the process of initializing an OnLine Dynamic Server instance. Every parameter of the $ONCONFIG file will be explained, with recommendations made on how to properly set them. Finally, I'll introduce the sysmaster database and the ability to query into the OnLine Dynamic Server shared memory structures used to operate the instance.

By the end of this chapter, you will be able to initialize an OnLine Dynamic Server instance with a solid baseline configuration. You will have a basic understanding of all the important tunable parameters and how they interact with each other. This will help in tuning the instance once databases are built and applications are running against them. Finally, you'll understand what the SMI is and how you can use it to monitor almost all aspects of instance activity.

The Onmonitor Utility

Having worked through the logical design phase of the applications and the database environment, completed a preliminary tune of the kernel, sliced up the disks, and set up the various files and environment variables, you're now ready to begin configuring and initializing an OnLine Dynamic Server instance.

There are two ways to do this. The first method involves manually editing the $ONCONFIG file, setting each value the way you want, then executing an "`oninit -i`" command. If everything is set properly, the instance will come up to full on-line mode. If not, you'll have to see what, if any, messages are output to the message file and continue modifying the $ONCONFIG file until you get it right.

The second method of initializing an OnLine Dynamic Server instance is to use the `onmonitor` utility. `Onmonitor` allows you to create dbspaces, and add or drop chunks, monitor various instance metrics, modify and tune almost all the configuration parameters, and change the operating mode of instances.

I recommend using `onmonitor` to initialize an instance because of the field level validation that occurs during the initialization process. It traps many errors or problems as you enter them, so you don't have to guess at why the instance didn't initialize. This is not to imply that it catches everything; it definitely does not, but it's better than blindly shooting in the dark.

warning

The root and informix userids have full access to all options within the `onmonitor` utility. End users, while they can invoke `onmonitor`, only have access to the reporting facilities of the utility. Be aware, however, that end users given access to `onmonitor` through an application or a shell menu can issue operating system commands or get to the command line through the "!" escape syntax from the `onmonitor` ring menus.

The `onmonitor` ring menu is only two levels deep, as illustrated in Table 3-1. With one major exception, the menu is almost identical to that in previous versions of the OnLine engine. As you might expect, there are a few new menu options for Dynamic Server functionality in some of the rings. Like any other Informix ring menu, you can use the capitalized letter in the menu option to jump to that menu option. For reference purposes, when indicating a specific menu option in this text, I'll use the following syntax: **top_level:second_level**.

The **Force-Ckpt** ring menu option does not have any other options. It simply asks if you want a checkpoint to occur. If you answer yes, it will initiate a checkpoint. This option and its command line alternative are very handy when migrating logical logs around the system or creating BLOBspaces and the active logical log must be changed. Obviously you cannot drop a logical log if it is the current log or it contains the last checkpoint. A new BLOBspace is not activated until a checkpoint occurs in the logical log following the one that was active when the BLOBspace was created. By executing an "`ontape -a`" command to archive the current logical log then selecting this menu option, you can force the instance to use a new logical log and it will contain the last checkpoint. New BLOBspaces will become active and/or you'll be able to drop the previous logical log.

Table 3-1 *The* onmonitor *ring menus.*

Top-Level Ring:	Secondary Ring Options:	Description:
Status	Profile Userthreads Spaces Databases Logs Archive data-Replication Output Configuration Exit	The status ring contains monitoring and reporting functions. It is what end users see when they invoke onmonitor.
Parameters	Initialize Shared-Memory perFormance data-Replication diaGnostics pdQ Add-log Drop-Log Physical-log Exit	The parameters ring contains initialization and modification options. The options to add or drop logical logs as well as to move and/or resize the physical log are in this ring as well.
Dbspaces	Create BLOBspace Mirror Drop Info Add_chunk datasKip Status Exit	The dbspaces ring has creation, modification, and reporting options for chunks and dbspaces within the instance.
Mode	Startup On-Line Graceful-Shutdown Immediate-Shutdown Take-Offline Add-Proc Drop-Proc deCision-support Exit	The mode ring contains options to change the operating mode of the instance and to add and drop CPU virtual processors.

continued

Top-Level Ring:	Secondary Ring Options:	Description:
Force-Ckpt		See text above
Archive		See text below
Logical-logs	<u>D</u>atabases <u>T</u>ape-Parameters <u>E</u>xit	See text below
Exit		Exits dbaccess

The **Archive** ring has changed the most from previous versions of OnLine. It now only contains the ability to change the instance archive and logical log tape devices. The ability to create an archive or restore from one has been moved to the ontape or onarchive command line utilities. I believe this was in preparation for the onbar API, where the instance only serves up data as requested by the outside application.

The **Logical-logs** ring has two options, **Databases** and **Tape-Parameters**. The first option allows you to change the logging mode of a particular database. As explained in the "Logging Modes" section of Chapter 5, Building a Database Environment, some changes take place immediately; others require the instance to be "quiesced" to single-user mode and an archive created before they take effect.

The second option on this ring menu generates the same screen display as the **Archive:Tape-Parameters** option, but only allows you to modify the logical log archive device entry.

Throughout this text, I will refer back to the onmonitor ring menu options as appropriate for any specific action needed in the discussion.

Stepping Through the Initialization Process

Using the onmonitor utility makes initializing an OnLine Dynamic Server instance a fairly easy process. If you invoke the **Parameters:Initialize** option, you'll automatically be guided from screen to screen for the entire process. Provided you have all the environment variables set correctly, the disk space set up, and the kernel tuned, you should finish the process with an instance in full on-line mode.

The figures in this chapter were taken from a 7.12.UC2 port of the engine. The configuration parameters are listed, for the most part, in the order in which you would see them when initializing an instance. In the following sections, I'll walk through every element of each screen of the onmonitor initialization process. Each field will be examined and explained; in most cases a recommended setting will be given.

In addition to listing the screen field name, I will also list the $ONCONFIG parameter name in parentheses.

Initial Device Configuration

On the first screen of the initialization process, shown in Figure 3-1, you enter information for the basic hardware devices needed to initialize or restore an instance. You define where the rootdbs can be found which contains the rest of the information required to bring the instance on-line.

```
 INITIALIZATION: Make desired changes and press ESC to record changes.
   Press Interrupt to abort changes.  Press F2 or CTRL-F for field-level help.
                              DISK PARAMETERS
Page Size      [    2] Kbytes                            Mirror [N]

Tape Dev.      [/dev/tapedev                                                  ]
Block Size     [     16] Kbytes        Total Tape Size [      10240] Kbytes
Log Tape Dev.  [/dev/tapedev                                                  ]
Block Size     [     16] Kbytes        Total Tape Size [      10240] Kbytes
Stage Blob     [                   ]

Root Name      [rootdbs            ]        Root Size [      20000] Kbytes
Primary Path   [/dev/online_root                                              ]
                                          Root Offset [          0] Kbytes
Mirror Path    [                                                              ]
                                        Mirror Offset [          0] Kbytes
Phy. Log Size  [      1000] Kbytes       Log. Log Size [        500] Kbytes
                                 Number of Logical Logs [         6]



Do you wish INFORMIX-OnLine to handle mirroring? (y/n)
```

Figure 3–1 The **Parameters:Initialize** *configuration screen from* onmonitor.

DO NOT PRESS THE "ACCEPT" KEY ON THIS SCREEN UNLESS YOU INTEND TO CREATE A NEW ROOTDBS OR OVERWRITE THE EXISTING ROOTDBS!

The engine will check for the existence of the physical devices entered in the ROOTNAME, MIRRORPATH, LTAPEDEV, and TAPEDEV fields on this screen. If cooked files are going to be used for the rootdbs and its mirror, the ROOTNAME and MIRRORPATH files will be enlarged to ROOTSIZE once the cursor leaves the ROOTSIZE field.

The Page Size field is set by Informix during the port of the product to the operating system and cannot be modified.

Mirror (MIRROR)

This enables or disables the ability to use OnLine Dynamic Server-based mirroring for the entire instance. This field should always be set to "Y". You will be required to define a mirror chunk for the rootdbs, but you can always drop the mirror later should you use another option to protect the integrity and availability of the rootdbs.

Setting this option to "N" prevents the use of OnLine Dynamic Server-based mirroring in the future without reinitialization of the instance.

Tape Dev (TAPEDEV)

The tape device to be used when creating instance archives. The device name entered here should be a symbolic link to the actual tape device name and needs to be fully pathed.

Block Size (TAPEBLK)

The block size for the archive device. Consult the documentation for the device to set this properly.

Total Tape Size (TAPESIZE)

The total amount of data to be stored on a tape. This number should not exceed Informix's limit of 2 TB.

 **ALWAYS** enter a storage amount less than that for which the tape is rated in this as well as the LTAPESIZE fields. For a more detailed explanation, please see the "Tape Devices" section of Chapter 6, *Archiving and Restoring*.

The Informix `ontape` utility does not handle end-of-tape conditions well at all. `Ontape` will abort the archive process if it encounters an EOT condition before it has written TAPESIZE (or LTAPESIZE) amount of data out to any tape. Enter a value about 5 percent less than the uncompressed storage capacity of the tape to avoid this problem.

Log. Tape Dev. (LTAPEDEV)

The fully pathed symbolic link to the tape device to be used for archiving the logical logs.

Block Size (LTAPEBLK) and Total Tape Size (LTAPESIZE)

See the notes on TAPEBLK and TAPESIZE.

Stage BLOB (STAGEBLOB)

The BLOBspace name for BLOBs awaiting transfer to optical media. This field should be left blank unless you're using the OnLine-Optical extension to the engine.

Root Name (ROOTNAME)

The name of the dbspace that will function as the rootdbs. Convention holds that the name of the dbspace is "rootdbs," but any name can be used. Allocation of disk space at this moment of the initialization process is at a single-chunk level. After the instance is active, additional chunks can be added to the rootdbs if needed.

If a cooked file is going to be used for ROOTNAME, it needs to be created via the "`touch`" command before continuing past this point. The file's permissions should be 660; group and owner privileges should be "informix."

Root Size (ROOTSIZE)

The amount of disk space to allocate for the rootdbs. In a properly built instance, no more than 15–25 MB should be allocated. This will allow for the initial creation of the logical and physical logs as well as the sysmaster database. The logs should be moved out of the rootdbs as soon after instance initialization as possible.

With a rootdbs of this size, some temporary table creation or sorting and order by work can still occur in the rootdbs, but not to any significant degree. Temporary dbspaces should be created to serve those purposes. If temporary dbspaces are not going to be created, ROOTSIZE will need to be adjusted upward to allow for this type of activity. Temporary dbspaces are discussed in greater detail in the "Temporary Dbspaces" section of Chapter 4, Basic Administrative Tasks.

Primary Path (ROOTPATH)

The fully pathed symbolic link to the first disk chunk to be used for the rootdbs. Please refer to the "Symbolic Links" section of Chapter 2, Preparing for Initialization, for a discussion about the value of using symbolic links.

Offset (ROOTOFFSET)

The offset value allows multiple dbspaces (or logical disk chunks to add to dbspaces) to be created within one physical disk partition. This option was of much greater value prior to the widespread release of logical disk management software available with most operating systems.

Prior to this software, disk partitions were created via hard partitioning of the drive. Because an administrator couldn't always foresee how each disk would need to be partitioned to meet future demands, Informix provided a way to use one larger physical disk partition to create several smaller disk chunks. Using the "offset" value, an administrator could mark the beginning point of a dbspace, or a logical chunk to add to a dbspace, within a larger disk partition, then have the dbspace (or chunk) extend contiguously for the chunk size entered.

With disk management software that allows disk partitioning on the fly, offsets have little value anymore. Should you use offsets to build your dbspaces, or chunks to add to other dbspaces, the OnLine Dynamic Server engine will prevent an offset and size allocation from overwriting another dbspace or allocated chunk. You will need to keep track of what dbspaces and chunks are on each individual disk partition, and where each offset begins and ends. This information is available via the "`onstat -d`" command. It can also be retrieved through `onmonitor` from the **Dbspaces:Info** option.

Mirror Path (MIRRORPATH)

If MIRROR is set to "Y," you will be prompted for the pathed name of the symbolic link pointing to the chunk that will mirror the rootdbs. Otherwise, the prompt will jump to the field for setting the size of the logical logs. Notice there is no sizing information for this (or any other) mirror chunk. The engine assumes that the mirror chunk will be at least the same size as the primary chunk.

Offset (MIRROROFFSET)

See the notes on ROOTOFFSET above.

Phy. Log Size (PHYSFILE)

I used to hate this field, as well as the logical log size field, when initializing instances with OnLine 5.x and earlier versions. These sizes could only be set once—during initialization. If system performance indicated they were the wrong size, there was no way to correct it but to reinitialize the instance.

In OnLine Dynamic Server you can tune the size of these logs like any other parameter. The physical log will be created in the rootdbs to begin with, so set this value to 1000 KB. The "Creating, Moving and Resizing Logs" section of Chapter 4, Basic Administrative Tasks, will explain how to tune the physical log and move it to another dbspace.

Log. Log Size (LOGSIZE)

During the initialization process, the logical logs will be created in the rootdbs. The initialization process uses very little log space; since the rootdbs is only 15–25 MB in size, set this field to 1000 KB as well.

Number of Logical Logs (LOGFILES)

This field determines how many logical logs are created during the initialization process. It is *not* the total number of logical logs allowed in the instance (LOGSMAX), which will be set on the next screen. Setting this value to 5 will provide more than enough logical log space for instance initialization. The "Creating, Moving, and Resizing Logs" section of Chapter 4 will explain how to move logical logs as well as how to tune their size once the instance is initialized.

With these fields populated, pressing the "accept" key will validate the TAPEDEV, LTAPEDEV, ROOTPATH, MIRRORPATH, and MSGPATH entries. If successful, the **Parameters:Shared_Memory** screen will be displayed.

Shared Memory Configuration

From the screen shown in Figure 3-2, the parameters affecting the instance's shared memory are set and tuned.

```
SHARED MEMORY: Make desired changes and press ESC to record changes.
    Press Interrupt to abort changes.  Press F2 or CTRL-F for field-level help.
                          SHARED MEMORY PARAMETERS
Server Number                           [    0]     Server Name [hpcs1              ]
Server Aliases [                                                                    ]
Dbspace Temp   [                                                                    ]
Deadlock Timeout                        [   60] Secs Number of Page Cleaners  [    1]
Forced Residency                           [N]       Stack Size (K)           [   32]
Non Res. SegSize (K)            [     8000]          Optical Cache Size (K) [      0]

Physical Log Buffer Size   [      32] K       Dbspace Down Option              [0]
Logical Log Buffer Size    [      32] K       Preserve Log For Log Backup      [N]
Max # of Logical Logs      [       6]         Transaction Timeout        [   300]
Max # of Locks             [    2000]         Long TX HWM                [    50]
Max # of Buffers           [     200]         Long TX HWM Exclusive      [    60]
                                              Index Page Fill Factor     [    90]
                                              Add SegSize (K)          [  8192]
                                              Total Memory (K)         [     0]

Resident Shared Memory size [      576] Kbytes     Page Size [    2] Kbytes

Enter a unique value to be associated with this version of INFORMIX-OnLine.
```

Figure 3–2   *The shared memory configuration screen from* onmonitor.

Several field-level validations take place in this screen. If you enter a value in one field that is out of range based on other entries, an error message will usually appear with a general recommendation to correct the error.

Server Number (SERVERNUM)

A value between 0 and 255 must be entered in this field. This value is used to create an offset into the general shared memory structures of the operating system to allocate the shared memory this instance will use. This value obviously needs to be unique if more than one instance of OnLine will be running on the same physical server. Sequentially numbering the instances is not required. Nor is it required that the number be unique across all instances on the network; it is physical-server-specific.

Server Name (DBSERVERNAME)

A unique name among all OnLine instances, not just OnLine Dynamic Server instances, on the network. The name is limited to 18 characters, and is also used as the value for the $INFORMIX-

SERVER environment variable if your application is connecting via a shared memory connection. The DBSERVERNAME is also entered in the first field of the $INFORMIXSQLHOSTS file. Required environment variables like $INFORMIXSERVER are covered in the "Environment Variables" section of Chapter 2. The $INFORMIXSQLHOSTS file is explained in detail in the "Required Files" section of the same chapter.

Server Aliases (DBSERVERALIASES)

Secondary names for the instance. Again limited to 18 characters and unique across the network, these aliases are commonly used for defining additional connection paths into the instance.

These connection paths are most commonly network-related, so the alias names should reflect that. For example, to provide a TCP/IP-based connection alias to the "amazon" instance, I used the name "amazon_tcp" and entered it in the DBSERVERALIASES field. These connection aliases need to have valid entries in the $INFORMIXSQLHOSTS file in order for them to work.

Dbspace Temp (DBSPACETEMP)

This field contains the names of the dbspaces to be used for sorting, order-bys, temporary tables, hash indexes, and so on. The names entered here need to be comma separated without any whitespace between them.

Dbspaces listed in the DBSPACETEMP field can be either explicitly created as "temporary" dbspaces or regular dbspaces. I recommend using "temporary" dbspaces so that any engine-generated activity in the temporary dbspaces is not logged in the logical logs, as would be the case if the engine-generated activity occurred in regular dbspaces.

During the initialization process, you can enter temporary dbspace names that do not yet exist. A single-error message written to the MSGPATH file, indicates an inability to find the dbspaces. A single-error message will be written to the log each time the instance is started until you create the temporary dbspaces and use the names entered in this field.

Only those dbspace names entered in this field, or those explicitly set by an application or by the $DBSPACETEMP or $PSORT_DBTEMP environment variables will be used by the engine as temporary space, regardless of their creation type.

Dbspaces created using cooked files cannot be used as temporary dbspaces.

Deadlock Timeout (DEADLOCK_TIMEOUT)

The number of seconds a server will wait while trying to acquire a lock or other resources in another instance while executing a distributed transaction. Accurately setting this value depends on the relative throughput and reliability of the network connections to the other instances. For servers on the same terrestrial-based network segment with little or no network saturation, the default value should be sufficient. Monitoring network loads and application performance will assist in the proper tuning of this parameter. Distributed transactions are discussed in greater detail in Chapter 11.

Forced Residency (RESIDENT)

This determines whether or not the resident portion of the instance's shared memory segment can be swapped out of the main operating system's shared memory. Whether or not this parameter works for your system is O/S-dependent. Check the ONLINE_7.x file in the $INFORMIXDIR/release directory to see if this is available for your port.

Assuming it is, and provided there is enough physical memory on the server, this should be set to "Y." Enabling residency will eliminate a fairly large I/O hit and context switch as the OnLine Dynamic Server memory structures get paged out and then back into main memory. The end result is an increase in the overall performance of the instance.

Obviously, the total memory size of the kernel, applications, and other user processes will determine whether or not there is enough physical memory to meet all system demands and still allow the instance's shared memory to remain resident. These factors need to be considered as well when setting this parameter.

Non Res. SegSize (SHMVIRTSIZE)

The size of the instance's virtual portion of shared memory. This value will require tuning over time. Initially it should be set at (num_user_threads x 350kb) or 8 MB, whichever is bigger. If the instance needs additional virtual memory, it will allocate another segment of SHMADD size. The addition of extra virtual memory segments can be monitored via the "`onstat -g seg`" command.

The efficiency of the virtual shared memory portion decreases as additional segments are added. If one or more additional virtual segments have been allocated during normal database operations, this parameter should be tuned to the sum of all the virtual segment allocations for the instance.

If an additional virtual memory segment is no longer needed by the instance, it will be released by the instance. Sometimes this release does not properly execute. You can force a release of an unused virtual memory segment by executing an "`onmode -F`" command.

Number of Page Cleaners (CLEANERS)

The guideline for this parameter is one cleaner per physical disk in the instance, to a maximum of 128 cleaners.

Stack Size (STACKSIZE)

This should be left at default. This specifies the amount of stack allocated by, and for, the instance to hold user-specific variables for database operations. These stack allocations can and will be chained together should more than one be required for a given user's operation.

Optical Cache Size

Leave at default or null if not using the OnLine-Optical extension to the engine. Otherwise, see the manuals that accompanied your distribution of the OnLine-Optical software for a discussion of this field.

Physical Log Buffer Size (PHYSBUFF)

The size of the two buffers used to buffer the writes to the physical log. These should be left at default unless there is a need for more or less I/O to the physical log.

Increasing the size of the buffer decreases the I/O load but increases the risk of lost data in the event of a catastrophic server crash. The efficiency at which the physical log buffers are operating can be monitored via the `oncockpit` graphical utility or by executing the "`onstat -l`" command.

Logical Log Buffer Size (LOGBUFF)

Performs the same function as PHYSBUFF, though for the logical logs. There are three logical log buffers. Their efficiency can be monitored by using the same tools as those to monitor PHYSBUFF.

Max # of Logical Logs (LOGSMAX)

The total number of logical logs the instance will allow to be created. This is NOT the number of logs created at initialization.

The maximum number of logs that can be created is 32,767. I recommend setting this to about four or five more than you really think you'll need. If you suddenly need to add a couple more logs for a database operation during production hours, you don't have to shut down the instance to retune this parameter.

Max # of Locks (LOCKS)

This parameter has some but not a large effect on the size of an instance's shared memory, so the tendency is to set it rather high—particularly in an OLTP environment, where a lack of locks will cause applications to fail.

As each lock needs to be monitored and accounted for, set this field to what appears to be a reasonable value, then monitor by executing the "`onstat -p`" and "`onstat -k`" commands. I generally start at about 100,000 for a busy instance and tune from there.

Each lock takes 44 bytes of memory. The minimum value you can enter is 2000; the maximum value is 8,000,000.

Max # of Buffers (BUFFERS)

These buffers are the single largest consumer of the resident portion of shared memory and have the greatest impact on the instance's shared memory size.

BUFFERS are used to buffer read and write requests. The more buffers you have in an instance, the greater the likelihood that the information a user needs will be in the buffers, eliminating a call to disk. At the same time, too many buffers can lead to unnecessary bloat and overhead within the instance as well as inefficient use of system resources. The extra buffers have to be maintained and checked during checkpoints for any impact they could have on the logical consistency of the data in the instance.

Informix used to recommend setting this parameter to between 20 and 25 percent of the physical RAM on the system. This recommendation did not take into account multiple residency. Currently Informix recommends allocating four buffers per anticipated user thread up to a maximum of 2000.

I do not generally follow this recommendation; instead, I use the read and write cache percentages to set and tune this parameter. The BUFFERS parameter directly affects the "%cache read" and "%cache write" values reported by the "`onstat -p`" command. You want to set this parameter so that during normal database operations, the "%cache read" value is greater than 95 percent and the "%cache write" is greater than 85 percent.

Dbspace Down Option (ONDBSPACEDOWN)

This parameter determines what the instance should do in the event there is a media failure in an unprotected, noncritical dbspace. A noncritical dbspace is one that does not contain either the rootdbs, logical logs, or physical log. The three possible values for this parameter are explained in Table 3-2.

Table 3–2 Possible values for the ONDBSPACEDOWN parameter.

Dbspace Down Value	Description
Continue	The dbspace is marked as "down." Depending on how the DATASKIP parameter is set, queries needing information stored in this dbspace will either fail or generate a warning.
Abort	The instance will automatically shut down.
Wait	The instance will continue processing requests for the instance until a checkpoint occurs. At that moment, instance activity will be suspended until the server is rebooted or an override is issued via the "onmode -O" command.

Preserve Log for Log Backup (LBU_PRESERVE)

This parameter applies mainly to those environments using the onarchive utility to create archives of the instance and/or logical logs. Normally, all logical logs are used to calculate the amount of free (or used) logical log space when determining whether a long transaction condition exists. LBU_PRESERVE reserves the last free logical log whenever a transaction begins for exclusive use by the instance to write instance-related log messages.

The onarchive utility generates logical log messages as it processes. This parameter reserves the log space necessary for these messages to be written out without having an impact on long transaction calculations.

Transaction Timeout (TXTIMEOUT)

The number of seconds a participant instance in a distributed transaction will wait for an instruction from the coordinating instance. When TXTIMEOUT seconds have elapsed, the participant instance will assume that the original communication thread was corrupted and spawn another thread to signal the coordinating server and determine the course of action to take.

This value should be left at default unless network saturation or throughput requires otherwise. Distributed transactions are discussed in greater detail in Chapter 11.

Long TX HWM (LTXHWM)

This value represents a percentage of the total logical log size and indicates the amount of logical log space a large transaction can fill before being rolled back. This value should never exceed 50 since the rollback itself will generate logical log entries.

If the logical logs fill up prior to a transaction completely rolling back, the instance will panic and crash. It will not come back up because the first thing the engine will do during fast recovery is attempt to complete the rollback and, in the process, write out messages to the logical logs. The logical logs will still be full because the rollback hasn't been completed, so the fast recovery process will abort.

The Advanced Support engineers at Informix's technical support centers have a number of utilities that can be used to help you bring the instance back on-line, though not without some risk to the logical integrity of the data. The various support options Informix can provide are explained in greater detail in the "Informix Technical Support Options" section of Chapter 10, Recovering from a Crash.

Long TX HWM Exclusive (LTXEHWM)

Another percentage of the total logical log space. This value represents the amount of logical log space that can fill up before a transaction in rollback or commit mode is given exclusive access to the logs. As a result, all other add, update, or delete operations are stalled while the rollback or commit completes. This value should not exceed 60.

Index Page Fill Factor (FILLFACTOR)

The original intent of this parameter was to allow for index growth by leaving a percentage of an index page unused at the time the index was created. As rows were added to the table, their index entries would be inserted into the unused space.

In actual use, however, this only works when the index keys are unique or if there is very little duplication. I recommend leaving this value at default until further refinements can be made to the operation of this parameter.

Add SegSize (SHMADD)

The amount of additional memory that will be added to the virtual portion of the instance's shared memory should the instance require more than that allocated via the SHMVIRTSIZE parameter.

Total Memory (SHMTOTAL)

The maximum amount of shared memory the instance can allocate. This total includes all three portions of shared memory: resident, message and virtual.

If the instance tries to allocate more memory than allowed by this parameter, the application whose database request caused the allocation attempt will fail. A message will be written to the MSGPATH file indicating which portion of shared memory requested another segment.

Setting this value to 0 will allow unrestricted shared memory allocation.

At the bottom of the screen are two fields that cannot be modified. **Page Size** is the size in KB of a data page in the engine. Informix has, for almost all ports, written to a 2 KB page size, although there are a few ports that use a 4 KB page size due to operating system constraints.

Resident Shared Memory Size simply reflects the amount of memory the resident portion will consume. The value of BUFFERS will have the greatest impact on the size of the resident segment.

Pressing the "accept" key will bring up the **Parameters:Performance** screen, whose configuration parameters I'll cover in the next section.

VP and Performance Configuration

From the screen shown in Figure 3-3, the CPU and AIO virtual processors will be configured as well as network connectivity and recovery threads.

```
PERFORMANCE: Make desired changes and press ESC to record changes.
  Press Interrupt to abort changes.  Press F2 or CTRL-F for field-level help.
                    PERFORMANCE TUNING PARAMETERS

    Multiprocessor Machine       [N]    LRU Max Dirty              [ 60]
       Num Procs to Affinity  [   0]    LRU Min Dirty              [ 50]
       Proc num to start with [   0]    Checkpoint Interval        [300]
                                        Num of Read Ahead Pages    [   ]
    CPU VPs                    [   1]   Read Ahead Threshold       [   ]
    AIO VPs                    [    ]
    Single CPU VP                [N]    NETTYPE settings:
    Use OS Time                  [N]       Protocol Threads Users VP-class
    Disable Priority Aging       [N]         [      ] [    ]  [    ] [    ]
    Off-Line Recovery Threads [  10]         [      ] [    ]  [    ] [    ]
    On-Line Recovery Threads  [   1]         [      ] [    ]  [    ] [    ]
    Num of LRUS queues        [   8]         [      ] [    ]  [    ] [    ]




Are you running on a multiprocessor machine?
```

Figure 3–3 *The virtual processor and performance configuration screen from* onmonitor.

Parameters such as the number of CPU vps (NUMCPUVPS), least recently used queues (LRUS), and read ahead pages (RA_PAGES) have a significant impact on the overall performance of the instance. Many of the parameters on this screen should receive as much review during general tuning as those on the shared memory screen.

Multiprocessor Machine (MULTIPROCESSOR)

This turns on or off the multiprocessor locking mechanisms, known as "spin locks," for the instance. If you have a dual-CPU system, try turning this on and off and test performance. If you have three or more physical CPUs in the server, set this to "Y."

Num Procs to Affinity (AFF_NPROCS)

This field is bypassed if MULTIPROCESSOR is set to "N," or if set to "Y" and the operating system does not support process affinitization.

Process affinity is the ability to bind a specific process to a physical CPU within the system. This increases the performance of the process that's bound because it has uninterrupted access to the CPU and, by extension, memory resources. This field sets the number of CPU vps that will be bound to physical CPUs.

It goes without saying that you should not attempt to bind four CPU vps in a four CPU server since there wouldn't be a processor left to support the operating system or any other processes.

Proc num to start with (AFF_SPROC)

CPUs are affinitized in sequential order. This value determines which physical CPU to start with when binding the instance's CPU vps. I recommend against starting with CPU 0 for obvious reasons.

CPU VPs (NUMCPUVPS)

The number of CPU vps to initialize for the instance. The number of CPU vps should match the number of physical CPUs on the server *if* MULTIPROCESSOR is set to "Y" and process affinitization is not used. If processor affinitization is active, this field should match AFF_NPROCS. On uniprocessor servers, set this parameter to 1.

AIO VPs (NUMAIOVPS)

Normally, the AIO vps handle all disk I/O for the instance. Initially set this to the number of active physical disks used by the instance. Monitoring the wait and sleep queues for this class of processor will enable you to tune this parameter.

If your port supports kernel asynchronous I/O (KAIO), and it's activated, the work required of the AIO vps is dramatically reduced. In this case, set NUMAIOVPS to no more than two since all they'll be doing is writing to the physical and logical logs.

Check the ONLINE_7.x file in the $INFORMIXDIR/release directory to see if KAIO is supported in your port of the engine and how to turn it on. KAIO only works with raw disk chunks and provides better I/O performance and throughput than I/O managed by the AIO vps to raw disk.

Single CPU VP (SINGLE_CPU_VP)

This value has a close relationship to MULTIPROCESSOR. Obviously, if the server only has one CPU this should be set to "Y." In a dual-CPU system I recommend setting this to "Y" and testing performance in conjunction with setting the MULTIPROCESSOR parameter to "N" and vice versa. You may find performance is actually better set this way because you avoid all the overhead associated with mutexes, the multiprocessing lock mechanism.

If your server has three or more processors, set this to "N" in conjunction with MULTIPROCESSOR set to "Y."

Use OS Time (USE_OS_TIME)

If applications require datetime stamps to fractions of a second, set this to "Y"; otherwise, leave this parameter at its default setting.

Disable Priority Aging (NOAGE)

This is another port-specific setting and will be documented in the ONLINE_7.x file.

Some ports of the UNIX operating systems will decrease the priority of processes that use a lot of CPU time. NOAGE, if available in your port, causes the operating system to disregard CPU usage when selecting processes to decrease in priority. This allows the `oninit` processes supporting the CPU vps to have more physical CPU time, resulting in better throughput in the instance.

Off-Line Recovery Threads (OFF_RECVRY_THREADS)

This sets the number of threads to perform roll-forward operations out of the logical logs when the instance is in recovery mode. In addition to being used during the fast recovery process when restarting an instance, these threads are also used in a recovery resulting from a restore from archive.

This value should be set close to the number of tables in the instance that have a high number of add, modify, or delete operations. In a system where SINGLE_CPU_VP is set to "Y," do not set this value any higher than 40.

On-Line Recovery Threads (ON_RECVRY_THREADS)

This is the number of threads used to perform roll-forward operations during a "warm" restore of a dbspace. This should generally be set to only 1 or 2.

Num of LRU queues (LRUS)

This sets the number of LRU (least recently used) queue pairs. The number of buffers set by the BUFFERS parameter will be evenly distributed through these queues to hold data pages for reading or modifying by an application. The LRU queues are divided among the page cleaner threads (CLEANERS) so that they can flush the data in the buffers to disk whenever required.

The minimum number of LRU queues a system can have is 3; the maximum is 128. Generally the number of LRU queues should match the number of CPU vps in a large multiprocessor machine (MULTIPROCESSOR = "Y" and SINGLE_CPU_VP = "N"). Uniprocessor or small multiprocessor machines in a heavy OLTP environment will need fewer than five LRU queues.

LRU Max Dirty (LRU_MAX_DIRTY)

This sets the percentage of the LRU queue that can be used before the page cleaning process begins to flush the buffers to disk. This type of write is called an "LRU write" and is one of the most efficient methods of writing to disk. Leave this parameter at its default value to begin with and monitor the disk writes that occur during a normal processing period. The number and types of writes the instance is processing can be monitored by executing the "`onstat -F`" command or through the `D/B Cockpit` graphical utility.

LRU Min Dirty (LRU_MIN_DIRTY)

The percentage at which the flushing of the LRU queue will stop. Leave at default and monitor by executing the "`onstat -F`" command or through the `D/B Cockpit` graphical utility.

Checkpoint Interval (CKPTINTVL)

This sets the maximum number of seconds between checkpoints if the instance is handling active user threads. Writes that occur during checkpoints are the most efficient method of writing to disk because the data is sorted and organized by chunk before being handed off to the page cleaners.

As I explain in the "What Is a Checkpoint?" section of Chapter 10, all other noncheckpoint activity in the instance is suspended during the checkpoint process. This makes the length of time a checkpoint takes to complete important to monitor.

For most environments, a checkpoint duration of less than five seconds is acceptable. This can be achieved by monitoring the LRUs and the percentages at which they start and stop flushing, the physical log size and percent used statistics, as well as the CKPTINTVL. Setting CKPTINTVL too low might decrease the duration of a checkpoint, but might increase the number of checkpoints that occur, causing more interruptions of database service. Setting CKPTINTVL too high could lead to a longer checkpoint duration if the buffers are not being flushed because the LRU settings are too high as well.

Num of Read Ahead Pages (RA_PAGES)

This sets the number of data and index pages that will be cached in the buffer pool during a sequential scan. While this can increase overall performance of some queries, setting this value too high can cause unnecessary thrashing of the LRU queues.

Thrashing the LRU queues occurs when a large amount of data is read in to satisfy one query thread, and then must be purged to accommodate other large data reads to satisfy other concurrent queries.

Set this parameter to 10 and monitor as explained in the discussion of the next parameter.

Read Ahead Threshold (RA_THRESHOLD)

The number of pages left in RA_PAGES before another call is made to read in more data pages. Setting this too low can decrease the efficiency of the read-ahead pool because the query process has to wait for data to come up from disk. Setting this too high will cause the buffer pool to fill up with unnecessary data and cause LRU thrashing.

To look at the overall efficiency of your read-ahead settings, review the output from the "onstat -p" command. Add the "ixda-RA," "idx-RA," and "da-RA" values. This sum should be fairly close to the value of "RA-pgsused." A high number of "buf-waits" could also result from too small a difference between RA_PAGES and RA_THRESHOLD.

NETTYPE Settings

What is entered in this section will determine not only the number of users that can access the instance, but how they connect to it. In earlier versions of OnLine Dynamic Server, there was a configuration parameter called USER_THREADS that could be used to limit the number of user threads to the licensed amount. In the current versions of OnLine Dynamic Server, this is controlled via NETTYPE settings.

There are two individual threads which make up the overall connection thread: a "poll" and a "listen" thread. The poll thread listens for messages from client connections, through either a network or shared memory connection. The poll thread in turn passes these messages to the listen thread. The listen thread performs all the work of authenticating the user and actually establishes the connection to the instance by starting a "sqlexec" thread to process the SQL statement. The results of the SQL statement are returned in reverse order along the thread path. The OnLine Dynamic Server engine starts a poll thread for every unique combination of type "NETTYPE" used in conjunction with an instance name listed in the $INFORMIXSQLHOSTS file.

The NETTYPE parameter also allows you to specify where a particular poll thread is run for greater throughput and efficiency. There are two vp classes on which a poll thread can run, CPU or NET. The greatest efficiency and highest throughput is achieved by using a CPU vp. This is called an "in-line" poll thread and should be used to service the protocol(s) through which the bulk of the client connections will occur. You cannot declare more in-line poll threads than there are CPU vps. Threads run on NET vps are called "net vp" poll threads.

The NETTYPE parameter is composed of four fields, as shown in Table 3-3.

Table 3–3 The nettype parameter fields.

Field Number	Field Name	Possible Values
1	connection protocol	Either ipcshm, tlitcp, tlispx, or soctcp.
2	threads	The number of threads to start.
3	users	The number of user connections *each* of these threads will service.
4	vp-class	The vp class the thread(s) will run on. Acceptable values are CPU or NET.

It is possible that not all connection protocols will be supported in your port of OnLine Dynamic Server. Check the ONLINE_7x file in the $INFORMIXDIR/release subdirectory to see which are available for your port.

When trying to determine the number of threads to configure, be aware that about 200 user connections can be serviced by a single shared memory thread (ipcshm), whereas only 50–100 connections can be serviced by a network thread.

Pressing the "accept" key in this screen will bring up the **Parameters:data_Replication** screen.

Data Replication

This screen, shown in Figure 3-4, will set up the timing, failure condition actions, and file location parameters involved in replicating instance activity to another server using the High-Availability Data Replication (HADR) mechanism. This mechanism is explained in greater detail in Chapter 9.

```
DATA REPLICATION: Make desired changes and press ESC to record changes.
   Press Interrupt to abort changes.  Press F2 or CTRL-F for field-level help.
                      DATA REPLICATION PARAMETERS
Interval         [   30]
Timeout          [   30]
Auto             [0]
Lost & Found     [/usr/informix/etc/dr.lostfound                            ]




















Enter the maximum time (in seconds) between data replication buffer flushes.
```

Figure 3-4 *The data replication configuration screen from* `onmonitor`.

If you will not be using HADR, skip down to the **Lost & Found** field, press the space bar to overwrite what's there, and press the "accept" key to move on to the **Parameters:diaGnostic** screen.

Interval (DRINTERVAL)

The maximum number of seconds between HADR data replication buffer flushes. If set to –1, replication occurs synchronously to the secondary server; when the primary server writes to the replication buffer, the buffer is immediately transferred to the secondary server.

Synchronous transfer mode is the most secure way of handling replication as far as transactional integrity on the secondary server is concerned. As explained in Chapter 9, transactions are not marked complete until confirmation is received back from the secondary server that the change records have been received by the secondary server for application to its copy of the instance.

Setting this to 0, or a positive number, causes replication buffer flushes to occur asynchronously. The logical log records are written to the replication buffer, but the buffer only gets sent to the secondary server whenever the replication buffer gets full, DRINTERVAL expires, or a transaction is committed by a database in unbuffered logging mode in the instance being replicated.

Because a significant amount of time can elapse before the replication buffer gets sent to the secondary server, transactions are immediately committed on the primary server without a check to verify receipt of the update records on the secondary server. This can lead to inconsistent database environments should the primary server crash prior to writing the replication buffer out to the secondary server.

Timeout (DRTIMEOUT)

The number of seconds the server will wait for confirmation of the replication buffer transfer. This should be set to 25 percent of the total time you want to elapse before a replication failure is declared to allow for several retry attempts.

Auto (DRAUTO)

This determines the behavior of the secondary database server in the event the primary server fails. The possible values for this field are listed in Table 3-4.

For the roles of the two servers to be coordinated, this value needs to be identical on both servers in a HADR pair.

Table 3–4   Possible values for DRAUTO.

Value	Description
0	Off. The secondary server does not change behavior at all. It remains a read-only server and waits for the primary server to reconnect and resynchronize. I generally recommend using this value.
1	Retain_type. The secondary server temporarily assumes the role of primary server. When the original primary server comes back on-line, the secondary server reassumes its original role after synchronization completes.
2	Reverse_type. The secondary server assumes the role of primary server and keeps that role even after the original primary server comes back on-line. The original primary server assumes the role of secondary server.

Lost & Found (DRLOSTFOUND)

Fill this field with whitespaces if not using data replication. Otherwise, it is the pathed file where transactions are listed that were committed on the primary server but not on the secondary server and were found during a fast recovery process after a replication failure occurred.

Pressing the "accept" key will bring up the **Parameters:diaGnostics** screen, which will be examined next.

Diagnostics

The parameters set from the screen shown in Figure 3-5 determine which diagnostic files are written to disk in the event of an instance failure. These diagnostic dumps can be of value to the Informix Advanced Support engineers to diagnose the cause and possible effects of an assertion failure or other crash condition.

The instance log file for routine operational messages is defined as well from this screen.

```
DIAGNOSTICS: Make desired changes and press ESC to record changes.
     Press Interrupt to abort changes.  Press F2 or CTRL-F for field-level help.
                        DIAGNOSTIC PARAMETERS
    Message Log    [/usr/informix/online.log                          ]
    Console Msgs.  [/dev/console                                      ]
    Alarm Program  [                                                  ]

    Dump Shared Memory         [Y]
    Dump Gcore                 [N]
    Dump Core                  [N]
    Dump Count                 [   1]
    Dump Directory             [/tmp                         ]




    Enter pathname for OnLine message log
```

Figure 3–5 *The diagnostic configuration screen from* `onmonitor`.

Message Log (MSGPATH)

One of the most important log files on the system, this file holds all the routine and error messages the instance generates. Each instance on a physical server must have its own MSGPATH file.

The MSGPATH will grow over time, so I have a simple shell script that gets executed via the system crontab to move the file into a rolling archive. See the "move_logs" section in Chapter 12, Scripts to Help Get the Job Done, for an explanation of this script.

Console Msgs (CONSOLE)

This is a useless parameter. In all my years of experience with the OnLine product, I have only seen one type of message displayed to the console—that the logical logs were full and needed archiving. This situation was already apparent because the instance had suspended operation while waiting for them to be archived. Point this parameter to a file or to /dev/null.

Alarm Program (ALARMPROGRAM)

The pathed name of a program that the OnLine Dynamic Server instance will run if a problem or error occurs. This program can either be a full executable or a shell script, but it must be able to receive five input parameters: severity, class id, class msg, specific msg, and a "see also" file. Please refer to the *OnLine Administrators Guide* for a full description of these parameters and how to implement an alarm program.

Dump Shared Memory (DUMPSHMEM)

Setting this to "Y" will dump a copy of the instance's shared memory into DUMPDIR whenever an assertion failure occurs. An assertion failure occurs when a check against internal instance or engine conditions returns false when it should have returned true.

The file created by this dump will be named "`shmem.some_number`" where "some_number" will be a unique number, probably based on a time stamp value. There must be sufficient disk space in the file system DUMPDIR points to hold the full size of the instance's shared memory. The dump can be read and analyzed with the `onstat` utility by executing the "`onstat shmem.some_number`" command.

Dump Gcore (DUMPGCORE)

Setting this to "Y" will create a "gcore" file, provided gcore is available on the system. Set this to "N."

Dump Core (DUMPCORE)

Setting this to "Y" will generate a core dump in the case of an assertion failure within a vp. Set this to "N."

Dump Count (DUMPCNT)

The number of shared memory dumps to preserve on disk. Set this to 1 unless you have a tremendous amount of disk space on which to save files the size of the instance's shared memory.

Dump Directory (DUMPDIR)

The directory in which OnLine will write shared memory and core dumps.

Pressing the "accept" key will bring up the **Parameters:pdQ** screen.

Parallel Data Query (PDQ)

Parameters for the Parallel Data Query (PDQ) mechanism are set in the screen shown in Figure 3-6.

```
PDQ: Make desired changes and press ESC to record changes.
     Press Interrupt to abort changes.  Press F2 or CTRL-F for field-level help.
                       PARALLEL DATABASE QUERIES PARAMETERS

PDQ Priority                          [    0]
Max PDQ Priority                      [100]
Decision Support Queries              [         ]
Decision Support Memory (Kbytes)      [         ]
Maximum Decision Support Scans        [  1048576]
Dataskip [off                                                               ]
Optimizer Hint                        [2]




Enter the pdq priority.
```

Figure 3-6 *The PDQ configuration screen from* `onmonitor`.

PDQ will be discussed in greater detail in the "PDQ and MGM" section of Chapter 8, Enhancing Performance. The query resource parameters set here are mainly of use to multiprocessor servers supporting OLAP environments.

PDQ Priority (PDQPRIORITY)

The amount of system resources the OnLine Dynamic Server engine will try to use to process PDQ queries within the instance.

This is a percentage that can vary between 0 (off) and 100. These resources include physical CPU time and memory.

If set to 1, parallel scan threads are used, but no other parallel features of the engine are enabled for the instance. If set to 2 or higher, more parallelism is employed to process the query.

This value needs to be set carefully to avoid causing resource contention problems with other processes that need to run on the server. It is important to turn this on, albeit at a low level, to increase the performance of the update statistics command, as discussed in the "Update Statistics and Data Distributions" section of Chapter 8.

Max PDQ Priority (MAX_PDQPRIORITY)

The percentage of total instance resources that can be used to service an individual PDQ query. Setting this to 0 (zero) turns off all the parallel features in the instance.

In OLTP environments, this should be set to 1 to enable parallel scans. In OLAP environments, the value entered here depends on the number of concurrent queries that need to be processed in the instance. If there are only two or three queries, set this to 35. If you need ten concurrent queries, set this to 10.

Decision Support Queries (DS_MAX_QUERIES)

The total number of PDQ queries that can be running at one time. This should correlate with MAX_PDQPRIORITY to manage concurrency.

Setting MAX_PDQPRIORITY to 100 will give the first person to run a PDQ type query almost all the resources of the instance. Setting DS_MAX_QUERIES = 5 and MAX_PDQPRIORITY = 20 will give five people the ability to process queries, though they could potentially use all of the instance's resources.

Decision Support Memory (DS_TOTAL_MEMORY)

The amount of shared memory that can be used to process PDQ queries. This shared memory is part of the total memory as configured via SHMTOTAL. Informix recommends using the following formula to configure this parameter:

```
DS_TOTAL_MEMORY = physical_memory - os_memory -
instance_resident_memory - ( 128 kb *
number_of_users ) - other_memory
```

where `physical_memory` is the total amount of memory on the server; `os_memory` is the amount of memory required by the kernel, including buffer caches; `instance_resident_memory` is the amount of memory allocated for the instance's resident portion of shared memory; `number_of_users` is the number of client connections expected on the instance; and `other_memory` represents the amount of memory required by non-Informix applications running on the server.

Informix recommends that this parameter be set to 20 to 50 percent of SHMTOTAL for OLTP environments and 80 to 90 percent for OLAP environments. Obviously, if the server will be supporting multiple instances, this formula will need to be adjusted to take into account the existence of these other instances when considering physical and O/S memory.

Dataskip (DATASKIP)

Used in conjunction with table fragmentation, DATASKIP permits the instance to ignore dbspaces or BLOBspaces that are unavailable due to media or other types of failure when processing queries. Refer to the "Setting or Modifying DATASKIP" section of Chapter 4, Basic Administrative Tasks, for a more detailed discussion of this parameter.

Optimizer (OPTCOMPIND)

Very few tunable parameters have been the subject of as much discussion and revision as OPTCOMPIND. This parameter is used to "hint" the query optimizer on how to perform index joins to determine the fastest way to query data. The value entered here for this parameter is the default hint guide for the instance, but an application can reset it for the application on a query-by-query basis by resetting the $OPTCOMPIND environment variable.

The three possible values for this field are shown in Table 3-5.

Table 3–5   Possible OPTCOMPIND values.

OPTCOMPIND Value	Description
0	The optimizer will choose a nested-loop join where the appropriate indexes exist. Query "cost" is not a factor. This is comparable to optimizer operation in OnLine versions 5.x and earlier.
1	The optimizer will use nested-loop joins if the transaction isolation level of the query is "repeatable read." Otherwise, the query will be processed based on costs alone as if OPTCOMPIND was set to 2. Isolation levels are explained in the "Concurrency and Isolation Levels" section of Chapter 5.
2	The optimizer uses a "cost" basis to determine how it will process the query. No one join method is *supposed* to have a higher preference than another.

Over the last several years, as newer versions of OnLine Dynamic Server have been released, the recommended default value of the OPTCOMPIND parameter has changed. As this book goes to print, the recommendation is to set it at 0 for OLTP environments, 1 if there are databases in the instance using "mode ANSI" logging mode or the applications use "repeatable read" isolation levels or 2 for larger OLAP environments. Setting OPTCOMPIND to 2 usually results in a greater predisposition to use hash joins and will generally require a greater amount of instance resources to complete a query because the query is preprocessed several times to determine the cost of each access method.

Pressing the "accept" key will clear the screen and present a confirmation prompt asking if you want to continue with initialization of the rootdbs and creation of the instance. Entering "Y" will start the process.

There will be several prompts to press "enter" as the instance goes through a fast recovery process. If all goes well, eventually the `onmonitor` screen will redisplay the **Parameter** ring menu, and the status line will indicate that the instance is in quiescent mode.

You can either continue on, and build dbspaces and perform other administrative tasks, or choose **Mode:Online** to bring the instance all the way on-line and complete the creation of the sysmaster database. I recommend moving to on-line mode, then monitoring the MSGPATH file with a "`tail -f`" command to see when the sysmaster database completes building before doing anything else in the instance.

Once the creation process of the sysmaster database has been completed, selecting the **Logical-logs:Databases** ring option should display a screen similar to that shown in Figure 3-7. This indicates that the sysmaster database exists and is in unbuffered logging mode. Logging modes will be explained in greater detail in the "Changing Database Logging Modes" section of Chapter 4.

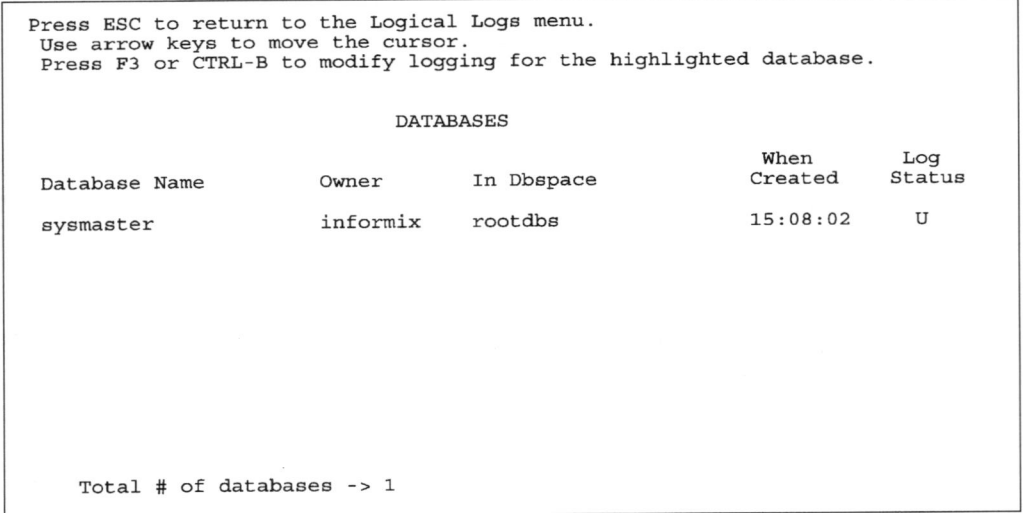

Figure 3-7 *The database information and status screen from* `onmonitor`.

The instance is now fully functional and ready for use. With the creation of the sysmaster database, the SMI interface can now be used to monitor what is happening inside the instance.

The Sysmaster Database and the SMI Interface

The sysmaster database/SMI interface is one of the best features of OnLine Dynamic Server. Through the SMI interface, an administrator can finally get at all the information needed to tune and manage an instance.

The sysmaster database is a combination of pseudo and real tables created in the rootdbs by the OnLine Dynamic Server engine when an instance is initialized. The real tables, for the most part, hold information generated by the `onarchive` utility. The pseudotables are pointers into the shared memory that OnLine Dynamic Server maintains.

Through the SMI interface, you have the ability to gather information from both the real and pseudotables of the sysmaster database through a subset of the SQL language. Almost all the information displayed by the `onstat` utility, and most displayed by the `oncheck` utility, is created by commands parsed through the SMI interface.

The full schema of the sysmaster database can be found in the $INFORMIXDIR/etc/sysmaster.sql file. This file contains a cursory description of what each table is and the purpose for each column. As just mentioned, the database is generated as part of the instance initialization sequence. There is, however, nothing to prevent the sysmaster database from being recreated at any time. A word of caution: since the real tables contain data generated by the `onarchive` utility, dropping and recreating the sysmaster database will result in the inability to retrieve previously created archive sets.

Beyond that, I think it would be a rather stupid idea to try to alter, or remove, structures so important to the overall health and welfare of the instance as the sysmaster shared memory tables.

The nature of the sysmaster database is such that a database schema cannot be created, nor tables unloaded, once it is built and operational. Because most of the tables are simply pointers redirected into shared memory, the data in the tables cannot be modified or deleted; nor can new data be added to them. The informix userid can, however, create stored procedures within the sysmaster database.

The sysmaster database can be queried like any other database from within an I-SQL or `dbaccess` query, or by an application. Unlike regular databases, selective user-based permissions cannot be enforced—"public" has connect privileges to all tables.

The sysmaster database is originally created using the unbuffered logging mode, but can be changed to a buffered log mode if desired. I don't recommend changing the logging mode since little or no performance increase will result from the change. The tables themselves are, for the most part, in shared memory, so why buffer them in shared memory again?

Since it functions like a regular database, data from the sysmaster database can be used in joins or selects with data from other databases. Unlike regular databases, selects or joins to the sysmaster database can occur with other databases of dissimilar logging modes. Quite a few of the scripts I've included in Chapter 12 utilize this cross-database connectivity functionality.

In becoming more familiar with the sysmaster database, you'll see that there are only a few actual tables; there are, however, quite a few views. As with any other view, these should be treated with caution as to how long they might actually exist from release to release.

Check the information in the $INFORMIXDIR/release directory as well as the printed materials that accompanied your distribution of the software to see which tables and views are officially supported and will be found in future releases. The supported schema for these tables and views will also be included in the printed documentation.

Summary

A lot of information was presented in a relatively short amount of space. You should have a good understanding of all the parameters that need to be set to initialize an OnLine Dynamic Server instance. Provided you have all the environment variables set correctly and the disk and tape devices set up, you should be able to use the `onmonitor` utility and, by going through each screen, actually initialize an instance. Finally, you should understand that the purpose of the sysmaster database is to allow you to look inside the instance to extract service-related information. While most of the sysmaster database is actually a pointer into shared memory, you can execute queries against it like any other database.

When initializing an OnLine Dynamic Server instance, keep the following points in mind:

- Always enable mirroring (MIRROR), even if you plan on using hardware- or software-based products to protect the dbspaces containing the rootdbs, the physical log, or logical logs against media failure.
- Always use symbolic links rather than actual device names when entering parameters such as ROOTPATH, TAPEDEV, LTAPEDEV, or any chunk location information.
- Set the TAPESIZE and LTAPESIZE values to about 5 percent less than the rated *uncompressed* capacity of the tape.
- The rootdbs only needs to be 15 to 25 MB in size since the physical and logical logs should be moved into other dbspaces after instance creation. The ability to create "temporary" dbspaces to contain, sort, order-by, and temporary tables further reduces the need for a large rootdbs.
- Since both the physical and logical logs can be moved and resized almost at will, set both initially at 1 MB and only create four to five logical logs. This is enough log space for the initialization of the sysmaster database.
- Set the transaction highwater marks at no more than 50 for LTXHWM and 60 for LTXEHWM.
- You will need to try different values for OPTCOMPIND to see which yields better results in your environment.

Coming Up

This chapter dealt with only one aspect of administering an OnLine Dynamic Server instance that occurs very rarely. There are, however, a number of tasks that need to be accomplished on a much more frequent basis. These tasks include changing database logging modes, administering dbspaces or BLOBspaces, and killing user threads. The next chapter will cover these and other topics.

Basic Administrative Tasks

- *Changing the Operating Mode of the Instance*
- *Changing Database Logging Modes*
- *Creating and Dropping Chunks, Dbspaces, or BLOBspaces*
- *Moving and Resizing Logs*
- *Safely Terminating a User Thread*
- *Starting and Stopping an Instance Automatically*

If you were to use this book as a kind of operational textbook and perform the tasks in each chapter, by now you would have designed and initialized an active OnLine Dynamic Server instance that could be worked with. In this chapter, I will cover the basic, day-to-day server-oriented administrative tasks you'll encounter. Some of these tasks will only be done once in an instance; other tasks will done with some degree of frequency depending on the level of activity and growth the instance experiences. By the end of this chapter you should be able to add and drop dbspaces, understand and be able to change database logging modes, move and resize the physical and logical logs, and safely terminate a user thread.

Changing Operating Modes

An OnLine Dynamic Server instance can run in several different operating modes with different levels of end-user functionality. The instance can operate in some modes for an extended period, other modes are transitional, but each mode has a specific function. In order to execute some instance administrative functions, the instance must be in a specific operating mode. As a result, it is important to understand what each operating mode is, what administrative or end-user access is allowed in each mode, and how to change operating modes at will.

You can tell what mode the instance is operating in a couple of different ways. The most laborious is to look through the MSG-PATH file for any messages indicating a change in mode. A slightly easier way is to invoke the `onmonitor` utility. The operating mode will always be displayed on the status line just under the ring menu, as shown in Figure 4-1.

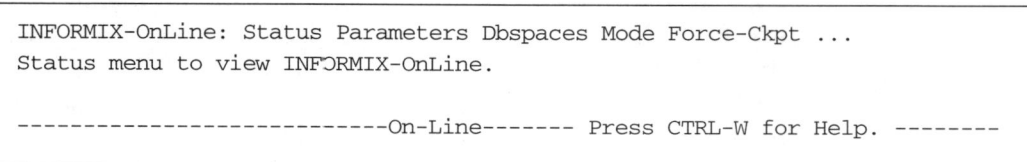

```
INFORMIX-OnLine: Status Parameters Dbspaces Mode Force-Ckpt ...
Status menu to view INFORMIX-OnLine.

---------------------------On-Line------- Press CTRL-W for Help. --------
```

Figure 4–1 The status line from the `onmonitor` utility showing the instance's operating mode.

Because the status line does not refresh, this message will not automatically update unless the menu is manually refreshed.

The easiest way to check the engine's operating mode is to run the "`onstat -`" command, which prints out the mode and up-time status information, as illustrated in Figure 4-2.

```
epaphus: onstat -

INFORMIX-OnLine Version 7.13.UC2 -- Quiescent -- Up 9 days 00:57:32 -- 44848
Kbytes
```

Figure 4–2 *The output of an "`onstat -`" command with the instance in quiescent mode.*

The top line of output from any `onstat` command always lists the operating mode of the instance. The only exception to this is if the instance is completely off-line, in which case a "shared memory not initialized" error message will appear.

Only the root and informix userids should be able to change the operating mode of an instance. Be aware, however, that any userid that is part of group informix, even if it is a secondary group, can change the operating mode of any instance on the server.

There are six different operating modes. They are:

- **Off-line**: The instance is not running. Shared memory for the instance has not been allocated or initialized. No virtual processors are running.
- **Recovery**: A transitional mode as the engine initializes the shared memory and starts the virtual processors for the instance. The fast recovery process executes in this mode. See the "What Is the Fast Recovery Process?" section of Chapter 10, Recovering from a Crash, for a discussion on fast recovery. Even though shared memory is initialized in this mode, the SMI interface is not available for use.
- **Quiescent**: The instance is fully active but access to user-created databases is suspended. This mode is somewhat equivalent to single-user mode in the UNIX environment. Unlike UNIX single-user mode, which allows root access to the operating system, all userids, including informix, are prevented

from opening new connections to any database structures other than those available through the SMI.

In shutting down an instance, all user threads have to be completely terminated for the engine to complete the transition to quiescent mode. Several administrative tasks such as adding or dropping logical logs require an instance to be in quiescent mode to complete.

- **On-line**: The instance is fully operational and available to all users with rights to access it. There are some administrative or tuning tasks that can be done with the instance in an on-line mode. These include adding a CPU vp or creating an archive via the `ontape` utility.
- **Shutdown**: A transitional mode as the instance moves from an on-line mode to either quiescent or off-line mode. Unless an immediate shutdown is being executed, all user threads are allowed to complete their tasks and terminate normally. New database connections are refused, however.

Once a shutdown command has been issued to take the instance to quiescent or off-line mode, it cannot be reversed or canceled.

- **Read only**: This mode only applies to the secondary server in an HADR data replication environment. In this mode, an application running on the secondary server (such as `dbaccess`) has the ability to query the secondary instance's databases tables directly, but insert, modify, or delete SQL commands are not processed.

The operating mode of the instance can either be changed through `onmonitor`, from the **Mode** option, or via the command line using `oninit` and `onmode` commands.

- `oninit -s` brings a configured instance from off-line mode to quiescent mode.
- `oninit` with no flags will bring a configured instance from off-line mode all the way to on-line mode.

The `oninit` utility also has a "`-p`" flag, which I do not recommend using when restarting an instance. With the "`-p`" flag set, the engine will not remove temporary tables in the rootdbs or other dbspaces during instance start up. Using this option does decrease the amount of time it takes for the instance to come online. However, since the disk space used by the temp tables is not freed up, and the temp tables cannot be accessed by user sessions, it's a waste of disk space. I don't think the extra ten seconds of waiting is worth the continual loss of disk space.

warning

There is one other flag to the `oninit` command that you should be aware of—the "-i" flag. Using this flag will initialize the rootdbs for the instance, wiping out anything that might have been there. Losing the information contained in the rootdbs will effectively wipe out the rest of the data structures in the instance. Do not use this flag unless you intend to rebuild the instance from scratch.

The `onmode` command can be used as follows:

- `onmode -m` changes the instance from quiescent to on-line mode.

- `onmode -s [-y]` transitions the instance from on-line mode through shutdown mode to quiescent mode. Using the "-y" flag will eliminate a confirmation prompt.

- `onmode -k [-y]` shuts the instance down from either an on-line or quiescent mode to off-line mode in an orderly fashion. User threads are terminated gracefully by the engine, buffers are flushed through a checkpoint process, and transactions are rolled back if necessary.

- `onmode -u [-y]` immediately terminates all instance activity and takes the instance off-line. This is the equivalent of pulling the plug on the instance, but transactions are marked for rollback in the logical logs. As with the "-k" option, using the "-y" flag will eliminate the two confirmation prompts that otherwise would present themselves.

There are other options to the `onmode` command such as "-z" to terminate user threads, "-a" to increase the shared memory segment size, and "-c" to initiate a checkpoint. These options will be covered later in this chapter or in other chapters as appropriate for the discussion. These and other options do not fit with what I'm covering in this section of the book.

Changing Database Logging Modes

As I will explain in the "Creating the Database" section of Chapter 5, when a database is created, a "logging mode" has to be selected. The logging mode of a database determines whether or not logical groups of database activity can be programmed to either succeed or fail as a complete unit. This is called a "transaction." A common example of a transaction can be found in the banking environment where, when depositing your paycheck, the bank must

1. Credit your account for the face value of the check
2. Debit the account of your employer for the face value of the check

Both actions must succeed or both must fail; otherwise, the bank will be in a real mess financially.

The logging mode of the database also determines whether or not records detailing the data changes that occur in the instance are created. If a database is in a "logged" mode, these changes are tracked by writing information into the physical and logical log structures. In the "What Is the Fast Recovery Process?" section of Chapter 10, I explain how the logical log records are used in the fast recovery process to ensure logical data integrity.

It is not uncommon to change the logging mode of databases. Quite often, a database will be created by using the `dbimport` utility; and, unless there is absolutely no data to import, the database will be created in an unlogged mode. Because the entire import is handled as a single transaction, this prevents a long transaction from occurring while the data is being loaded into the tables. Once the database is imported, the logging mode will usually be changed to another mode.

Because of the way different logging modes operate, from time to time it might be advantageous to temporarily change back to an unlogged mode if major structural changes need to be made to tables while in a maintenance period. See the "Logging Modes" section of Chapter 5 for a full description of the logging modes available in OnLine Dynamic Server. For the purposes of the discussion here, there are two types of logging modes: logged and nonlogged.

In earlier versions of the engine, all changes to database logging modes had to be made while the instance was in quiescent mode via the `tbmonitor` utility. OnLine Dynamic Server still allows some changes to the logging mode to be made via the `onmonitor` utility, although there are some logging mode changes that have to be made from the command line via the `ontape` utility. In the 7.2 release of OnLine Dynamic Server, a new utility called `ondblog` was introduced to mark databases for a logging mode change. The change does not occur until an archive is created. Finally, an application or individual user can make some limited logging mode changes that only affect their own particular application or user thread. Using the "`set log`" SQL syntax, a user or application can change the session environment from an "unbuffered" log mode to a "buffered" log mode, or vice-versa.

From the `onmonitor` **Logical-Logs:Databases** option, a database can immediately be changed from any of the three "logged" modes (buffered, unbuffered, mode ANSI) to another of the three. The `ontape` and `ondblog` utilities can be used as well to make these changes without requiring the creation of an archive.

Changing a database from any of the logged modes to a nonlogged mode, or vice versa, requires using the `ondblog` and/or the `ontape` utility and creating an archive. I recommend creating an archive whenever changing the logging mode of a database, so I never use the `onmonitor` utility to change logging modes. Instead, I invoke the `ontape` utility, create an archive, and change the logging mode with one command line string.

Using the `ontape` utility to change logging modes is fairly straightforward. To change a database between one of the three logging modes, use the "`-U` *dbname*" flag for unbuffered logging, "`-B` *dbname*" for buffered logging, or "`-A` *dbname*" for mode ANSI.

To completely change from a nonlogged or logged mode to the other requires creating a level 0 archive. Simply append one of the three flags just mentioned or "`-N` *dbname*" for a nonlogged mode change to an "`ontape -s -L 0`" command.

The `ondblog` utility sets a flag to change a database's logging mode to whatever option is requested when the next level 0 archive occurs. The `ondblog` utility options are as follows:

- ansi—mode ANSI logging mode
- cancel—cancels the logging mode changes previously requested

- buf—buffered logging
- nolog—changes the database to a nonlogged environment
- unbuf—unbuffered logging

These options can be followed by one of two additional parameters. The first is simply a space-delimited list of databases the logging mode change is to affect. The other option is an "-f" flag followed by a pathed filename. This file would contain a list of database names the change is to affect. The databases would be listed individually in the file, one to a row.

In the absence of the "-f" flag and filename or a list of space-delimited database names, the `ondblog` utility will change all the databases in the instance to the requested level at the next level 0 archive.

Whether you use the `ontape` utility or a combination of the `ondblog` and `ontape` utilities to change the logging mode of a database, the instance does not need to be in quiescent mode, but there cannot be any active user threads attached to the instance at the time the logging mode change is attempted. Otherwise, a rather cryptic "-107" error is generated.

If an `ontape` command is issued to change the logging mode on a database and is interrupted, the database will remain closed as far as user connectivity is concerned until a full instance archive is generated—with or without changing the logging mode.

In situations where I need to change the logging mode of a database to perform maintenance activities, I speed up the process of creating an archive and changing the logging mode by setting the archive device temporarily to /dev/null. The archive completes immediately, and the logging mode change is made. Of course, prior to this I created a full archive of the instance in its native logging mode to tape in case I have to restore the instance environment. Once I complete all the maintenance tasks, I change the logging mode back to the original state by executing the proper `ontape` command with the tape device still pointing to /dev/null. Then I change the tape device back to the real device and create a full archive of the instance to a tape that I save along with the archive created before I started the maintenance period.

Managing Dbspaces and BLOBspaces

Like changing the logging mode of a database, the creation or removal of dbspaces is pretty straightforward using the `onmonitor` or `onspaces` utility. As I mentioned in the "Dbspace Design Issues" section of Chapter 2, the creation and population of dbspaces is a mixture of common sense, intuition, and guesswork. In creating and placing dbspaces within disk spindles, you need to know how the tables those dbspaces will contain will lay across the disks, how active they will be, and at what rate they're anticipated to grow. These anticipated growth rates and performance expectations will determine how and where tables get built.

In OLTP environments, the highly volatile tables should be fragmented across a number of smaller high-performance drives. Other tables can be placed in larger dbspaces on larger drives where response is not so critical. In a DSS environment, the volume of data to store will require larger drives. The division of that data across the drives will be driven by the logical grouping and association of columnar elements rather than performance.

Offsets

There are two ways of dealing with disk chunks as well as dbspaces. The first is that any individual chunk or dbspace is a subset of a larger disk partition. Using this approach, the O/S disk partitioning tool is used to create the largest possible hard partition the O/S can support on a disk. Single-chunk dbspaces, or chunks for adding to dbspaces on the same or other drives, are created by using disk space allocated at various starting points, or "offsets," within the hard partition. This approach requires keeping track of all the chunks, their offsets, and sizes for each hard disk partition.

In an environment where design and implementation processes are happening "on the fly" throughout the life of a project, this approach can take some measure of the guesswork and administrative headaches out of the disk partitioning and dbspace sizing tasks. Because there are fewer hard disk partitions to work around, the size of any given dbspace can be increased by as little or as much space as is left in the partition by adding more chunks at different offsets.

Another positive aspect of using offsets is that you have more control over where on a disk a chunk is located. A chunk can be created closer to or further away from the center of the spindle, depending on performance needs, through the offset value itself.

On the other hand, using offsets can be a record-keeping hassle. On more than one occasion in environments using offsets, I ran into situations where the creation of dbspaces failed because other chunks were "temporarily" created in areas of disks that were supposed to be free.

Using offsets requires constantly remapping the layout by perusing the output from the "`onstat -d`" command or the **Dbspaces:Info** option of `onmonitor`. Offsets also make it more difficult to monitor drive hotspots if your port of the engine does not include all the instance graphical monitoring utilities. While you can monitor total dbspace and chunk activity through the `onperf` or `D/B Cockpit` graphical utilities, O/S monitoring tools are of little value because they function at the hard partition level. Because there would generally only be one hard partition per drive, it would be difficult to monitor which OnLine chunk on a given drive was more active than another and be able to make whatever changes might be required to increase performance. OnLine Dynamic Server's graphical monitoring utilities are covered in Chapter 7, Monitoring the Instance.

Partitions

The second approach to handling disk chunks and dbspaces is to create one or more physical partitions on the disk and use each partition as a single chunk. This approach requires more design work up front so that the disk partitions are sized correctly. I prefer this approach because it makes it easier to monitor disk bottlenecks with either OnLine Dynamic Server or O/S tools. The mapping of logical instance structures to the physical implementation is also cleaner and easier to follow.

A frequently asked question by those new to OnLine Dynamic Server is how big can any individual raw disk chunk be. The answer is 2 GB, although there is a condition that could affect the actual size of the chunk. To understand what this condition is and its impact on chunk creation, let me share with you a portion of e-mail from John Lengyel at Informix:

> The real deal here is that the last byte in any chunk must be less than two gigabytes from the beginning of the device. So it's not enough to say that a chunk must be smaller than 2 gig. The chunk "offset" must also be taken into account.
>
> A chunk's offset, plus its size, must be "less than" 2 gigabytes, which is 2147483648 bytes. The practical limit will depend on your OnLine page size, which is either 2K or 4K. For systems with 2K pages, the maximum combination of chunk offset and chunk size is 2097150 kilobytes. For 4K systems that maximum is 2097148 kilobytes.
>
> Note that OnLine protects you if you try to go out of bounds. Some examples:

```
onspaces -a dbs1 -p /dev/online1 -o 0 -s 2097150
```

That chunk comes in just under the wire. As does this next fairly small one:

```
onspaces -a dbs1 -p /dev/online1 -o 2092150 -s 5000
```

These examples show errors caught by onspaces:

```
unix%> onspaces -a rootdbs -p /dev/online1 -o 0 -s
    2097152
```

Chunk size (2097152k) greater than 2097151k limit.

```
unix%> onspaces -a rootdbs -p /dev/online1 -o
    2092150 -s 5002
```

Chunk size + offset (2097152k) greater than 2097151k limit.

```
unix%> onspaces -a rootdbs -p /dev/online1 -o 0 -s
    2097151
```

The size must be a multiple of the page size.

Temporary Dbspaces

There are two types of dbspaces, "regular" and "temporary." Regular dbspaces contain standard database table and index data structures. They can be mirrored, activity in them is logged to the logical logs if the database is in a logged mode, and they are included in archives created by the `ontape` or `onarchive` utilities.

OnLine Dynamic Server uses "temporary" dbspaces to create temporary tables for hash joins as well as index, sort, and order-by operations instead of flat files, as previous versions of OnLine did. End-user applications can also use temporary dbspaces for creating explicit or implicit temporary tables resulting from a "`select blah into temp`" type of query.

Temporary dbspaces cannot be mirrored, are not archived, and are completely initialized at each reboot of the instance. Engine-caused activity in temporary dbspaces is not logged in the logical logs, regardless of the database logging mode.

Unlike engine-generated activity, some user-generated temp table activity in a temporary dbspace can, and will be, logged in the logical logs, depending on the database logging mode and the DDL syntax used. If a database is not in a logged mode, obviously nothing will be logged. In a logged mode, *all* database activity is considered crucial unless explicitly stated otherwise; this includes the creation and use of user-generated temporary tables.

To create an unlogged temporary table, the phrase "`with no log`" must be appended to the create table statement. For example:

```
create temp table ex_ample
  ( div_no integer,
    area_no smallint,
    tot_sales decimal(12,2)
  ) with no log;
```

The OnLine Dynamic Server engine will not use temporary dbspaces for user-generated or engine-generated temporary tables unless explicitly told to do so. To do so requires setting the DBSPACETEMP parameter in the **Parameters:Shared-Memory** `onmonitor` screen or the $DBSPACETEMP user environment variable.

Creative use of the $DBSPACETEMP environment variable can result in greater instance performance when multiple data-manipulation-intensive applications are running simultaneously. Because you can create any number of temporary dbspaces, applications that make heavy use of, or cause the creation of, temporary tables could then be coded to use different temporary dbspaces. This would reduce the amount of disk contention for the same temporary dbspaces from all the applications.

In an instance environment where a number of temporary dbspaces are available and there are no special restrictions made by the application to the temporary dbspaces to use, they will be used in rotation. Statements that can be parallelized will cause the creation of several temporary tables in several temporary dbspaces. These temporary tables will then be merged to create the desired result set.

This merge occurs quickly because each data set in a temporary table is already in sorted order. All that is required at this point is a comparison of the sort orders for each temporary table. This is one of the reasons OnLine Dynamic Server is so much faster than previous versions of the engine.

Creating a Dbspace or BLOBspace

When you create a new instance, you create a dbspace commonly called the "rootdbs." This occurs when valid data is entered into the ROOTNAME, ROOTSIZE, and ROOTPATH parameters, as well as the ROOTOFFSET and MIRRORPATH parameters if needed, from the **Parameters:Initialize** onmonitor screen. As you can tell from the `onmonitor` dbspace creation screen shown in Figure 4-3, the creation of a new dbspace once an instance is up and running is not much different or more difficult than creating the rootdbs.

```
Press ESC to build a new DBspace.
Press Interrupt to cancel the option and return to the Dbspaces menu.
Press F2 or CTRL-F for field level help.
                         CREATE DBSPACE
    Dbspace Name [              ]    Mirror [ ]    Temp [ ]
PRIMARY CHUNK INFORMATION:
   Full Pathname [                                              ]
        Offset [       0] Kbytes           Size [       0] Kbytes
MIRROR CHUNK INFORMATION:
   Full Pathname [                                              ]
        Offset [       0] Kbytes
```

Figure 4-3 *The dbspace creation screen from* `onmonitor`*.*

As I explained in the "Using Symbolic Links" section of Chapter 2, symbolic links should always be used to point to disk partitions or tape devices instead of real device names. I will follow that philosophy in the examples given here and in the rest of the chapters in the book.

Looking at this screen and how it operates, if mirror was not set to "Y" when the instance was initialized, the "Mirror" field in the dbspace creation screen will be ignored. If the "Temp" field is set to "Y," the dbspace is created and flagged as a temporary dbspace. See the previous section of this chapter for information on temporary dbspaces.

Including the name of the newly created temporary dbspace in either the $DBSPACETEMP environment variable or the $ONCONFIG file will activate its use by the engine for the instance. Pressing the "accept" key after the applicable fields have been filled in will create the dbspace. If mirroring was enabled, the mirror will be built as well. The creation of the dbspace takes very little time, regardless of its size.

If the dbspace is to be mirrored, the dbspace will not be accessible until the creation of the mirror has completed. The length of time required to build a mirror can vary depending on the size of the primary dbspace, the type and speed of the I/O bus, and general I/O contention with other processes running on the server.

The initial creation of a mirror puts a very high I/O load on the system because the mirror creation process does a series of bitmap copies from the primary device to the mirror. Watch the overall system load and I/O pipelines when creating a number of mirrored dbspaces, especially if you're using a shell script to invoke a series of onspaces commands. You can easily max out the disk I/O subsystem causing severe performance problems that will affect your dbspace creation process and any other applications running on the server.

To create a dbspace from the command line, use the onspaces utility with the following flags:

- -c indicates that this is a "create" action
- -d *dbspacename,* name of the dbspace
- -p *pathedname,* the pathed name of the symbolic link pointing to the disk partition
- -s *size,* the size of the dbspace in KB

- `-o` *offsetvalue,* the offset value, if any, into the disk partition; 0 for none
- `-t` (optional) if the dbspace is to be a temporary dbspace; not required otherwise

If the dbspace is to be mirrored, include the following flag:

- `-m` *pathedname offsetvalue,* the pathed name of the symbolic link pointing to the mirror disk partition followed by the offset value, if any, into the disk partition; 0 for none

For example, to create a 100 MB mirrored dbspace called index_1, you would enter the following type of command:

```
onspaces -c -d index_1 \
-p /usr/informix_72/amazon/ama_chnk_1 -o 0 -s 100000 \
-m /usr/informix_72/amazon/ama_chnk_12 0
```

To create a 150 MB temporary dbspace called work_space_1 that is offset 200 MB into the disk partition, the command would look like:

```
onspaces -c -d work_space_1 \
-p /usr/informix_72/amazon/ama_chnk_20 \
-s 150000 -o 200000 -t
```

If you need to create a BLOBspace, eliminate the "`-d` *dbspacename*" flag from the `onspaces` command and add the following:

- `-b` *blobname,* the BLOBspace name
- `-g` *pagesize,* the size of the BLOBspace page **in pages**, not KB

For example, to create a 1 GB nonmirrored BLOBspace using 3 OnLine pages as a BLOBpage size, the command would be:

```
onspaces -b blob_world \
-p /usr/informix_72/amazon/ama_chnk_3 -s 1000000 \
-o 0 -g 3
```

You cannot create "temporary" BLOBspaces, but they can be mirrored. BLOBspaces function almost like regular dbspaces, although there are a couple of differences. Unlike a regular dbspace, which is available for use immediately after creation, and mirroring if done through the engine, the logical log entries detailing the creation of a BLOBspace and its activation for use must occur in two separate logical logs. This means you'll probably have to force a switch in the active logical log via the `ontape` utility using the "`-a`" option. This would be followed by forcing a checkpoint to occur by using the "`onmode -c`" command to completely activate the new logical log and complete the BLOBspace creation process.

The other major way BLOBspaces differ from regular dbspaces is that the page size of the BLOBspace can be set to any multiple of the engine's page size. The ability to create an enlarged page size within a BLOBspace improves the storage efficiency and I/O transfer of the BLOB data. The smallest BLOBspace page size you can use is 1, or the same size of the page size for your port of the engine.

While a BLOB could fill one or more BLOBpages, only one BLOB will be stored to a BLOBpage. To get the most efficient use of the BLOBspace pages, they should not be set too large or too small. Ideally, the BLOBpage size should be set as close as possible to the average size of the BLOB. This way, you're not wasting as much disk space when the BLOB is smaller than the BLOBspace page size, or when the BLOB is larger than the BLOBspace page size and an additional BLOBpage is allocated within the BLOBspace to store the BLOB.

I realize that using the term "average size" can be misleading. This implies, in my mind anyway, a standard average. Sum up the individual sizes of each BLOB, divide by the number of BLOBs, and *voila*—the average size. The problem with this is that there could be a number of BLOBs significantly larger in size than the majority. These BLOBs could skew the calculation of the average. It is more appropriate to look at the average BLOB to be stored in terms of volume and size, and calculate the BLOBpage size from that. Treat the occasional larger BLOB as an exception. Although they will require more than one BLOBpage for storage, the amount of disk space wasted on the last BLOBpage allocated to store these larger BLOBs should be relatively small when compared to the total amount of space used.

If a table contains more than one BLOB column, or several tables contain BLOB columns, build several BLOBspaces of varying BLOBpage sizes if the "average" size of the different BLOB columns vary significantly. To check how well you calculated the BLOBpage size, the "`onstat -pB`" command will display the storage efficiency of the BLOBpages in each BLOBspace.

Adding a Disk Chunk

Expanding a dbspace or BLOBspace by adding a disk chunk is not much different than creating a dbspace or BLOBspace. To add a disk chunk using the `onmonitor` **Dbspaces:Add_chunk** option, you first see a list of active dbspaces or BLOBspaces similar to Figure 4-4.

```
Press ESC to return to the Dbspaces menu.
Use arrow keys to move the cursor.
Press F3 or CTRL-B to choose the highlighted DBspace/BLOBspace.

                       LIST OF DBSPACES/BLOBSPACES

                                  When
    Dbspace/BLOBSpace Name        Created               Status
       rootdbs                    15:06:51                M
       logs                       15:11:28                M
       tempdb1                    15:14:35                N T
       db0                        15:15:23                M
```

Figure 4-4 *A list of active dbspaces generated by the* `onmonitor` **Dbspaces:Add_chunk** *option.*

To continue the process, highlight one dbspace or BLOBspace by scrolling up or down the screen. Press "ctrl-b" when the appropriate dbspace or BLOBspace is highlighted, enter the disk information for the new chunk to add, and press the "accept" key. The chunk will be added to the dbspace.

To accomplish the same task from the command line, use the `onspaces` utility with the following flags:

- `-a` *dbspace/blobname,* name of the dbspace or BLOBspace
- `-p` *pathedname,* the fully pathed symbolic link pointing to the disk chunk to add
- `-o` *offsetvalue,* the offset value, if any, into the disk partition; 0 for none
- `-s` *chunksize,* the size of the chunk in KB

If the dbspace or BLOBspace is mirrored, the new chunk will need to be mirrored as well. In this case, add the following to the onspaces command:

- -m *pathedname offsetvalue,* the fully pathed symbolic link pointing to the disk chunk to add, the offset value in KB, if any, into the disk partition; 0 for none

For example, to add another 1 GB chunk to the blob_world BLOBspace created in a previous example, you would execute:

```
onspaces -a blob_world \
-p /usr/informix_72/amazon/ama_chnk_20 \
-s 1000000 -o 0
```

Dropping a Disk Chunk

The ability to drop a disk chunk from a dbspace or BLOBspace that was added after the dbspace was created is a new feature in OnLine Dynamic Server. In OnLine versions 5.x and earlier, a chunk added to a dbspace was irretrievable unless the entire dbspace was dropped. Now, if an additional chunk is empty, it can be removed from the dbspace or BLOBspace with the onspaces utility.

Unlike regular dbspaces, dropping an additional chunk from a BLOBspace requires the instance to be in quiescent mode.

To determine if a chunk is completely empty, execute an "oncheck -pe" command. Save the output to file and review it. Each chunk of every dbspace will be listed individually along with any table or index allocation that exists in the chunk.

If a table or index has space allocated in the chunk you want to drop, try to remove the allocation or move it to another chunk. Tables that have multiple extents can be concatenated somewhat by altering an index to cluster, which will remove unnecessary extents; or the tables can be unloaded, dropped, and rebuilt in other dbspaces. Changing the fragmentation strategy will cause the affected fragments to be rebuilt, possibly removing allocations in the chunk to be dropped. See the "Altering Fragments" section of Chapter 5 to learn how to alter fragmentation schemes.

Once the chunk is free, use the `onspaces` utility with the following flags to drop the chunk:

- `-d` *db/BLOBspacename,* name of the dbspace or BLOBspace containing the chunk to be dropped
- `-p` *pathedname,* the fully pathed symbolic link pointing to the disk device
- `-o` *offsetvalue,* the offset value in KB, if any, into the disk partition; 0 for none
- `-y` to answer the confirmation prompt

If for some reason the chunk is *not* completely empty, the drop process will be aborted and an error message returned.

Dropping a Dbspace or BLOBspace

To drop a dbspace or BLOBspace, follow the same procedure when dropping a chunk to make sure there are no tables or indexes in the space to be dropped. The "`where_are_tables`" script, discussed in Chapter 12, Scripts to Help Get the Job Done, can be used to determine if tables are stored in any given dbspace as well.

The **Dbspaces:Drop** `onmonitor` option will display a list of dbspaces, similar to that shown in Figure 4-4. Select the dbspace to drop by scrolling up or down the screen and following the directions printed at the top of the screen.

To drop a dbspace or BLOBspace from the command line, use the `onspaces` utility with the following flags:

- `-d` *db/BLOBspacename,* name of the dbspace or BLOBspace to be dropped
- `-y` to answer the confirmation prompt

Similar to the procedure for dropping a disk chunk, if the dbspace is not completely empty, the drop process will be aborted and an error message returned.

Adding or Dropping a Mirror

If mirroring was enabled at the time the instance was created, and a dbspace or BLOBspace was created without a mirror, a mirror can be added at any time. Likewise, mirroring can be dropped from a dbspace or BLOBspace if it is no longer needed.

The **Dbspaces:Mirror** onmonitor option will either create or stop mirroring on any dbspace or BLOBspace listed. The selection procedure for this option is similar to the dbspace add or drop options just discussed.

Using the onspaces utility to add a mirror to a dbspace or BLOBspace requires adding the mirrors on a chunk-by-chunk basis using the following flags:

- -m *db/BLOBspacename,* the name of the dbspace or BLOB-space
- -p *pathed_name_of_primary_chunk,* the fully pathed symbolic link pointing to the disk partition
- -o *offset_value_of_primary_chunk*, the offset value in KB, if any, into the disk partition; 0 for none
- -m *pathed_name_of_mirror_chunk offset_value_of_mirror_chunk,* the fully pathed symbolic link pointing to the mirror disk partition, the offset value in KB, if any, into the disk partition; 0 for none
- -y to answer the confirmation prompt

If the chunk in the dbspace to be mirrored is using cooked space rather than a raw partition, the syntax would be:

- -m *db/BLOBspacename,* the name of the dbspace or BLOB-space
- -f *filename,* the fully pathed filename of the mirror disk chunk

For example, suppose the dbs_1 dbspace was created using cooked space. To create a mirror of that dbspace, you would execute the following command:

```
onspaces -m dbs_1 -f /home2/mirrors/dbs1_mirror -y
```

 *note*

The same procedure must be followed to prepare a cooked-file-based mirror chunk as to use cooked file space for the primary dbspace chunk. The mirror file needs to be created with the "touch" command and given 660/informix/informix permissions, ownership, and group privileges. Only then can the onspaces *command be executed.*

When you drop a mirror, you drop all the mirrors on the dbspace. To drop a dbspace's mirrors using the onspaces utility requires the following flags:

- -r *db/BLOBspacename,* the dbspace or BLOBspace name
- -y to answer the confirmation prompt

Changing the Status of a Chunk

Either part of an OnLine Dynamic Server mirrored chunk pair can be brought off- or on-line at will, provided the other half of the pair is completely functional. One possible reason for doing this would be to enable you to physically move data around within your disk environment without requiring a total shutdown of the system to rebuild the database. Once again, using symbolic links to point to the physical devices rather than the actual device names when creating the chunks and/or dbspaces makes this migration transparent to the instance.

Either the **Dbspaces:Status** onmonitor option or the onspaces utility can be used to make the change. When using the onspaces utility to change the status of one half of a mirror pair, you need to append either a "-D" to take the chunk down or an "-O" to bring the chunk back on-line to the command string. The flags for this type of action would be:

- -s *db/BLOBspacename,* the name of the dbspace or BLOBspace to be affected
- -p *pathed_name,* the pathed name of the symbolic link pointing to the disk chunk to be taken down or brought on-line
- -o *offset_value,* the offset value in KB, if any, into the disk partition; 0 for none
- -D OR -O to indicate the action required on the chunk
- -y to answer the confirmation prompt

Setting or Changing DATASKIP

The DATASKIP parameter determines how the instance handles queries requesting data from dbspaces or BLOBspaces that are unavailable. If turned OFF, the query fails. If turned ON for all, or for specific dbspaces and the query needs to access those down dbspaces for data, the query completes with the data it has access to but an error message is generated. The **Dbspaces:datasKip** onmonitor option can be used to set or modify this parameter.

The onspaces utility can be used to change the DATASKIP parameter as well. There are only two flags, but the first can be followed by a set of values. The syntax is as follows:

- -f ON OR OFF
  [*list_of_db/BLOBspacenames*] (optional)—a comma-delimited list of dbspaces to be affected by the command
- -y to answer the confirmation prompt

Using the "ON" or "OFF" option alone will turn DATASKIP on or off for all spaces in the instance. If you need to set DATASKIP functionality at a dbspace or BLOBspace level, individual spaces can be listed in a comma-delimited format within the command.

Creating, Moving, and Resizing Logs

One of the first tasks to complete after initializing an instance that will contain databases in a logged mode is to create one or more dbspaces to hold the physical and logical logs, then relocate the logs out of the rootdbs and build new logical logs. If all the databases will be in unlogged mode it's not as critical, but should be done anyway. Moving the logs out of the rootdbs eliminates a significant amount of I/O all pointing at that one device and helps prevent a disk I/O bottleneck from occurring.

A nice new feature of OnLine Dynamic Server is that not only can both sets of logs be moved at will, they can also be resized. In OnLine versions 5.x and earlier, the sizes were set at instance initialization and were unalterable unless the instance was reinitialized. This was very frustrating when trying to tune the instance's log usage as applications were being deployed and used by the full complement of users.

If you follow the guidelines I give in the "Initial Device Configuration" section of Chapter 3, Initializing an OnLine Dynamic Server Instance, when you create a new instance you'll create a 1 MB physical log and five logical logs, each 1 MB in size, in a rootdbs of about 25 MB. The number and size of the logs are adequate for the creation of the sysmaster database and other initialization functions.

If all the databases in the instance will be unlogged, there is no pressing need, other than to free up space in the rootdbs, to move the logs to different dbspaces, since there will be little or no activity in them. There will probably not be any need to increase the number of logical logs either. The physical log will also be okay if simply moved into another dbspace.

In an instance with one or more databases in a logged mode, more logical logs will be needed—quite possibly in a larger size. The number and size of the logical logs as well as the size of the physical log will need to be tuned over time. In addition, both types of logs *must* be moved out of the rootdbs and into separate dbspaces from each other. These logs should be located in dbspaces created on some of the highest performing disks in the system because the logs will be subject to a considerable amount of activity.

The Physical Log

The relocation of the physical log, as well as the creation and dropping of logical logs, requires the instance to be in quiescent mode. Moving or changing the size of the physical log requires an immediate instance shutdown to complete, so only make changes to the physical log during a maintenance window. Figure 4-5 shows what the `onmonitor` **Parameters:Physical-Log** screen looks like to accomplish this task.

All you need to do is enter the new size of the physical log, and/or the dbspace the log should be in, press the "accept" key, and the instance will shut down and reinitialize with the log resized and/or moved.

You would use the following flags with the `onparams` utility to achieve the same result:

```
              MODIFY PHYSICAL LOG


      Physical Log Size [      1000] Kbytes

      Dbspace Name     [rootdbs           ]
```

Figure 4-5 *The* onmonitor *physical log tuning screen*

- -p -s *size_in_kbytes,* the new size of the physical log in KB; if you are not changing its size, reenter the current size
- -d *dbspacename,* the name of the dbspace to contain the physical log
- -y to answer the confirmation prompt

A level 0 archive should always be created immediately after moving the physical log.

The physical log, as well as the physical log buffers, can be monitored for efficiency through the D/B Cockpit graphical utility or via the command line with the "onstat -l" and "oncheck -pr" commands. Using either option, look for the percentage of the log used at checkpoint. Look at the MSGPATH file, also known as the OnLine message log, as well to see how long it takes for a checkpoint to complete.

A checkpoint will occur when the physical log becomes 75 percent full. If the physical log is too small, checkpoints will occur too often, though hopefully they will complete quickly. Even though the pages in the physical log are used serially, during a checkpoint the entries need to be sorted before writing into the logical logs. If the log is too large, checkpoints will occur every CKPTINTVL seconds, but will take a long time to complete while all the pages in the physical log are sorted.

In an OLTP environment, a checkpoint duration of more than five seconds will probably be unacceptable because all activity in the instance is paused during the checkpoint. Tuning the physical log size as well as the CKPTINTVL parameter will result in a balance of checkpoint duration and frequency.

The Logical Log

Logical logs are just as easy to resize or move as the physical log. If the instance is in quiescent mode, logical logs can be dropped, added, and/or resized.

At no time can there be less than three fully active logical logs in an instance. As a result, moving logical logs is a process of creating new logs in new dbspace(s), activating them through a level 0 archive, then deleting the old logs in the old dbspace(s).

The **Parameters:Add_Log** screen from the `onmonitor` utility is shown in Figure 4-6.

```
Press ESC to add a logical log.
Press Interrupt to cancel the option and return to the Parameters menu.
Press F2 or CTRL-F for field level help.

                    ADDING A LOGICAL LOG

            Logical Log Size   [       10000] Kbytes

            Dbspace Name       [                    ]
```

Figure 4-6 *The Parameters:Add_Log* `onmonitor` *screen to add and/or change logical logs.*

Similar to moving or changing the physical log, to create a new logical log enter the name of the dbspace as well as the desired size and press the "accept" key. Be aware that you cannot create all the logical logs you want. The instance will only allow LOGSMAX logical logs to be built in the instance. This parameter can easily be tuned if necessary, but it requires an instance shutdown to take effect.

Using the `onparams` utility to add a logical log would require the following flags:

- `-a -d` *dbspacename*, the name of the dbspace to contain the logical log
- `-s` *log_size* (optional), in KB—use only if you want a logical log sized larger or smaller than the instance "default"

If the "-s" option is not used, the new logical log will be created using the LOGSIZE parameter from the physical device initialization screen of the instance initialization process. This size is considered the "default" size for all logical logs in the instance.

When created, a logical log is not immediately activated for use by the instance, a level 0 archive is required to change the status of newly added logical logs. When I add logical logs, I usually create a quick-and-dirty archive using `/dev/null` as the tape device to activate the logs. I follow this by creating another archive to the real archive device to capture the instance with all the logs created and in an active state.

Only logical logs that are not currently recording transactions, or the one containing the last checkpoint, can be dropped from the instance. Dropping a logical log involves selecting it by its physical number, not its logical id.

Each logical log has a physical number that never changes as well as a logical number assigned to it when the log becomes the "current" log in the instance. This logical number is incremented serially and is assigned to each logical log as it becomes active log throughout the life of the instance.

The physical log number for each log, as well as the currently active log and the log containing the last checkpoint, can be identified from the output of an "`onstat -l`" command. Figure 4-7 contains the output of an "`onstat -l`" command from one of my production machines.

In this figure, you can see that the logical log with physical number 24 and logical id 213 is the current log by virtue of the "C" status flag. It also contains the last checkpoint record because of the "L" flag. The logs are 10 MB in size and have been moved around a couple of times right after initialization because the physical number starts at 7. As the logical logs fill, they are archived automatically and marked available for reuse by the presence of the "B" flag.

Using the `onparams` utility to drop a logical log requires the following flags:

- `-d -1` *physical_log_number*, the physical number of the logical log to drop
- `-y` to answer the confirmation prompt

```
INFORMIX-OnLine Version 7.13.UC2 -- On-Line -- Up 12 days 02:59:55 -- 44848
Kbytes

Physical Logging
Buffer      bufused    bufsize    numpages    numwrits    pages/io
 P-2           0         16         93827       6380        14.71
    phybegin   physize    phypos    phyused    %used
     300035     2500       1861        0        0.00

Logical Logging
Buffer   bufused   bufsize   numrecs   numpages   numwrits   recs/pages   pages/io
 L-2        0        16       3876706    549841     486442       7.1         1.1

address    number    flags      uniqid    begin      size      used      %used
c1625304     7       U-B----     196      200035     5000      5000     100.00
c1625320     8       U-B----     197      2013bd     5000      5000     100.00
c162533c     9       U-B----     198      202745     5000      5000     100.00
c1625358    10       U-B----     199      203acd     5000      5000     100.00
c1625374    11       U-B----     200      204e55     5000      5000     100.00
c1625390    12       U-B----     201      2061dd     5000      5000     100.00
c16253ac    13       U-B----     202      207565     5000      5000     100.00
c16253c8    14       U-B----     203      2088ed     5000      5000     100.00
c16253e4    15       U-B----     204      209c75     5000      5000     100.00
c1625400    16       U-B----     205      20affd     5000      5000     100.00
c162541c    17       U-B----     206      20c385     5000      5000     100.00
c1625438    18       U-B----     207      20d70d     5000      5000     100.00
c1625454    19       U-B----     208      20ea95     5000      5000     100.00
c1625470    20       U-B----     209      20fe1d     5000      5000     100.00
c162548c    21       U-B----     210      2111a5     5000      5000     100.00
c16254a8    22       U-B----     211      21252d     5000      5000     100.00
c16254c4    23       U-B----     212      2138b5     5000      5000     100.00
c16254e0    24       U---C-L     213      214c3d     5000      2147      42.94
c16254fc    25       U-B----     190      215fc5     5000      5000     100.00
c1625518    26       U-B----     191      21734d     5000      5000     100.00
c1625534    27       U-B----     192      2186d5     5000      5000     100.00
c1625550    28       U-B----     193      219a5d     5000      5000     100.00
c162556c    29       U-B----     194      21ade5     5000      5000     100.00
c1625588    30       U-B----     195      21c16d     5000      5000     100.00
```

Figure 4-7 *Output generated by the "onstat -l" command.*

The **Parameters:Drop_Log** onmonitor option will display a list of the logical logs with their size and dbspace information as illustrated in Figure 4-8.

```
Press ESC to return to the Parameters menu.
Use arrow keys to move the cursor.
Press F3 or CTRL-B to drop the highlighted logical log.
                    INDIVIDUAL LOGICAL LOGS
  Number    Uniqid    Flags      Pages      Used    % Used    Dbspace
     1         1      U---C-L     5000      1093    21.86     rootdbs
     2         0      F------     5000         0     0.00     rootdbs
     3         0      F------     5000         0     0.00     rootdbs
     4         0      F------     5000         0     0.00     rootdbs




         Total # of logical logs -> 4.
```

Figure 4–8 *The* onmonitor *drop logical log screen.*

Highlight the logical log to drop, press "cntl-b," and follow the prompts. As with any major instance change, I recommend creating a level 0 archive after dropping logical logs.

The size of logical logs is as important as the size of the physical log. Rather than having an impact on the checkpoint process, the size of the logical logs affects transaction concurrency. The LTXHWM and LTXEHWM parameters identify what percentage of the logical logs can fill prior to forcing a rollback of an open transaction, or pausing other instance activity to allow a transaction to commit or finish rolling back.

If the logical logs are too small, they will fill too quickly. While the log information will be copied out to tape quicker, there is a greater possibility of triggering a long-transaction error condition, depending on how long a transaction element in an application or a user-initiated action takes to complete.

On the flip side of the size issue, a bigger logical log size means that you don't have to worry as much about long transaction conditions. However, logs will take longer to fill, and as a result will not be archived off to tape in as timely a manner. Should an absolutely catastrophic disk error occur, however, all that could be used to restore from would be the instance archive tapes and the logical logs archived to tape. If only one logical log was filled per day, it would make it very difficult to use it to restore from since the log would still be on disk.

Depending on your level of paranoia, logical logs should be sized to fill, and be archived to tape, every 30 to 60 minutes of average instance use.

Killing a User Thread

One of the greatest things about the multithreaded design of the OnLine Dynamic Server engine is that there aren't any sqlturbo processes on which a braindead administrator, or user, can execute a "`kill -9`" command. That's enough justification in and of itself to upgrade to OnLine Dynamic Server! To be sure, someone with root or "`su`" privileges can still kill the `oninit` processes that run the entire instance, but they had better be prepared to accept the ensuing wrath of users and DBAs.

Short of shutting down the instance, terminating a user thread can only be accomplished by executing an "`onmode -z` *session_id*" command. The nice thing about the "`onmode -z`" command in OnLine Dynamic Server when compared to earlier versions of the engine is that it actually works!

There is also a "–Z" flag that can be used if the thread is coordinating a distributed transaction. See Chapter 11, Distributed Transactions, for more information on when, if ever, to use this flag.

As with OnLine versions 5.x and earlier, if the user thread is listed as being in a "critical section," it should not be interrupted if at all possible. Figure 4-9 contains the output of an "`onmode -u`" command. This command would indicate whether or not a thread was in a "critical section."

From the data in the figure, the thread for userid "paf" is in a "critical section" of the OnLine code.

A "critical section" is defined as being that part of OnLine Dynamic Server code that handles the completion of a transaction and ensures all disk updates have occurred as requested. Interrupting a thread in a "critical section" will force a rollback of that particular transaction to occur. If the rollback cannot be ensured, the instance will immediately shut down rather than

```
INFORMIX-OnLine Version 7.13.UC2--On-Line--Up 55 days 05:27:15--22848 Kbytes

Userthreads
address     flags   sessid   user   tty    wait         tout  locks  nreads  nwrites
c0fb9010   ---P--D  0        root   -      0            0     0      25295   15992
c0fb9444   ---P--F  0        root   -      0            0     0      0       0
c0fb9878   ---P--B  9        root   -      0            0     0      2026    1755
c0fb9cac   ---P--D  0        root   -      0            0     0      0       0
c0fbd350   ---PX--  14942    paf    ttyq7  c1405098     0     1      13      0
5 active, 128 total, 22 maximum concurrent
```

Figure 4-9 Output from an "onstat -u" command showing a thread in a "critical section."

allow an incomplete transaction to be marked as completed or rolled back.

Upon restarting the instance, the fast recovery mechanism can usually clean up the problem. That notwithstanding, the user or administrator should still verify the data that was being worked on at the time of the involuntary server shutdown to make sure data was not lost or corrupted.

While the output from the "onstat -u" command will list all the user threads in an instance, additional information on a particular thread can obtained by executing an "onstat -g ses session_id" command and querying through the SMI into the instance's shared memory. To look at the UNIX and OnLine Dynamic Server activity of a user, you can run the "checkon" script found on the accompanying media. Its functionality is described in Chapter 12.

Starting and Stopping OnLine Dynamic Server Automatically

If you're lazy like me, shutting down each instance prior to rebooting the server machine, then restarting them once the server comes back up, is a task to delegate as quickly and as permanently as possible. I use the UNIX system's own shutdown and initialization routine to handle these chores for me.

There are two simple shell scripts called "`start_online`" and "`stop_online`," which I've included on the accompanying media. A description of each can be found in Chapter 12. These scripts are placed in the rc2.d and rc0.d directories, respectively, to automatically start and stop instances on a physical server during a server shutdown or reboot. These directories are usually found under the /etc directory, but can also be found under the /sbin directory in some versions of UNIX.

The number in the directory name refers to the run level of the operating system which will trigger the scripts in that directory to execute. Level 0 is server shutdown, while level 2 is the first multi-user level.

Scripts or programs in the rc0.d directory are executed in numerical order provided they are prefaced with a "K" (capital letter) rather than a "k" (lower case) as the machine is shut down. Likewise, in the rc2.d directory, scripts or programs prefaced with an "S" rather than an "s" are executed on reboot and when the machine enters multi-user mode.

You can use any number and name combination (e.g., S95_start_online) for these two instance-oriented scripts. I usually choose a rather low number for the rc0.d script to shut the instances down early in the server shutdown sequence. This gets the OnLine Dynamic Server processes cleaned up and out of the way before other subsystems on the server start shutting down. It also allows for a rollback of moderate length to occur before it is affected by other server actions.

I use a high number for the script in the rc2.d directory so that the instances are one of the last systems to be started. This allows almost all the other system daemons to take their portion of shared memory and other processes started at boot to stabilize prior to starting OnLine Dynamic Server.

Summary

Most of the more common OnLine Dynamic Server administrative functions were covered in this chapter. Noticeably absent, of course, were the instance performance tuning and general monitoring tasks. Tuning information will be covered throughout the book in conjunction with the instance features or mechanisms that are affected by specific tunable procedures. Monitoring utilities will be covered in greater detail in Chapter 7, Monitoring the Instance.

You should understand the different engine operating modes and be able to bring an instance on- or off-line at will. You should understand the difference between logged and nonlogged database modes. You should be able to create and drop dbspaces, and understand the differences between regular and temporary dbspaces. Finally, you should be able to move or resize both the physical and logical logs, and to kill a user thread safely.

When executing these basic server-oriented administrative functions, keep the following points in mind:

- Once an instance shutdown command has been issued, it cannot be aborted or reversed.
- Changing the database logging mode to an unlogged mode will allow you to complete major database modifications without worrying about long transaction conditions.
- Any time a major change is made to the instance or databases, always create a level 0 archive to tape.
- Several temporary dbspaces should be created in the instance for temporary tables created by order-by, sort, or user-directed "into temp" commands.
- Activity in user-directed temporary tables will logged if the database is in a logged mode. This can be avoided if the temporary table is created using the "with no log" syntax.
- The physical and logical logs should be moved out of the rootdbs into different dbspaces to help prevent I/O bottlenecks.
- Use the "onmode -z session_id" command to terminate a user thread.

Coming Up

In the next chapter, we're going to step away from being an *OnLine* administrator and look at some of the basic tasks a *database* administrator would execute in a configured instance. Included in that discussion is the creation of databases, tables, and indexes. Table and index fragmentation will be covered, the differences between indexes and constraints will be explained, and new or improved SQL commands will be introduced.

Chapter 5

Building a Database Environment

- *Database, Table and Index Creation*
- *Understanding and Using Fragmentation*
- *Proper Usage of Constraints and Indexes*
- *Loading Data*
- *Controlling and Protecting Multi-user Access to Data*
- *New or Improved SQL Statements*

The majority topics of this book covers relate to the administration of OnLine Dynamic Server instances. This chapter will depart from that focus a little bit. In this chapter I'll be discussing *database* administration issues and what impact the features and mechanisms of OnLine Dynamic Server have on administering a database.

To that end, database and table creation, fragmentation, table population issues, and new or improved SQL statements will all be covered. By the end of the chapter, you should have a solid understanding of the basic tasks involved in creating and operating a database within an OnLine Dynamic Server instance.

When performing DBA tasks, my preference has always been to create and execute database administrative commands (or DDL statements) through direct SQL statements via the `dbaccess` query language option or the I-SQL tool. Although I will use that approach in my examples in this chapter, the `dbaccess` utility in OnLine Dynamic Server now has ring menu options for almost all the database administrative work covered in this chapter.

Ultimately, it's a matter of taste and convenience to choose a method you'll prefer to use. Even though it requires more keystrokes to achieve the same result, I feel as though I have greater control and can get things done quicker by using SQL statements rather than using the `dbaccess` ring menus.

Logging Modes

As mentioned in the "Changing Database Logging Modes" section of Chapter 4, Basic Administrative Tasks, changes made to data within a database can be recorded to disk to ensure data integrity in the event of a system failure. The creation (or lack thereof) of these records occurs by virtue of setting databases in the instance to use what is referred to as a "logging mode."

If a database is "logged," the physical and logical log structures of the instance are used to record changes to its data. Each database in an instance can operate in a different logging mode. The logging mode for a database is set at its creation, but can be changed at any time if necessary as explained in Chapter 4. An individual user or application can make a minor logging mode change within a logged database environment for the duration of a session by using the "`set log`" command.

There are four different logging modes, though two of them are very similar, only differing in when the log buffers get flushed to disk. The first mode, "no logging," writes very little information to the logical logs. The only records written are DDL statements such as `create/drop table, create/drop index, create/drop procedure, rename table/column, alter table` statements, and so on. The changes to rows affected by these statements are not logged, just that the command was given and the result code returned. An unlogged database environment has a very high throughput rate but no ability to reconstruct database changes over time in the event of a critical instance failure. Changes written to disk is all the information that will be available. Recovery of unlogged databases in an instance is limited to the last instance archive created.

"Mode ANSI" logging operates like unbuffered logging, discussed next, but also enforces ANSI transaction processing compliance. ANSI compliance includes such features and rules as unique owner naming for table references, different defaults for table level privileges, differences in the update and read capability of cursors, and differences in how character and decimal data types react to data type overflows or definition statements.

Be aware that OnLine Dynamic Server does not strictly enforce all the ANSI standards in a mode ANSI database environment. If you issue non-ANSI SQL statements, the instance will generate a warning message but continue to process them. Unless your operating environment *requires* the use of ANSI standards, there is little to be gained from using mode ANSI.

"Unbuffered logging" and "buffered logging" operate in an identical fashion except for the moment in time when the logging records are written to disk. Both logging modes capture DDL statements. In addition, all DML statements (e.g., `insert, update,` and `delete` commands) are logged, with the exception of select statements.

There is one exception regarding the logging of select statements: "`select into temp`" statements *are* logged. The logging of "`select into temp`" statements can cause problems if an application or a query extracts a large subset of data to manipulate then discard. The best way to avoid this problem is to create a temporary table using the keywords "`with no log`" in a temporary dbspace. See the "Temporary Dbspaces" section of Chapter 4 for more information on temporary dbspaces.

The difference between these two logging modes occurs in the writing of log data to the logs on disk. A database environment using unbuffered logging will flush the logical and physical log buffers containing transaction information whenever a transaction is committed. A buffered log database environment will hold transaction information in the logical and physical log buffers until the buffer fills, a checkpoint occurs, or the user connection that generated transactions is closed when the transactions have not been written to the logs.

There is one other condition that will force a buffered log database to release its transaction information: because there is only one set of logical log buffers in an instance, if an unbuffered database in the instance commits a transaction, the buffered log information will be written out to disk along with the unbuffered log information.

There are advantages and disadvantages to both of these logging modes. With unbuffered logging, data integrity and consistency can be guaranteed to the transaction level, even in the event of a critical instance failure. However, because every committed transaction causes a buffer flush to disk, there is increased disk I/O. In addition, because the flush will write information out of the buffer to the logical logs about transactions currently in process, the logical log pages will fill with redundant data over time. The logs fill faster, but contain less "real" data than is written by a buffered database environment.

In a buffered logging database environment there is significantly less disk I/O involved with each transaction, so the instance will run faster. However, because the transaction information is held in shared memory, it is at risk should a critical instance failure occur. The transaction information not written to disk will be lost when the instance's shared memory is released.

As Malcolm Weallans, a fellow member of the IIUG Board of Directors, states, "What's the difference between buffered and unbuffered logging? Your paranoia!" There are few environments that can tolerate the loss of committed transaction data, so I use unbuffered logging in all my environments except for large OLAP installations. In these environments there is very little transaction-oriented activity, so the need for logging is minimal.

When deciding on logging modes, be sure to take into consideration

- the volatility of the data
- the overall database throughput needed
- the business impact of losing individual transactions
- the ability to recreate individual transactions

so that you can choose the mode that's right for your particular environment.

Creating the Database

A database can be created in one of three ways: through the `dbaccess` ring menu options, the `dbimport` utility, or a SQL statement run, for example, from `dbaccess`. When creating a database, the dbspace in which it is to be created and the logging mode need to be specified.

The **Database:Create** option in `dbaccess` prompts you through this process. After the database name is entered, a ring menu appears with options for specifying the dbspace and logging mode. The **Database:Create:Dbspace** option presents a list of the dbspaces in the instance. The rootdbs is the default selection. Select one of the dbspaces listed, and press the "enter" or "return" key.

The **Database:Create:Log** option permits the selection of one of the four logging modes discussed earlier in this chapter from a ring menu. "None," or no logging, is the default. Exiting without making a selection in either of these two screens will invoke the database creation process using the defaults for both settings.

When exiting from the **Database:Create** option, you are given the option to either create the database (the default) or discard the information entered and abort the creation process entirely. If created, the new database becomes the "current" or "active" database for the `dbaccess` session.

The second method to create a database, the `dbimport` utility, creates not only the database but also tables, indexes, and constraints. The utility continues, and populates the database with data saved in ASCII format in files saved either on disk or tape.

Be aware that OnLine Dynamic Server treats a `dbimport` session as a single transaction. If the log mode flag is set to create a logged database within the `dbimport` session, and there are a large number of data rows to load, a long transaction will occur and the import will be rolled back. As a result, I strongly recommend *not* setting the log mode flag when using `dbimport` and changing the logging mode afterwards.

The selection of a creation dbspace and logging mode is handled via flags to the command. The syntax for these two options is as follows:

```
dbimport db_name -d creation_dbspace [ -l | -l
    buffered | -ansi ]
```

The "`-l`" option specifies unbuffered logging, and the "`-l buffered`" option specifies that the database should use buffered logging. If a log mode flag is not used, the database is created in a nonlogged state. If no creation dbspace is specified, the database will be created in the root dbspace.

Using a SQL statement in `dbaccess` is the fastest way to create a database. If `dbaccess` is invoked without specifying a database name, selecting **Query:New** will automatically invoke the **Database:Selection** screen since SQL statements have to be directed toward a database. Pressing the "interrupt" key will bypass this screen and bring up the **Query:New** screen. The SQL syntax is pretty straightforward:

```
create database db_name
  [ in creation_dbspace ]
  [ with log | with buffered log | log mode ansi ]
```

Similar to the `dbimport` utility, the database will be created in the rootdbs with no logging unless otherwise specified. For example, if you execute the following:

```
create database chap5_db in dbs_0 with log;
```

you would create a database called "chap5_db" in the dbs_0 dbspace that operates in an unbuffered logging mode.

Table and Index Creation and Fragmentation

Once a database is created, it's time to create the tables that will actually hold the data. How they are built and what methods, if any, are employed to preserve the integrity of the data, or speed up access to the data, will have an impact on the overall ability of the database to meet whatever design goals were established. In this section we'll look in detail at how tables can be built to balance disk I/O loads and enhance performance without creating indexes and suffering the insert and update overhead they bring with them.

Creating Tables and Indexes

Tables and indexes can be created using the same three methods outlined in the previous section to create databases. While tables can be fragmented using all three options, setting up index fragmentation requires using SQL statements only available through the `dbimport` or `dbaccess` utilities.

Because the `dbimport` utility uses a database schema generated during the export process, tables and indexes are created using statements found in the schema. If the "-ss" or "server-specific" flag was used during the export process, dbspace placement and extent sizing information was preserved for use during the import—another major administrative feature of OnLine Dynamic Server. If any changes to table placement or sizing need to be made prior to importing the database, those changes can easily be made by editing the schema file. Columnar information, other than column name, cannot be modified in the dbschema script. Otherwise, you would risk incurring datatype mismatch problems as the data was read back into the table.

Using `dbaccess` menu options to create and/or partition tables is similar in look and feel to creating a database by using the same functionality. The **Table:Create** and **Table:Alter** options bring up a screen where the column definitions are entered or altered through a series of ring menu options. When creating a table, additional options for creation dbspace, extent sizing, lock mode, and fragmentation are presented as well.

Unless specified otherwise in these screens, a table will be created in the same dbspace in which the database was created, have page-level locking, and be 16 KB in size. Constraints and indexes can be created as well through `dbaccess`, but the process is cumbersome in my opinion; use SQL statements instead.

The syntax rules to create tables or indexes by direct SQL statements can be found in the *Informix Guide to SQL—Syntax* that accompanied your distribution of the product. For the purposes of this discussion, rather than detailing all the syntax to create tables and indexes, I'll focus on the application of the syntax. In-depth schema design and normalization will not be covered; however, the correct application of fragmentation is dependent on both. I'll use a table and indexes created with statements such as the following:

```
create table store_sales
( division smallint,
  store smallint,
  category char(3),
  sales_date date,
  amt_sold decimal(8,2)
) in dbs_12
    extent size 550000 next size 55000
    lock mode row;

create index ix_strsls_div on store_sales (division);
create index ix_strsls_cat on store_sales (category);
create index ix_strsls_dt on store_sales (sales_date);
```

Fragmenting Tables

One of the new features in OnLine Dynamic Server is the ability to fragment tables and indexes. As the term implies, tables and indexes can be broken up and distributed across several dbspaces to achieve performance or design goals. Unlike RAID level 0 (striping), logical rules can be applied to the fragmentation scheme, usually resulting in greater I/O performance and enhanced availability. The latter benefit stems from the fact that under OnLine Dynamic Server, the DATASKIP parameter can be set such that fragmented tables can still be accessible, even if one or more of the table's fragments are on dbspaces that are down.

Both tables and indexes can be fragmented. There are two types of table fragmentation, "round-robin" and "by expression."

Round-robin fragmentation cannot be applied to indexes. Indexes can be fragmented by expression into several dbspaces, fragmented into a single dbspace other than where the table is, or, as the previous script would have created the indexes, left "in table" or in the same dbspace as the table.

Regardless of the fragmentation method used, it is important to remember the impact extent sizing will have on the fragments and the dbspaces they are in. In the table sizing discussion in Chapter 2, I said that tables need to be correctly sized to prevent interleaving of extents and a decrease in performance as the disk heads move all over the place to read the data. In setting the initial and next extent sizes for a fragmented table, remember that all of a table's fragments, except those created using the information in the tip that follows, will be created and expanded with the same settings. As a result, extent sizes should be set such that when a little-used table fragment needs to expand the amount of space it takes by virtue of the "next size" parameter in the table creation statement, its new size does not completely fill up the dbspace in which it was created.

> *tip*
>
> *There is one way to create fragments of different initial sizes. You must create two or more "rogue" tables with identical schemas. Create each table with different initial and next extent sizes. Then use the* "alter fragment" *command, which will be explained later in this chapter, to create a new table by "attaching" the rogue tables together. Use the* "alter fragment" *command again to modify the fragmentation expressions to what you need. This will create a table fragmented into several dbspaces, with each fragment having its own unique sizing parameters.*

Round-Robin Fragmentation

Data loaded into a table after round-robin fragmentation has been applied will be evenly distributed to all the dbspaces specified by the fragmentation command. If the table already contains data, that data will *not* be redistributed. The data will remain in place unless unloaded, deleted, and reloaded, at which point the data stream will be treated as new rows being inserted.

Round-robin fragmentation has all the weaknesses and strengths of RAID stripping. Even with an index to assist queries, the engine must still search all the dbspaces for the requested data. That said, depending on the size of the table, fragmenting a table by round-robin can still provide an increase in performance over leaving a table in a single dbspace.

 *If a table is fragmented by round-robin, any indexes created on the table **MUST NOT** be created "in table." If left "in table," indexes will be fragmented like the table causing the index pages to be distributed serially through the fragmentation dbspaces.*

The result is a significant performance penalty because the engine searches all the index fragments in all the dbspaces to find the necessary information. At the very least, indexes of tables fragmented by round-robin should be left whole but fragmented off into another dbspace.

The syntax to recreate the test table using round-robin fragmentation would look like this:

```
create table store_sales
(   division smallint,
    store    smallint,
    category char(3),
    sales_date date,
    amt_sold decimal(8,2)
)   fragment by round robin in
        dbs_9, dbs_10, dbs_11, dbs_12
    extent size 95000 next size 9500
    lock mode row;
```

Even though the extent sizes used are completely fictitious, the initial and next extent sizes changed to take into account data being spread across four dbspaces as well as the relocation of indexes into another dbspace.

"By Expression" Fragmentation

Fragmentation "by expression" occurs when table or index data is divided into multiple dbspaces based on logical rules. The rules are created using simple SQL statements, and can be applied at table creation or any time thereafter.

Except for the data type listed in the "Evaluating the Expression" section of this chapter, almost any column in the table can be used in the fragmentation expression. Unlike round-robin fragmentation, adding "by expression" fragmentation to a table or index containing data will cause rows to be redistributed according to the fragmentation rules. Depending on the logging mode of the database and the number of rows to be moved, this can cause a long transaction to occur. A row will also be moved between dbspaces if the value(s) in the column(s) that make up the fragmentation expression change and the row no longer qualifies to be stored in the same dbspace as prior to the change.

One of the best things about fragmentation by expression is that it can be leveraged to reduce the number of indexes created on a table and still provide equivalent if not better query response. The query optimizer will use the table's fragmentation expression when processing queries to eliminate dbspaces from the read request. If the fragmentation expression precludes one or more dbspaces from having the data requested, those dbspaces will not be searched.

Using the test table previously created, suppose there were six divisions that could have data. Of those divisions, only four of them were really active. A fragmentation expression could be built to put each of the four active divisions in separate dbspaces and the two less active divisions together in another dbspace. This would eliminate the index on division since the data would already be segregated by division. The syntax for this action could look something like this:

```
create table store_sales
(  division smallint,
   store    smallint,
   category char(3),
   sales_date date,
   amt_sold decimal(8,2)
)  fragment by expression
   division = 1 in dbs_9,
   division = 2 in dbs_10,
   division = 4 in dbs_11,
   division = 5 in dbs_12,
   (division = 3) or (division = 6) in dbs_13
extent size 950 next size 95
lock mode row;
```

In this case, the extent sizes were set to accommodate the fragment containing divisions 3 and 6. The smaller extent sizes will help prevent this fragment from overwhelming the dbs_13 dbspace in the event that another table extent is required. In the fictitious dbspace design we're using here, the other division's fragments are the only table structures in their respective dbspaces, so table extent interleaving caused by small extent sizes is not a concern; the additional extents will simply concatenate together.

Evaluating the Expression

Fragmentation expressions are evaluated from the top down, and from right to left. Needless to say, they should be mutually exclusive, but, if not, a row will be placed according to the first condition satisfied.

Any column of a table can be used in expression statements with the exception of BLOB columns. With one exception made in the "Dropping Fragments" section later in this chapter, I would recommend against using serial, date, and datetime data types in expressions because the distribution of rows becomes lopsided very quickly. These data types can be used in fragmentation expressions, but the expressions will need to be rewritten on a regular basis to redistribute the rows in the table. In addition, using a date or datetime data type in an expression slows down expression parsing because the data type must be converted to an integer to be evaluated.

Any of the SQL relational operators can be used to create expression statements, including the mod operator. Using the mod operator in expressions is commonly called creating a "hash" expression, and results in an even distribution of rows in a newly fragmented table that already had data stored in it. A hash expression in a table creation statement would look something like:

```
.
.,
cust_id integer
)  fragment by expression
   mod(cust_id, 3) = 2 in dbs_8,
   mod(cust_id, 3) = 1 in dbs_7,
   mod(cust_id, 3) = 0 in dbs_6
   lock mode row;
```

A fragmentation expression should be as simple as possible, since the expression will be evaluated every time a row is added to or modified in the table. In expressions where ranges need to be used, they should be listed in order of restrictiveness, with the most restrictive condition listed first. This will prevent rows from bunching up in the first dbspace. For example:

```
.
.,
region_code smallint
)   fragment by expression
    (region_code >= 200) in dbs_4,
    (region_code >= 150) in dbs_3,
    (region_code >= 100) in dbs_2,
    remainder in dbs_5;
```

In this example, I also use the "`remainder`" attribute. Although liberally used in examples provided by Informix, it should be avoided whenever possible.

The reason behind this is that "remainder" fragments are always searched for each query into the table. Even if the rest of the fragmentation expression would appear to indicate the dbspace or dbspaces that should have the data requested, the "`remainder`" clause implies variability in what it might contain. As a result, the query optimizer always searches remainder fragments in case a row might be there that matches the query parameters.

Depending on the size of the remainder fragment, this could have a negative impact on query performance. Rather than using a "`remainder`" clause, write your fragmentation expression so that rows outside of the other defined attributes fall into another dbspace. For example, to rewrite the previous fragmentation expression and eliminate the "`remainder`" clause, you could do the following:

```
.
.,
region_code smallint
)   fragment by expression
    (region_code >= 200) in dbs_4,
    (region_code >= 150) in dbs_3,
    (region_code >= 100) in dbs_2,
    (region_code < 100) in dbs_5;
```

Fragmenting Indexes

As mentioned earlier in this chapter, indexes can be fragmented by expression but not by round-robin. The simplest expression simply creates the index in a dbspace other than where the table was created. This is often called "partitioning off" the index. For example:

```
create index ix_strsls_cat on store_sales (category)
   in idx_space_1;
create index ix_strsls_dt on store_sales (sales_date)
   in idx_space_2;
```

Partitioning indexes away from the tables they reference can result in a significant increase in performance. I always try to put indexes in dbspaces on disks where the other dbspaces contain seldom referenced tables or table fragments. With this type of design, index-based queries complete much faster because there is no contention in the dbspace containing the table for reads or writes to complete on the table and index.

Just as the busiest tables in a database need to be distributed around the available disk spindles, the busiest indexes should also be distributed among the available disks.

When moving to a more sophisticated fragmentation scheme for an index, with the same data type exceptions mentioned in the previous section, any column listed in the index can be used to create the expression. For example:

```
create index major_idx on store_sales (division,
    store, category)
fragment by expression
   division > 4 in idx_space_4,
   category = "A" or category = "F" in idx_space_5,
   division <= 4 in idx_space_1;
```

Unlike fragmenting tables, extent sizes cannot be set for indexes. OnLine Dynamic Server allocates an initial extent proportional to the size of the initial table extent and that of the data types in the index.

Altering Fragments

The fragmentation of a table or index can be altered at any time by executing the "alter fragment" command. Fragments can be added, dropped, modified, or completely eliminated using this command. The "alter fragment" command can be used to join two tables having identical schemas together to form a fragmented table. A table fragment can also be detached from a table to create a new table.

*The "*alter fragment*" command should not be used when a database is in a logged mode or the table to be altered is active. Altering table fragments executes as a single transaction and locks the table in exclusive mode. This can cause a long transaction to occur, depending on the amount of data to be moved by the "*alter fragment*" command.*

While fragments are being altered, the "double disk space" condition will exist. When executing a table alter, the old fragment(s) will continue to exist in their original state on disk until the new fragments are created. Only after the new fragments are completely built, and any indexes resynchronized, will the original fragments be deleted. This ensures data integrity for the alter fragment transaction. In the event of a rollback, the new fragments are deleted and the old fragments reactivated. Prior to altering a fragment, make sure there is sufficient room in the affected dbspaces to contain the old and new fragments.

Initializing, Adding, or Modifying Fragments

To illustrate the alter fragment command, let's use the store_sales table created at the beginning of the chapter. To change it from its original state to a fragmented table, you would use the following type of syntax, depending on the desired fragmentation scheme:

```
alter fragment on table store_sales
   init fragment by round robin in dbs_2, dbs_3, dbs_4;
```

or

```
alter fragment on table store_sales
  init fragment by expression
    division = 1 in dbs_9,
    division = 2 in dbs_10,
    division = 4 in dbs_11,
    division = 5 in dbs_12,
    (division = 3) or (division = 6) in dbs_13;
```

Unlike the "alter table" *command, you cannot mix actions in an* "alter fragment" *statement. As a result, adding a fragment to a table and modifying another fragment's expression on the same table requires two separate statements to be executed.*

To change the table back to being nonfragmented, the syntax would look like:

```
alter fragment on table store_sales init in dbs_12;
```

To modify the fragmentation conditions:

```
alter fragment on table store_sales
  modify dbs_11 to ((division = 4) or (division = 3)),
  modify dbs_13 to division = 6;
```

To add additional fragments:

```
alter fragment on table store_sales add store > 400
    in dbs_11;
```
  (by expression fragmentation)
```
alter fragment on table store_sales add dbs_7;
```
  (round-robin fragmentation)

Adding another dbspace to a table using round-robin fragmentation will not cause a redistribution of rows already stored. The new dbspace will simply be added to the rotation to receive new rows as they are added.

The fragmentation syntax resulting from either modifying fragmentation conditions or adding a new fragment with an expression will be placed at the end of the expression statement for the table. Create a dbschema of the table after modifying or adding

fragments to make sure the expressions are in the correct order to properly distribute the data. A series of add, modify, and drop fragment commands might be needed to achieve the proper order of expressions.

Dropping Fragments

Fragments can be dropped, but attention must be paid to where the data that the fragment contained will go. By default, the data will be placed in the "remainder" fragment if it was created. As I mentioned earlier, remainder fragments should be avoided if possible because of the impact they have on query processing.

This creates a situation where dropping a table fragment is not much different than moving the logical logs out of the rootdbs when the instance was originally created. Either the existing fragment expressions must be altered or new fragments added with conditions that would allow them to receive rows from the fragment to be dropped. After this is completed the fragment can be dropped.

If the new or modified fragment conditions prevent a row from the dropped fragment being stored elsewhere, a "-776" SQL and "-772" ISAM error will result, and the drop fragment transaction will be rolled back. An example of code to drop a fragment would be:

```
alter fragment on table store_sales drop dbs_12;
```

Attaching Tables

Two or more tables with identical schemas can be joined together to create a single table by using the "attach" SQL command. This single table will be fragmented by round-robin since each of the original tables will keep any rows they had prior to being "attached." This can be changed by creating a whole new fragmentation scheme and using the "init" keyword in the "alter fragment" statement.

Changing from round-robin to "by expression" fragmentation on a table with "attachments" will have an impact on making additional attachments, as explained in the notes that follow. Each table that gets attached to another table retains its original extent size parameters. Review these values prior to attaching to make sure there won't be any space problems in the dbspaces as the fragments grow.

The syntax for attaching tables looks like:

```
alter fragment on table store_sales attach
    store_sales, midwest_sales;
```

In looking at the syntax for attaching tables, the second table listed (midwest_sales) becomes the "secondary" table and loses its identity, while store_sales is the "primary" table and keeps its name.

A couple of notes on attaching tables:

- When attaching tables, remove any constraints that have been created. Trying to attach tables with constraints will generate a SQL "-888" error.
- If the fragmentation scheme of a primary table is changed from round-robin (the default) to by expression, the ability to attach additional tables is lost. A "-782" SQL error is generated. This happens because there is no expression statement to determine the action of the new fragment.
- While both tables can have indexes, even on different columns, after attachment all indexes on the secondary table are lost. Only those indexes on the primary table remain.

Detaching Fragments

Fragments of tables can be separated from a "primary" table to create new, "detached" tables. Provided the primary table was fragmented by expression, and, as a result, the ranges of rows in any given fragment can be determined, detaching a fragment can allow for more focused manipulation of the data in that specific fragment.

Depending on how the fragmentation expression was written, detaching fragments into new tables can be an easy way to create historical tables. In this case, using date or serial data types in the fragmentation expression would be of value. A fragment expression could be created using a date column from the table. When the fragment receiving rows contains dates greater than a specific date, or grows to a predetermined size, a new fragment is added with a more current date range for its expression. The newly inactivate fragment could then be detached from the primary table to create a new table containing "historical" data.

Detached tables inherit any extent size and lock mode parameters given to the primary table. Nothing else is inherited from the primary table. Indexes, keys, and constraints will need to be created on the newly detached table. The syntax for detaching tables simply requires the name of the dbspace containing the fragment to be detached and the new table name; for example:

```
alter fragment on table store_sales detach dbs_12
    div3_sales;
```

Constraints, Referential Integrity, and Indexes

Next to the actual creation of databases and tables, maintaining the integrity of the data in the database is the most important responsibility of any DBA. Data integrity can be defined as the correct and accurate storage of data that maintains any interdependent relationships and/or semantic rules defined for the data. Stored procedures and the various types of constraints play a key role in achieving and maintaining this type of integrity as well as enhancing the performance of the database. Because it's part of your job, let's look briefly at what constraints and indexes are and how they function.

While stored procedures can have a significant role in ensuring data integrity and enhancing performance, the topic is too broad to receive more than a cursory mention in this book. For more information on using stored procedures, please refer to Informix Stored Procedure Programming *by Michael Gonzales, also published by Informix Press.*

Stored Procedures

Stored procedures are functions written in a combination of SQL and Stored Procedure Language (SPL). Procedures are stored in compiled form within the database engine for an individual instance and can be used to maintain security, log actions to tables, manipulate data, or enhance database performance.

While the general syntax of a stored procedure looks very much like C, there isn't more logic to SPL than variable assignment commands and basic program control statements such as "`if-then-else`," "`while,`" and "`for`" structures. The rest of the functionality in a stored procedure is derived from SQL statements.

Procedures can be called and executed by end user applications or activity-based triggers also written and stored in the database engine.

Triggers are written in the same SQL and SPL hybrid as stored procedures, and can have some of the same type of functionality as stored procedures. Triggers cannot be called by users; instead, they are activated when their "triggering action" is executed.

For example, a trigger could be created to execute whenever a row in a table was modified. A trigger could also be written to execute if a specific column of a row within a table was modified. When the specific action for a trigger occurs in the database, the trigger will execute its logic. Often a trigger calls a stored procedure that can have a more robust set of programming statements.

With the amount of logic triggers and stored procedures can have, business rules can be enforced at the database level rather than in applications. For example, the specific query statements to determine the gross margin of sales can be coded into a stored procedure and kept in the database engine rather than coded into a number of user applications, ensuring consistency of results and simplified application code. A combination of an insert trigger and stored procedures can be used to ensure that appropriate cross-reference information exists in a number of tables before a row is inserted into a particular table. A modify trigger and stored procedures can be used to automatically recalculate the totals of open orders whenever a price is changed on products in the products table. I trust you get the picture of what these can do for your application or data.

Constraints and Indexes

Constraints and indexes can also be used to enhance query performance, maintain relationships between data elements, and define ranges of values for data. As a short historical note, constraints were introduced in version 4.10, but not really touted until the 5.x versions of the OnLine engine. At the time there was a bit of confusion regarding constraints, especially because it appeared as though they just built an index with a funny name on the table. Some confusion still exists today, especially among those new to Informix. An often-asked question is "What's the difference between a unique index, primary key, and unique constraint?" The answer is twofold in nature. First, from a logical database design perspective, each performs a different function. Second, while all three are enforced through an index, there are differences in how the OnLine Dynamic Server engine handles and administers indexes as opposed to keys or constraints.

From a design perspective, I view keys, constraints, and indexes as follows:

- Constraints are used to enforce business rules in a table and fall into two categories. First, constraints enforce uniqueness of rows. For example, customer name must be unique in the customer table, or a combination of customer ID and shipping address must be unique in the address table. These constraints are enforced through the creation of indexes and are referred to as "index-based" constraints. The second type of constraint, commonly called a "check" constraint, is used to specify a range of values for a column or to derive values for columns. For example, the value in the price field must be greater than or equal to 50.00 to ensure minimum order cost; or the value in the maintenance cost field is equal to product cost times 18 percent. These types of constraints are not enforced by indexes; they are enforced by rules embedded in the engine.

- Keys, both primary and foreign, are another type of constraint and are used to define referential integrity, or data relationships, between tables. This is also referred to as a "parent-child" table relationship. The keys prevent the addition of data to child tables where a valid cross-reference to the parent table does not exist. Keys can also prevent the deletion of data from a parent table when child rows exist in other tables.

An example of this type of design relationship can be found in an order processing system. A customer is identified within the system by a unique customer ID—a primary key. A row in the order table must contain a valid customer ID(a foreign key) as well as a unique order number—a primary key. The order detail table must have a valid order number (a foreign key) for the order line items that table contains. As shown in this example, a table can have both primary and foreign keys. If a row were to be deleted out of any of these three tables without the related rows being deleted, the entire order system would collapse.

note

Preventing the deletion of a row from a parent table assumes that cascade delete has not been enabled on any child tables. By default, OnLine Dynamic Server will not allow rows from a parent table to be deleted if rows exist in child tables that refer to the parent rows. If "`on delete cascade`*" is added to the foreign key constraint statement on a child table, when a row is deleted from the parent table, all the associated rows in that child table will be deleted automatically. This can be used to reduce coding overhead in applications.*

All child rows must be deleted before the parent row will be deleted. Thus, if a `delete` *statement is issued for a row in a parent table and most of the child tables have cascade delete enabled but one does not, the continued existence of child rows in that one table will cause the entire delete transaction to roll back, and no rows will be deleted.*

- Indexes, as an entity, should only be used to enhance query performance. With this in mind, I feel that a DBA should never allow the creation of a unique index as a standalone entity on a table. If uniqueness is required, it's a business rule and should be coded as a constraint. As mentioned in the first bullet, some constraints are enforced through index structures. The indexes supporting these constraints can be used by the query optimizer to enhance performance. This should be viewed as a secondary benefit of constraints rather than the primary reason for their existence. If additional query performance is needed outside of the business rules, use indexes rather than constraints.

OnLine Dynamic Server enforces constraints differently than indexes. This will have an impact on how SQL operations will operate and, as a result, how applications should be written. As an OnLine administrator, part of your job is to help application developers with these kinds of nuances. The functional differences between indexes and constraints are as follows:

- Indexes are enforced immediately, regardless of the transaction state or engine logging mode.
- Constraints are enforced at the end of a transaction.

For example, in a customer information table there is a customer ID column of type integer populated with rows numbered 1 through some number. Suppose you decided to keep the first 10 customer ID numbers unused. To make the change, you would run a SQL statement such as:

```
begin work;
lock table customer in exclusive mode;
update customer set cust_id = (cust_id + 10);
```

If a unique index existed on the cust_id column, the update statement would fail when attempting to update the first row. The cust_id of the first row would be changed to 11, but a cust_id of 11 already exists in the index structures, so the index would prevent the row from being changed.

If a unique constraint existed on the cust_id column, the transaction would complete because all rows would be updated to their new value before uniqueness was checked. If the cust_id column was a parent column to other tables, the child tables would need to be updated first, followed by an update to the cust_id column. This would require setting constraints to "deferred" mode in order to complete the transaction.

By default, constraints are enforced at the end of a transaction. This is not a problem for such single-statement transactions as the cust_id update shown previously. Constraint enforcement changes slightly when multiple statements are executed in a single transaction. In this case, constraints are enforced at the conclusion of each add, update, or delete statement in the transaction.

In the case where parent and child tables need to be updated, enforcing the constraint after each statement will cause a rollback of the transaction because the data has not been updated in all the tables. This can be avoided by using the "`set constraints deferred`" phrase at the beginning of the transaction. With constraints deferred, constraint enforcement will revert to the end of the transaction for a multistatement transaction. Setting constraints to deferred mode only lasts for the transaction in which the statement is made. At completion or rollback of a transaction, constraints are reset to "immediate" mode.

*When experimenting with constraints, **NEVER** delete the index created by a constraint, or information about a constraint from the sysconstraints table, in an attempt to remove the constraint.*
ALWAYS *use the alter table statement and the constraint name you entered or the instance created for you when the constraint was created. Attempting to delete constraints by any other method will ultimately require restoring from an archive. I know; I tried it. Once.*

Fragmenting Constraints

Looking at the syntax for creating constraints, you'll quickly see that there aren't any provisions for fragmenting constraints as you can indexes. This would appear to limit the usefulness of index-based constraints on fragmented tables since the indexes created to enforce the constraint would be built "in table." For a table created with round-robin fragmentation, these constraints would have a significant negative impact on performance. For "check" constraints, this is not a problem. There aren't any indexes to worry about.

There is a way around the problem. The only way I can explain it is to say that indexes are "upgradable" in terms of functionality. An index can be turned into a constraint, but the opposite is not true. This means you can, for example, create a unique index with some sort of fragmentation scheme for a table. Then you can run an "`alter table`" statement and add a unique constraint on the same columns used to create the unique index. The instance will take the existing unique index and upgrade (or promote) it to act as a constraint.

The name of this constraint will *not* be the name of the index. You will need to name the constraint or allow the instance to generate a name for you. After upgrading a unique index to a unique constraint or primary key, if you look at the table information from I-SQL or `dbaccess`, only the original index with its original name will be shown. However, a dbschema of the table will show both the index and the constraint statements.

As mentioned in the previous warning, even though you created the original index, do *not* simply delete the index to drop the constraint created by upgrading the index unless you want to restore from archive. Drop the constraint first; then you can drop the index.

This method of fragmenting constraints will work for all index-based constraints. A primary key constraint can be created by upgrading a unique index, while foreign keys can be created from duplicate indexes.

I highly recommend this method of creating constraints even if the tables or indexes are not fragmented. This method yields a database schema that can easily be stripped of indexes and constraints with utilities such as `strip_index`, included in Chapter 12, Scripts to Help Get the Job Done, in preparation for exporting a database to another system. This is explained in greater detail in the "Dbimport" subsection of the following section.

Populating the Database

Once a database is built, tables created and fragmented, and business rules established that will be enforced through the use of constraints and stored procedures, data needs to be inserted. There are several utilities to do this, each with advantages and disadvantages that will have an impact on your choice in any given situation. Several of these utilities will be discussed in this section.

Dbimport

The first utility, `dbimport`, was discussed in the database creation section of this chapter. `Dbimport` is the companion utility to `dbexport` and is used to create a complete database environment, then populate it by loading from ASCII flat files containing data for each table in the database. Because the database itself is created as part of the import, there aren't any problems about allowing or denying users access to the database while the utility runs. The database is locked in exclusive mode during the import and, as I have mentioned before, should be created without any logging to prevent a long transaction from occurring.

Minor edits of the `dbimport` schema file can be made as long as the table order in the schema is not changed, data types within a table are not materially changed (e.g., character to integer); nor are columns added or deleted. Doing any of the aforementioned will undoubtedly cause failures when loading the data files.

You can add or delete indexes and constraints, but I recommend altering the import schema to delete indexes and index-based constraints in order to decrease the amount of time required to import a database. There is a utility called `strip_index` on the media accompanying this book that will do this for you. When the `dbimport` utility processes the schema file, it will create the tables, then load them. Because the tables do not have any indexes, the data rows will load quite quickly. Once the import is over, the index file created by the `strip_index` utility can be run from I-SQL or dbaccess to create the indexes and constraints.

If the export data was stored on tape, save the schema file to a disk file rather than to tape. In looking at the schema file from this type of export, there will be a load table flag placed in the schema to trigger the read from tape. The load flag looks like "***load table***," If you elect not to strip the schema file of index and constraint creation statements, this load flag can be moved from just below the index creation statements for the table to just before them, resulting in a nonindexed table load.

Another advantage of the `dbimport` utility is that the creation of triggers and stored procedures occurs last in the import file. As a result, there isn't any overhead resulting from the execution of triggers and stored procedures during table loads. In a practical real-world sense, you really wouldn't want these database objects executing anyway, because the data being imported has already been processed by the stored procedures in the original database. The data should have the correct "value" already.

The SQL "load" Statement

The SQL "load" command has the least amount of flexibility of all the utilities discussed in this section of the chapter. It can be used for small to medium data sets in a logged database or large data sets in an unlogged database. Users can access the table while a load is occurring if the person running the load has not locked the table in exclusive mode. The `load` command reads a delimited ASCII flat file and simply loads it in column order into the target table. Depending on the number of indexes on the target table, data does load fairly fast using this command.

There are a couple of potential problems when using the `load` command. In a logged database, the load is handled as a transaction. Depending on the amount of data to load, a long transaction could occur, or there could be a lock table overflow. The table can be locked in exclusive mode to get around the lock issue, but that eliminates any other user activity from occurring in the table.

Another problem is that there aren't any mechanisms to handle exceptions in the data file. If, for whatever reason, a field to load into a numeric column contains a character, the engine will catch the data type conversion error and simply abort the load. The utility does indicate how many rows were loaded, which makes it easier to find the problem row in the load file.

The Dbload Utility

`Dbload` has more flexibility when working with ASCII flat files. `Dbload` can

- Load delimited or fixed length, nondelimited files,
- Load columns out of table order,
- Skip N rows of the load file before beginning to load,
- Write bad rows out to a log file for fixing while continuing the load process,
- Load ASCII BLOBS,
- Issue a `commit work` statement every X rows to prevent long transactions from occurring,
- Substitute a value instead of null into a "not null" column.

A "command" file is used to control the `dbload` utility and its functionality. In it, the file name to be loaded, target table, column order, and manipulation statements are listed. You can also specify how many error rows can be encountered before the load process is aborted.

Dbload does not require a table to be locked in exclusive mode because it can send a commit statement at a regular interval during the load process. It will suffer the same performance problems if indexes exist on the table as the "load" command would experience.

For an excellent overview of the dbload utility (as well as other topics), please refer to the Informix Press book *Programming Informix-SQL/4GL: A Step-By-Step Approach* by Cathy Kipp.

The OnLoad Utility

The onload utility is one of the fastest utilities to load data. The companion to the onunload utility, it reads a binary copy of the table in from tape and places the table and indexes in the requested dbspaces. You can set parameters for dbspace creation, to rename indexes, or to rearrange table or index fragmentation dbspaces.

Onload executes as a single transaction, but locks the table in exclusive mode so that concurrent user access is not allowed. Because the data is written out in a format not unlike that of the ontape archive utility, you cannot alter or modify the data or its order of load in any way.

Onload preserves original extent information as well as the total table extent size at the time of export. This makes it an excellent tool to use when trying to decrease the number of table extents in dbspaces. Simply use the onunload utility to copy all the tables out to tape, drop the tables, then reload them using the onload utility. When completed, all the tables will occupy a single extent within the dbspaces.

The High-Performance Parallel Loader

New to OnLine Dynamic Server in the 7.2 release is a loader utility called onpload that provides flexibility in the types of data files it can process, manageability in what can be done with the data during the load process, and incredible load speeds. I have just begun to work with the loader and don't have enough experience to write more than a cursory introduction to the product at this time. If, between now and the end of this book, I can work with it enough, I'll expand on what is written here.

`Onload` can load as well as unload tables. In load mode, it can either keep the tables accessible to other users (deluxe mode) or it can lock the tables in exclusive mode (express mode). If the load is performed in express mode, a level 0 archive must be created before the table is available for use. In either case, at the conclusion of a load, indexes are rebuilt and constraints evaluated.

Input files can read from disk or tape, format conversions (e.g., EBCDIC to ASCII) can be made, and the ability to "scrub" the data as it comes through the loader is also available. Data elements can be combined or parsed out for loading into different tables as well.

`Onload` has received high praise from several large Informix accounts who were involved in the beta test. I'm looking forward to really putting it to the test and seeing how it works.

Flat File Loads Through 4GL Applications

Loading tables through 4GL applications in many respects doesn't really qualify for inclusion in the list of utilities already mentioned. Informix 4GL was not intended to be used for creating data load programs, though in using it you can create very robust error handling and data manipulation functionality. I think it needs to be included because prior to `onload`, there really was nothing else available to read data from ASCII flat files, scrub it intelligently, and insert the data into tables. I also include it to show off a little piece of 4GL functionality buried in the product with only a cursory mention in the Informix *4GL by Example* manual.

A friend of mine, now an Informix System Engineer, was reading the *Example* manual and happened across two commands included in the 4GL demo distribution libraries ($INFORMIXDIR/demo/4glbe) that enable a 4GL application to read data in directly from ASCII flat files. `Fglgets` takes a file name as a parameter, opens the file if not already open, and returns the first row of the file. If the file is already open, it returns the next row of the file. The `fglgetret` command checks the return code of the C language `pop` command that actually gets the row out of the file.

The best way to explain how it all works is to show a small snippet of code with the commands implemented. I'll follow with some additional comments.

```
database something_or_another

main
  define fname varchar(30)
  define in_str varchar(255)
  define nrecs integer
    ## please be aware that no error handling is
    ## included in this snippet of code.
  prompt "Please enter pathed file name to load: "
    for fname
  let fname = fname clipped
    ## open file and get first row
  call fglgets(fname) returning in_str
    ## check the status of the open and "pop"
  while fglgetret() = 0
    let nrecs = nrecs + 1
    if nrecs mod 100 = 0 then
      display "Loading row: ", nrecs using "###,###"
        at 8,2
    end if
    call process_row(in_str)
          ## continue to get rows until EOF
    call fglgets(fname) returning in_str
  end while ## fglgetret = 0
end main
```

Some notes on using 4GL to load ASCII flat files:

- In order to use `fglgets` and `fglgetret`, you'll need to compile the fglgets.c file into object form and include it with any other standard libraries you reference in makefiles.
- The `fglgets` code opens but does not close the file.
- `Fglgets` only travels *down* the file. You cannot "rewind" the pointer in the file as you can in C.
- The maximum string length that can be read is 256 bytes.
- The Informix code only allows eight files to be opened and processed at a time before you have to terminate the applica-

tion using the library and restart it. This is controlled by the MAXOPEN parameter in the code and can be changed if you wish.
- Each time `fglgets` is invoked with a new file name it is counted toward the MAXOPEN total, even if the file does not exist or cannot be opened.
- If the total number of files opened exceeds MAXOPEN, the Informix code does not return an error message to the application. It does not return any data either. From the perspective of the application, it will appear as though the file was empty. As a result, you will need to either increase MAXOPEN or count the number of times an attempt is made to open a new file and stop any further attempts to open a file once MAXOPEN has been reached.
- Placing the call to `fglgets` in a called function has no effect on the MAXOPEN counter. The counter acts at an application level rather than a module level.

Concurrency and Isolation Levels

Once a database is built and populated, controlling and protecting multi-user access to data becomes important. The protection part is implemented through the use of locks in the OnLine Dynamic Server instance. The control part is largely controlled by the application and determines how the instance implements the different types of locks, as well as how the instance responds to application requests for locked data. The logging mode of the database does have an impact on both of these, as will be explained shortly.

Concurrency refers to the simultaneous accessing of data by multiple users. *Isolation levels* refer to the impact a database action request should be allowed to have on other database action requests. Obviously, how these two are designed and implemented are highly integrated and reciprocal. A very restrictive isolation level will significantly decrease the amount of concurrent access to the database. A demand for a large number of concurrent users will require either a very low isolation level or very small, tightly written transactions in an application, or several levels of isolation control being used in the application, depending on the operation in question.

Lock Types and Modes

To understand both issues, you must first understand how the OnLine Dynamic Server engine handles the locking of data and how locks can be placed. A lock can be placed on an entity as small as an index key value or as large as an entire database.

OnLine Dynamic Server has three lock types, as illustrated in Table 5-1.

Table 5-1 OnLine Dynamic Server lock types.

Lock Type	Description
Exclusive	All access to the data element is denied to users other than the user locking the element in this mode. It is placed at a row level by update or delete operations, and at a table or database level by user command.
Shared	Placed by read operations to make sure data elements have been committed to disk. Setting shared locks can be used to prevent data elements being read from being deleted or changed while the elements are still in use by the application requesting the read.
Upgradable or promotable	A shared lock that can be modified into an exclusive lock when requested. This is the type of lock used by update cursors.

Users can, through SQL statements, place a shared or exclusive lock on tables or databases. OnLine Dynamic Server itself will invoke an exclusive table lock if major DDL commands such as "`alter/rename/drop table`," "`create/drop index`," or "`rename column`" are executed. The instance releases its locks as soon as the action is completed, provided the user does not preface the DDL action with a separate lock statement. User-initiated locks remain in place for the length of the transaction in a logged database or, in an unlogged database, until the lock is manually removed.

Understanding and Setting Isolation Levels

An isolation level affects how read requests are handled by the instance. These levels have the greatest impact on concurrency or multi-user access to data. There are four isolation levels as shown in Table 5-2.

Table 5–2   OnLine Dynamic Server isolation levels.

Isolation Level	Description
Repeatable read	The most restrictive level, all rows read are locked with a shared lock for the duration of the entire transaction. Locks are also placed on those rows that were read because of a nonindexed read or sequential scan to determine eligibility for the select statement. It is important to note that these shared locks are only placed if there is an *explicit* transaction surrounding the read. Simply setting the isolation level to repeatable read, then running a select statement, does not invoke the protection this isolation level provides. Without the transaction in place, rows selected can be altered by other processes. This is the default isolation level for mode ANSI databases.
Cursor stability	Similar to the repeatable read isolation level, shared locks are placed on rows read by a cursor. However, once the cursor statement requests the next row of data, the lock on the previously read row is released—provided, of course, the row was not altered. As with the repeatable read isolation level, the shared lock is only placed if the cursor is inside an *explicit* transaction. This level, while it can be set by a SQL statement, is ineffective in an I-SQL or `dbaccess` session—it only applies to cursors declared in applications like those created through I-4GL.

Isolation Level	Description
Committed read	The default level invoked by a logged database except for mode ANSI. This level ensures that rows read and returned to the application have been committed to disk. The instance checks to see if shared lock *could* be placed on the row in question before it is returned to the application. It does not actually lock the row, so it acts like a dirty read in terms of speed. Committed read isolation does not prevent data being read from being changed by another process, even if the read is inside an explicit transaction. All a committed read isolation prevents is the return of data locked for update, insert, or deletion.
Dirty read	The least restrictive level, a dirty read allows all rows, whether they're committed or not, to be returned to the application. This includes rows whose values could change because of an update, or newly inserted rows in a table that have not been committed. The risk of requesting data at this isolation level is that the rows returned could change or be deleted either because of a transaction rollback or by the actions of another user.

To set any of these levels, use the "`set isolation`" command. Various isolation levels can be used throughout an application depending on integrity requirements of the data being read or restrictions that might need to be imposed while the application runs a particular piece of functionality.

Where nonchanging reference data is concerned, dirty reads are acceptable. When requesting more critical data elements, consider using cursor stability or repeatable read, depending on the concurrency needs, to prevent data from changing due to outside actions while being used by the application.

OnLine-Specific SQL Statements

With the release of OnLine Dynamic Server version 7.1.UD1, several new SQL statements were introduced, and several existing SQL statements were slightly modified. While all of the changes are explained in the *Guide to 7.1 Feature Enhancements* manual that came with your distribution of the software, I would like to briefly cover some of the statements I feel are the most significant. Changes to some statements that were made in this release, such as to the "`update statistics`" command, will be covered in other chapters.

Violations and Diagnostics, Constraint and Index Enabling, and Filtering

Prior to version 7.1.UD1, any errors due to updating or inserting rows into tables with unique indexes or index-based constraints had to be handled manually. The `sqlca.sqlerrd` codes had to be trapped to determine what error had occurred and what should be done to correct the problem. Generally, the offending row was kicked out to a holding table for manual intervention and processing.

Now the engine can handle a large part of this work for you, decreasing the amount of error-handling code required in the application. This is accomplished by setting up violation and diagnostic tables for specific target tables, then turning on the newly added error-handling features of unique indexes and index-based constraints.

Invoking the "`start violations table`" statement causes the engine to create two tables fragmented like the target table in the instance. One table contains "violation" information, the other "diagnostic" information. While you can set the name for each of these two tables if you wish, the default names are the target table name with "_vio" and "_dia" appended, respectively. You can also set the total number of rows these tables will hold.

The schema of the violation table is a duplicate copy of the target table with a couple of extra columns. These columns include a numeric counter, an abbreviation of the action taken that resulted in a failure, as well as the userid of the person requesting the action that failed.

The diagnostic table has a numeric column, which holds the numeric cross-reference to the row in the violations table. This column and the column in the violations table are not linked by a primary-foreign key relationship, however. The diagnostic table also has a column that indicates whether an index or constraint error occurred, the name of the index or constraint that was violated, and the owner of that constraint or index.

With these two tables in place, the next step is to activate the "object mode" of the constraints and indexes on the table, as well as the "error option." The term "object mode" simply refers to the operating state of the object. In this case, the "objects" I'm referring to are only indexes and constraints. Object modes can be set globally for all indexes or constraints on a table, or individually on a constraint-by-constraint basis. The three object modes are shown in Table 5-3.

Table 5-3   Constraint and index object modes.

Object Mode	Description
Enabled	The instance recognizes the existence of the index or constraint and factors those rules into its processing. Processing stops whenever a requested action (update, delete, or insert statement) fails. This is the default mode.
Disabled	The instance behaves as if the index or constraint does not exist.
Filtering	The engine acts as if the indexes or constraints are in enabled mode; however, only those rows that satisfy the action requested are successfully processed. Those that fail are copied out to the violation table for the target table, with appropriate information inserted into the diagnostic table as well.

You can specify what the instance sends an application should a constraint or index be in filtering mode and an action request fails. This is called setting the "error option." You can either have the instance return an error code to the application ("`with error`") or not ("`without error`"). Your application logic and follow-up procedures will determine the most appropriate option for your environment.

The violation and diagnostic tables should not be deleted until the object mode has been changed back from filtering mode to enabled or disabled mode, and the "`stop violations`" statement has been issued. At this point, the violations and diagnostic tables can be dropped like any other normal table.

It should also be noted that while duplicate indexes and triggers can be enabled or disabled by using the "`set`" command, they cannot be put in filtering mode; nor will any actions pertaining to them be logged in the violations or diagnostic table.

Roles

"Roles" within the database environment are similar to "groups" in the UNIX environment. As such, roles can be used to manage table, column, or stored procedure security and access.

In OnLine versions 5.x and earlier, user management could only be handled on a per-userid basis. This quickly became an administrative nightmare if specific permissions needed to be granted or denied within a database. Quite often, sites used a generic login ID for users to accomplish specific tasks. This made auditing almost impossible without coding it into the applications because there was no way to easily identify the user executing the database actions.

With OnLine Dynamic Server, an administrator can still manage permissions at a userid level if needed, but users can now be included in larger administrative entities called "roles." Permissions can be granted or denied to roles and, because the individual userid is used, meaningful auditing can be accomplished.

Session Authorization

"Set session authorization" is the equivalent of the UNIX "su" command. If a user has DBA privileges on the database, they can assume the functional identity of another user. With this new functional identity, the user can execute statements on tables or columns normally denied to the user. The user can also grant access privileges on tables or columns owned by the assumed user's identity.

Rename Database

This is not earth shaking, but it sure is handy to finally have this command! As an administrator, you could always rename columns, tables, indexes, constraints, and so on rather easily. Your only option to rename a database was to drop and recreate it with the new name. This was a painful way to migrate environments from development or test to production if you only had one server to work with and not enough resources to run several instances.

If you are the *original creator* of the database, and have DBA privileges, this command allows you to change the name of a database provided the database is not currently being used.

By using the "set session authorization" *SQL command you can rename the database even if you are not the original creator. To rename the database without being the owner:*

1. *Connect to the database to be renamed via I-SQL or* dbaccess.
2. *Reset your functional identity to that of the creator through the* "set session authorization" *command. This presupposes that you have DBA privileges on the database in question, as explained in the "Set Session Authorization" section of this chapter.*
3. *Close the database connection and connect to another database OR use the* "select database" *ring menu as if you were going to select a new database; use the interrupt key to abort. This leaves you without a current database connection but in the query language tool.*
4. *Execute the* "rename database" *command.*

Summary

A wide range of topics oriented toward administering a database were covered in this chapter. While not all of the administration functions were explained, you should now be able to create a database as well as tables and indexes. You should be able to determine whether or not the fragmentation of indexes or tables would be effective for your environment. You should be able to implement round-robin and "by expression" fragmentation on tables and indexes, and to populate the tables in a database in the most efficient manner. Finally, you should be able to understand the balance between data integrity and multi-user access that resolves itself through isolation levels.

When administering your databases, keep the following points in mind:

- Even though it requires more keystrokes to achieve the same result, you might find that you have greater control and can get things done quicker using SQL statements rather than the `dbaccess` ring menus.

- While round-robin fragmentation has all the weaknesses of RAID stripping, using this method can still provide an increase in performance over leaving a table in a single dbspace. Just remember that any indexes created on tables using round-robin fragmentation **MUST NOT** be created "in table" but should be, at the very least, partitioned off to another dbspace.

- Write fragmentation expressions with the most restrictive conditions first. Remember to keep the expressions simple because they are evaluated each time data is updated or inserted.

- Avoid using the "`remainder`" attribute whenever possible in fragmentation expressions. Its use implies variability of the data it contains and will result in this fragment being sequentially searched by each query.

- Review the notes in the "Attaching Tables" section of this chapter for some points to consider when attaching tables.

Coming Up

In looking at the jobs a DBA performs, a large number of them were covered in this chapter. One of the most important jobs, though, is ensuring the recoverability of the database in the event of a catastrophic failure. In the next chapter we'll move back to being an OnLine administrator and look at archiving and restoration schemes, and how to create archives as well as restore from them.

Part 3

Planning for Database Recovery and Performance Tuning

By now you should have an operational OnLine Dynamic Server instance and have created one or more databases with various logging modes and table and index fragmentation strategies. So what do you do now? It's time to look at the additional administrative tasks regarding instance maintenance and enhancing performance.

In these chapters, I'll cover archiving and restoring instances as a whole or individual tables if required. I'll introduce and illustrate the four major instance and database monitoring utilities. With these utilities you can look inside the OnLine Dynamic Server engine and see what an individual user session is doing, or at what level of efficiency the shared memory or various vps are operating at. Finally, I'll explain how the OnLine Dynamic Server query optimizer works, parallel database operations and environments, and the resource maintenance activities that support this technology.

With what you learned in the previous section, at the end of this section you should understand, and be able to perform, all of the basic and intermediary, to somewhat advanced, functions required of OnLine and database administrators. You should feel comfortable in taking your instance out of development and into test mode preparatory to going live. There's still a few more odds and ends required to complete your understanding but you should be feeling confident in your ability to use the OnLine Dynamic Server engine.

Chapter 6

Archiving and Restoring

- *Archive Design Methodologies*
- *Archiving the Logical Logs*
- *What Tape Devices Can You Use?*
- *How Does the Archiving Process Work?*

In every job there is a mundane task or set of tasks that have to be done on a regular basis regardless of how dull, boring, or quotidian they might be. In some cases the task itself is not terribly significant; it's just part of a larger process. In other cases, that task is important enough that its completion, or failure, can have a serious and irrevocable impact on other processes.

The OnLine Dynamic Server archive and restoration tasks fit into the latter category. A relatively boring task when viewed individually, few people make it their life's goal to handle the process of archiving OnLine Dynamic Server instances. Yet whenever a restore from archive is required, nothing is more important to the enterprise than the existence and stability of the archive created by that process.

In this chapter I'll discuss several different philosophies regarding the archiving process. I'll describe how OnLine Dynamic Server can create archives while the instance is on-line and active, as well as the types of tape devices Informix supports. Finally, I'll cover the syntax required to create or restore from archives using the `ontape` utility. By the end of the chapter you should be able to design and implement an archive process that will work in your environment.

Archiving Strategies

It's a fact of life that from time to time a partial or complete restore will be required. Whether due to a major mistake made by a user or some sort of catastrophic mechanical failure, the inability to recover an instance back to a particular moment in time could cost you your job. It only makes sense, then, to make sure the proper archiving strategy is in place as well as the hardware to support it.

OnLine Dynamic Server has two utilities to archive an instance: "`ontape`" and "`onarchive`." In this chapter, I will only be discussing the `ontape` utility. `Onarchive` will not be covered since it was a dead product when delivered and never got much better. As evidenced by the comments made in Appendix C, I am not alone in thinking this.

I do give Informix credit for having their heart in the right place in trying to produce a flexible, robust archival tool. It just didn't work right, or well, depending on to whom you talk. The engineers realized this, and to their credit decided against fixing it. In the upcoming 7.2 releases of the engine, `onarchive` will be replaced with an API interface called "`onbar`."

`Onbar` will incorporate the best features of `onarchive` into an `ontape` foundation. The media management and constraints that now exist within OnLine Dynamic Server will disappear. It will be handled by third-party vendors who will write software to interface their archiving hardware and media management systems to the OnLine Dynamic Server `onbar` API. As this book goes to press, I have only seen introductory information on the `onbar` API and its functionality. I am looking forward to what it appears to be able to provide in terms of flexibility and the ability to archive and restore to a moment in time. I also like the fact that the tape management piece will no longer be handled by the engine—no longer will basic archive commands have to be bundled in elaborate wrapper scripts to produce carriage returns for confirmation prompts and so on.

In establishing an archiving strategy, a number of factors can and should influence its creation. Among these are:

- What granularity of restore could be required?
- How much data is there to archive and possibly restore in the instance?
- How easily could lost data be recreated?
- How much time is available to create an archive if the archive process was required to occur in a quiet or maintenance period?
- What would be an acceptable amount of time to restore from archive?
- What physical devices are available on which to create the archive?
- What are the "retention" and "recycle" periods?

The importance of each of these factors, and their interrelationship, will determine whether you use what I call a "whole-istic" approach to database archiving, a more individualized or focused approach, or a combination of the two.

While most sites use the "whole-istic" approach, there are advantages to taking a more focused approach. The most important advantage is that you can direct your efforts at those tables which really need archiving rather than having to deal with the entire instance. This yields a higher degree of granularity when faced with having to restore. This approach does tend to be more complicated to implement and maintain because it requires significantly more manual intervention.

The Focused Approach

Because the OnLine Dynamic Server engine does not natively support table-level restores from `ontape` (though with a proper fragmentation it is possible to do), if specific tables require special attention from a restoration point of view, most often this calls for a series of table-oriented archiving procedures.

A table-oriented archiving procedure usually involves some sort of table unloading. Depending on the size of the table and the need for concurrent access during the archive, this can be achieved by using either the SQL "`unload`" command to create an ASCII dump to disk, or the "`onunload`" command to create a binary copy of the locked table to tape. These key tables can be unloaded and archived several times a day, or week, depending on need. This type of focused archive could also be run to generate table copies for the updating of remote servers if full data replication is not possible or required.

Another variation on this method of archiving is particularly relevant in OLAP environments; that is, to archive the load data rather than the database itself. This is helpful when multiple aggregate tables are affected by a single load file, as is often the case.

Simply reloading the source files will regenerate the same aggregate values as before, so there's no need to capture the changes with an instance archive. On the other hand, the restoration process will take longer to complete depending on the number of source files that need to be processed and the length of time required to process each one.

To be sure, from time to time a baseline archive should be created. In this way the number of source files to carry forward for potential use in restoring the data can be reduced. Those source files can then be removed to permanent off-site storage.

The "Whole-istic" Approach

This is the most common way to approach archiving an instance. Using the `ontape` utility, the entire instance is archived to tape or disk on some sort of a regular basis. Unfortunately, there is not a great deal of flexibility when it is necessary to restore from these archives.

In OnLine versions 5.x and earlier, archives and restores were limited to the entire instance. With OnLine Dynamic Server you have to archive the entire instance, but you can restore to a dbspace level if needed. Going one step further, most dbspace restores can be executed with the instance on-line and fully functional.

On-line dbspace restores are only possible for dbspaces not containing critical OnLine Dynamic Server structures like the logical logs, physical log, or rootdbs. If you lost a dbspace containing those structures, the instance would crash and you would have to restore the entire instance.

The frequency and depth of the archives created with `ontape` is bounded by the amount of time required to create the archive, the acceptable amount of time to effect a restore, and, to a lesser degree, the tape device itself. While I'll be discussing tape devices in somewhat greater detail later in the chapter, for now it's the speed of the device that's important.

The speed of the tape device has a direct impact on the time required to archive or restore an instance. That said, if you have a slow device, don't be completely discouraged. Unlike other major database vendors, OnLine Dynamic Server archives can be created while the instance is on-line and actively being used. Provided there is not a requirement for complete inactivity in an instance during an archive, you can still use a slow device to create your archives. The archive process normally has little to no effect on the normal processing that occurs in an instance.

The only case where archives have an impact on normal instance processing occurs when the archive device (TAPEDEV) and logical log tape device (LTAPEDEV) are the same, and databases in the instance are in a logged mode. In this case, it is possible for the logical logs to fill up with records from database activity while the archive is

running. With the logical log archiving process terminated in order to create the instance archive, the instance will suspend all activity until the logs get written out to tape. All user sessions will stall until the archive process is canceled, and the logical logs are archived. Once the logs are written to tape, the instance will resume normal processing. The instance archive will need to be restarted during a period of lower instance activity, since it was aborted and unusable.

Ontape has three "levels" of granularity to its archiving process, as shown in Table 6-1.

Table 6–1 Ontape *archive levels.*

Archive Level	Description
Level 0	All used pages in the instance are written to tape.
Level 1	Only those pages that have changed since the time stamp of the last level 0 archive are written to tape.
Level 2	Only those pages that have changed since the last level 0 or level 1 archive time stamp, which ever occurred last, are written out to tape.

Your job as an administrator is to strike a balance between what can be achieved with these three levels of archives and your requirements to protect and recover your data. For a production OLTP environment, I would recommend that:

1. The databases be in an unbuffered logging mode
2. The logical logs be archived to tape continuously
3. A daily level 2 archive of the instance be created

Depending on your level of paranoia and the length of time to create and restore a full archive, a level 0 archive would be created either at the first of the month or on the first and fifteenth of the month. In addition, a level 1 archive could be created once a week to decrease the length of time required to create the daily level 2 archive.

With this type of design, a restore would require the level 0 tape from either the first or the fifteenth, the closest intervening level 1 (if any), the last level 2, and the logical logs written out to tape following the level 2 archive. How and when to archive logical logs will be discussed in the next section of this chapter.

In an OLAP environment, there are a couple of additional factors to consider. First, the size of the data store is usually much larger than for an OLTP environment. This means the amount of time required to create or restore from an archive will be longer. Second, as the warehouse grows, there will be an ever *decreasing* percentage of pages in the database that will be changing over time. This probably should require a different approach to archiving.

Unbuffered logging of the databases in the instance and the archiving of logical logs to tape is less important. Archives can be made less frequently than on a daily basis depending on the frequency of updates to the warehouse, the average amount of data loaded, and the rate at which the load and update process occurs.

As I mentioned earlier in this chapter, it might make more sense to archive the raw data load files rather than the instance itself. Certainly an instance archive needs to be made occasionally to establish some sort of a moment-in-time baseline against which the raw data is reloaded. In this case, a level 0 might be generated once or twice a quarter rather than once or twice a month. A level 1 archive could be created perhaps once a month, with level 2 archives created once a week.

Restoration with this type of design is similar to that for the OLTP environment mentioned in the previous paragraph. However, instead of using logical log archives to restore back to the last recorded moments in time, data load files would be used to reload the warehouse.

The impending release of the `onbar` API will undoubtedly have an impact on the archive designs I've just discussed. Should the utility allow for multiple concurrent archive threads to be active in an instance, and these threads could feed a series of tape devices in a DLT jukebox, for example, the designs expounded in the previous paragraphs will need to be revisited. With enough tape devices thrown into the archive design, and each device able to store more data than older devices, a data warehouse could be completely archived much more frequently. This would reduce the amount of tape management required to store load files as well as the effort to use these load file archive tapes in a restore.

In an OLTP environment, level 0 archives could be created daily, or at least weekly with level 1 archives created the other days of the week. A total restore would require less time to complete because at least one complete archive level would have been eliminated from the process.

Logical Logs

As I explained in the "Logging Modes" section of Chapter 5, Building a Database Environment, the physical log and logical logs are used to store information about the changes that occur to data in an instance. Depending on the logging mode of a database, either very little information will be stored in these logs, as is the case with a database in unlogged mode, or every action (save most queries) will be tracked and recorded, as happens with a database in a logged mode.

These data changes might, or might not, be of value to you in terms of recovering to a moment in time, and will determine which logging mode you choose for an individual database. Generally speaking, most environments (except OLAP) cannot sustain a loss of transaction information and will require these records. As a result, we need to know when, and how, logical logs can be archived.

Depending on whether you are using buffered or unbuffered logging, transaction information is stored for a period of time in the physical and logical log buffers, then written to the log structures on disk. Naturally, these structures, particularly the logical logs, will fill up over time. Without any archiving of the logical log information, the instance will continue writing information into the logs until the logs fill up. At that moment in time, transactions will be suspended, and a message indicating that the logical logs are full will be entered into the MSGPATH.

So we need to decide how and when to archive the logs. There are three choices to consider:

> One "feature" I was glad to see go away in OnLine Dynamic Server is the "logical log full" message that used to be entered into the MSGPATH file about every 5 seconds in earlier versions of the OnLine engine. It was obnoxious, unnecessary, and could have been potentially fatal to an instance should the MSGPATH file have grown large enough to fill the file system in which it resided. Although I don't have firsthand experience with this type of condition, I can only imagine that the instance would have shut down if it was unable to log messages to its log file.
>
> In OnLine Dynamic Server, a simple error message indicating that the logical logs are full and require archiving is placed in the MSGPATH file. Instance activity is suspended as a result of this condition. Archiving the logical logs to tape (or /dev/null if necessary) will allow instance activity to resume.

1. Never. This is accomplished by setting LTAPEDEV to /dev/null. As each logical log fills, it is immediately marked as though it was archived off to tape. The log is immediately made available for use whenever the instance cycles back to it. This option should be considered for an OLAP environment, where the volume of change is high but also easy to track or recreate. I also set my LTAPEDEV to /dev/null in development instances where I need a logged database environment but I don't care about capturing the changes that occur to the test data the database contains.
2. On demand. The logical logs are archived to tape as a result of executing the "`ontape -a`" command. Full logs as well as the current logical log are archived to tape and marked free for reuse. This choice is acceptable for instances containing unlogged databases because the logs will not fill quickly enough to justify continuous archiving. Extreme care must be taken using this option in instances with logged databases. If the logical logs are not archived off frequently enough, a log-full condition could occur that will affect the entire instance.
3. Continuous. As each logical log fills, it is automatically archived to tape. Accomplished by executing the "`ontape -c`" command, this will invoke a log archive process which runs in foreground mode on a terminal or in a terminal window. The archive process will indicate when an archive tape has filled and request that a new tape be used. This is the best option to choose for instances with databases in logged mode

in a production environment. The tapes used to archive the logical logs need to be switched out on a regular basis in conjunction with the daily archive process.

There are those who disagree with the interface design and the requirement to dedicate a terminal of some sort, as well as a tape device, to the logical log archive process. Unfortunately, there are not too many other ways of handling it in my opinion. It's also easy to deal with. Character-based terminals are inexpensive and simple to install on the system's serial ports. If rack or desktop space is at a premium, use an X-terminal to run all the logical log archive processes out of a separate xterm window, or buy some character-based windowing software and run the archive processes out of windows on the system console or other device. As far as tape devices are concerned, 4mm DAT devices are inexpensive and more than fast enough to handle the amount of logical log data that will be pushed to it under normal and reasonable conditions.

There is one other factor to consider in deciding on when and how to archive the logical log records: the impact BLOBs will have on the process. Because BLOBs bypass the instance's shared memory structures, writes of BLOBs are not considered committed until the BLOB information has been written to the logical log. Depending on the size of the BLOBs, the frequency at which they are written, and the size of the logical logs themselves, a logical log could fill quickly. Remember, too, that deletes of BLOBs are not considered committed, and the disk space freed up, until the logical log containing the delete record has been archived. This could require more effort to archive the logs if you elect to use the "on demand" method. Continuous logging would be easier and better in this type of situation. Heavy BLOB activity will fill log space in a shorter amount of time, so the archive terminal must be monitored to make sure the tape is not filled up and needing to be swapped out.

Tape Devices

The market today seems to be able to provide a number of different technologies and media to archive your instances and logical logs. There are QIC, 4mm DAT, and 8 mm helical-scan tape technology, all of which have traditionally been used to store archives. Each of these has their own particular advantages and disadvantages, ranging from size of the tape itself to the amount of data each type of tape can hold. New floppy/cartridge drives can hold from 100 MB to 1 GB, making them excellent candidates for table-driven, focused archives or even logical log archives.

With data warehouses becoming more popular and larger, as well as larger production OLTP environments, DLT technology has become the hottest tape commodity in the market today. Boasting a compressed capacity of close to 70 GB and an acceptably fast transfer rate, it would appear that DLT should be able to work with almost any archive design in either database environment. In addition, you can select WORM optical disks and even rewritable optical media for long-term storage of data accessed so infrequently that response time is not a factor.

With all these choices it would seem to be easy to implement the best technology for the task, rendering this section of the chapter irrelevant. Unfortunately, tape technology support is the Achilles heel of OnLine Dynamic Server, at least until the `onbar` API is available.

The biggest weakness in OnLine Dynamic Server, and with the `ontape` utility, is its tape-handling and tape technology support. Basically there is none. A double-edged sword, this is both a good and a bad thing.

On the down side, you have no direct device support. You are at the mercy of whatever devices have a valid driver for your version of the operating system. On the positive side, Informix is not spending valuable engineering time fiddling around with tape drive commands, robotic control extensions, and other related issues. They do not have to make sure they have support ported into each release of the product for every possible tape/cartridge/optical device that could be attached to a machine, thereby bloating the code. Instead, they concentrate on what they do best and use their engineering resources to improve and enhance the functionality, performance, and scalability of the engine.

So what can you use to archive with? The bottom line on tape devices is this: you can use any *single*-tape device you want as long as you have a driver for it and it operates in *native, uncompressed* mode. There is no support for auto-changers or juke boxes. You either need to manually swap tapes or write shell scripts to wrap around the `ontape` utility to get it to work with multitape devices. Informix also does not support archives made using hardware or software compression.

A commonly asked question by those new to OnLine Dynamic Server, is how much data will the engine support via the TAPESIZE and LTAPESIZE configuration parameters. Though current technology allows you to put anywhere between 1 and 35 GB to a tape in uncompressed mode, the engine was designed to accommodate much larger uncompressed tape sizes. Quoting John Lengyel from Informix:

> The wrinkle here is that the settings for LTAPESIZE and TAPESIZE are in units of "kilobytes." So although it's true that LTAPESIZE can have a maximum value of 0x7fffffff (2147483647), that value doesn't specify a tape capacity of 2147483647 bytes (2 gig), but of 2147483647*1024 bytes (2 terabytes).

There is one other option for a tape device that can be used quite effectively from time to time — /dev/null.

Setting TAPEDEV or LTAPEDEV to /dev/null allows archive commands to completely execute in just a few seconds. This is handy when you need to change logging modes on a database, or archive and close the current logical log so newly created BLOBspaces can be activated. In making the change to /dev/null, you do not need to erase the information regarding tape size or block size for that tape device; these values are ignored.

Needless to say, you cannot restore anything from an archive created to /dev/null.

Should you temporarily change either of your tape devices to /dev/null to execute some commands, remember to change it back to the symbolic link pointing to the valid device as quickly as possible.

Even though your choices of supported tape devices is somewhat limited, you are not limited to where the tape device is located depending on how you want to use it. You can elect to use tape drives physically attached to a UNIX server other than the one supporting the instance. Simply preface the device path with the system name followed by a colon. For example:

```
perseus:/usr/informix_721/tapes/logtape_1
```

There are two conditions that must be observed if you want to use a "remote" tape device for instance archives. The first is that the remote system name must be resolvable through /etc/hosts or a DNS lookup. The second condition is that because the instance has no direct system connection to the device, it cannot tell when the tape device closes or completes a write. As a result, an archive written to the remote device is not considered complete until the archive process is manually terminated after all the data is written to tape. This limits the use of remote tape devices to full instance archives or automatic logical log archives using the "ontape -a" command. Continuous logical log archives to remote tape devices will not be successful since the instance has no way of receiving back the "write-close" result code from the tape device at the end of the logical log data stream in order to mark the log backup complete. Without interrupting the logical log archiving process (and forcing a close to be recorded in the instance), the logs will not be considered free for reuse. This could lead to a "logical log-full" condition in the instance.

Using remote tape devices does incur additional overhead because you're going across a couple of network connections yielding a slower overall throughput rate. Still, you can leverage the tape devices purchased and installed on other systems, if necessary, for the right kind of archive task.

You can archive to hard disk as well, though you must work with constraints such as the operating system's limit on file system or individual file sizes. To archive to disk, create the file to receive the archive by using the "touch" command, set TAPEDEV to the pathed name of the file, and start the archive. Naturally, this "flat file" type of an archive can then be copied to tape during an operating system archive. Some people have reported archiving their raw dbspaces to tape using the "dd" command. This is completely unsupported by Informix.

These limitations on tape devices should disappear with the onbar API and the ability to use third-party tape management systems. With onbar, the engine simply supplies a data feed to a device name, undoubtedly with some sort of flow control. Third-party tape management software is used to control the tape devices as well as any robotic extensions. The full storage capacity of the devices will be utilized, custom archive scripts can be implemented, and, I believe, a lower level of dbspace granularity in the archive creation process will be available. Needless to say, I am excited about what `onbar` will allow to be done in designing and implementing an archiving process.

warning

When setting up or changing tape devices, always enter a tape size value about five percent lower than the tape's actual raw, uncompressed storage capacity. For example, if you're using a 525 MB QIC tape device as a logical log archive device, set LTAPESIZE to 500 MB. If you're using a 4mm DDS2 tape which can store about 4 GB of data, set the tape size value to 3800 MB.

Setting the value lower than actual capacity allows for some flexibility should a cartridge's tape length be a little short as well as any tape label information `ontape` writes out to the tape. Archives encountering an EOT condition prior to writing out the amount of information equivalent to the device tape size for any given tape in the archive set will fail and be aborted. Better to err on the conservative side of tape sizes than to find out the hard way that your sixth tape in a multitape archive is a little short and have to restart the archive all over again!

There is one additional caveat to selecting a tape device to use with the `ontape` utility: the device must automatically rewind the media when the device is opened or closed. Prior to writing to or reading from a tape, `ontape` performs a series of compatibility checks. Media rewind is one of the checks.

Understanding the Archiving Process

A commonly asked question by administrators new to OnLine Dynamic Server is how the engine can create archives at all, much less at different levels, while an instance is fully active and in a multi-user state. This is one of the nice features OnLine Dynamic Server enjoys over its competitors in the market today. The answer lies in a part of the data page structures called the "page header" and "page-ending time stamp." In this section I will briefly explain how the on-line archive process works.

Every time an element on a data page changes, an overhead structure on the page called a "time stamp" is updated. There are, in fact, two time stamps on a page, but for the purposes of the discussion here, I'll treat them as a single entity.

The relative value of any given page's time stamp to another page in an instance determines whether or not one page was modified before or after another. The time stamp is also used by the engine to determine if a page was modified before or after any given moment in time. This is the key to creating on-line archives.

When you initiate an archive at any of the three levels, the first thing that happens is a checkpoint. The checkpoint flushes all the buffers to disk and synchronizes the disk images to those in the logical log buffers if buffered logging is set on any databases in the instance.

Then the engine sets what I'll call the "archive time stamp" for the instance. This is the moment in time the checkpoint completed and can be one of the standards against which all page time stamps will be evaluated to determine qualification for archiving.

Depending on the archive level requested, the engine will copy out to tape either of the following:

- Pages with time stamps greater than the archive time stamp of a previous archive of a lower number, as happens with a level 1 or level 2 archive
- All used pages, but the pages copied will be as they were when their page time stamp was less than or equal to the archive time stamp, as occurs in a level 0 archive

As the archive process continues, a couple of other procedures occur that are not relevant to this discussion, and then the engine begins to copy data out of the instance to tape.

BLOBspaces are copied to tape after the rootdbs and logical log records since BLOBspaces need to be locked in exclusive mode until their contents are written to tape in order to maintain consistency. Once the rootdbs, logical log information, and BLOBspaces are archived, the other dbspaces are copied out in chunk-creation order. Chunk-creation order simply means that each chunk is archived to tape in the same order in which it was added to the instance.

The archive process then looks at each used page in a chunk; the time stamp on the page is evaluated to see if it matches the criteria for archiving. If it does, it is copied out to tape. But what happens when the next checkpoint needs to occur and pages are going to be updated that haven't been archived yet? This is where the physical log assumes a role other than that of ensuring the ability to rollback a transaction.

Prior to the checkpoint flush to disk, `ontape` looks at all the pages in the physical log. In looking at a page in the physical log, if `ontape` has already evaluated that page in the chunk to determine whether or not it should be archived, nothing more happens with that page and the next page from the physical log is read. If the page stored in the physical log belongs to a chunk that has not yet been processed by `ontape`, `ontape` will jump to and evaluate the existing time stamp on that page in the chunk. If the time stamp qualifies the page for archiving, the page is written to tape immediately.

Once all the pages from the physical log are read, and qualifying pages are archived off to tape, the checkpoint is allowed to continue and `cntape` resumes work from where it stopped prior to the checkpoint. As part of the checkpoint process, the page time stamps of all pages affected by the checkpoint are updated. As the `ontape` archive process gets to one of those pages that was archived as part of the checkpoint process, the time stamp on the page will be greater than the archive time stamp, disqualifying it for archiving. `Ontape` will continue and evaluate the next page in the chunk. This is of little consequence to us because the page, as it existed prior to the start of the archive, was already copied out to tape.

As you can see, OnLine Dynamic Server archives are literally a moment-in-time snapshot of the instance's contents. The last two reserved pages in the rootdbs contain all the relevant information about the last two archives, of different levels, created within the instance. The archive level, the real time the archive occurred, the archive time stamp, and information about the current logical log at the time the archive started are stored. This can be checked by extracting the information in the reserved pages with the "`oncheck -pr`" command.

Using the Ontape Utility

The `ontape` utility is used to archive and restore all or part of OnLine Dynamic Server instances and logical logs. In this section, we'll look at the required syntax to perform these operations. You'll see that one of the great things about this utility, as opposed to the `onstat` utility, for example, is that it is easy to use in terms of command options.

Creating Archives

First let's look at how to archive the logical logs. As I mentioned in the "Logical Logs" section of this chapter, you can either archive the logs "on demand" or "continuously." To archive the logs "on demand," execute the "`ontape -a`" command.

This will copy all the full logs to tape, then ask if you want to archive the current log as well. If you answer yes, the current active log will stop recording transaction information and be copied to tape, regardless of how much of the log was used. While this is occurring, the next unused log becomes the active log and begins to record transaction information.

To continuously archive the logical logs, execute the "`ontape -c`" command. This will start the log archive process in foreground mode on the terminal, or terminal window, in which it was invoked.

There are almost no status messages displayed from this command. When a tape is filled to LTAPESIZE, a message stating the log numbers that the tape contains appears, followed by a prompt asking for a new tape to be inserted. Other than that, there are no other messages or reports.

Now let's look at the syntax required to archive the instance itself. The only flag that needs to be set is the archive level. The syntax is as follows:

```
ontape -s -L archive_level
```

where "archive_level" is replaced with a 0, 1, or 2.

In truth, there is one other flag that can be set in conjunction with this command. As explained in the "Changing Database Logging Modes" section of Chapter 4, Basic Administrative Tasks, database logging modes are changed in conjunction with a level 0 archive. This can involve appending a flag for the desired logging mode as well as the name of the database to this command. If a logging mode change needs to be made to more than one database in the instance, using the `ondblog` utility eliminates the need to execute a level 0 archive for each database that needs to be changed. With `ondblog`, all the databases are flagged with their new logging mode, then the change occurs when one level 0 archive is executed.

While an instance archive is running, the approximate percent completed will be displayed. This number may or may not be completely accurate. Prior to writing archive data to tape, the engine will sum up all the allocated table extents. As the archive reads through the pages, it will calculate what percentage of the total allocation has been read. The percentage calculation can be skewed if a large number of tables have actually used only a small amount of the total number of pages allocated. Because unused table pages will not need archiving, the archive process will bypass the rest of the pages in that table and move to the next set of used pages. As a result, the percent complete calculation will appear to display erratic and inconsistent progress. This should not cause you any concern.

Restoring from Archives

There are only two options when restoring from an archive. You can either restore the entire instance, commonly called a "cold restore," or you can restore one or more dbspaces, referred to as a "warm" or "on-line" restore. The conditions requiring the restore will dictate which option, or if a combination of the two, is appropriate.

A cold restore is required if a catastrophic failure occurs on an unprotected disk containing the rootdbs, logical logs, or physical log. The engine will crash due to this failure and will not come back on-line. A complete restore or reinitialization is your only option. Cold restores require the instance to be completely offline.

If unprotected disks containing other dbspaces fail, or you simply need to recover a dbspace (other than the rootdbs or one containing the physical or logical logs), an on-line or warm restore would be best. This type of restore can occur with the instance in an on-line, fully active operating mode, though the dbspaces to be restored must be in a down state. See the "Changing the Status of a Chunk" section of Chapter 4, Basic Administrative Tasks, for information on changing the status of a dbspace or chunk.

The syntax to execute a restore is as straightforward as the syntax for an archive:

```
ontape -r
```

performs a cold restore, while

```
ontape -f -D dbspace_name
```

restores the named dbspace or BLOBspace. Multiple dbspaces can be restored at one time by replacing "dbspace_name" with a white-space-separated list of dbspace names.

Summary

For the moment, the archiving of an OnLine Dynamic Server instance is a relatively uncomplicated process. The `onbar` API, when it's released, should allow for more flexibility in creating archives as well as eliminate the tape device limitations we have to work around now. Although the `ontape` command archives the entire instance, you can still create table level archives by using SQL commands or OnLine Dynamic Server utilities such as `onunload`.

When designing or implementing an archive and restore methodology, keep the following points in mind:

- Regardless of the size of the instance or archive methodology used, a complete baseline archive needs to be created periodically. The amount of time between these baseline archives will vary depending on
  — the size of the instance
  — the amount of time required to create the archive
  — the amount of change that occurs in the instance
  — the acceptable amount of risk and time required to recreate changes occurring after the baseline archive
- Informix will not support archives created on tape media with hardware or software compression.

- Set the TAPESIZE and LTAPESIZE parameters to about 5 percent less than the rated capacity of the tapes to be used. Informix supports uncompressed tape sizes up to 2 TB.
- By using /dev/null as an archive device, certain functions, like changing database logging modes or automatically freeing logical logs, can be accomplished. Archives created to /dev/null cannot be restored.
- When using the `ontape` utility, various archive levels can be employed to reduce the total time required to create or restore from an archive.
- If an instance has databases operating in logged mode, and only one tape device is available to the system, make sure archives are run during a period of time that will allow them to complete without the logical logs filling up.
- Some DML and DDL statements, such as dropping a BLOB or creating a BLOBspace, require the current logical log to be closed and archived before completing. `Ontape` has a flag to invoke this process.

Coming Up

In the next chapter, I'll discuss the various utilities to look inside the instance as a whole, or into an individual user session, to see what tasks are being executed and resources used. Both the command line and the new graphical utilities will be covered.

Chapter 7

Monitoring the Instance

- *What SQL statement is a user thread executing?*
- *How efficiently is the instance reading or writing data?*
- *How much table interleaving is occurring in the dbspaces?*
- *How do I check to see if an index is corrupted?*
- *I just corrupted the $ONCONFIG file, how can I see what values the instance was brought on-line with?*
- *Can I monitor key engine elements or functionality from a graphical interface in real time?*

Database environments are not plug-and-play ready. Database engines require daily care, feeding, and maintenance.

This chapter will introduce four utilities to help you look into the bowels of the OnLine Dynamic Server engine and monitor what's happening. Two of the utilities are command-line-oriented; the other two are Motif-based. By the end of the chapter you should understand the purpose of each tool and how to use them to generate the type of information you want.

Command Line Utilities

Unlike the graphical utilities I'll be covering later in this chapter, every port of OnLine Dynamic Server contains the `onstat` and `oncheck` utilities. The functionality of these two utilities has increased substantially over that in OnLine 5.x and earlier ports, where they were called "`tbstat`" and "`tbcheck`," respectively. The old names still exist, with full OnLine Dynamic Server functionality, in the $INFORMIXDIR/bin directory for the sake of backward compatibility.

The `onstat` utility is used to monitor the operational "status" of an instance or a thread. This utility displays information derived almost exclusively from queries into the SMI. See "The Sysmaster Database and the SMI Interface" section of Chapter 3, Initializing an OnLine Dynamic Server Instance, for more information on the SMI. The `onstat` utility shows moment-in-time snapshots that can be highly volatile.

`Oncheck` is used to verify instance or database configuration information that primarily resides on disk. There is much less volatility in the information it displays.

Both of these utilities and their flags are explained fairly well in the *OnLine Administrator's Guide* that accompanied your software. I will not, in this chapter, attempt to reexplain every flag option or what the output generated by each flag looks like. What I will do, however, is cover some of the flag options of each utility that I find most helpful to use. A couple of commands, such as "`onstat -p`," are covered in other chapters and will not be covered again in this chapter.

Engine Status Reports: The Onstat Utility

For newcomers to OnLine Dynamic Server, the `onstat` utility is the most difficult to master. Not because it is complicated to use, it's just that there are so many flags and options to remember and use. Some of the options are single-flag-driven (a - f, h - z), while the "–g" flag requires additional parameters. A complete list of all the flags is shown in Figure 7-1.

```
usage: onstat [-abcdfghklmpstuxzBCDFRX][-i] [-r seconds] [-o file] [infile]
     -a      Print all info
     -b      Print buffers
     -c      Print configuration file
     -d      Print DBspaces and chunks
     -f      Print dataskip status
     -g      MT subcommand (default: all)
     -i      interactive mode
     -k      Print locks
     -l      Print logging
     -m      Print message log
     -p      Print profile
     -s      Print latches
     -t      Print TBLspaces
     -u      Print user threads
     -x      print transactions
     -z      Zero profile counts
     -B      Print all buffers
     -C      Print btree cleaner requests
     -D      Print DBspaces and detailed chunk stats
     -F      Print page flushers
     -R      Print LRU queues
     -X      Print entire list of sharers and waiters for buffers
     -r      Repeat options every n seconds (default: 5)
     -o      Put shared memory into specified file (default: onstat.out)
     infile  Use infile to obtain shared memory information
                                                              continued
```

Figure 7–1 *Flags and parameter options for the* `onstat` *utility.*

```
MT COMMANDS:
    all     Print all MT information
    ath     Print all threads
    wai     Print waiting threads
    act     Print active threads
    rea     Print ready threads
    sle     Print all sleeping threads
    spi     print spin locks with long spins
    sch     print VP scheduler statistics
    lmx     Print all locked mutexes
    wmx     Print all mutexes with waiters
    con     Print conditions with waiters
    stk <tid>     Dump the stack of a specified thread
    glo     Print MT global information
    mem <pool name|session id>    print pool statistics.
    seg     Print memory segment statistics.
    rbm     print block map for resident segment
    nbm     print block map for non-resident segments
    afr <pool name|session id>    Print allocated pool fragments.
    ffr <pool name|session id>    Print free pool fragments.
    ufr <pool name|session id>    Print pool usage breakdown
    iov     Print disk IO statistics by vp
    iof     Print disk IO statistics by chunk/file
    ioq     Print disk IO statistics by queue
    iog     Print AIO global information
    iob     Print big buffer usage by IO VP class
    ppf [<partition number> | 0]    Print partition profiles
    tpf [<tid> | 0]    Print thread profiles
    ntu     Print net user thread profile information
    ntt     Print net user thread access times
    ntm     Print net message information
    ntd     print net dispatch information
    nss <session id>    print net shared memory status
    nsc <client id>     print net shared memory status
    nsd     print net shared memory data
    sts     Print max and current stack sizes
    dic     print dictionary cache information
    opn [<tid>]    Print open tables
    qst     print queue statistics
    wst     print thread wait statistics
    ses <session id>    print session information
    sql <session id>    print sql information
    dri     Print data replication information
    pos     Print /INFORMIXDIR/etc/.infos.DBSERVERNAME file
    mgm     Print mgm resource manager information
    ddr     Print DDR log post processing information
    dmp <address> <length>    Dump shared memory.
    src <pattern> <mask>      Search memory for (mem&mask)==pattern
```

Figure 7-1 continued

The new functionality given to the onstat utility gives you the ability to look inside the OnLine Dynamic Server engine and see what's happening in the current instance to which your environment points. This type of functionality has existed for years in mainframe-based databases but was sorely lacking on UNIX-based engines. With the expanded capacities, dramatically improved performance, significantly greater ability to access data, lower software and hardware costs, and new reporting and analysis functions, there is little advantage to a mainframe-based database engine when compared to OnLine Dynamic Server. Let's take a look at what some of these commands do.

One new option to the onstat *command you might find particularly handy is the "*-i*" flag. By executing an "*onstat -i*" you put the* onstat *command in interactive mode. Your system prompt changes to reflect that the* onstat *command is running. At this point, simply enter the flags and qualifiers for the command you want to run as shown in this brief example:*

```
epaphus: onstat -i

INFORMIX-OnLine Version 7.13.UC2 -- On-Line -- Up 1 days 07:48:32 -
    - 52656 Kbytes
onstat> -

INFORMIX-OnLine Version 7.13.UC2 -- On-Line -- Up 1 days 07:48:36 -
    - 52656 Kbytes
onstat> -u

INFORMIX-OnLine Version 7.13.UC2 -- On-Line -- Up 1 days 07:48:39 -
    - 52656 Kbytes

Userthreads
address  flags     sessid   user       tty  wait tout locks nreads nwrites
c4a0b010 ---P--D   0        informix-0      0    0    723   2894
c4a0b444 ---P--F   0        informix-0      0    0    0     0
         [SNIP]
21 active, 128 total, 55 maximum concurrent

onstat> -d
```

```
INFORMIX-OnLine Version 7.13.UC2 -- On-Line -- Up 1 days 07:51:31 -
- 52656 Kbytes

Dbspaces
address      number    flags    fchunk   nchunks   flags    owner       name
c4a090e8     1         1        1        1         N        informix    rootdbs
c4a09a98     2         1        2        1         N        informix    logfiles
c4a09b00     3         1        3        1         N        informix    phylog
             [SNIP]
onstat>
```

Since the onstat *command is already running and attached to the instance's shared memory, the response back to commands entered will be almost instantaneous. All the* onstat *command flags are available in this mode, including the "*-r seconds*" flag. There is a new option, "*-rz seconds,*" available only in this mode. This command combines the "repeat every x seconds" option with the "zero statistics" option to repeat the command at the specified interval and to zero out the statistical counters between each iteration of the command. Typing* ctrl-c *will interrupt a repeating command while* ctrl-d *will abort the* onstat *interactive mode interface.*

Looking at User Threads

Prior to OnLine Dynamic Server, about the only information you could get about user activity was that there was a database connection via a sqlturbo process as shown by the output of an onstat -u command. That's changed; a lot! You can now look at what any given user thread is doing and the resources it is taking to complete its tasks. Figure 7-2 shows the output of the onstat -u command, but this is only the first step in looking at a user thread.

The output is not much different than that of earlier versions of OnLine with one major difference—instead of PID numbers for the sqlturbo processes, there are now "sessid" numbers listed. These session ID numbers correspond to thread identification numbers. You can use these session IDs to query information about a specific thread. This requires using the "-g" flag with extra parameters. In this case, because I'm interested in session-related information, I'd

```
INFORMIX-OnLine Version 7.13.UC2 -- On-Line -- Up 18 days 15:46:16 -- 44848
Kbytes

Userthreads
address    flags     sessid   user       tty     wait       tout  locks  nreads  nwrites
c23d9010   ---P--D   0        root       -       0          0     0      3357    4662
c23d9444   ---P--F   0        root       -       0          0     0      0       0
c23d9878   ---P--F   0        root       -       0          0     0      0       0
c23d9cac   ---P--F   0        root       -       0          0     0      0       0
c23da0e0   ---P--F   0        root       -       0          0     0      0       0
c23da514   ---P--F   0        root       -       0          0     0      0       0
c23da948   ---P--B   16       root       -       0          0     0      419     3877
c23dad7c   ---P--D   0        root       -       0          0     0      0       0
c23dbe4c   Y--P---   15712    ssbennio   ttyp4   c286d7e0   0     1      4       1
c23dc6b4   Y--P---   14848    djw        ttypc   c29d2238   0     0      42      6
c23dcae8   Y--P---   15784    dallas     -       c2928bd8   0     1      0       0
c23dd350   Y--P---   14858    djw        ttypc   c28de570   0     1      1       0
c23dd784   Y--P---   15648    ssbennio   ttyp4   c279c130   0     0      15      4
c23de420   Y--P---   15570    dallas     ttyp2   c27c6580   0     0      29      13
c23df0bc   Y--P---   15776    dallas     ttyp2   c279c5c0   0     1      15      7
15 active, 128 total, 25 maximum concurrent
```

Figure 7–2 Output generated by the "onstat -u" command.

use "-g ses sessid" where "sessid" is replaced with a valid user session ID. For example, to look at what the "dallas" userid is doing in the session 15570, I executed an "onstat -g ses 15570" command and received the result shown in Figure 7-3.

We can see that, among other things, this session is running an update statement from within a 4GL or other client application which is running on the same server as the OnLine engine. I know this because the Front End Version (F.E. Vers) has a valid value that is not at the same release level as the engine. This indicates that the SQL statement is not executed from within dbaccess. There isn't an isolation level specified other than the default for the database, but the lock mode was set to "not wait." You can also see statistics about the virtual memory being used as well as the type, state, and thread IDof the actual thread handling the request.

Many times, though, you're only going to be interested in the SQL statement being executed by a thread instead of all the statistical information about the session. Perhaps the session is showing a high number of reads or writes, or it's dying unexpectedly. In

```
INFORMIX-OnLine Version 7.13.UC2 -- On-Line -- Up 18 days 15:48:23 -- 44848
Kbytes

session                              #RSAM   total      used
id        user    tty     pid   hostname  threads memory     memory
15570     dallas  ttyp2   16953 epaphus      1    65536      28000

tid          name       rstcb     flags    curstk        status
15605        sqlexec    c23de420  Y--P---  34552    cond wait(sm_read)

Memory pools count 1
name     class    addr     totalsize    freesize  #allocfrag   #freefrag
15570    V        c25f7010 65536        37536     139          15

name         free    used      name       free       used
overhead     0       112       scb        0          80
opentable    0       5032      filetable  0          864
ru           0       224       log        0          2120
temprec      0       1608      ralloc     34600      0
gentcb       0       192       ostcb      0          2216
net          0       3720      sort       0          56
sqscb        0       8800      rdahead    0          296
hashfiletab  0       280       osenv      0          808
sqtcb        2936    1552      fragman    0          40

Sess      SQL         Current   Iso    Lock     SQL    ISAM    F.E.
Id        Stmt type   Database  Lvl    Mode     ERR    ERR     Vers
15570     -           -         -      NotWait  0      0       6.03

Last parsed SQL statement:
update system : snavp set ( navto_tran_id , navto_prg_id ) = ( " " , " ")
where user_id = user
```

Figure 7–3 *Output generated by the* "onstat -g ses" *command.*

this case, use the "-g sql *sessid*" flag. It only showed the SQL-related information shown in Figure 7-4 when I ran it against session ID15869.

Disk and Chunk Information

As I explained in the "Dbspace Design Issues" section of Chapter 2, Preparing for Initialization, one of the more important tasks when deciding on the physical implementation of the logical database design is to balance disk I/O. Tables need to be fragmented or dis-

```
INFORMIX-OnLine Version 7.13.UC2 -- On-Line -- Up 18 days 16:24:28 -- 44848
Kbytes

Sess        SQL         Current     Iso     Lock        SQL     ISAM    F.E.
Id          Stmt type   Database    Lvl     Mode        ERR     ERR     Vers
15869       -           -           -       Not Wait    0       0       6.03

Last parsed SQL statement :
 update system : snavp set ( navto_tran_id , navto_prg_id ) = ( " " , " ")
 where user_id = user
```

Figure 7-4 *Output generated by the "*`onstat -g sql`*" command.*

tributed in such a way as to prevent the instance from becoming disk-bound from either the sheer volume of reads or writes, or having too many tables or table fragments located on too few drives, causing waits to occur. In order to monitor for these types of hot spots, you need to be able to look at disk access statistics.

The "`onstat -d`" command is handy to use when you want to look at the overall disk configuration for the instance. The "`chk_chunks`" script in the "Monitoring the Instance" section of Chapter 12, Scripts to Help Get the Job Done, highlights disk chunks that could have a problem. Neither of these, however, provide the type of information you need to monitor the I/O load within the instance. There are two onstat command flags which do provide that type of information. The first one is "`onstat -D`." Figure 7-5 contains some sample output generated by this command.

Some of the information shown is the same as that shown by the "`onstat -d`" command, the "`-D`" flag also displays pages read and written at a chunk level. This is particularly helpful when a dbspace has more than one chunk allocated to it. As will all the other instance's statistical counters, these values can be reset to zero by executing an "`onstat -z`" command if necessary.

The second command to use when monitoring disk I/O is "`onstat -g iof`." This command is only effective if your instance's I/O is being handled through the AIO vps rather than with KAIO (kernel asynchronous I/O) which is available in some ports of the engine. As shown in Figure 7-6, this command displays total *disk operations* rather than pages read or written.

Using these two commands, I can look at the volume of data reads and writes as well as total disk activity for any given chunk

```
INFORMIX-OnLine Version 7.13.UC2 -- On-Line -- Up 36 days 05:08:24 -- 17384
Kbytes

Dbspaces
address    number  flags  fchunk  nchunks  flags  owner     name
c20b10e8   1       2      1       1        M      informix  rootdbs
c20b1df8   2       2      2       1        M      informix  l_logs
c20b1e60   3       1      3       1        N      informix  columbia_1
c20b1ec8   4       1      4       1        N      informix  columbia_2
c20b1f30   5       1      5       1        N      informix  columbia_3
c20b1f98   6       1      6       1        N      informix  columbia_4
c20b2000   7       1      7       1        N      informix  columbia_5
c20b2068   8       1      8       1        N      informix  columbia_6
c20b20d0   9       1      9       2        N      informix  col_index_1
c20b2138   10      1      10      1        N      informix  col_work_1
c20b21a0   11      1      11      1        N      informix  col_work_2
c20b2208   12      1      12      1        N      informix  col_work_3
 12 active, 2047 maximum

Chunks
address    chk/dbs  offset  page Rd   page Wr  pathname
c20b1150   1  1     0         15756    654579  /usr/informix_711/columbia/col_chnk_1
c20b1228   1  1     0         11533    654579  /usr/informix_711/columbia/col_chnk_2
c20b1300   2  2     0          8567    404494  /usr/informix_711/columbia/col_chnk_3
c20b1d20   2  2     0         16098    404494  /usr/informix_711/columbia/col_chnk_4
c20b13d8   3  3     0        845937     10079  /usr/informix_711/columbia/col_chnk_5
c20b14b0   4  4     0        200491      4564  /usr/informix_711/columbia/col_chnk_6
c20b1588   5  5     0       1143439      7055  /usr/informix_711/columbia/col_chnk_7
c20b1660   6  6     0        821585     14675  /usr/informix_711/columbia/col_chnk_8
c20b1738   7  7     0        840939     12864  /usr/informix_711/columbia/col_chnk_9
c20b1810   8  8     0        577042     16231  /usr/informix_711/columbia/col_chnk_10
c20b18e8   9  9     0       1592706    388041  /usr/informix_711/columbia/col_chnk_11
c20b19c0   10 10    0        254398    255271  /usr/informix_711/columbia/col_chnk_12
c20b1a98   11 11    0        237157    238658  /usr/informix_711/columbia/col_chnk_13
c20b1b70   12 12    0        261266    265901  /usr/informix_711/columbia/col_chnk_14
c20b1c48   13 9     0       1466755    272954  /usr/informix_711/columbia/col_chnk_15
 13 active, 2047 maximum
```

Figure 7-5 *Output generated by the "onstat-D" command.*

about which I am concerned. Potential disk bottlenecks, such as the col_chunk_11 chunk in these figures, are pretty easy to spot. The dbspace created by using this as well as another chunk contains all the indexes for one of the databases in this instance. With that information, you would expect to see a significant amount of activity in these chunks. Under some conditions, I would probably rec-

```
INFORMIX-OnLine Version 7.13.UC2 -- On-Line -- Up 36 days 05:20:16 -- 17384
Kbytes

AIO global files:
gfd    pathname      totalops    dskread    dskwrite    io/s
 3     col_chnk_1      63482       2410       61072      0.0
 4     col_chnk_2      63734       2662       61072      0.0
 5     col_chnk_3     323149       2045      321104      0.1
 6     col_chnk_5     908873     899552        9321      0.3
 7     col_chnk_6     883109     878870        4239      0.3
 8     col_chnk_7      86869      80159        6710      0.0
 9     col_chnk_8      86396      72785       13611      0.0
10     col_chnk_9      45531      33694       11837      0.0
11     col_chnk_10     46905      31690       15215      0.0
12     col_chnk_11   1777354    1394242      383112      0.6
13     col_chnk_12    127115      64270       62845      0.0
14     col_chnk_13    116461      57712       58749      0.0
15     col_chnk_14    129100      63569       65531      0.0
16     col_chnk_15    716270     448983      267287      0.2
17     col_chnk_4     323604       2500      321104      0.1
```

Figure 7-6   Output generated by the "onstat -g iof" command.

ommend spreading the indexes around to different dbspaces and chunks. In this particular instance, there are usually less than six concurrent users at any one time. Continued monitoring of chunk activity levels indicated that most of the activity to the chunk in question occurs during the weekly data loads, aggregation, and "update statistic" activity—as you would expect from the database structures stored in those chunks. As a result, I'm comfortable with the apparent lopsidedness in the values displayed.

Another command that could be of interest when monitoring disk activity is "onstat -C." As displayed in Figure 7-7, the output from this command shows the number of backlogged index deletions. At the moment in time the output displayed in Figure 7-7 was generated, there weren't any index entries to delete.

When a row is deleted from a table, and there is an index on that table, the index information for that row is not automatically deleted. The index element is marked for deletion, and a lock is placed on the element that prevents it from being used by another thread. When the transaction that deleted the row is committed, a request to delete the index element is handed off to the Btree cleaners. The workload of these cleaners can be monitored with this command.

```
INFORMIX-OnLine Version 7.13.UC2 -- On-Line -- Up 18 days 16:08:25 -- 44848
Kbytes

Btree Cleaner Info
btcleanr     pool       flags    pools    npend    busypnum   head    tail     free
c23da948     c2657010   1        1        0        0          0       0        c26598d8

nreqs        dups       success  dfrmv    unnec    ditems     ditlks cmprs     palcs
2775872      2662227    112817   112809   372      1438335    171192 10633     1

outstanding requests
address      next       partnum pagenum keynum

0 pending, 1024 total, 1024 hash buckets, 1 pools
```

Figure 7-7 *Output generated by the "*onstat -C*" command.*

General Instance Monitoring

When it comes to monitoring the general health and performance of an instance, it's difficult to draw an imaginary cutoff and say that flags 1, 2, and 7 are important enough to cover in this chapter while others are not. Depending on your situation, any number of flag options could be more important to run than the three I will mention here. That said, these three are fairly important and should be used on some sort of a regular basis for all instances.

The first command, "onstat -g seg," displays general shared memory statistics. As illustrated in Figure 7-8, this command shows the three different portions of shared memory (resident, virtual, and message), the size of each segment, and the number of free blocks for each segment.

It is important to monitor the number of virtual shared memory segments allocated within an instance. This is the portion used to support end user threads, and its efficiency decreases with each new segment allocation. If you see two or more segments of virtual shared memory during the normal processing cycle, at the next maintenance period increase the value of SHMVIRTSIZE to whatever the total value of the virtual shared memory segments are and restart the instance.

```
INFORMIX-OnLine Version 7.13.UC2 -- On-Line -- Up 36 days 04:56:49 -- 17384
Kbytes

Segment Summary:
  (resident segments are locked)
  id         key         addr      size      ovhd   class   blkused   blkfree
  3082       1381451777  c1753000  9609216   1000   R       1169      4
  3083       1381451778  c207d000  8192000   732    V       599       401
  275483     1381451779  c5109000  573440    616    M       67        3
```

Figure 7-8 *Output generated by the "*`onstat -g seg`*" command*

The second command you should run on a regular basis is "`onstat -R`." As shown in Figure 7-9, this command generates statistics on the use and efficiency of the LRU queues.

LRU queues come in pairs and contain all the shared memory buffers specified by the BUFFERS parameter in the $ONCONFIG file. In each LRU queue pair, one half of the pair is "free," the other "modified." New or modified data to write out to disk is stored in the modified portion of the LRU queues for processing by the page cleaners. The writing of this data out to disk can be triggered by several conditions, including checkpoints and tripping the LRU_MAX_DIRTY parameter defined in the $ONCONFIG file.

```
INFORMIX-OnLine Version 7.13.UC2 -- On-Line -- Up 36 days 05:09:33 -- 17384
Kbytes

5 buffer LRU queue pairs
    #     f/m    length    % of      pair total
    0      f      150     100.0%        150
    1      m       0        0.0%
    2      f      150     100.0%        150
    3      m       0        0.0%
    4      F      150     100.0%        150
    5      m       0        0.0%
    6      f      150     100.0%        150
    7      m       0        0.0%
    8      f      150     100.0%        150
    9      m       0        0.0%
 0 dirty, 750 queued, 750 total, 1024 hash buckets, 2048 buffer size
 start clean at 60% (of pair total) dirty, or 90 buffs dirty, stop at 40%
```

Figure 7-9 *Output generated by the "*`onstat -R`*" command.*

Depending on the condition that triggers the write to disk, the write will be handled more or less efficiently as far as the engine is concerned. Writes caused by the LRU queues overflowing and triggering the LRU_MAX_DIRTY parameter, while not the least efficient, are not the most efficient way to flush data to disk. As a result, this command should be run periodically during heavy database activity to see how full the queues become. While you should always expect some LRU writes to occur, if the "dirty" value constantly exceeds the "start clean at" percentage (the LRU_MAX_DIRTY configuration parameter), the number of LRU queues and/or buffers should probably be increased.

The third command I'll cover in this section is "onstat -g glo," the output from which is illustrated in Figure 7-10.

This command displays information about the instance's vps as well as the multithreading counters. As with the other commands, monitor the workload of each of these elements and tune if appropriate.

Database Integrity Reports: The Oncheck Utility

Because I think I'm a better database administrator than OnLine administrator, I have a greater affinity for the oncheck utility than for the onstat utility. Just as the onstat utility allows you to look inside an instance and check its configuration and status, the oncheck utility allows you to look inside a database or table for configuration and status information. Unlike the onstat utility's interaction with the instance, there are options in the oncheck utility that allow you to make modifications or repairs to databases. This repair mechanism is limited to index structures only, however. As illustrated in Figure 7-11, there are fewer command flags to the oncheck utility.

Each of these command flags is explained in detail in the *OnLine Administrator's Guide* that accompanied your port of the software, including a description of the multifaceted nature of the utility. By that I mean the ability to check, repair, or simply generate a report. That this utility can be used to perform three different types of functions explains why there are two major flags, "-c" and "-p," and a number of identical subflags available under both major flags.

```
INFORMIX-OnLine Version 7.13.UC2 -- On-Line -- Up 36 days 05:18:26 -- 17384
Kbytes

MT global info:
sessions      threads    vps     lngspins
    7            27       12         0

         sched calls   thread switches    yield 0    yield n   yield forever
total:    282677064       76331210       229523351   9091879      7641892
per sec:      5               3              2          2            0

Virtual processor summary:
 class vps    usercpu       syscpu        total
  cpu   1    17495.16      1155.01      18650.17
  aio   3     1065.75      3125.57       4191.32
  pio   2      317.37       920.14       1237.51
  lio   2      365.60      1186.24       1551.84
  soc   2      556.61      1466.68       2023.29
  tli   0        0.00         0.00          0.00
  str   0        0.00         0.00          0.00
  shm   0        0.00         0.00          0.00
  adm   1      265.18       541.86        807.04
  opt   0        0.00         0.00          0.00
  msc   1        0.23         0.14          0.37
  adt   0        0.00         0.00          0.00
 total 12    20065.90      8395.64      28461.54

Individual virtual processors:
   vp        pid       class     usercpu      syscpu       total
    1       15898       cpu     17495.16     1155.01     18650.17
    2       15899       adm       265.18      541.86       807.04
    3       15901       lio       183.54      594.69       778.23
    4       15902       pio       164.51      462.53       627.04
    5       15903       aio       470.74     1348.91      1819.65
    6       15904       msc         0.23        0.14         0.37
    7       15905       aio       319.82      968.57      1288.39
    8       15906       aio       275.19      808.09      1083.28
    9       15907       soc       408.46     1009.60      1418.06
   10       15908       soc       148.15      457.08       605.23
   11       15912       lio       182.06      591.55       773.61
   12       15913       pio       152.86      457.61       610.47
                        tot     20065.90     8395.64     28461.54
```

Figure 7-10 *Output generated by the* "onstat -g glo" *command.*

As with the onstat utility, it is difficult to arbitrarily decide which flags are more or less important and should be covered in this chapter, but the focus of the chapter is oriented more toward

```
Usage: oncheck [-clist] [-plist] [-qny]
         [ { database[:[owner.]table[,fragdbs|#index]] | TBLspace number
              | Chunk number } { rowid | page number } ]

-c - check
 r - reserved pages
 e - extents
 c - database catalogs [database]
 i - table indexes database[:[owner.]table[#index]]
 I - table indexes and rowids in index database[:[owner.]table[#index]]
 d - TBLspace data rows including bitmaps
       database[:[owner.]table[,fragdbs]]
 D - TBLspace data rows including bitmaps, remainder pages and BLOBs
       database[:[owner.]table[,fragdbs]]

-p - print
 r - reserved pages (-cr)
 e - extents report (-ce)
 c - catalog report (-cc) [database]
 k - keys in index (-ci) database[:[owner.]table[#index]]
 K - keys and rowids in index (-cI) database[:[owner.]table[#index]]
 l - leaf node keys only (-ci) database[:[owner.]table[#index]]
 L - leaf node keys and rowids (-cI) database[:[owner.]table[#index]]
 d - TBLspace data rows (-cd) database[:[owner.]table[,fragdbs]] [rowid]
 D - TBLspace data rows including bitmaps, remainder pages and BLOBs (-cD)
       database[:[owner.]table[,fragdbs]] [page number]
 t - TBLspace report database[:[owner.]table[,fragdbs]]
 T - TBLspace disk utilization report database[:[owner.]table[,fragdbs]]
 p - Dump page for the given
       [table[,fragdbs] and rowid | TBLspace and page number]
 P - Dump page for the given chunk number and page number
       [chunk num and page number]
 B - BLOBspace utilization for given table(s)
       database[:[owner.]table[,fragdbs]]

-q - Quiet mode - print only error messages
-n - Answer NO to all questions
-y - Answer YES to all questions
```

Figure 7-11 *Flag options for the "*oncheck*" utility.*

monitoring than troubleshooting, so I'll focus on a couple of flags that best illustrate the reporting functionality of this utility.

Instance Reserved Pages

The first command, "`oncheck -pr`," checks and prints out the entire contents of the reserved pages in the rootdbs of the instance. Figure 7-12 contains a heavily abridged copy of what is generated. I will explain each of the seven major sections.

There are actually 12 major sections in the output of this command although several are combined and appear as the seven sections illustrated in Figure 7-12. Each section begins with the keywords "`Validating INFORMIX-OnLine reserved pages`" followed by a somewhat cryptic description of the information that section contains. The seven sections of the "`oncheck -pr`" command can be described as follows:

- Instance Creation Information—the date and time the instance was created as well as its page size. There are several other fields in this section that are not being used at this time.
- Instance Configuration Information—a copy of all the information in the $ONCONFIG file.
- Logical Log Information—contains a complete physical description of all the logical logs created in the instance, and checkpoint information.
- Dbspace Information—contains logical information about all the dbspaces in the instance. It does not contain any physical information, such as locations of the physical chunks that make up the dbspace. That information is stored in the next section. There are several status flags which indicate whether or not the dbspace is mirrored, whether or not the dbspace is really a BLOBspace, and date, time, and creator information.
- Primary Chunk Information—contains all the physical information for each primary chunk in the instance. Information on chunks defined as "mirror" chunks is not included in this section. There are a series of status flags indicating, for example, whether or not the chunk is down or on-line, if it is a raw or block device, or if the chunk is part of a BLOBspace.
- Mirror Chunk Information—this section contains the same type of information as the Primary Chunk section but this section is restricted to chunks defined as "mirror" chunks.

```
Validating INFORMIX-OnLine reserved pages - PAGE_PZERO

Identity                    INFORMIX-OnLine
Database system state           0
Database system flags           0
Page Size                       2048
Date/Time created       05/04/96 00:05:34
Version number of creator       4
Last modified time stamp        0

Validating INFORMIX-OnLine reserved pages - PAGE_CONFIG
ROOTNAME        rootdbs
ROOTPATH        /usr/informix_711/columbia/col_chnk_1
ROOTOFFSET      0
ROOTSIZE        40000
MIRROR          1
MIRRORPATH      /usr/informix_711/columbia/col_chnk_2
        [snip]

Validating INFORMIX-OnLine reserved pages - PAGE_1CKPT & PAGE_2CKPT
Using check point page PAGE_1CKPT.

Time stamp of checkpoint        89247577
Time of checkpoint              11/21/96 11:37:02
Physical log begin address      10003f
Physical log size               1000
Physical log position at Ckpt   306
Logical log unique identifier   1985
Logical log position at Ckpt    1bf018
DBspace descriptor page         100005
Chunk descriptor page           100006
Mirror chunk descriptor page    100008

Log file number                 2
Log file flags                  15   Log file in use
                                     Logfile has been backed up
                                     Log written to archive tape
Time stamp                      89068936
Date/Time file filled           11/18/96 20:26:51
Unique identifier               1976
Physical location               100a03
Log size                        1500
Number pages used               1500
        [snip]
```

continued

Figure 7–12 *Abridged output generated by the "*`oncheck -pr`*" command.*

```
Validating INFORMIX-OnLine reserved pages - PAGE_1DBSP & PAGE_2DBSP
Using DBspace page PAGE_2DBSP.

    DBspace number          1
    Flags                   2    DBspace uses mirror chunks
    First chunk             1
    Number of chunks        1
    Date/Time created       05/04/96 00:05:34
    DBspace name            rootdbs
    DBspace owner           informix

    DBspace number          2
    Flags                   2    DBspace uses mirror chunks
    First chunk             2
    Number of chunks        1
    Date/Time created       05/04/96 00:21:53
    DBspace name            l_logs
    DBspace owner           informix

    DBspace number          3
    Flags                   1    No mirror chunks
    First chunk             3
    Number of chunks        1
    Date/Time created       05/04/96 00:24:25
    DBspace name            columbia_1
    DBspace owner           informix

Validating INFORMIX-OnLine reserved pages - PAGE_1PCHUNK & PAGE_2PCHUNK
Using primary chunk page PAGE_1PCHUNK.

Chunk number            1
Next chunk in DBspace   0
Chunk offset            0
Chunk size              20000
Number of free pages    16795
DBspace number          1
Overhead                0
Flags                   40   Chunk is online
Chunk name length 37
Chunk path              /usr/informix_711/columbia/col_chnk_1

Chunk number            2
Next chunk in DBspace   0
Chunk offset            0
Chunk size              26000
Number of free pages    447
DBspace number          2
Overhead                0
Flags                   40   Chunk is online
Chunk name length 37
Chunk path              /usr/informix_711/columbia/col_chnk_3
        [snip]
```
continued

Figure 7–12 *continued*

```
Validating INFORMIX-OnLine reserved pages - PAGE_1MCHUNK & PAGE_2MCHUNK
 Using mirror chunk page PAGE_1MCHUNK.

    Chunk number           1
    Next chunk in DBspace  0
    Chunk offset           0
    Chunk size             20000
    Number of free pages   0
    DBspace number         1
    Overhead               0
    Flags                  50    Mirror chunk
    Chunk is               online
    Chunk name length      37
    Chunk path             /usr/informix_711/columbia/col_chnk_2

    Chunk number           2
    Next chunk in DBspace  0
    Chunk offset           0
    Chunk size             26000
    Number of free pages   0
    DBspace number         2
    Overhead               0
    Flags                  50    Mirror chunk
    Chunk is               online
    Chunk name length      37
    Chunk path             /usr/informix_711/columbia/col_chnk_4

Validating INFORMIX-OnLine reserved pages - PAGE_1ARCH & PAGE_2ARCH
 Using archive page PAGE_2ARCH.

    Archive Level              0
    Real Time Archive Began    11/20/96 17:05:02
    Time Stamp Archive Began   89238994
    Logical Log Unique Id      1982
    Logical Log Position       49e3e0

 DR has not been initialized.
```

Figure 7–12   *continued*

- Archive Information—the last section of the command, it contains information generated when an instance archive is created using the `ontape` utility. Only the archive information required to execute a complete restore to the last fully consistent archive is maintained in these reserved pages. Included in this information is the active logical log and checkpoint-related records as you would expect. In the example output included in Figure 7-12, the last archive completed in the instance was a level 0 archive. In this case, only the level 0 and the logical log information is stored in the archive-related reserved pages. Had the last archive created been a level 1 or a level 2 archive, the level 0 and the level 1 or level 2 information, as well as the logical log information, would have been stored and displayed. These archives would be required to execute a full restore back to fully consistent instance environment. Only one full set of archive-related information, the current set, is maintained in these archive-related pages.

System Catalog Tables

Executing "`oncheck -pc`" checks the integrity of the system catalog tables and prints out statistical information. The command, if executed as shown in the previous sentence, will check all the *real* catalog tables in the instance. This includes the real tables in the sysmaster database that contain, among other things, `onarchive` utility information. As I stated in the "Sysmaster Database and SMI Interface" section of Chapter 3, some tables in the sysmaster database are simply pointers into shared memory. As a result, quantifiable information such as number of pages allocated, number of pages used, and physical location is impossible to capture because the information does not exist. These shared memory tables are listed in the output of the "`oncheck -pc`" command, but only by table name.

Figure 7-13 contains a very small part of the output generated by the "`oncheck -pc`" command. In this illustration, only the first two tables of the sysmaster database are included.

For tables or indexes that are fragmented, each table and index fragment is considered separately, and information for each fragment is printed out. As a result, the output from this command looks very much like the tablespace report I'll be covering next.

```
Database: sysmaster
  Owner              informix
  Date created       05/04/96  00:08:13

TBLspace sysmaster:informix.systables
  Physical Address              100010
  Creation date      05/04/96  00:08:13
  TBLspace Flags                2      Row Locking
  Maximum row size              104
  Number of special columns     0
  Number of keys                2
  Number of extents             3
  Current serial value          227
  First extent size             8
  Next extent size              8
  Number of pages allocated     24
  Number of pages used          18
  Number of data pages          9
  Number of rows                156
  Partition partnum             1048579
  Partition lockid              1048579

Extents
  Logical Page     Physical Page     Size
       0              1015bf           8
       8              1017e1           8
      16              1017a1           8

Index information.
  Number of indexes       2
  Data record size        104
  Index record size       2048
  Number of records       156

TBLspace sysmaster:informix.syscolumns
  Physical Address              100011
  Creation date      05/04/96  00:08:13
  TBLspace Flags                2      Row Locking
  Maximum row size              36
  Number of special columns     0
  Number of keys                1
  Number of extents             7
  Current serial value          1
  First extent size             8
  Next extent size              8
  Number of pages allocated     64
  Number of pages used          61
  Number of data pages          34
  Number of rows                1700
  Partition partnum             1048580
  Partition lockid              1048580
```

continued

Figure 7-13 *Output generated by the "*`oncheck -pc`*" command.*

```
Extents
  Logical Page    Physical Page  Size
        0            1015c7       16
       16            10171f        8
       24            1017d1        8
       32            101831        8
       40            1016c7        8
       48            1016df        8
       56            1017b1        8

Index information.
  Number of indexes       1
  Data record size       36
  Index record size    2048
  Number of records    1700
```

Figure 7–13   *continued*

Tablespace Report

The "oncheck -pt" and "oncheck -pT" commands are very similar in terms of the output created. Both enable you to look at statistical information on a table-by-table basis within a database as opposed to an entire database, or instance as with the "oncheck -pc" command. The difference between the two commands is that the "-pT" option includes information about data page usage and index level information. Figure 7-14 contains an illustration of the output generated by an "oncheck -pt" command on a fragmented table.

The table has two indexes on it. Both indexes are partitioned off into dbspaces other than where the table fragments are located. For your information, the unique index, "ix_strpur_1," was "promoted" to being a constraint using the method described in the "Fragmenting Constraints" section of Chapter 5, Building a Database Environment.

The "-pT" flag produces the same type of output as shown in Figure 7-14; however, additional storage efficiency information is included for each table fragment. Information on the depth and breadth of index levels is included for each index as well. This information follows after the general tablespace information for each fragment of the table. Figure 7-15 contains an example of the table storage efficiency information followed by index-related information generated by the "oncheck -pT" command.

```
TBLspace Report for spar:db_a.str_purchase

            Table fragment in DBspace columbia_1

    Physical Address            300025
    Creation date       08/24/96 13:48:01
    TBLspace Flags              2       Row Locking
    Maximum row size            42
    Number of special columns   0
    Number of keys              0
    Number of extents           4
    Current serial value        1
    First extent size           32500
    Next extent size            3250
    Number of pages allocated   46250
    Number of pages used        43944
    Number of data pages        43938
    Number of rows              1889315
    Partition partnum           3145762
    Partition lockid            3145762

Extents
    Logical Page   Physical Page   Size
         0              3062e5     23500
         23500          300ee1     6500
         30000          30bf19     3250
         33250          30cd33     13000

            Table fragment in DBspace columbia_2

    Physical Address            400008
    Creation date       08/24/96 13:48:01
    TBLspace Flags              2       Row Locking
    Maximum row size            42
    Number of special columns   0
    Number of keys              0
    Number of extents           1
    Current serial value        1
    First extent size           32500
    Next extent size            3250
    Number of pages allocated   32500
    Number of pages used        19098
    Number of data pages        19095
    Number of rows              821082
    Partition partnum           4194309
    Partition lockid            3145762

Extents
    Logical Page   Physical Page   Size
         0              406ba9     32500                          continued
```

Figure 7–14 *Output generated by the "*`oncheck -pt`*" command.*

```
                Index ix_strpur_1 fragment in DBspace col_index_1

    Physical Address              90001b
    Creation date     10/09/96  14:09:46
    TBLspace Flags                2     Row Locking
    Maximum row size              42
    Number of special columns     0
    Number of keys                1
    Number of extents             3
    Current serial value          1
    First extent size             18571
    Next extent size              1857
    Number of pages allocated     44569
    Number of pages used          44030
    Number of data pages          0
    Number of rows                0
    Partition partnum             9437208
    Partition lockid              3145762

Extents
   Logical Page   Physical Page    Size
        0            912020        27856
     27856            918fdc       14856
     42712            d08103        1857

                Index xyz fragment in DBspace col_index_1

    Physical Address              90001c
    Creation date     10/09/96  14:15:39
    TBLspace Flags                2     Row Locking
    Maximum row size              42
    Number of special columns     0
    Number of keys                1
    Number of extents             1
    Current serial value          1
    First extent size             8511
    Next extent size              851
    Number of pages allocated     14468
    Number of pages used          14303
    Number of data pages          0
    Number of rows                0
    Partition partnum             9437209
    Partition lockid              3145762

Extents
   Logical Page   Physical Page     ize
        0            91c9e4        14468
```

Figure 7–14 continued

```
[Table fragment information]

Type            Pages    Empty  Semi-Full  Full   Very-Full
Free            2306
Bit-Map            6
Index              0
Data (Home)    43938
Total Pages    46250

Unused Space Summary

  Unused data slots                        19
  Unused bytes per data page               42
  Total unused bytes in data pages    1845396


[Index information]

Type            Pages    Empty  Semi-Full  Full   Very-Full
Free             539
Bit-Map            6
Index          44024
Data (Home)        0
Total Pages    44569

Unused Space Summary

  Unused data slots                         0
  Unused bytes per data page               42
  Total unused bytes in data pages          0

Index Usage Report for index ix_strpur_1 on spar:db_a.str_purchase

                   Average     Average
Level    Total    No. Keys   Free Bytes
  1         1         8         1851
  2         8        72          354
  3       580        74          297
  4     43435        62          272
Total   44024        62          273
```

Figure 7-15 *Fragment storage efficiency and index level information generated by the "oncheck -pT" command.*

Chunk Free List and Tablespace Interleaving

The "oncheck -pe" command produces a comprehensive list of page usage in every chunk of the instance. When used in combination with the "oncheck -pt" command and/or the `where_are_tables` script from Chapter 12, you can see to what degree there is tablespace interleaving occurring within chunks and dbspaces. Figure 7-16 contains a small section from the output generated by the "`oncheck -pe`" command. The output is generated in the same order in which the chunks were created and allocated to dbspaces. Thus, the output of this command starts with the rootdbs and continues until the last chunk that was added to the instance.

```
DBspace Usage Report: columbia_6  Owner: informix  Created: 05/04/96

Chunk: 8 /usr/informix_711/columbia/col_chnk_10      Size    Used    Free
                                                     76000   18610   57390

  Disk usage for Chunk 8         Start      Length
  OTHER RESERVED Pages             0           2
  CHUNK FREE LIST PAGE             2           1
  TBLSPACE TBLSPACE                3          50
  spar:db_a.strpld_info           53          25
  spar:db_a.category              78           8
  spar:db_a.fisc_mth_sum          86         500
  FREE                           586        2500
  spar:db_a.fisc_mth_sum        3086        3000
  FREE                          6086       16500
  spar:db_a.afs_tables         22586           8
  spar:db_a.bad_invdts         22594           8
  spar:db_a.str_errors         22602           8
  FREE                         22610         500
  spar:db_a.cal_ytd_sum        23110       15000
  FREE                         38110       37890
```

Figure 7-16   *Abridged output generated by the "`oncheck -pe`" command.*

Table and index searches occur significantly faster if there is very little or no interleaving of table or index extents in a dbspace. In fact, an increased performance penalty occurs when a table has more than eight interleaved extents and gets worse as each extent is added. At the very top of the output generated by this command (not shown in the example above), there will be a list of all tables that have eight or more extents.

In the example illustrated in Figure 7-16, the fisc_mth_sum table has two extents in this dbspace separated by a block of free pages. This usually indicates that an extent from another table occupied those 2500 pages when the fisc_mth_sum table needed to allocate another extent. When the table occupying those 2500 pages was deleted, the space taken up by that table remained "free" because the engine does not automatically concatenate adjacent extents of the same table since it would require recalculating all the hidden rowids stored in all the page headers and index structures. You can rejoin all the extents into one larger extent by either unloading the table, dropping it, recreating it with the proper extent sizing to represent the current size of the table and reloading the data or altering one of the indexes on the table to "cluster" mode. Altering an index to "cluster" mode physically rearranges the rows in the table to conform to the index keys and will cause a concatenation of extents within dbspaces if possible. You can, if you want, change the index back to regular mode after concatenating the extents.

Verifying Data and Index Consistency and Integrity

The last two sets of commands I will cover while discussing the `oncheck` utility verifies the integrity and consistency of data and index pages. The "`oncheck -ci`" and "`oncheck -cI`" commands will verify the general linkage between all nodes in the Btree index structure. The "`-cI`" option goes one step further and verifies that the key values stored in each index element actually match the values of the row to which the index element refers.

Unlike all the other commands I've covered in this chapter, these two commands not only generate a report but can also effect repairs if they find errors. There are, of course, conditions that need to be met before the command will attempt to make these repairs. First, the command must be invoked by the root or informix userid, and second, the instance must be in quiescent mode. Experience has taught me not to believe a corrupted index can be repaired by running an "`oncheck -cI`" against it. There have been too many cases where the command indicated the index was repaired, but running a query against the index reported errors. As a result, I usually drop the index and recreate it. This way, if the index builds, I know everything is in order within the index. Besides, it takes about the same amount of time as running the repair option.

The "`oncheck -cd`" and "`oncheck -cD`" commands verify the consistency of data pages within a table. The "`-cD`" command also reads the reference information for any BLOB columns in a table and verifies that the BLOB exists where specified in the reference information. There are the corresponding "`-pd`" and "`-pD`" commands, which actually print out the consistency check information. I would strongly suggest *against* using these flags if redirecting the output to a flat file rather than standard out because there is a significant amount of output generated. If the table only has a few rows, it might be okay to capture the output in a flat file; otherwise, you risk creating a file large enough to fill the file system and possibly cause other system problems. It is not worth the risk.

Graphical Utilities

In addition to the command line utilities, OnLine Dynamic Server contains two Motif-based utilities to display performance or diagnostic information. These two utilities, `onperf` and `D/B Cockpit` display information in real-time mode like the `onstat` utility. Each of these graphical utilities has a set of parameters and default settings used to determine alarm conditions and check database metrics. These defaults can be modified as needed for your specific environment.

It is my understanding that all ports of Dynamic Server contain the `onperf` utility, but `D/B Cockpit` was only released in the more popular ports of the engine. While both utilities display `onstat` utility type information, `onperf` must be run local to the server. Its focus is oriented more toward device-level or session-specific performance analysis and reporting. `D/B Cockpit` is a two-tiered application designed to provide an instancewide view of performance and activity. `Onprobe`, the data-gathering application, runs locally on the target instance. `Oncockpit`, the client or display application, can be invoked on any supported machine within the network and communicates with the `onprobe` application through a named instance alias. This will be explained in greater detail in the "D/B Cockpit" section of this chapter.

D/B Cockpit

The `D/B Cockpit` utilities allow you to perform distributed monitoring of instance performance and activity levels. Originally released in a limited number of ports of the engine, the utilities will soon be bundled together as a separate stand alone product orderable from Informix. It will remain a Motif-based application, but some functionality will eventually migrate to the Windows 95-based Enterprise Command Center utility. While I will only give a high-level overview of D/B Cockpit in this chapter, more detailed information can be found in the D/B Cockpit manual that accompanied your software if your port included the utility.

The D/B Cockpit utility is actually a full-fledged client-server application. Onprobe, the "server" portion, executes locally within the target instance. Its outbound communication connection operates through a separate instance service from the standard user thread connection services described in the "NETTYPE Settings" section of Chapter 3. As a result, the onprobe "service" requires its own instance alias and corresponding entries in the $SQLHOSTS file and /etc/services files. Oncockpit, the client portion, can be executed from within any supported Motif-based user environment on the network. Because oncockpit communicates directly with the onprobe service, the client machine's $SQLHOSTS and /etc/services files need entries defining the onprobe service as well.

Besides displaying general instance activity information, various metrics can be established in either onprobe and/or oncockpit that constitute error or alarm conditions. Depending on the metric and the severity level assigned to the metric, any number of actions can be performed. These actions can range from a simple display of an alarm condition, as illustrated in Figure 7-17, to the execution of a shell script or application.

When defining error or alarm conditions, the metrics that define these conditions can be either session-based or universally oriented. A session-based metric set is specified when the oncockpit utility is invoked and overrides the universal, or permanent, metrics onprobe uses for that session of oncockpit. These session-based metrics are passed to onprobe for use when gathering information for that specific session of oncockpit. This means that two oncockpit sessions connected to the same instance can be using different metrics for alarm or error conditions. On the onprobe side of the connection, several different universal metric files can be defined for any given instance. Onprobe can only use one universal metric set at a time, and must be stopped and restarted to use another set.

By default, session and universal metric files are stored in the $INFORMIXDIR/etc subdirectory and are called "sessalrm" and "permalrm," respectively. Individual metrics can be modified from

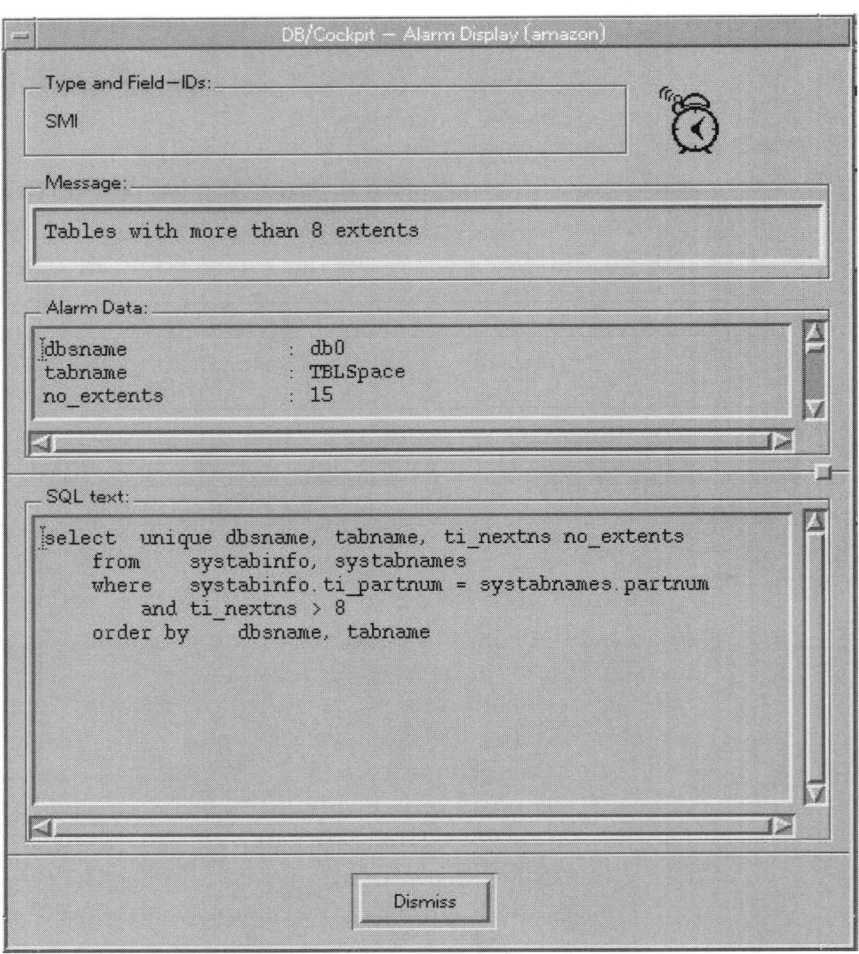

Figure 7-17 *An alarm condition display from the* D/B Cockpit *utility.*

within the oncockpit utility and either replace the default metric files or are saved in new files for later use. Severity codes for alarm conditions are defined in a file usually called "severity" in the same directory. These too can be modified and saved. Figure 7-18 contains a syntax diagram for the onprobe utility, and shows the flags to use in order to select an alarm and/or severity metric file other than the default. The "-service" and "-log" parameters are required when invoking onprobe. If the "-severity" and "-alarms" parameters are not specifically set when onprobe is invoked, the utility will automatically use its default settings.

```
onprobe [ -severity severity_file ] [ -service service_name ] [ -alarms
alarm_file ] [ -log log_file ]

 -severity Load the severity file 'severity_file'. $INFORMIXDIR/etc
    is added to any file name that does not begin with a dot (.) or a
    slash (/). The default file is $INFORMIXDIR/etc/severity.

 -service Accept oncockpit clients using the service 'service_name'.
    The default service is named 'cockpit'.

 -alarms Load the permanent alarm file 'alarm_file'. $INFORMIXDIR/etc
    is added to any file name that does not begin with a dot (.) or a
    slash (/). The default file is $INFORMIXDIR/etc/permalrm.

 -log Append log messages to the file 'log_file'. If 'log_file' is
    hyphen (-), log messages will be printed to the standard output.
```

Figure 7–18 *Syntax diagram for the* onprobe *utility.*

Onprobe is like the little pink bunny that just keeps going and going. Once started, onprobe continues to function and gather information about its target instance regardless of the instance's operating mode. While the instance is on-line, onprobe gathers information from both the instance's SMI interface as well as through direct shared memory calls. Its SMI interface will show up as a user thread in the output of an "onstat -u" command. When the instance is shut down to quiescent mode, onprobe releases its thread to allow the instance to complete the shutdown process. Prior to releasing the thread, onprobe will send an alarm message to all connected oncockpit sessions, alerting them that the operating mode of the instance is changing. While the instance is in quiescent mode, onprobe executes direct shared memory queries to gather information. If the instance is shut down to off-line mode, the onprobe process, which runs in background mode, does not terminate, but stops all shared memory queries and waits for the instance to be restarted. It will periodically send out an alarm message to any attached oncockpit sessions that the instance is down. When the instance comes back on-line, onprobe will restart its information gathering and begin retransmitting to any attached oncockpit sessions.

The oncockpit utility can attach to any active onprobe service on the network, provided the machine supporting the oncockpit session can resolve the onprobe servicename through its local $SQLHOSTS file and the hostname of the machine running the onprobe service. The syntax diagram for the oncockpit utility is illustrated in Figure 7-19. The "-host", "-service", and "-log" parameters are required when invoking oncockpit. If the "-alarms" and "Xtoolkitoptions" parameters are not set at the time oncockpit is invoked, default settings will automatically be used.

```
oncockpit [ -host host_name ] [ -service service_name ] [ -alarms alarm_file ]
  [ -log log_file ] [ Xtoolkitoptions ]

-host Connect to the onprobe server running on the host 'host_name' . The
   default is the local host.

-service Connect to the onprobe server using the service 'service_name'. The
   default service is named 'cockpit'.

-alarms Load the session alarm file 'alarm_file'. $INFORMIXDIR/etc is added
   to any file name that does not begin with a dot (.) or a slash (/). The
   default file is $INFORMIXDIR/etc/sessalrm.

-log Append log messages to the file 'log_file'. If 'log_file' is hyphen
   (-), log messages will be printed to the standard output.

Xtoolkitoptions Any standard Xt options.
```

Figure 7-19 *Syntax diagram for the* oncockpit *utility.*

When oncockpit connects to an onprobe service, it displays what I call a summary "dashboard" of engine activity similar to that shown in Figure 7-20.

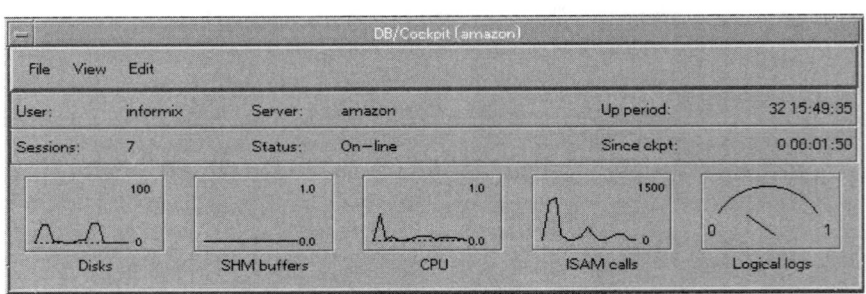

Figure 7-20 *The top-level or "dashboard" screen from* oncockpit.

While there isn't a tremendous amount of activity reflected in Figure 7-20, it does serve to illustrate that the major indicators of instance activity are displayed and refreshed in real time. What I generally do is have a dashboard display open for all my instances during the day. That way I can, with a quick glance, see how busy any instance is. At the same time, the alarm program will generate error messages to which I can respond before users start calling and wondering "why the database is slow/stuck/not working." It certainly helps your credibility when users call to complain to be able to say that you're already aware of the problem and are working on it. It beats saying "Really!? It's doing what?"

From this dashboard view, you can select the "View" dropdown menu to look at more specific information about the instance from a list of choices that includes session, shared memory, logical and physical log, dbspace, virtual processor, database, and data replication. For example, selecting the "Dbspaces" menu option generates a screen like that displayed in Figure 7-21.

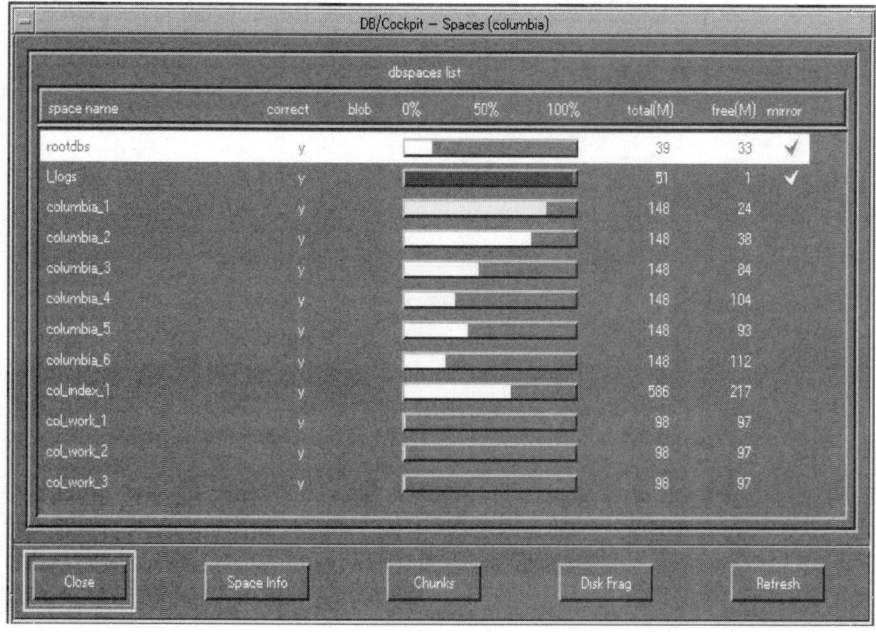

Figure 7-21 *The dbspaces display from* `oncockpit`.

The information, similar to that generated by an "`onstat -d`" command, is displayed in such a way that dbspace fill percentages, mirroring status, and dbspaces sizes can be easily interpreted. Highlighting a dbspace in the list and selecting one of the buttons at the bottom of the screen will quickly generate a display of the physical device information for the dbspace.

In the "Onstat" section of this chapter, I covered two commands that allow you to get information about a specific user thread. Oncockpit has several screens that display the same type of information. Selecting the "Sessions" menu option displays information similar to that in Figure 7-22.

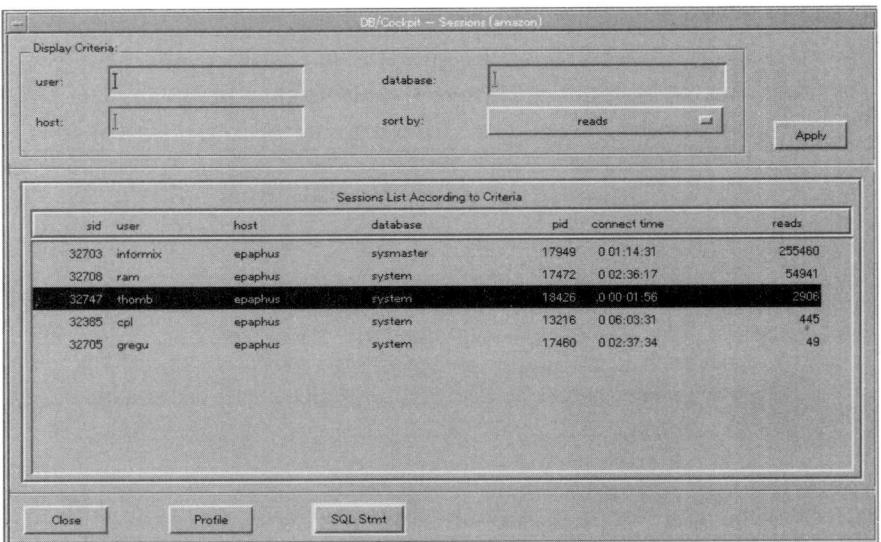

Figure 7-22 *The sessions screen from* oncockpit

Initially, this screen is empty. You have to select the criteria by which you would like to see the active sessions sorted and displayed. You can enter a specific userid, host, database, and type of activity ("sort by") criteria prior to clicking on the "Apply" button to look at one user's activity. Or, by simply selecting the "sort by" criterion and clicking on the "Apply" button, a list of all active sessions in the target instance will be generated, as illustrated in Figure 7-22.

At the bottom of the screen, there are buttons to drill down and look at the SQL statements as well as the general resources being used by any selected session. To look at this type of information, simply highlight a session and select the option that interests you most. For example, selecting session #32747 and clicking on the "SQL Stmt" button lists the last parsed and current SQL statement for that session as well as optimizer information for the current SQL statement. This is illustrated in Figure 7-23.

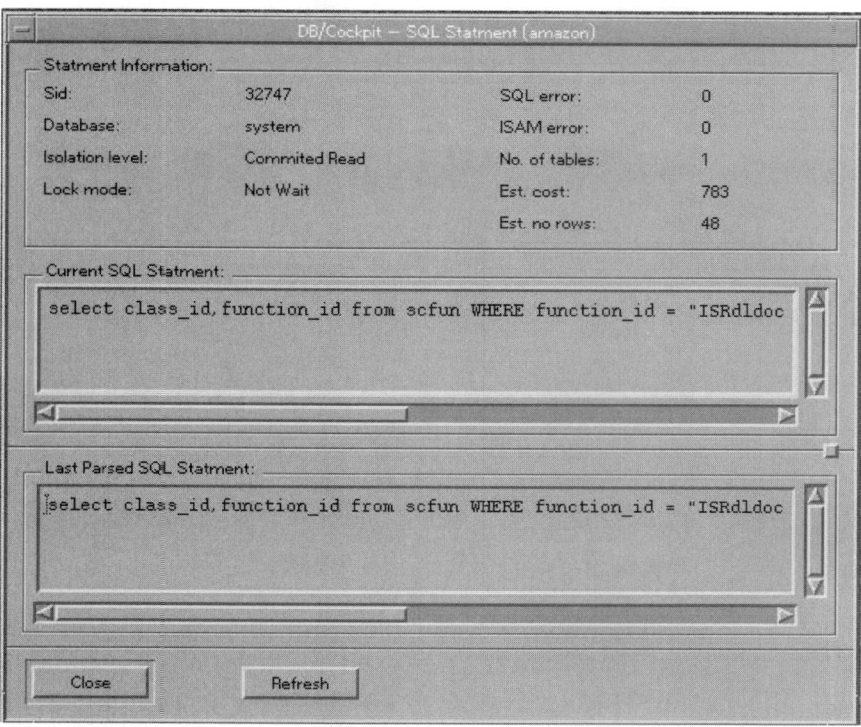

Figure 7–23 *The session SQL screen from* `oncockpit`.

Returning back to the main dashboard display and selecting the "Logical Log" menu option generates a display similar to that in Figure 7-24.

The most attractive feature of this screen is the "percent full" bar graph for each logical log. One of the problems with the "`onstat -l`" command in OnLine Dynamic Server is that once used, a logical log always displays as 100 percent full even if archived off to tape. In the strictest technical sense this is true—a log is not erased until it becomes the active log again. However, when trying to determine how much log space is required to process a transaction, it was easier in the 5.x versions of OnLine because archived logs without an active transaction were listed as 100 percent free. Executing an "`onstat -l`" command in OnLine versions 5.x only showed log space taken by uncommitted transactions in the logical logs or the current, unarchived log.

The graphical display from `oncockpit` acts the same way. According to the `oncockpit` screen shown in Figure 7-24, logical

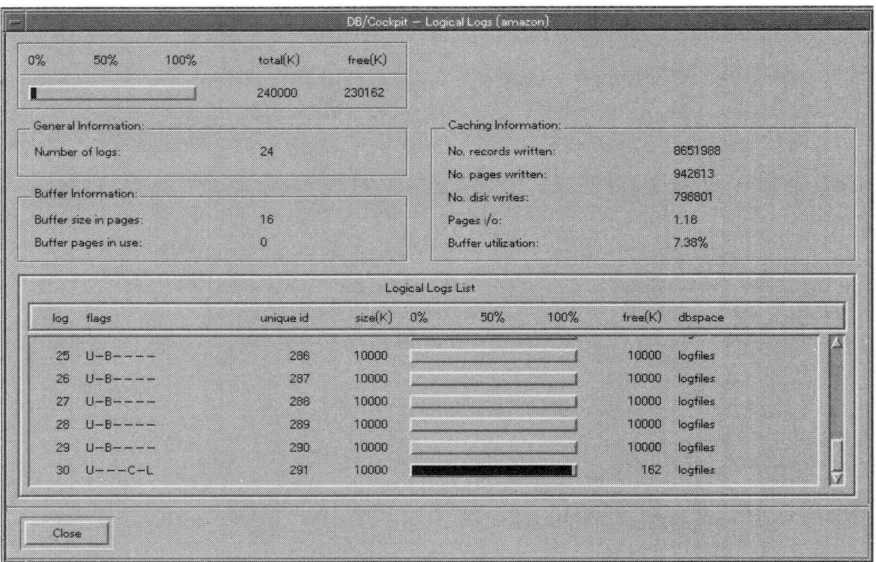

Figure 7–24 *The logical log screen from* `oncockpit`.

log number 290 has filled and been archived to disk. The bar graph for that log shows it available for use. Tracking log use by a transaction is as easy as watching the bar graphs for the logical logs when you use the `oncockpit` utility.

Of course, this information can be derived from looking at the "`onstat -l`" utility and looking for the "Begin Transaction" flag; it's just a little harder to find in the output generated under OnLine Dynamic Server. You can also use the "`transaction_size`" script described in Chapter 12. This script shows the amount of logical log space used to record a user's current transaction as well as the largest amount of log space used to record any transaction for that same user's session.

Selecting the "Physical Log" menu option from the dashboard "View" menu will generate a screen display similar to that in Figure 7-25.

This screen displays the physical information as well as usage statistics that can help you tune the efficiency of your physical log and decrease the duration of your checkpoints.

Selecting the "Shared Memory" menu option generates a screen similar to that displayed in Figure 7-26.

Like the main dashboard display, this screen provides an overview of shared memory utilization. There are bar graphs indicating

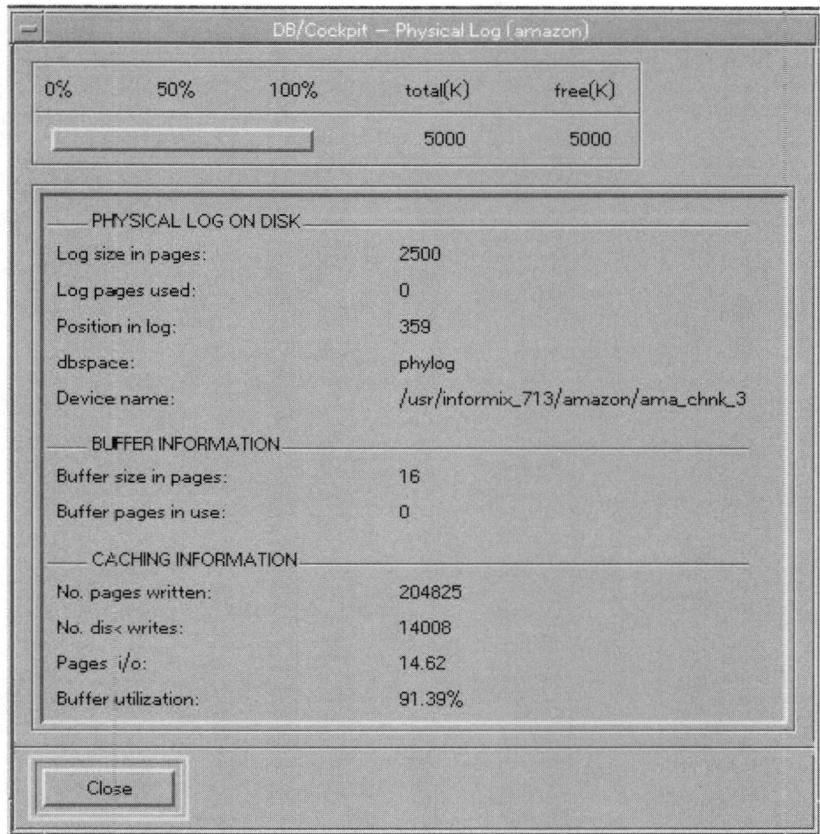

Figure 7–25 *The physical log screen from* `oncockpit`.

such factors as read and write efficiency, read ahead utilization, and waits verses requests ratios. There are buttons at the bottom for a more detailed view of a number of components of the OnLine Dynamic Server shared memory environment, such as the individual portions shown in Figure 7-27.

I like the `D/B Cockpit` utilities; they have been helpful to me in understanding what's happening in an instance. It is not because `D/B Cockpit` is a point-and-click type of interface that I find it valuable to use. Rather, it is the ability to have performance information from several different components in the engine displayed simultaneously in easy-to-understand graph forms. It is much easier to interpret activity occurring on the fly in a graphical format than by using a series of repeating `onstat` commands. At least for me, I can lose perspective of how compo-

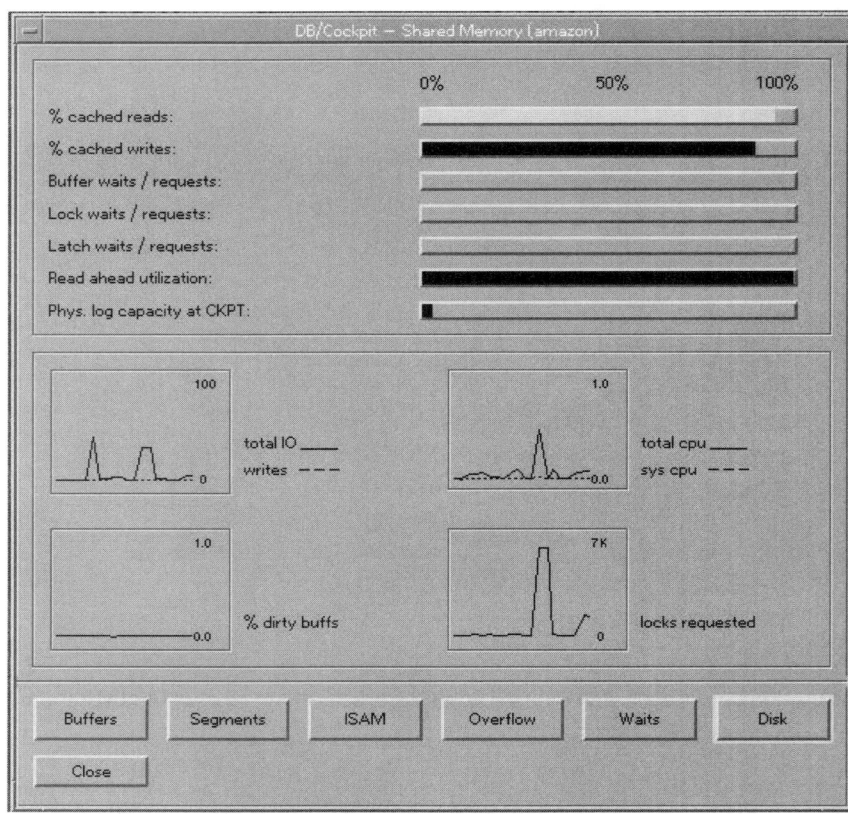

Figure 7–26   *The shared memory* oncockpit *screen.*

nents are interacting if I'm trying to dig columnar data out from character-based reports. With overlapping graphs, I can see correlations and patterns much more easily. Be aware, though, that when I need specific, quantifiable results, I always use the onstat utility.

Onperf

Onperf is, in many ways, like the D/B Cockpit utilities in that onperf creates real-time graphical displays of performance information. Onperf distinguishes itself from D/B Cockpit by the level of granularity in the graphs it generates. Where D/B Cockpit tends to look at more general instancewide performance, onperf graphs can be set up to report only on certain types of

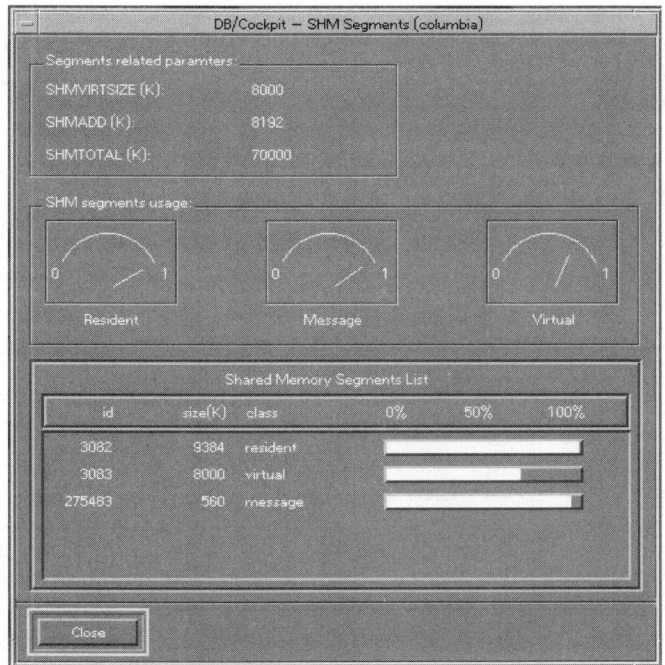

Figure 7-27 *Shared memory portion screen from the* oncockpit

ISAM calls, for example, and ignore other related ISAM calls. If you want to look at chunk activity, you can specify just disk reads, or writes, rather than all disk operations for the chunks selected. In addition to this selectivity, there are tools such as the "query tree" that have been built into the utility and create graphical reports without any user input.

Onperf's top-level display is a graph similar to that shown in Figure 7-28.

In the graph displayed in Figure 7-28, I removed the default graph parameter of ISAM operations and added in its place AIO, PIO, and LIO reads and writes plus semaphore operations. This graph, like all others created by onperf, can be displayed in several forms, including pie, vertical bar, and line graphs, by selecting the appropriate option from the "View" pull-down menu.

Selecting "New" from the "Graph" pull-down menu opens another window with a top-level graph. The values these top-level graphs display can be modified by selecting one of the options from the "Metrics" pull-down menu, as shown in Figure 7-29.

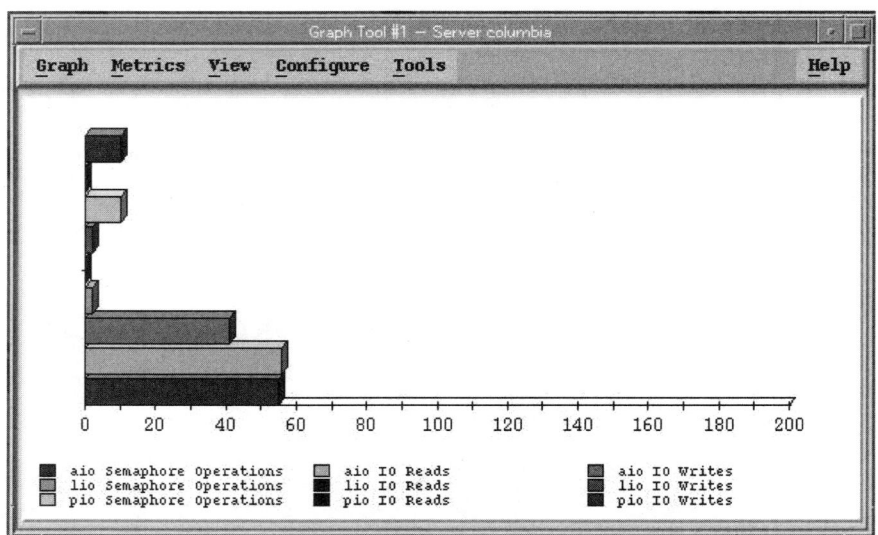

Figure 7–28 *The* `onperf` *utility top-level graph.*

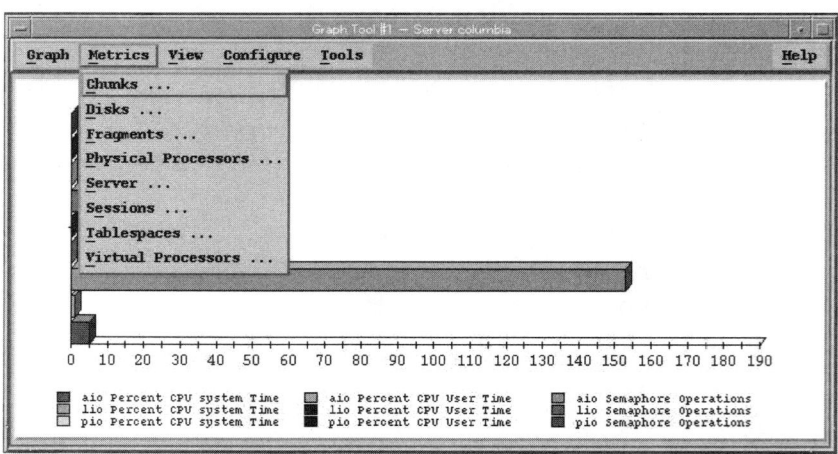

Figure 7–29 *Metric options available for* `onperf` *graphs.*

Selecting one of these metrics will open one or more additional windows similar to the window shown in Figure 7-30. These windows allow you to select the specific parameters you want graphed.

As Figure 7-30 illustrates, for the "Chunk" metric you need to select not only the chunks you're interested in, but the specific operations or conditions that affect the chunks as well. The

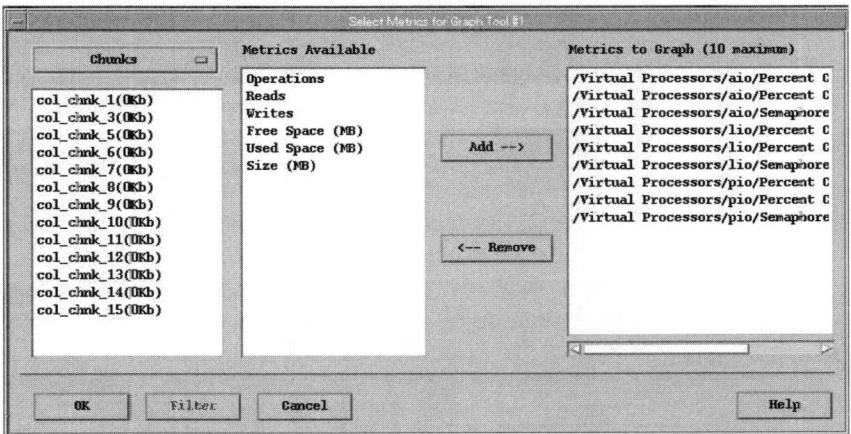

Figure 7-30 *Metric detail selection screen from* `onperf`.

graphing tool can only support ten parameters at a time, so you must be somewhat selective in your choices of what to display. If I wanted to add more than one chunk parameter to the current graph selections shown in Figure 7-30, I would have to remove one or more of the virtual processor parameters currently selected to be graphed.

Along with the top-level graphing tool, there are several other pre-prepared activity-based graphs or tools available under the "Tools" pull-down menu. The metrics that support these graphs cannot be altered. One of these tools is the "Disk Activity" graph shown in Figure 7-31.

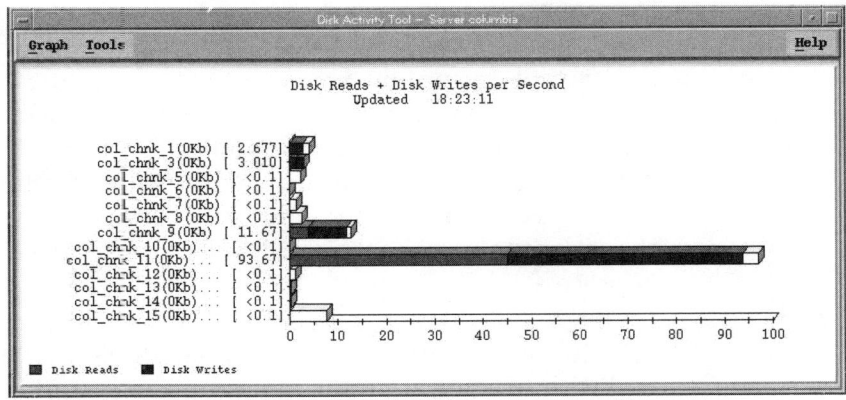

Figure 7-31 *The "Disk Activity" tool from* `onperf`.

This graph shows general I/O activity at a disk chunk level. While the same type of graph can be constructed using metrics from the top-level graph, this tool is not limited to ten parameters in its display. It will display read and write activities for all chunks in the target instance.

My favorite `onperf` tool, though, from the "Tools" menu is the "Query Tool." An example of the output this tool generates is shown in Figure 7-32.

If you are trying to track the impact a specific SQL statement has on an instance and need to know how the statement is being processed by the engine, this tool is pretty valuable. Each little box in Figure 7-32 represents a processing component involved in returning the result of the query. By following the boxes up from the bottom of the screen, you can see the manner in which the query is processed. This information can be used in conjunction with that gathered from the "`set explain on`" SQL command. This SQL command is discussed in Chapter 8, Enhancing Performance.

There is a little speedometer dial in each box as well as a numeric value. The speedometer indicates the number of rows per unit of time that particular component is processing. The numeric value represents the number of rows processed through that particular component.

From the example shown in Figure 7-32, it becomes pretty clear that several elements of the selected query are being parallelized by the engine and executing simultaneously. This is one of the goals of OnLine Dynamic Server and its multithreaded architecture. Be aware that not all query statements can be parallelized. Statements that can be parallelized will execute significantly faster, though, as a result of "divide and conquer" processing.

This tool, in conjunction with the "`set explain on`" SQL statement, can help you build your SQL statements to achieve the best performance possible by spotting if, where, and how the engine is using its various query processing mechanisms to process the query. It can also help you check on the statement's efficiency by monitoring the number of rows affected by each phase of process.

Like `D/B Cockpit`, `onperf` has its place and function in monitoring or resolving performance problems. Like any tool, the skill with which it is used will have a significant impact on the usefulness and effectiveness of the tool in solving any problem that may arise.

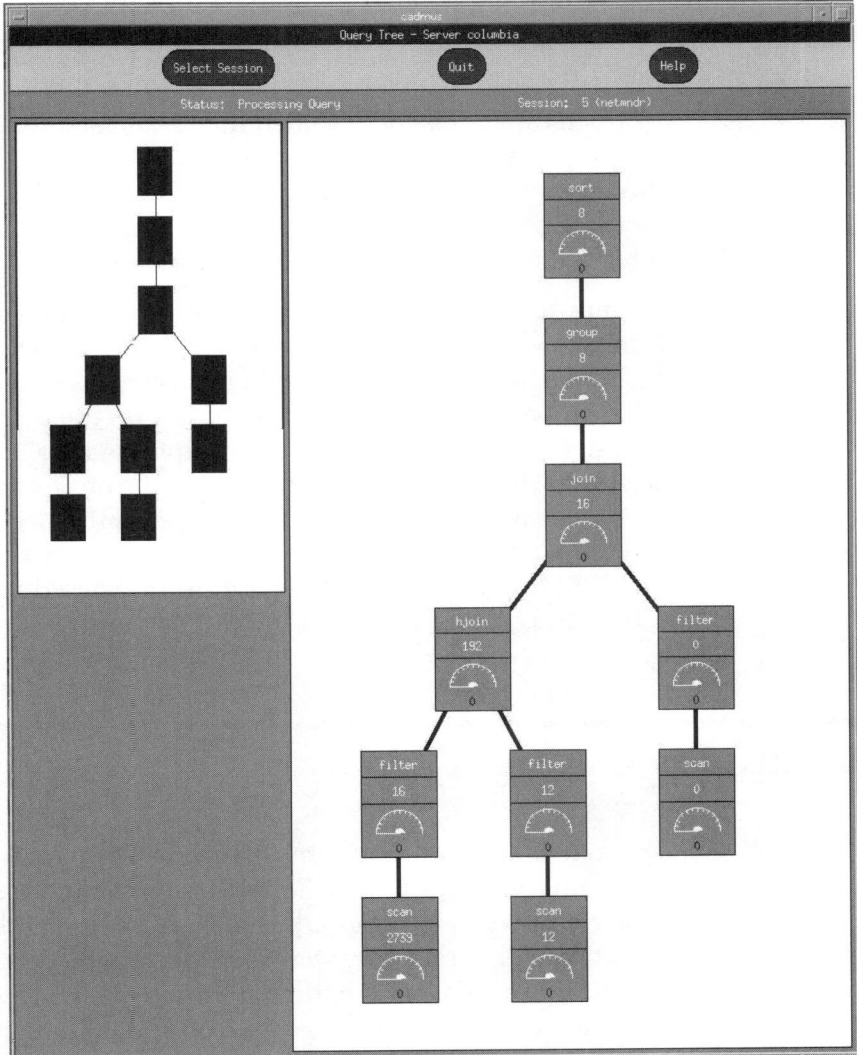

Figure 7-32 *The "Query Tool" tool from* `onperf`.

Using the Sysmaster Database

In the "Sysmaster Database and SMI Interface" section of Chapter 3, I explained that with the release of OnLine Dynamic Server, administrators could now query information held in the shared memory segment that the OnLine engine controlled. Access to this information comes by connecting to the sysmaster database and having queries processed through an interface simply called the "SMI."

Much of what is today called the "sysmaster database" has always existed in the OnLine product. Prior to Dynamic Server, though, only the `onstat` utility could access this information. In fact, the `onstat` utility is nothing more than a repackaging of information returned from queries through the SMI.

You can create your own `onstat`-like utilities by becoming familiar with the real and pseudosysmaster tables and writing your own SQL queries against them. This is precisely what I and others have done in the scripts included on the media that accompanies this book. These scripts are explained in Chapter 12, Scripts to Help Get the Job Done. Consult the *OnLine Administrator's Guide* and the release notes that accompanied your port of the software, as well as the "`sysmaster.sql`" script in the $INFORMIXDIR/etc directory for a list and description of all the tables and columns in the sysmaster database.

Summary

The four major utilities for monitoring instance performance and checking the integrity of instance-level and database-level database elements were reviewed. While only a few of the many flags or options for each utility were explained in this chapter, the most important were covered with illustrations of the type of output each flag or option will generate. You should understand the difference between the `onstat` and `oncheck` utilities and what each was designed to accomplish. You should understand what the `D/B Cockpit` and `onperf` graphical utilities were designed to accomplish and their relationship to the command line utilities. Finally, you should understand that almost all the information these utilities provide is gathered by queries to the sysmaster database through the SMI interface. You should know where to look for more information on the tables and columns in this database and, as a result, be able to write SQL queries against these tables to gather the specific information you need.

Coming Up

With an understanding of what tools and utilities to use to gather performance information, OnLine administrators can begin to look at ways of enhancing the performance of OnLine Dynamic Server instances. In the next chapter we'll look at engine mechanisms such as PDQ and MGM, and query optimization procedures such as "`update statistics`" and the OPTCOMPIND parameter, which can have a direct impact on the performance of queries or the instance in general.

Chapter 8

Enhancing Performance

- *How are Virtual Processors added and removed?*
- *What does the "*`update statistics`*" SQL command do?*
- *How does the optimizer work?*
- *What is PDQ and MGM?*

While a chapter such as this is needed in any book attempting to explain how to use a piece of software, it's difficult to treat the subject fairly in just a few pages. Many of the engine mechanisms covered in this chapter deserve complete chapters in and of themselves to fully explain all the nuances in their configuration and implementation that could have an impact on how the mechanism functions. The scope of this book does not permit this kind of analysis. Nonetheless, in this chapter I'll cover what virtual processors are, how to monitor and tune them, how to increase the effectiveness of indexes and index-based constraints by using the "update statistics" command and incorporating data distributions, briefly explain how the OnLine Dynamic Server query optimizer works, and introduce the engine mechanisms that manage OLAP queries. By the end of this chapter you should be familiar with, and know how to tune, many of the basic components that affect the performance of an instance.

To really understand how to tune an instance environment created by OnLine Dynamic Server requires a fairly even mixture of understanding the engine architecture, the study of performance guides for the engine, and hands-on experience. For the second part of this equation I strongly recommend you purchase and read the Informix Press book *OnLine Performance Tuning, Second Edition* by Liz Suto. She has written a well balanced book, backed by case studies, explaining in greater detail all the concepts covered in this chapter as well as many others.

Tuning Virtual Processors

As I mentioned in the "Processor Component" section of Chapter 1, Introduction to OnLine Dynamic Server, virtual processors, or vps as they are commonly called, are the workhorses of the OnLine Dynamic Server engine. Vps are what process the various engine-related tasks generated by internal and external threads. As indicated in Appendix C, their architecture is what differentiates OnLine Dynamic Server from the other major database engines on the market today. The efficiency with which they operate has a significant impact on the performance of the instance. In this section, we'll look at what vps are and how to tune them.

What Are Virtual Processors?

Individual vps are, as entities, UNIX processes. Unlike many UNIX processes, though, they were written to be what is called "multi-threaded." To appreciate what that means requires a brief, very high-level explanation of how processes are handled by the UNIX operating system.

While UNIX is a fully multi-user, preemptive, multitasking operating system, when you get down to the most fundamental aspects of how UNIX handles processes, only one thing is really happening at any given moment in time in the operating system. While new hardware and software technologies are coming out that allow different components of the system CPU to be working on different tasks for different users, for our purposes let's leave it a one-at-a-time model.

What happens is that the operating system switches around, processing elements of each user's program so fast that it appears as though the computer is working on every user's requests at the same time. This switching between tasks is called a "context switch." When a task is given to the system CPU to be worked on, the operating system has to tell the CPU where in the program code to get its instructions as well as what data is to be used when executing the instruction.

For the most part, tasks are allocated a specific amount of time by the operating system on the system CPU for processing. Regardless of what is happening in the code, when that amount of time has passed, a context switch occurs. The information in the CPU registers about where in the program code the task was, as well as the values of all the data elements, is copied out into system memory. This information stays in memory until the task receives another allotment of CPU time. Then the information gets copied back into the system CPU registers to continue processing.

Tasks execute faster on a computer with fewer users not because it's easier for the operating system or CPU to handle the request load, but because each task waits a shorter amount of time before getting another turn on the system CPU. While from a human perspective this is perhaps not the most efficient way to complete a task, there isn't any other option available in computer technology today to handle multiple tasks from multiple users.

Previous to OnLine Dynamic Server, user connections were handled as UNIX processes. Identified as the "sqlturbo" process, the UNIX operating system handled these processes like all the other processes in the system. Regardless of the operating state of the process or the actual time needed on the CPU to process an instruction, when the timeslice of a sqlturbo process on the system CPU expired, the operating system switched out the process and loaded another one. The design and implementation of virtual processors significantly reduced this inefficiency in task processing.

As I said at the beginning of this section, vps are UNIX processes. As such, they are subject to being switched out at the expiration of their timeslice on the system CPU. However, these vps are multithreaded as well as task-specific in design. Briefly, that means the following:

- Vps act somewhat like the UNIX operating system in that any vp will be processing multiple requests from multiple sources and will, in fact, execute a type of context switch themselves.
- Because vps are task-specific, significantly less information needs to be copied out in a thread switch. The vp reexecutes the same stream of code for every request it services, so only the data being processed for the request and an abbreviated program pointer needs to be copied out—or in. This allows them to do more work in the same amount of time.
- Vps are not timeslice-driven. Rather than giving a task a specific amount of time, the vp works on the task for as long as it is efficient to do so. If one task needs more or less time than another, the vp will adjust its processing workload accordingly.
- Finally, vps can be given the power to partially override a request by the operating system to be switched out at the expiration of the vp's timeslice on the system CPU. If the vp determines that it is about to compete a task, it will delay the system's context switch request until the task is completed.

The last two items in this list are what make OnLine Dynamic Server so much more efficient at database processing and so much faster than any other database engine on the market today.

VP Classes

Virtual processors are organized into 11 logical groups called "classes." More than one individual vp can be running in any of these classes for any instance you create. The virtual processor classes are as follows:

- CPU—executes all end-user-oriented threads as well as some internal engine threads. As I explained in the "VP and Performance Configuration" section of Chapter 3, Initializing an OnLine Dynamic Server Instance, a single connection thread (referred to as a "poll" thread) can also be allocated to run on a CPU vp. On systems with KAIO enabled, the disk I/O to database tables or instance logs residing in raw disk space runs through the KAIO thread attached to the CPU vp.
- AIO—in cases where KAIO is not supported or running, or disk I/O is occurring to a cooked filesystem, the AIO vp class handles all disk I/O.
- LIO—in the absence of a KAIO thread, this vp handles disk I/O to the logical logs. Should these logs be stored in cooked filesystems, the I/O is handled by the AIO vp.
- PIO—in the absence of a KAIO thread, this vp handles disk I/O to the physical log. Should the log be stored in cooked filesystems, the I/O is handled by the AIO vp.
- ADM—maintains the system timer used to wake up threads that are on the sleep queue.
- ADT—used in conjunction with the OnLine Dynamic Server auditing process, this thread is started by setting the ADTMODE parameter in the $ONCONFIG file to the value of "1."
- MSC—services operating system calls by the engine.
- OPT—used by the Optical extension to the OnLine Dynamic Server engine.
- SHM—handles client communication tasks for shared-memory-based poll threads.
- SOC—handles client communication tasks for socket-based poll threads.
- TLI—handles client communication tasks for TLI-based poll threads.

Every vp, when spawned, is identified as an "oninit" process in the operating system. Figure 8-1 illustrates this correlation. At the top of the figure is part of the output generated by an "onstat -g glo" command. This is followed by a "ps -ef" command.

```
Virtual processor summary:
  class      vps      usercpu    syscpu     total
  cpu        3        4754.59    429.45     5184.04
  aio        5        203.57     655.96     859.53
  pio        1        12.69      53.64      66.33
  lio        1        18.19      90.44      108.63
  soc        1        31.03      114.50     145.53
  tli        0        0.00       0.00       0.00
  str        0        0.00       0.00       0.00
  shm        0        0.00       0.00       0.00
  adm        1        27.96      80.24      108.20
  opt        0        0.00       0.00       0.00
  msc        1        6.99       4.80       11.79
  adt        0        0.00       0.00       0.00
  total      13       5055.02    1429.03    6484.05

Individual virtual processors:
  vp     pid    class    usercpu   syscpu    total
  1      972    cpu      1270.52   144.52    1415.04
  2      981    adm      27.96     80.24     108.20
  3      999    cpu      1552.98   142.92    1695.90
  4      1000   cpu      1931.09   142.01    2073.10
  5      1001   lio      18.19     90.44     108.63
  6      1002   pio      12.69     53.64     66.33
  7      1003   aio      64.52     200.19    264.71
  8      1004   msc      6.99      4.80      11.79
  9      1005   aio      49.54     158.62    208.16
  10     1006   aio      39.08     119.72    158.80
  11     1007   aio      28.52     95.84     124.36
  12     1008   aio      21.91     81.59     103.50
  13     1012   soc      31.03     114.50    145.53
                total    5055.02   1429.03   6484.05

epaphus:ps -ef|grep oninit
  root    1007    999     0    Dec 8  ?     2:03 oninit
  root    999     972     0    Dec 8  ?     28:14 oninit
  root    1002    1000    0    Dec 8  ?     1:05 oninit
  root    1012    1000    0    Dec 8  ?     2:25 oninit
  root    1008    972     0    Dec 8  ?     1:42 oninit
  root    1000    972     0    Dec 8  ?     34:33 oninit
  root    1005    972     0    Dec 8  ?     3:27 oninit
  root    1003    972     0    Dec 8  ?     4:24 oninit
  root    1006    1000    0    Dec 8  ?     2:38 oninit
  root    1001    999     0    Dec 8  ?     1:48 oninit
  root    972     1       0    Dec 8  ?     23:34 oninit
  root    981     972     0    Dec 8  ?     1:47 oninit
  root    1004    999     0    Dec 8  ?     0:10 oninit
epaphus:
```

Figure 8-1 *The correlation of virtual processors to UNIX "oninit" processes.*

Notice the correlation in Figure 8-1 between the actual system process time, reflected in the "`ps`" command of the CPU vp processes, and that reflected in the "`onstat -g glo`" command. Compare this with the vps of other classes. While all classes of vps need to be monitored and tuned, it is particularly important to the overall performance of the instance to properly tune the CPU class of virtual processors. This will be covered in the next section.

Monitoring and Tuning Virtual Processors

If vps actually do the work within the OnLine Dynamic Server engine, it is critical that enough are spawned to meet the instance's needs. When tuning vp classes, it is not accurate to say "if some are good, then more are better." Remember that each process still gets its timeslice on the system CPU. Each process will also receive more or less the same amount of time on the system CPU regardless of whether or not the process has anything to do. Having too many vps defined in an instance, many of them not having any tasks to work on, could cause a situation where vp processes with work to accomplish must wait a longer amount of time to get another timeslice. Once switched onto the system CPU, these vp processes without work to accomplish will simply waste CPU time that could be used to process work by other vps. This is not exactly a model of efficient operation.

Conversely, too few vps in the more critical classes will create an ever-growing backlog of requests to be serviced. This can lead to a decrease in the processing throughput of the instance. So how do you determine the right number of vps? There are a couple of guidelines to allocating vps:

- Never allocate more CPU class vps than you have physical CPUs. In multiprocessor systems, I recommend allocating *at least* $n - 1$ (n = physical CPUs) CPU class vps, if not fewer, to start off with, then monitoring the instance's performance.
- If your port of the engine does not support KAIO, or you have not enabled it, allocate one AIO vp for each physical disk device. If KAIO is enabled, allocate one AIO vp.
- When allocating vps to support network-based poll threads, allocate one vp for each 50–100 anticipated user connections. See the "NETTYPE Settings" section of Chapter 3 for

more information about setting the required configuration parameters.

Working from these guidelines, you can then monitor vp efficiency and tune as activity reports indicate a need.

The most effective tool to monitor how well the vp classes are performing is the "onstat -g ioq" command. An abridged example of the output generated by this command is shown in Figure 8-2.

```
INFORMIX-OnLine Version 7.13.UC2 -- On-Line -- Up 3 days 18:14:57 -- 44848
Kbytes

AIO I/O queues:
  q name/ id   len   maxlen   totalops   dskread   dskwrite   dskcopy
       adt  0    0      0           0         0         0         0
       opt  0    0      0           0         0         0         0
       msc  0    0      2       24870         0         0         0
       aio  0    0      4      128679         4    128669         0
       pio  0    0      1        2841         0      2841         0
       lio  0    0      1       73462         0     73462         0
       gfd  3    0     16        2645      1784       861         0
```

Figure 8-2 Abridged output generated by the "onstat -g ioq" command.

Of particular interest in the output from this command are the "len" and "maxlen" columns for the AIO vp class. The "len" column shows the current number of backlogged requests. The "maxlen" column shows the historic high-water number of backlogged requests since the last time the engine statistics-gathering mechanism was zeroed out. In order to properly monitor the possible existence of a backlog of I/O requests, the performance statistics for the instance should be reset to zero, then monitored for a period of time. Executing an "onstat -z" command will reset the instance's statistics back to zero.

During the monitoring period, if a value greater than zero exists on a regular basis in the "len" column, or the "maxlen" column value is increasing, you should consider adding another AIO vp. As will be discussed in the next section, you cannot add or remove vps to the LIO or PIO class. Monitor the current and maximum queue length of these two vp classes from the "onstat -g ioq" report simply to be aware of what's happening in the instance rather than in preparation for tuning these two vp classes.

To monitor the activity of the CPU vp class, you need to look at the backlog of requests on the "ready" queue. To see this type of backlog, execute an "onstat -g rea" command. If there are constantly tasks waiting to be processed, you might consider adding another CPU vp to the instance—provided you have a physical CPU to support it.

Never allocate more CPU vps to an instance than there are physical CPUs in the computer system. On multiprocessor systems supporting multiple residency, you might have to allocate far fewer CPU vps than the number of physical CPUs per instance due to system CPU saturation. Systems supporting both applications as well as the OnLine Dynamic Server engine are particularly vulnerable to this type of CPU saturation. Monitor your system's physical activity reports, such as "sar" or "top," to determine if this type of condition exists on your system. If it does, you might have to reduce the number of CPU vps or add more physical CPUs to the system if possible.

Adding or Removing Virtual Processors

Vps can be added to an instance and begin to actively process tasks while the instance is on-line and supporting active user threads. With the exception of the CPU vp class, an instance must be shut down to remove vps from service. Vps can be added or dropped either from within the onmonitor utility or from the command line using the onmode utility.

Adding VPs

The proper onmode utility syntax to use to add a vp is as follows:

```
onmode -p +number_to_add vp_class
```

where *number_to_add* is replaced with the number of additional vps of class, *vp_class*, you want to add. You cannot string together the addition of vps to several vp classes with one iteration of the onmode command; you must execute the onmode command for each vp class.

Selecting the **Mode:Add-Proc** option from the onmonitor utility displays a screen similar to that shown in Figure 8-3.

```
ADD VIRTUAL PROCESSORS: Press ESC to add virtual processors.
Press Interrupt to cancel and return to the modes menu.


                     ADDING VIRTUAL PROCESSORS

  Number of CPU Virtual Processors to add                    [  0]

  Number of Asynchronous IO Virtual Processors to add        [  0]

  Number of Logical log IO Virtual Processors to add         [  0]

  Number of Physical log IO Virtual Processors to add        [  0]

  Number of Network Virtual Processors to add        [ ]  [   ]
                                                     [ ]  [   ]
                                                     [ ]  [   ]

Enter the number of cpu processors to add
```

Figure 8-3 *The Add-Proc screen from* `onmonitor`.

From this screen, you can enter the number of additional CPU and/or AIO class vps you would like to add to the instance. You can also add connection-oriented vps to handle user connections to the instance through poll threads by entering the number of additional vps followed by the PROTOCOL type at the bottom of the form. See the "NETTYPE Settings" section of Chapter 3 for more information about entering values in these fields.

While the screen would appear to allow you to add more LIO and PIO class vps, values entered here are ignored. The engine will spawn one LIO and one PIO vp within the instance to handle the I/O needs to and from the physical and logical logs when the instance is initialized or restarted. If the dbspace these logs are in is mirrored, the engine will spawn a second LIO or PIO vp to maintain the mirrored copy of these logs.

Once you have entered the type and number of vps you want to add to the instance, pressing the "accept" key will add the vps to the instance and activate them.

In order to add additional CPU vps, you need to make sure the MULTIPROCESSOR and SINGLE_CPU_VP configuration parameters are set correctly. If not, you will receive an error from the engine in response to your request to add the vp.

Dropping VPs

As I mentioned at the beginning of this section, only CPU class vps can be dropped while the instance is up and running. To remove vps from other classes requires shutting down the instance. You can use either the `onmode` command or the `onmonitor` utility to drop CPU vps.

The correct syntax for the `onmode` command is

```
onmode -p -number_to_drop cpu
```

where *number_to_drop* is replaced with the number of CPU vps you want removed from the instance. Attempting to delete a vp of a different class with this command will return an error message.

The engine will not let you remove all the CPU vps for an instance; nor will it allow you to remove a CPU vp that is supporting a poll thread. See the "NETTYPE Settings" section of Chapter 3 for more information on pool threads running on a CPU vp.

Selecting the **Mode:Drop-Proc** `onmonitor` option will display a screen in which you enter a value for the number of CPU vps to drop. Pressing the "accept" key after entering a value will remove that number of CPU vps from service. To reduce the number of vps in other classes requires shutting the instance down and editing parameters such as NUMAIOVPS in the $ONCONFIG file.

Update Statistics and Data Distributions

In the "Parallel Data Query" section of Chapter 3, as well as later on in this chapter, the OnLine Dynamic Server query optimizer is discussed. This engine component attempts to find the most efficient way of gathering and processing queried data. You can assist the optimizer in performing its tasks by generating the statistical information it uses to calculate the costs of various paths to the data by executing the "`update statistics`" command on a regular basis. A complete explanation of what this command does can be found in the *Informix Guide to SQL, Syntax* manual that accompanied your distribution of the software. In this section, I'll briefly cover the most important aspects of this command.

Modes and Distributions

The "`update statistics`" command has changed significantly from OnLine versions 5.x and earlier. It now does more than simply count the number of rows in a table—it gathers information on the uniqueness of the data and how skewed the data is in the table, reoptimizes stored procedures, and assists in the conversion of indexes when version upgrades occur. The syntax diagram for the command looks something like the following:

```
update statistics
    | for procedure proc_name
    | low
        | for table [table_name | synonym_name]
            | (column_name,)
        | drop distributions
    | medium
        | for table [table_name | synonym_name]
            | (column_name,)
        | resolution res_percent
            | confidence_value
                | distributions only
    | high
        | for table [table_name | synonym_name]
            | (column_name,)
        | resolution res_percent
            | distributions only
```

The "`update statistics low`" command performs the same type of work done by the "`update statistics`" command in OnLine versions 5.x and before. Total row counts for database tables are updated; minimum and maximum column values, and index level information is updated in the database system catalog tables as well.

Distributions and Resolution

Beginning with the "`medium`" and "`high`" keywords, the "`update statistics`" command can be expanded to include two additional resources for the optimizer, "data distributions" and "accuracy resolution."

Data Distributions Data distributions is a procedure where the actual data in one or more columns is sampled, then compiled into a series of what Informix calls "bins." There are a fixed number of bins for the data sampled. The number of bins and the accuracy of the data ranges each bin contains is determined by the value entered for the accuracy resolution. How the optimizer uses these bins will be explained in the "The OnLine Query Optimizer" section of this chapter.

The bins and the values they contain can be reviewed by executing the "`dbschema -d db_name -hd table_name`" command. An abridged sample of the output this command generates is shown in Figure 8-4.

```
        Distribution for db_a.str_purchase.trans_date
        Constructed on 1996/12/09
        High Mode, 0.500000 Resolution

        --- DISTRIBUTION ---
                (                       1993/12/01)
            1:(    14072,     22,    1994/01/05)
            2:(    14072,      7,    1994/01/13)
            3:(    14072,      8,    1994/01/21)
            4:(    14072,     10,    1994/01/31)
            5:(    14072,      9,    1994/02/09)
            6:(    14072,      9,    1994/02/18)
            7:(    14072,     10,    1994/02/28)
            8:(    14072,      8,    1994/03/09)
            9:(    14072,      8,    1994/03/17)
           10:(    14072,      9,    1994/03/26)
           11:(    14072,      9,    1994/04/05)
           12:(    14072,      7,    1994/04/13)
           13:(    14072,      7,    1994/04/21)
```

Figure 8–4 *Data distribution bin information generated by the* `dbschema` *utility.*

In this distribution report, there are two sections. The data distributions section is illustrated in Figure 8-4. The columns in this section indicate the number of rows in each bin, the number of unique values found within the range of values for that bin, and the maximum data value for that bin. For example, in the example shown in Figure 8-4, bin 8 has 14072 total "rows," 8 unique data values, and a data range spanning from 12/1/1993, found by looking at the first row of the report, to 3/9/1994.

The second section of this report, which was not included in Figure 8-4, contains what are called "overflow" values. The values included in this section are ones for which there is a great amount of duplication in the sampled data set.

These overflow values are listed in two columns. The first column is the number of times the value occurs in the data set; the second column is the data value itself. The command issued to create the distributions ("high" or "medium") will affect what the output looks like. If data distributions are created using the "update statistics high" command, the output by the data distributions option to the dbschema utility will be sorted.

Data Resolutions The "resolutions" flag in the "update statistics" command determines the number of distribution bins that are created and the accuracy of the data ranges in the bins. The value entered for the "resolutions" flag represents an approximate percentage of the data set you want each bin to contain. Acceptable values for this flag are from 10 to .005; the default, as shown in Figure 8-4, is .5.

Your need for accuracy within the bins will determine the "resolutions" value you enter and the "update statistics" command you run to create the distributions with. Obviously, a smaller "resolutions" value will increase the number of bins holding values and, in theory, increase the bin's effectiveness when used by the optimizer.

Update Statistics Modes The mode of the "update statistics" command has an impact on how the data distribution bins are created and populated. This could affect the potential effectiveness of the bins. In "high" mode, the distributions are created after all the rows are read and their values sorted. From there, any highly duplicated values are pulled out and flagged as overflow values. The remaining values are divided into the distribution bins according to the desired resolution. As a result, the statistical information for these distributions is very accurate. You should be aware, though, that creating this type of distribution is very resource intensive from the instance, engine, and computer system perspectives.

Prior to invoking an "`update statistics high`" command for a multi-column distribution, set the $DBUPSPACE environment variable to an amount that should allow for the distribution to be created by one pass through the data. The $DBUPSPACE variable sets the amount of disk space, in KB, that the engine can use to build the sorts and joins needed in creating the distributions. For example,

```
styx: DBUPSPACE=5000; export DBUPSPACE
```

will allow the engine to use up to 5 MB of disk space while it updates the instance's statistics.

There is no feedback from the "`update statistics high`" command on whether it took one or more passes to create the distributions. As a result, when setting the $DBUPSPACE variable you really don't know if the value entered was sufficient. The only way to tune this is to start with a small value, then run and rerun the command, each time increasing the value of $DBUPSPACE, and time how long each iteration of the "`update statistics high`" command takes to complete. Eventually you'll hit a value for DBUPSPACE where the "`update statistics`" command executes significantly faster than the previous iteration.

In "`medium`" mode all the rows are read, but after that a random sample of rows are taken to create the data distribution information. If the data value you are creating a distribution on is fairly evenly distributed, using sampling to create the statistical information should be acceptable. If not, the statistical information could be less accurate.

If you do not enter a value for the "`resolutions`" flag, the default is 2.5. You can hedge the process a bit by specifying a "`confidence`" value when executing an "`update statistics medium`" command. The "`confidence`" value affects how small, or large, a random sample is taken to create the distribution. The acceptable range for this value is .80 to .95. This value is more of a statistical measure than actual. If set to .90, it does not mean that 90 percent of the rows will be read to create the sample. Rather, it is an indication of how similar this distribution would be to one created using the "`high`" keyword of the "`update statistics`" command.

Your use of the "`resolutions`" and "`confidence`" values can significantly impact the number of rows sampled when creating the distribution. For example, by setting the "`resolutions`" *high* and the "`confidence`" *low*,

```
update statistics medium for table table_name
    (column_name) resolutions 10 .80
```

very few rows will be sampled to create the distribution. As you *decrease* the "`resolutions`" and *increase* the "`confidence`," the sample size grows. In general, and depending on the "`resolutions`" and "`confidence`" values selected, using this mode to create the distributions should be less resource-intensive.

Usage Recommendations

As with almost everything else, your particular instance requirements will affect when, and at what level, the "`update statistics`" command is run. In versions 5.x of the OnLine engine, Informix formerly recommended dropping and recreating indexes if the total table size changed by more than 25 percent, and running "`update statistics`" about once a week. While I think it's an excellent idea to drop and recreate the indexes to even up the Btree layers, with proper data distributions this will have less of an impact on query performance than in earlier versions. This is particularly true if the total row count in the table does not change that much but the data turns quite a bit. In this case, you need to refresh the distributions.

You can drop and recreate data distributions at will without refreshing the rest of the instance's statistics by executing

```
update statistics [high | medium] resolutions
    resolution_value distributions only
```

and if run in "`medium`" mode, a "`confidence`" value can be included as well.

Rather than running the "`update statistics`" command from a time-based perspective (e.g., once a week or monthly), I tend to follow a usage and statistically significant model. If the row count or overall amount of data has changed by more than about 10 percent in a highly used table, I update the statistics and distributions. If the table is not used that often and 25 percent of the data experiences changes, I update distributions. If the same table experiences a 25 percent change in row count, I update statistics and distributions.

Of course, this process of updating statistics varies and can change based on overall query performance. Like anything else when it comes to tuning, I don't have any hard and fast rules, just general guidelines to follow.

I use the following general procedure for executing the "update statistics" command:

- "high" mode on the first column listed in an index or index-based constraint. This column is sometimes referred to as the "head" column in the index.
- "high" mode on any non-"head" column frequently used as a join column or is on the left side of an "=" filter.
- "medium" mode on other columns infrequently used in query conditions
- "low" for tables with less than 1000 rows. It's faster to scan the table or run down any indexes that might exist. With less than 1000 rows, though, I generally resist creating indexes unless the row length is very long.

There is another factor that will affect how quickly the "update statistics" command executes—the PDQPRIORITY parameter. In creating the statistical information to load into the distribution bins, a significant amount of scanning and sorting is required. Some of this work can be done in parallel if PDQPRIORITY is enabled, as will be explained in the "PDQ and MGM" section of this chapter. Even if the predominant function of an instance is OLTP, you should still set PDQPRIORITY to a value of 1 to allow the "update statistics" command to take advantage of the advanced PDQ scanning algorithms. Set MAX_PDQPRIORITY to 10 in a predominantly OLTP environment to limit the total amount of shared memory resources the "update statistics" command can allocate.

The combination of sensible data fragmentation and periodic statistical updates and data distribution refreshes will enable the query optimizer to quickly and accurately find the best possible path to the queried data. The Informix OnLine Dynamic Server optimizer will be discussed in the next section.

The OnLine Query Optimizer

The job of the query optimizer is to figure out the quickest and least expensive way to select requested data. It is a complicated procedure that can be affected by a number of seemingly unrelated factors. While I make no claim to understanding all the nuances of the optimizer, I'll cover the most important aspects of how the optimizer works.

Factors Affecting Optimization

When a request is made for data, especially for data that resides in several tables yet shares some sort of relationship, a number of different approaches (also known as "paths") can be used to retrieve, sort, and/or aggregate the result. Each approach will vary in terms of the amount of instance resources required to process the request as well as the amount of time that will be required to complete the process. The optimizer evaluates each approach, guided by the constraints within which it must operate and the statistical information available, and selects the approach it thinks will be the most efficient. For the most part, the optimizer is fairly accurate in its assessments, although this evaluation phase can take longer to complete than the actual query.

The optimizer relies on the following baseline information when evaluating different query paths:

- The OPTCOMPIND parameter
- Baseline table statistics such as row counts, min and max values, and index values generated by an "update statistics" command
- Data distribution information generated by the "medium" and "high" modes of the "update statistics" command.

In addition, the optimizer recognizes and factors in any conditions placed on the data in the "where" clause of the query.

The optimizer uses the data distributions information to determine which table has the fewest number of rows that will match the query conditions. This could lead the optimizer to use a nested-loop join to join the table's data together. If indexes do not exist, or the data is distributed somewhat unevenly, a hash or sort-merge join might be more appropriate. Without this type of data, the optimizer simply cannot function properly and will undoubtedly use a less efficient query path.

Although the optimizer will, in effect, rewrite your SQL statement to eliminate such things as duplicate conditions, the way in which the "where" conditions are written will have an impact on the optimizer. This will be illustrated in the case study that follows. If the query requires the data to be sorted or grouped, the sorting and grouping requirements will affect the work the optimizer performs as well.

The query path selected by the optimizer can be reviewed by issuing the "set explain on" command prior to running a query. The query path selected is output to a file called "sqexplain.out" in the current working directory along with some diagnostic information—not all of it readily understandable. To illustrate how to use the output of this command, as well as the effect an ambiguous "where" clause can have on the optimizer, consider this case study of a simple query written in pseudocode:

```
select financial aggregations by category out of the
    store purchase table for stores in divisions 1
    or 4 with transaction dates between November 3,
    1996 and November 9, 1996
```

This appears to be a fairly simple query to write and should execute fairly quickly. Only one table is involved, the data is already stored at the category level, and there are indexes "headed" by division number and transaction date. The query was written as follows:

```
select division_no, str_no, category_id, sum(purchase_amt),
    sum(purchase_cost), sum(quantity_filled), sum(quantity_out),
    sum(service_charge)
  from str_purchase
  where division_no = 1
     or division_no = 4
     and (trans_date >= "1996.11.3" and trans_date <= "1996.11.9")
  group by 1,2,3
```

When this query was run, it seemed to take forever to return any values. Once the values were returned, they did not even approximate what was originally requested by the user.

To figure out how the query was being processed, it was rerun after setting "`explain`" on. The query path chosen by the optimizer was written to the "sqexplain.out" file and is shown in Figure 8-5.

```
QUERY:
------
select division_no, str_no, category_id, sum(purchase_amt),
       sum(purchase_cost), sum(quantity_filled), sum(quantity_out),
       sum(service_charge)
   from str_purchase
   where division_no = 1 or division_no = 4 and
       (trans_date >= "1996.11.3" and trans_date <= "1996.11.9")
   group by 1,2,3

Estimated Cost: 670079
Estimated # of Rows Returned: 140382
Temporary Files Required For: Group By

1) db_a.str_purchase: SEQUENTIAL SCAN (Serial, fragments: ALL)

    Filters:   (db_a.str_purchase.division_no = 1 OR
               (db_a.str_purchase.division_no = 4 AND
               (db_a.str_purchase.trans_date>= 1996/11/03 AND
                db_a.str_purchase.trans_date <= 1996/11/09 ) ) )
```

Figure 8–5 *Query path report from the "*`set explain on`*" command*

I've cleaned up the "Filters" section to make the optimizer's choice more obvious, but first a couple of other pieces of information. The "Estimated Cost" is an optimizer-oriented value and has no "real" relevance to us. Included in the creation of that number is the estimated number of I/Os, shared memory requirements, sorting or grouping overhead, and the amount of system time. You should use this figure only for comparative purposes with other tuning iterations. The "Estimated # of Rows Returned" represents the approximate number of rows the optimizer estimates it will have to process to complete the query. Finally, there is a "`group by`" statement in the SQL, so temporary tables will be used to create the groupings in the order requested.

The real meat in the information shown in Figure 8-5 is the actual path to be used in querying the data. In this case, the optimizer interpreted the conditions to be

all rows for division number = 1

OR

rows for division number = 4 transacted between 11/3/1996 and 11/9/1996

There weren't any indexes that matched this set of criteria so a sequential scan of all the table's fragments was ordered. The store purchase table has well over 2 million rows, so this took some time to complete.

It should also be obvious to you that the manner in which the "`where`" clause was written caused the optimizer to return inappropriate data by using incorrect data filters. While the data returned was accurate, and while the division 1 data for the requested date range could be extracted manually, the query was too time-consuming to run and was "expensive" in terms of impact on the system.

Making a slight change to the SQL statement resulted in a major difference in how fast the query performed and the appropriateness of the values returned. This is illustrated in Figure 8-6.

By isolating the division number condition to an integral unit by enclosing it in parentheses, the optimizer correctly interpreted the desired conditions and used the two indexes on the table to process the query. Simply comparing the "Estimated Cost" and "Estimated # of Rows Returned" values between this iteration and the previous iteration depicted in Figure 8-5 should give you an idea of how much faster the query performed. It now executes in under five seconds, as opposed to well over a minute for the first iteration.

This simple case study should illustrate that the key to overall query performance will not necessarily be in tweaking all the engine components covered in this section. No doubt about it, they are important, but often writing good, accurate SQL statements will have as large an impact, if not larger, on the performance of the SQL statement.

```
QUERY:
------
select division_no, str_no, category_id, sum(purchase_amt),
       sum(purchase_cost), sum(quantity_filled), sum(quantity_out),
       sum(service_charge)
  from str_purchase
  where (division_no = 1 or division_no = 4) and
       (trans_date >= "1996.11.3" and trans_date <= "1996.11.9")
  group by 1,2,3

Estimated Cost: 27698
Estimated # of Rows Returned: 1890
Temporary Files Required For: Group By

1) db_a.str_purchase: INDEX PATH

 Filters: (db_a.str_purchase.division_no = 1 OR db_a.str_purchase.division_no
 = 4 )

 (1) Index Keys: trans_date division_no str_no category_id inv_no (Serial,
fragments: ALL)
    Lower Index Filter: db_a.str_purchase.trans_date >= 1996/11/03
    Upper Index Filter: db_a.str_purchase.trans_date <= 1996/11/09
```

Figure 8–6 *Output from the "*`set explain on`*" command after tuning the query.*

OPTCOMPIND and Joins

The OPTCOMPIND parameter plays a key role in query optimization because it will force the optimizer to use different methods for joining data between two tables. In the "Parallel Data Query" section of Chapter 3, I listed the acceptable values for this parameter and the effect each would have on the optimizer's choice for joining tables. Let me briefly review the available join choices:

- Nested-loop—This is a one-to-many join. One table's values are used as the control value. These values are read once, but for each control value, every matching value in the second table is returned. The optimizer uses this method if forced to by OPTCOMPIND and there is an available index on the second table. The presence of an index on the second table prevents recurring sequential scans of that table.

- Dynamic-index—If, after a cost determination made by the optimizer, it is determined that a nested-loop join would be the most efficient way to get at the requested data, and an index does not exist on the second table of the join condition, the engine will create a temporary index on that table and then proceed with a nested-loop join. Dynamic-index joins are listed as such in the output generated by the "`set explain on`" command. If these occur fairly frequently as you are debugging various SQL statements, you should create an index on the columns used for the dynamic-index join.
- Sort-merge—As the name implies, the appropriate data from both tables is selected into temporary tables, then sorted. These temporary tables are then merged together by a sequential scan to generate the values to return.
- Hash—A new indexing strategy added to OnLine Dynamic Server, it is very similar to a sort-merge join, but its overhead costs are slightly less because there is no sorting involved. One table's data is read, and placed into what is called a "hash index." This is similar in nature to the distributions bins discussed earlier in this chapter. The second table's data is read, and each row is evaluated against the various components of the hash index to see if a join can be made.

When OPTCOMPIND is set to 0 (zero), the optimizer will always use nested-loop joins when an index exists on a join column in the second table. If an index does not exist, the optimizer will choose whichever of the other three choices is the least expensive. While nested-loop joins may not be the least expensive option to execute when you consider the I/O overhead of possibly reading index pages and data pages, they are relatively fast for the optimizer to structure and execute. It is for this reason that Informix recommends setting OPTCOMPIND to 0 (zero) in OLTP environments. For the most part, OLTP queries will use indexed columns from all the tables for selection criteria. This makes implementing a nested-loop join quite easy and getting to the data relatively fast despite the cost involved.

If OPTCOMPIND is set to 1, the isolation level of the query will have an impact on the join method selected by the optimizer. Isolation levels were explained in the "Understanding and Setting Isolation Levels" section of Chapter 5, Building a Database Environment. In Table 5.2, I showed that when a query is run using the "repeatable read" isolation level, each row read receives a shared lock. This could lead to a lock table overflow problem should a query join plan call for a sequential scan of one or both tables. To avoid this condition, the optimizer will act as if it were set to 0 (zero) and use a nested-loop join first if indexes are available. By using indexes, fewer actual rows might need to be read, resulting in fewer locks used. If a nested-loop join is not possible, the least expensive of the remaining options is used.

If the query is *not* using the "repeatable read" isolation level and OPTCOMPIND is set to 1, *or* OPTCOMPIND is set to 2, all join methods are evaluated equally without any preference being given to one method over another. This evaluation procedure does take time to perform, although the selected query path should execute quickly enough that it's not noticeable.

As explained in the "Parallel Data Query" section of Chapter 3, setting the OPTCOMPIND parameter when initializing the instance provides a baseline from which the optimizer operates. Any application can alter this parameter for the duration of the application thread by resetting the $OPTCOMPIND environment variable. Make sure your application developers do this, if indeed they do it at all, with care; the change could have an impact on the instance, possibly resulting in a decrease in total performance for the instance.

Once the query path has been determined, how the path is followed and actually executed is highly dependent on whether or not the parallelism mechanisms of the engine have been turned on in the instance. These features will be discussed in the next section.

PDQ and MGM

In this section, a new feature called PDQ, added to the OnLine Dynamic Server engine to improve the overall performance of OLAP queries, will be introduced. The parameters that control PDQ and the impact PDQ queries can have on an instance will also be discussed.

PDQ

PDQ, or Parallel Data Query, is an OnLine Dynamic Server function that, where possible, executes the various tasks of returning queried data simultaneously (or "in parallel") rather than serially, as was done in earlier versions of the engine. As you can imagine, this can have a tremendous positive impact on the overall performance of the instance.

This is not a cost-free feature, however. There is an impact on shared memory that requires a limitation on the number of PDQ-type queries that the instance can process at any moment in time. This restriction of concurrent queries might or might not be a factor in your environment, but it is real. For this reason, PDQ is most often used in OLAP environments, where fewer actual users are querying the data. In addition, OLAP queries are, by nature, more likely to be candidates for parallelization because they typically require multiple table joins and "`sort`" or "`order by`" statements that OLTP queries do not.

You can think of PDQ as a "divide and conquer" approach to query processing. The various tasks involved in processing the query are subdivided into individual threads for processing. As this process continues, results from each task are joined together upstream.

Figure 7.32 provides an illustration of a query that's been parallelized. In that diagram of the query, there are duplicate scan, sort, and merge operations sometimes taking place at the same time. As soon as some data is available to pass up the processing tree, the next level begins its work. In watching queries execute with this tool, it is not uncommon to see two to three directly joined levels of the tree actively processing data. Each level passes off data to the next higher level while continuing to work with new data coming in. The data elements continue to be filtered and merged together higher up the diagram until, finally, there is a single thread returning the result.

If you do not want to use the "Query Tree" tool in the `onperf` utility to see if a query is being processed in parallel, executing the "`onstat -u`" command can help answer the question. If there are multiple lines all with the same session id, the query is being processed in parallel. Multiple threads have been allocated by the engine to process the various components of the query.

PDQ works best on servers with more than one physical processor and, as a result, more than one CPU vp. This is not to say a

PDQ environment cannot be set up on a uniprocessor system; there simply wouldn't be that much of a return in doing so. There would only be one CPU (both physical and logical [CPU VP]) doing all the work. Although the query was parallelized, only one part of the query would be worked on at a time instead of several parts being processed simultaneously. In fact, it might actually take longer for results to be returned to the user from a PDQ environment on a uniprocessor system since each section of the parallelized query would be processed in a round-robin manner.

So how does the instance know which are OLAP queries that should be processed in parallel and which queries are OLTP-oriented and probably wouldn't benefit from parallelism? It doesn't. It's an all or nothing proposition for the instance depending on the PDQPRIORITY and MAX_PDQPRIORITY parameter settings. The engine will either attempt to process all queries in an instance in parallel mode, or it won't. As you might expect, there are some exceptions to that statement. For some query statements, there is no attempt made to process them in parallel. These include

- Queries performed as part of a "`for update`" application cursor.
- Queries executed with an application cursor declared "`with hold`."
- Queries executed using the "`cursor stability`" isolation mode. See the "Concurrency and Isolation Levels" section of Chapter 5 for a discussion of isolation modes.
- "`for each row`" queries executed as part of an "`update`" trigger

There are several configuration or tunable components that effect PDQ and how the instance is affected by parallelized queries. Most of these are grouped together into a component called the "MGM," discussed in the next section.

MGM

The "Memory Grant Manager," or MGM, is what controls the PDQ resources within the instance. While PDQ is turned on or off by the PDQPRIORITY and MAX_PDQPRIORITY parameters, the MGM controls memory use, activity on the CPU vps, disk I/O prioritization, and scan threads for the actual processing of PDQ queries. As each query is prepared within the instance for processing, the MGM allocates resources to the query and acts, quite literally, as a gatekeeper. Based on the MGM-oriented parameters, it controls how many and when queries are released into the instance.

This is particularly important when you realize that even though you, as an administrator, can set PDQ parameters, each user can, if they use the "`set pdqpriority`" SQL command or reset the $PDQPRIORITY environment variable, try to run a query at a different level than you set as the default for the instance. If the user sets their priority too high and there isn't a gatekeeper of system resources, that one query could use all the instance's resources, forcing all other queries to wait. Be aware that depending on how you set up your MGM parameters, you will limit the number of concurrent queries in the instance.

The MGM parameters are as follows:

- DS_TOTAL_MEMORY—the maximum amount of the instance's virtual portion of shared memory that can be allocated for PDQ query processing. Memory for processing of PDQ queries is allocated in units called "quantums." A quantum of memory is calculated using the following formula:

    ```
    quantum = DS_TOTAL_MEMORY / DS_MAX_QUERIES
    ```

    For example, if DS_TOTAL_MEMORY was set to 10000 KB and DS_MAX_QUERIES was set to 20, the "quantums" of memory allocated for query processing would each be 500 KB in size.

- DS_MAX_QUERIES—the number of concurrent PDQ queries the instance will process. DS_MAX_QUERIES only affects queries with a PDQPRIORITY greater than 0 (zero). Queries specifically set to a $PDQPRIORITY of 0 (zero) are not limited in any way by this configuration parameter. Obviously, the speed in which a non-PDQ query executes will be affected by other PDQ queries running in the instance, particularly if most of the instance's resources are allocated to process PDQ queries.

- DS_MAX_SCANS—available in the 7.2 release of OnLine Dynamic Server, the number of concurrent scan threads that can be used to satisfy PDQ queries. This can have both a positive and negative impact on the speed of query processing. If set too high, fewer queries can be executing read scans to get the data they need, causing other queries to wait for their turn to read data. If set too low, more queries can be reading data, but the read phase will take longer to execute because there are not enough scan threads to get all the required data simultaneously. Several sets of reads will need to be executed in a serial fashion, resulting in an overall slowdown in performance. Since each table fragment to be scanned during a query requires a unique scan thread, I use the following formula to set this parameter:

```
(DS_MAX_QUERIES * (avg_num_tables *
avg_num_frags)) * 1.1
```

where *avg_num_tables* is the average number of tables to be scanned in a query and *avg_num_frags* is the average number of fragments a table to be scanned will have. I add on an extra 10 percent as a fudge factor by multiplying the result by 1.1

- MAX_PDQPRIORITY—places a limit, in terms of a percentage, on the total amount of instance resources that can be allocated to a specific PDQ query. In reality, this acts as a "percent of a percent." When a query is processed by the instance, it requests a certain amount of resources via its $PDQPRIORITY setting. The MAX_PDQPRIORITY parameter setting allocates up to MAX_PDQPRIORITY percent of the $PDQPRIORITY percent of instance resources. For example, a query with a $PDQPRIORITY of 90 is processed in an instance with a MAX_PDQPRIORITY of 15. The query will be allocated up to 90 percent of the possible 15 percent, or, in other words, just under 14 percent of instance resources.

You can also look at this parameter as the companion to DS_MAX_QUERIES. If you only want five simultaneous queries to be executing in an instance, these two parameters should match each other. Assuming that each query was executed with a $PDQPRIORITY of 100, you would, in this example, set DS_MAX_QUERIES to 5 and MAX_PDQPRIORITY to around 20.

MGM parameters can be set permanently by editing the $ONCONFIG file, or temporarily through the onmode utility. The onmode flags to alter MGM parameters are:

- -D *value* to alter MAX_PDQPRIORITY
- -M *value* to alter DS_TOTAL_MEMORY
- -Q *value* to alter DS_MAX_QUERIES
- -S *value* to alter DS_MAX_SCANS

You can monitor the effectiveness of your MGM settings by reviewing the output of the "onstat -g mgm" command as illustrated in Figure 8-7.

The illustration in Figure 8-7 obviously comes from an instance without PDQ enabled. It does show, however, the general format of the output generated by this command.

In the first several sections, the command lists the MGM parameter settings and how they are being used. The number of active queries, memory quantums allocated or free, and the number of active scan threads are listed. This is followed by what I call the "gatekeeper" statistics. I explained earlier in this section that the role of the MGM was to act as a gatekeeper, allowing queries to be processed as resources allowed. The fifth section of the output generated by the "onstat -g mgm" command shows the number of inactive queries and the resource they are waiting on as a result of this gatekeeping mechanism.

These resource checks are referred to as "gates," and the MGM must be able to provide the minimum amount of the resource referred to at each gate in order for the query to be processed within the instance. If, for example, there aren't any memory quantums available to allocate, the query will stall at the first gate and the "Queue Length" value for that gate will increase by one. As a memory quantum becomes available, the query with the highest $PDQPRIORITY is allocated the quantum and proceeds to the next gate, where a check is made to see if enough scan threads can be allocated. This continues until the query can be released into the instance for processing.

Because queries are processed in $PDQPRIORITY order, it is important to enforce a coding standard by which queries are assigned their $PDQPRIORITY. This will ensure that less critical queries are processed after more critical queries.

```
INFORMIX-OnLine Version 7.13.UC2 -- On-Line -- Up 03:11:31 -- 14656 Kbytes

Memory Grant Manager (MGM)

MAX_PDQPRIORITY:   0
DS_MAX_QUERIES:    485
DS_MAX_SCANS:      1048576
DS_TOTAL_MEMORY:   62144KB


Queries:  Active    Ready    Maximum
          0         0        485

Memory:   Total     Free     Quantum
(KB)      62144     62144    128

Scans:    Total     Free     Quantum
          1048576   1048576  2162

Load Control:  (Memory)    (Scans)    (Priority)    (MaxQueries)    (Reinit)
               Gate 1      Gate 2     Gate 3        Gate 4          Gate 5
(Queue Length) 0           0          0             0               0

Active Queries: None

Ready Queries: None

Free Resource       Average #       Minimum #
Memory              0.0+-0.0        7768
Scans               0.0+-0.0        1048576

Queries             Average #       Maximum #   Total #
Active              0.0+-0.0        0           0
Ready               0.0+-0.0        0           0

Resource/Lock Cycle Prevention count: 0
```

Figure 8-7 *Output generated by the "`onstat -g mgm`" command.*

The last two sections list the number of active queries as well as some averages of the actual amount of resources being used. By monitoring the various resource queues, you can tune the various MGM parameters as needed to achieve what ever level of performance and concurrent access is required for your environment.

Summary

As I was developing the general outline for this chapter, I had initially included a section called "General Tuning Guidelines." As I thought about what I would write in that section, I realized that if there was a specific value of a tunable parameter, or a logical or physical design consideration important enough to include in that section, it should be covered in the section of the book discussing tunable parameters or logical and physical design issues. So all my accumulated wisdom and suggestions for improving performance are widely distributed throughout the book in the sections to which they are most relevant.

To look back at what *was* covered in this chapter: by now you should have a good understanding of what virtual processors are, the classes that define their functionality, and how to monitor and tune them. You should understand the role the "`update statistics`" command plays in enhancing query performance. You should understand how to create data distributions of varying degrees of statistical accuracy and the importance these distributions have in influencing and guiding the OnLine Dynamic Server query optimizer. You should also understand the factors that influence the optimizer and what effect the OPTCOMPIND parameter has on choosing a join method. Finally, you should understand what PDQ is and, from a very high level, how it operates. You should be able to monitor and tune the resources controlled by the MGM to balance query access and throughput.

In looking back over the information covered in *this* chapter to increase performance, keep the following points in mind:

- Virtual processors are the key to overall instance performance. Monitor their effectiveness constantly to maintain overall instance performance.
- Never allocate more CPU vps in an instance than you have physical CPUs. In systems supporting multiple residency, watch the physical system load when all the instances are up and running as well as the vp wait states to see if there are too many total CPU vps allocated for the system to handle.
- If KAIO is available in your port of the engine, configure and use it to virtually eliminate the AIO vps and increase I/O throughput to and from the disks in your system.

- The "update statistics" command should be run on a regular basis and at different levels to create the data distribution information to enable the query optimizer to find the most efficient path to the requested data.
- Tuning query throughput is as much a process of writing correct SQL statements as it is tweaking shared memory, PDQ, or MGM parameters. If you're having a problem with a query's performance, examine the SQL first, then instance parameters.
- The OPTCOMPIND parameter and environment variable determines which type of join the optimizer will consider when processing a query. Nested-loop joins are used when OPTCOMPIND is set to 0 (zero) and a usable index is available on the second table. All other join methods are treated equally when OPTCOMPIND is set to 1 or 2 and the query is not in "repeatable read" isolation level.
- PDQ is best employed in multiprocessor systems where there are enough physical CPUs to adequately parallelize the query. The usual requirement for PDQ to be effective is more than two physical CPUs.
- In OLTP environments, set PDQPRIORITY to 1 to enable parallel sorting. Set MAX_PDQPRIORITY to 10. This will improve the efficiency and speed of execution for certain parallelized actions such as updating statistics and creating indexes. In OLAP environments, these parameters can be set much higher, in conjunction with other MGM parameters, to achieve a balance of throughput and concurrent access.

Coming Up

In the next chapter, the concept of data replication will be introduced. I'll explain what is involved in replicating an instance between two different servers and keeping the data elements in them synchronized.

Part 4

Expanding Your Horizons, Additional Topics and Technologies

With the possible exception of Chapter 10, which could be considered a part of the previous section, this section contains chapters on other technological elements of the OnLine Dynamic Server engine. These elements are covered to expand your knowledge of the OnLine Dynamic Server engine, provide additional insight into its operation, and attempt to make your job a little easier to perform.

I'll cover the fast recovery process and explain the process the engine uses to restart an instance. One of the two methods OnLine Dynamic Server uses for replicating an instance will be covered along with cross-instance transactions, called distributed or "global transactions." I'll explain the benefits, and the risks, associated with using either of these two technologies. Finally, I'll describe or document a series of utilities and other information included on the disc that accompanies this book. Some of the material is oriented towards DBAs, the rest is focused more towards instance maintenance and administration. Some general purpose documentation is included courtesy of Informix Software and Kerry Sainsbury.

By the end of this section, you should have a well-rounded understanding of the OnLine Dynamic Server engine; its operation, maintenance, and other administrative requirements. While there is always more to learn and understand, real-world hands-on experience is required. This experience will enable you to test many of the principals suggested in this book and to put them in their proper perspective. Other books, particularly those in this Informix series, will help round out your theoretical knowledge and enable you to put it to practical use with the OnLine Dynamic Server instances you learned to create and administer here.

Chapter 9

Providing High Availability and Reliability

- *What is High-Availability Data Replication?*
- *How is it set up?*
- *What steps are required to recover from a failure while in replication mode?*
- *How do applications communicate with replicated instances?*

With the release of OnLine Dynamic Server, Informix introduced a feature called High-Availability Data Replication (HADR) that enables you to create a duplicate copy of an instance on another physical server. It is not used too often because, to be perfectly honest, getting this feature to work correctly is quite a challenge. It is very sensitive to any variation in the conditions that must be met prior to invoking replication as well as the sequence of steps that must be followed to invoke replication mode. By the end of this chapter, you should understand what HADR is and the role it plays in Informix's efforts to make the engine more fault tolerant. You should understand and be able to follow the sequence of steps required to initialize HADR and how to recover from failures that occur while in replication mode. You should also understand what, from an application perspective, is required to communicate with a replicated instance.

As this book is going to print, Informix has released another, more sophisticated data replication product called Continuous Data Replication (CDR). Informix also announced support for a product called OmniReplicator from Praxis International. The Praxis product enables you to replicate or update selected data elements between OnLine Dynamic Server instances and other vendors' database products. I do not have any experience with either product and will not cover any of their features or functions in this chapter.

What Is High-Availability Data Replication?

Unlike disk mirroring, discussed in the "Disk Drive Issues" section of Chapter 2, Preparing for Initialization, which creates a copy of all or some of the dbspaces within an instance on the same physical server, High-Availability Data Replication (HADR) creates and maintains a complete copy of an instance on a separate physical server. HADR is another mechanism in OnLine Dynamic Server's fault-tolerant suite of functionality that includes transaction logging in the physical and logical logs, the fast recovery mechanism that reads those logs during instance reinitialization, and physical disk mirroring.

The physical and logical logs, fast recovery mechanism, and disk mirroring were all designed to protect against physical media failures on the server. If you consider the ability to execute "warm" restores of selected noncritical dbspaces or moment-in-time restores (only available with the `onarchive` utility), an instance is fairly well protected against the possible effects of a disk drive failure.

HADR was designed to protect the instance against the total failure of the physical server. When HADR is successfully implemented, an instance, with its activity, is completely mirrored on another server on the network. This replicated copy can and will, depending on how you set it up, automatically take over the role and workload of the original instance in the event the original should suffer a catastrophic failure.

In setting up HADR, you have the ability to set when, during the normal processing cycle, the secondary server is updated to accurately reflect the production server. You can also establish the actions each server will take in the event the other server fails or drops off-line.

HADR is not inexpensive to operate. You need an additional physical server that in many ways is an exact clone of the original server. You must also have a *very* reliable and stable network connection between the two servers. Don't think, though, that the mirror server is just some sort of contented cow out on the network chewing up its own resources without providing anything in return. The mirror server can provide value back to the data processing environment by acting as a read-only database server for localized or distributed queries, depending on the replication frequency invoked. Connecting an application to use this server is as simple as changing the $INFORMIXSERVER environment variable.

HADR has a couple of key words associated with it that you need to understand. An instance that is *not* using replication is said to be in "standard" mode. In HADR, there are "primary" and "secondary" servers. The primary server, as its name implies, is the master server in the replication pair. Its activity is copied to the secondary server as specified by the instance administrator through the DRAUTO configuration parameter. See the "Data Replication" section of Chapter 3, Initializing an OnLine Dynamic Server Instance, for more information about this configuration parameter. "Lost-and-Found" transactions are database transactions that are committed on the primary server but might not be committed on the secondary server due to a failure of either server or the network. How this can occur will be explained in the next section.

How Does HADR Work?

HADR, as a concept, is not that difficult to understand. During normal database processing in an instance containing databases in logged mode, transactions are recorded in the instance's logical logs. The HADR mechanism takes the logical log records on the primary server and copies them into the replication buffer in the resident portion of shared memory on the secondary server. Using these logical log records, the HADR mechanism on the secondary server initiates a logical restore against its databases. In the event of a failure—and depending on the replication mode enabled—the remaining server will either stay functional and assume the role of the primary server, or shut down database access gracefully. When the two servers are reconnected, one server will assume the primary role, the other will become the "replicant."[1] Which of the two servers assumes what role is also dependent on configuration parameter settings that will be discussed later.

Logical Log Transfer Modes

The transfer of log records can occur in one of two modes, synchronously or asynchronously.

Synchronous Transfer Mode

In synchronous mode, when records on the primary server are flushed from the logical log buffer to the logical logs themselves, the log records are also written to the replication buffer in the resident portion of the instance's shared memory. Then this replication buffer is flushed immediately to the secondary server, where it is written into its replication buffer in order for that server's databases to be updated. Once the records are received into the replication buffer at the secondary server, an acknowledgment is sent to the primary server. When the acknowledgment is received by the primary server, the buffer flush is considered complete and

---

[1] Sorry, the Ridley Scott movie reference was too good to pass up.

the database transactions themselves are considered fully committed on the primary server.

In synchronous mode, should acknowledgment from the secondary server not be received in the configured amount of time, the transactions are rolled back on the primary. In this transfer mode, there are no committed transactions on the primary server that have not been received, and eventually written to disk, on the secondary server.

Asynchronous Transfer Mode

When asynchronous mode is used to transfer the logical log records, transactions are flushed from the logical log buffers on the primary server to the logical logs as well as to the replication buffer. At this moment, the flush is complete and the transactions are fully committed as far as the primary server is concerned. The replication buffer itself gets flushed to the secondary server independent of the primary server's logical log buffer flush. As a result, the secondary server only receives a replication buffer flush when any of the following occurs:

- A transaction is committed within a database in unbuffered logging mode.
- An amount of time equal to the DRINTERVAL configuration parameter has elapsed since the last replication buffer transfer to the secondary server occurred.
- The data replication buffer on the primary server fills up.
- A checkpoint occurs.

From the "Logging Modes" section of Chapter 5, Building a Database Environment, you will recall that whenever a transaction is committed in a database in unbuffered logging mode, the logical log buffers are immediately flushed to the logical logs. In synchronous transfer mode, this also causes a replication buffer flush to the secondary server. Since the commitment of a transaction in a database in unbuffered logging mode causes a replication buffer flush to occur in asynchronous transfer mode as well, it would appear at first glance that these two actions behave exactly alike in the two HADR logging transfer modes. There is an important distinction, however, which needs to be made when comparing these two situations.

Unlike synchronous transfer mode, when the replication buffer in an asynchronous replication pair is flushed to the secondary server, the primary server continues to process transactions. It does not wait for an acknowledgment from the secondary server that the buffer was received and is being processed. If, for some reason, the buffer flush is never received at the secondary server, it has no effect on the actions of the primary server. There is one exception to this, which occurs when a checkpoint occurs on the primary server. In this situation, the primary server transfers the replication buffer, then waits until the checkpoint completes on the secondary server.

The important point I'm trying to make is that asynchronous transfer mode does not absolutely guarantee that the secondary server will be an exact duplicate of the primary. It only provides for a general approximation. If the network stays up, as well as the servers, a secondary server in an HADR environment using asynchronous transfer mode will, from time to time, be an exact mirror of the primary.

For some environments, the ambiguity in the exactness of the copy between the secondary and primary servers by using asynchronous transfer mode will be acceptable for several reasons. There is significantly less network traffic because a lower amount of communication is occurring between the servers. If all the databases in the instance use buffered logging, the replication buffer won't be transferred that often anyway. These two factors contribute to a decrease in processing overhead on the primary server. In addition, the overall throughput of the primary server increases because there is no latency involved with replication buffer flushes for confirmation messages to be received from the secondary server.

Server Actions When a Failure Occurs

Although you hope it never happens, there will probably come a time when one of the servers in the replication pair fails. What happens in this situation depends on a number of factors, not least of which is whether or not a failure actually occurred, and the values set for several key HADR configuration parameters such as DRTIMEOUT and DRAUTO. In this section, I'll describe what happens in greater detail.

What Is a Failure?

The first thing to understand is what constitutes a failure condition for HADR. Is it a server that crashes unexpectedly? Does a disruption in the network constitute a failure? When you take into consideration recovery procedures, do either of these situations make a difference in what you do? The answer to all three questions is a qualified "yes."

Obviously, if a server experiences a physical failure, there's a condition that exhibited itself and caused the failure. However, it is not immediately recognized as a failure from the logical point of view of the HADR process on the surviving server. Some time passes before a failure condition is declared.

In the case of network disruption, both servers can, depending on conditions, declare a failure condition to exist on the other server. The value set for the DRTIMEOUT configuration parameter will have an impact on what happens in this situation. The recovery process for both servers in either of these two situations will most likely be completely different depending on how the DRAUTO configuration parameter was set.

The HADR mechanism defines a failure as any situation that prevents both servers from acting in concert. This includes physical failures such as system crashes and nonmirrored media failures on either server. The definition of a failure extends to include the inability to communicate with the other server as well as simply breaking the replication connection by shutting a server down and turning off the HADR parameters. It is this logical definition of what constitutes a failure that makes recovery afterwards different depending on the situation.

A failure is declared by the HADR mechanism when the two servers cannot or do not communicate for a given period of time. That amount of time is determined by the value set for the DRTIMEOUT configuration parameter. When the replication buffer is flushed to the secondary server in synchronous transfer mode, the primary server will wait for DRTIMEOUT seconds to receive a confirmation message back from the secondary server. If the message is not received in that amount of time, the HADR mechanism on the primary server will declare a failure condition to exist.

If replication communication appears to cease between two instances, each will execute a sanity check for the existence of the other by issuing a type of connection ping to the other instance every DRTIMEOUT seconds. Should either server fail to receive a response back in DRTIMEOUT seconds, the server will retry three more times, at DRINTERVAL seconds, before declaring a failure condition to exist. As a result of this last condition, you should always set DRTIMEOUT to no more than one-quarter the amount of time you think you would need to overcome a temporary network interruption or would want to wait before failure mode changes set by the DRAUTO configuration parameter begin in the event of a physical failure. What actually happens in a failure condition will be explained in the next section.

What Happens in a Failure Condition?

When you begin to evaluate the possible actions that can occur in a failure condition, you should quickly realize that these options apply mainly to the secondary server in the replication pair. The primary server's role is only affected by one of the three possible actions—and then only if *it* is the server that fails. Provided the primary server doesn't fail, its role never changes. With this in mind, the actions taken in a failure condition should be driven more by the logical design of the replication process than by the possibility of physical failure.

By this I mean that if you anticipate more network irregularities than actual physical failures, set up the HADR environment so that the secondary remains in read-only mode until a connection can be reestablished. If you have little or no concerns about the stability and robust nature of the network, but are worried about physical failures and have to continue to provide almost nonstop database services, have the secondary server assume the role of primary server. Whether or not it is important from an application and network bandwidth perspective to connect to one physical server or the other will determine whether the secondary server keeps its role as primary when the original primary server comes back on-line.

The actions of the servers in a failure condition are determined by the value set for the DRAUTO configuration parameter. Table 3-4 in Chapter 3 lists the possible values for this parameter. How the value of DRAUTO affects recovery after a HADR failure is addressed later in this chapter. To briefly recap, when DRAUTO is set to 0 (zero) or "off," the secondary server continues to operate as a read-only server. While the HADR communication connection is lost, the secondary server continues to listen for connection messages from the primary server. The secondary server will automatically reconnect to the primary whenever the primary server attempts to reconnect. It will then continue its role as secondary server. This is the setting I use most often and recommend to others.

When DRAUTO is set to 1 (one) or "retain_type," the secondary server will assume the role of primary server whenever the secondary server declares a failure condition to exist. It will continue to listen for connection messages from the primary server and, if any work was done on the secondary server during the time the failure condition existed, will transfer its logical logs to the primary server when they reconnect. It will then reassume the role of secondary server. Setting DRAUTO to 1 can be fraught with danger and should be avoided if the network is at all unstable, as will be explained in the "Effect of the DRAUTO Parameter on the Recovery Process" section of this chapter.

When DRAUTO is set to 2 or "reverse_type," the secondary server will assume the role of primary server in the event it declares a failure condition to exist. It will listen for connection messages from the primary server and, when received, transfer its changes to the primary server when they reconnect. The primary server will then be expected to assume the role of secondary server while the original secondary server continues in its role as primary server. This setting, too, can be fraught with danger if the network is not extremely reliable, as will be explained later in this chapter.

HADR is without a doubt the most complicated of all the fault-tolerant mechanisms discussed so far to set up and operate. I have to admit that my own experience with HADR is somewhat limited. I have successfully set it up a couple of times, but only after a number of failed attempts. In the next section, I will explain the conditions that need to be met and the steps required to successfully initialize HADR.

Initializing HADR

The process of initializing HADR is not difficult, although there are a number of conditions that must be met prior to beginning the process of initializing HADR. There is a step-by-step initialization process that must be carefully followed as well in order for HADR to successfully initialize. In this section, these conditions and the initialization process will be explained in greater detail.

Server and Software Conditions

As a general rule, let me say this: the primary and secondary servers have to be identical in almost every way. The operating systems have to be at the same release level with the same patches installed. Several network-related files, such as /etc/hosts, need to be modified to permit trusted communication between the servers. This condition will be covered in the "Network Conditions" section.

The physical hardware also needs to match very closely. For example, if you are using an HP Series 9000/800 for a primary server, you cannot use an HP Series 9000/700 for a secondary server. Within the same family of machine, though, you can use different models for the primary and secondary servers provided there are similar physical resources on the secondary server to match those used by the instance running on the primary server. To better understand the other physical conditions that need to be met, consider the Informix conditions that need to be met to initialize and run HADR.

OnLine Dynamic Server Conditions

From the engine's perspective, the two instances have to be exact and identical matches in every way except for the server names (and aliases) and the number of vps allocated. In fact, the best way to configure the secondary server is to copy the $ONCONFIG file from the primary server to the secondary and change the DBSERVERNAME and DBSERVERALIASES fields. This ensures that, among other things, the replication configuration parameters such as DRAUTO and DRINTERVAL are set identically so that each server will take the appropriate action in the event of a failure.

There are several implications to be made about the secondary server when you consider that both instances have to be configured identically. From a physical server perspective, if the primary instance's logical logs are being archived to tape, the secondary server will need an identically pathed tape device, even though the secondary is not archiving its logs. This device will be used when HADR is initialized and if a logical recovery is required after a HADR failure occurs.

If the primary instance uses three CPU vps because there are four physical CPUs, the secondary will have to be able to support three CPU vps as well—requiring the secondary server to be a multiprocessor server like the primary. One of the big differences allowed between the secondary and primary servers is that the secondary server does *not* have to allocate the same number of vps in any vp class. Using CPU vps as an example, although the primary might have three CPU vps, the secondary could operate with just one CPU vp. Of course, this will vary depending on the load placed on the secondary server. If its sole function is to replicate the instance, one CPU vp will be sufficient. If it is to act as a read-only server by reporting-only applications, additional CPU and other classes of vps might need to be allocated. If the server is expected to take over the role of the primary server for any length of time in the event of a failure, the secondary system had better have enough physical resources to be able to retune the secondary server to match the primary server's configuration; otherwise, there will be an impact on performance.

Disk requirements, in terms of total storage required on both servers, are the same as well, with one important exception: if mirroring is enabled on one server, you do not have to enable it on the other server. As far as the primary chunks are concerned, you will need to create the same number of similarly sized chunks on the secondary server as are on the primary server. Their physical path names and offsets must be identical as well. Here, again, is another important reason to use symbolic links rather than the actual physical device names when identifying chunks for use when creating or adding to dbspaces. By using symbolic links you do not have to replicate the exact physical disk set that exists on the primary server—especially if you have access to a logical disk manager. As long as the final device accessed through the symbolic link appears identical to that on the primary server, it will work. See the "Using Symbolic Links" section of Chapter 2, Preparing for Initialization, for more information on symbolic links.

Only databases in logged mode will continue to be replicated after the initial physical restore to initialize HADR. Because unlogged databases do not generate much in the way of logical log records, there is nothing to cache in the replication buffer and transfer to the secondary server. Logging mode changes to databases are not allowed while the instances are in replication mode. If you need to change the logging mode for one of the databases in a replicated instance, interrupt replication by taking the secondary off-line, make the logging mode change in the primary instance, and then reinitialize the secondary server and HADR communication as if you were starting HADR for the first time.

BLOBs stored in BLOBspaces are not replicated either, because writes to BLOBspaces do not pass through the buffer pool in the resident portion of shared memory. However, BLOBs stored "in table" are replicated because the BLOB data written out to disk passes through the shared memory pools like the rest of the data in the table.

Needless to say, storing BLOBs "in table" can have a significant impact on overall system performance in both real and statistical terms. The BLOB data can wipe out all the data cached for other threads, forcing rereads to occur. As the BLOB data floods into the buffers, foreground writes, the most inefficient of all the disk write mechanisms, might be required to write modified data already in the buffers out to disk. A large number of rereads and uncached writes will severely skew the read and write efficiency numbers reported by the "`onstat -p`" command. In turn, you might be inclined to retune BUFFERS and other parameters, yet not recognize any positive results of your actions.

Obviously, if you need to replicate an environment containing BLOBs you don't have much of a choice in how to set it up. Just be sure to take into account the ramifications of storing BLOBs "in table" when you look at your statistical reports as well as the overall throughput and performance of the system.

Network Conditions

I couldn't stress enough the importance of having a stable and robust network when trying to initialize and run HADR. Earlier in this chapter I explained that, depending on the replication mode used, the commitment of every transaction in a database in unbuffered logging mode would also trigger a replication buffer transfer from the primary server to the secondary server. In synchronous transfer mode, an acknowledgment from the secondary server must be received before the primary server continues its work. Since every database action (except queries) is an implicit transaction in a database in a logged mode, this means there will be a replication buffer flush and acknowledgment wait for every add, delete, or modify action that occurs in the database. Needless to say, the network needs to be able to handle that amount of communication between the two servers as quickly and reliably as possible. Isolating the communication between the two servers to their own subnet is always the best approach to eliminating contention from other traffic that travels across the general-purpose backbones of your network.

From a network perspective, the two servers must be able to use the informix userid to communicate with each other as trusted hosts. To enable this functionality, you either need to modify the /etc/hosts.equiv file or, at the very least, the .rhosts file in the informix userid's home directory. See the documentation that accompanied your O/S for instructions on how to properly set up these files.

Since the replication buffers are transferred via a network-based connection thread, a network protocol instance service needs to be defined in the $INFORMIXSQLHOSTS and /etc/services file, as well as DBSERVERALIAS in the $ONCONFIG file, for the instances on the primary and secondary servers. Like all other network-based services that need to communicate, the service numbers used in the /etc/services file for a given instance's service need to be identical on both servers for the two-way connection to be established. See the "Required Files" section of Chapter 2 for more information on configuring these files.

A Step-by-Step Approach to Initializing HADR

Once all the server, Informix, and network conditions have been met, you can begin the initialization process. This process is not difficult, provided each step is executed in order. I have organized these steps into Table 9-1. The table is organized such that actions which need to be taken on the primary server are isolated from those required to be taken on the secondary server. In some cases these actions are identical. Each action is listed in the order in which it is to be accomplished with regard to actions on the other server. There is one action on the secondary server that might not be required, depending on the amount of work that has occurred on the primary server following the initialization of its HADR mechanism. This will be explained below.

You will not get the secondary server in a HADR pair to properly connect or initialize unless all communication with it, including your HADR configuration commands, occurs through its network-based instance alias. If you attempt to configure and bring a secondary server up through the instance's shared memory connection, the secondary server will hang after the physical restore.

if you do not use the network-based alias, an error indicating a checkpoint is required will occur yet one cannot be forced. A logical restore, as explained in Table 9-1, will not succeed even if triggered by executing the "onmode -d secondary primary_instance" *command. The MSGPATH will log a message that recovery is beginning but logical log information will not be applied within the secondary server regardless of how long you wait.*

Provided that all the other prerequisites have been met, and you follow the procedure outlined in Table 9-1, using the network-based connection on the secondary server will enable you to successfully initialize a HADR pair. This step is explicitly called out in Table 9-1 but is implied in all the failure recovery mechanisms discussed later in the chapter.

Depending on the amount of work processed on the primary server following its HADR initialization, the logical recovery on the secondary server from tape might not be required. After the HADR mechanism is enabled on the secondary server via the "onmode -d secondary" command, the secondary server attempts to connect to the primary server. Once connected, the servers will exchange information about their relative state and what each considers to be the active logical log. If it is determined that the primary instance is using log number 245 and the secondary instance shows the active log to be number 240, the primary will check to see if logs 240 through 244 are still available. If they are, the logs will be transmitted to the secondary server and the logical recovery will be initiated automatically. As a result, you will not need to manually invoke the logical restore with the "ontape -l" command.

Table 9-1   Actions required to initialize HADR.

Primary Server	Secondary Server
• Edit the HADR configuration parameters (DRAUTO, DRTIMEOUT, DRINTERVAL, DRLOSTFOUND) in the $ONCONFIG file. • Add entries to the $INFORMIX-SQLHOSTS and /etc/services files for network connections to primary and secondary instances. • Modify the /etc/hosts.equiv or the .rhosts file for the informix userid to enable trusted communication with the other server. • Make sure the databases to be replicated are in logged mode. • Send a copy of the primary instance's $ONCONFIG file to the secondary server. • Create at least one (1) temporary dbspace if one does not already exist in the instance.	• Add entries to the $INFORMIX-SQLHOSTS and /etc/services files for network connections to primary and secondary instances. • Modify the /etc/hosts.equiv or the .rhosts file for the informix userid to enable trusted communication with the other server. • Create primary physical disk chunks identical to those on the primary server. Mirror chunks are optional. At least one (1) temporary dbspace will be required. • Create identically pathed symbolic links to tape device(s) and disk chunks as those on the primary server. • Modify the $ONCONFIG file received from the primary server. Change DBSERVERNAME, DBSERVERALIASES, and possibly MIRROR. • Install the file. • Set up general Informix environment variables.

Primary Server	*Secondary Server*
	• Initialize secondary and bring it all the way on-line to test access to all base physical devices. Execute an "oninit" command followed by the "onmode -m" command.
	• Make sure the sysmaster database builds.
	• Shut down the instance ("onmode -ky").
	• Change your $INFORMIX-SERVER environment variable to use the network-based instance connection alias.
• Create a level 0 archive ("ontape -s -L 0").	
• Archive the current logical log ("ontape -a").	
• With the instance in on-line mode, initialize the HADR mechanism in this instance and set it to primary mode. To do this, execute the "onmode -d primary secondary_instance" command, where secondary_instance is replaced by the network-protocol-based instance name of the secondary server. The MSGPATH file should reflect this change and contain the following messages: DR: new type = primary, secondary server name = secondary_instance DR: Trying to connect to secondary server ... DR: Cannot connect to secondary server DR: Turned off on primary server	• Perform a physical restore using the archive generated on the primary server ("ontape -p"). Do NOT archive the logical logs when prompted by the command. There are no other archive levels to restore. This will leave the instance in recovery mode, with all dbspaces created, but in an inconsistent state. This is normal. • Initialize the HADR mechanism in this instance and set it to secondary mode. To do this, execute the "onmode -d secondary primary_instance" command, where primary_instance is replaced by the network-protocol-based instance name of the primary server.

Initializing HADR

Primary Server	*Secondary Server*

	• The MSGPATH file should reflect this change and contain the following messages:
	`DR: new type = secondary, primary server name = primary_instance`
	`DR: Trying to connect to primary server ...`

	This step might NOT need to be taken. See the text preceding the table.
	• Perform a logical restore using the logical log archive tape generated on the primary server ("ontape -l"). This will complete the connection process to the primary server. The MSGPATH file should contain the following messages:
	`DR: Secondary server connected`
	`DR: Start failure recovery from tape`
	`DR: Secondary server operational`

• The primary server should show the connection completed. The MSGPATH file should contain the following messages: `DR: Primary server operational`	

You can see quite easily if this type of transfer and action is taking place. In the MSGPATH file on the primary, messages such as the following will be written:

```
DR: Sending log 240, size 1250 pages, 100.0% used
DR: Sending log 241, size 1250 pages, 100.0% used
DR: Sending log 242, size 1250 pages, 100.0% used
DR: Sending log 243, size 1250 pages, 100.0% used
DR: Sending log 244, size 1250 pages, 100.0% used
```

On the secondary server there will be messages like the following, indicating that the logical recovery process has begun:

```
DR: Secondary server connected
DR: Failure recovery from disk in progress ...
Logical Recovery Started.
Start Logical Recovery - Start Log 240, End Log ?
Starting Log Position - 240 0x891a0
```

If the number of logs used on the primary server since HADR was initialized is sufficient to have caused some to be overwritten, a logical recovery from tape will be required. In this case, the "ontape -l" command shown in Table 9-1 will need to be executed against a logical log archive tape generated on the primary server.

Once HADR is initialized, the status lines of both the primary and secondary instances will change to reflect their specific replication mode. Executing an "onstat -" command on the primary will return the following type of reply:

```
INFORMIX-OnLine Version 7.13.UC2 -- On-Line (Prim) -
 - Up 00:26:10 -- 9712 Kbytes
```

The secondary server's status line will have "Sec" in the parentheses.

Recovering After a HADR Failure

The process of recovering from a HADR failure condition will vary depending on the following:

- The value of the DRAUTO configuration parameter
- If the failure was logical in nature (in other words, network-related), the amount of work processed on the primary after the failure condition was declared, the actions of the secondary server (set by DRAUTO), and the amount of work, if any, executed on the secondary server
- If a physical failure occurred, the server that failed and the extent of the failure

In this section, I will attempt to explain all the possible recovery scenarios you might face in the event of a HADR failure condition.

Effect of the DRAUTO Parameter on the Recovery Process

In the "What Happens in a Failure Condition?" section of this chapter, I covered what actions the secondary server will take in the event of a HADR failure condition. Unfortunately, these actions all assume that the primary server suffered a physical failure that forced it off-line. These parameters do not, nor were they intended to, take into account the possibility of a logical or network-related failure. As a result, the type of failure condition that occurs and the value used for the DRAUTO configuration parameter will have an impact on what you do to recover from the failure.

Setting DRAUTO to "off" (0 [zero]) is the safest of the three options in terms of recoverability regardless of the type of failure or the server that fails. It is for this reason that I strongly recommend setting DRAUTO to 0. If the secondary server physically fails, there is no impact on the primary server. If the primary server fails or the failure condition is network-related, the secondary server will just sit there in read-only mode. Once the primary server reconnects, the two servers will automatically resynchronize. If the failure condition was network-related, depending on the amount of work processed on the primary server, you might need to perform a logical restore manually from the logical log archive tapes generated on the primary server to completely recover the secondary server.

If the primary server physically failed and will be down for an unacceptable amount of time, you can force the secondary server out of read-only mode into either standard mode or primary mode by executing the "`onmode -d standard`" or "`onmode -d primary new_secondary_server`" commands, respectively. Once either command is executed, normal data processing activities can begin on that server. You will need to make the necessary application environment variable changes such as $INFORMIX-SERVER or $DBPATH before the applications will connect to this database instance. You might also have to retune the instance to handle the workload if it previously acted as a quiet copy of the primary instance.

Setting DRAUTO to "retain_type" (1 [one]) or "reverse_type" (2 [two]) is very risky unless the network connection between the two servers is absolutely rock solid. I realize that no network is 100 percent bulletproof, and I do not expect complete and total uptime in any networked environment, but you shouldn't connect your replication servers across the main corporate backbone handling the e-mail, DOS-based file and print server chores, and intranet WWW access. This network segment will be busy enough without the added replication traffic. You also don't want to subject the replicated servers to the network throughput degradation that occurs on and off throughout the normal processing day of the corporation, especially if you're using synchronous log transfers.

The biggest risk in setting DRAUTO to either "retain_type" or "reverse_type" is the amount of work that the secondary server will process as the result of a HADR failure condition that is logical or network-based in nature. This is particularly true if the users who used to access the primary server are not in the same physical location as the primary server and the applications they use have been written to automatically reconfigure and connect to the secondary server. For more information on setting up applications to reconfigure automatically, please refer to *Optimizing Informix Applications*, written by Robert D. Schneider and published by Informix Press.

With DRAUTO set to "retain_type," in the event of a logical failure, you will have a situation where there are two primary servers, each thinking the other failed. Since the secondary server assumes the role of being a primary server following a failure condition, it is capable of processing changes to its copy of the database. Once the network connection is reestablished, the reconnection negotiation will fail because each server will try to assert to the other that it has the changes that need to be applied in order to synchronize the servers.

When DRAUTO is set to "reverse_type" and a logical failure occurs, the connection renegotiation will fail because the two servers will demand that the other assume the secondary role and accept the changes being sent to it.

If a physical failure occurs and DRAUTO is set to "retain_type" or "reverse_type," there is almost nothing to worry about. The recovery process is very similar to the HADR initialization process, as will be explained later in this chapter. Recovery from logical failures, on the other hand, will generally be a messy process, as is explained in the next section.

A Step-by-Step Approach to Recovering from HADR Failure Conditions

In this section, I will explain the process you should follow to recover from logical and physical failures. The impact of the DRAUTO configuration parameter on the recovery process will be illustrated as well. As you will see, recovering from a physical failure is easiest to accomplish, regardless of to what the DRAUTO configuration parameter is set. Recovery after a logical failure requires more effort and coordination.

If there is any key factor that should influence the actions you take in recovering from a failure, it would be the disparity in data between the two servers. If too many changes have occurred in the surviving server since the failure condition began, it will be easier and faster to completely reinitialize the server coming back on-line.

How much change is "too much"? That's your decision. Logical recoveries are a slow process. If I am faced with having to use a logical log tape to roll forward logs, I will always reinitialize with a physical restore, then reconnect the servers. Even if I don't have to use a logical log tape because the surviving server was configured with a large number of logs and they still exist on the system, I will be more disposed to reinitialize than to wait for each of the logs to roll forward.

In speaking of physical failures, I'm referring to a condition in which the server as a whole goes down. This could be caused by media failure in a critical dbspace that was not mirrored or a failure in the processing or memory component of the hardware. For the secondary server, any nonmirrored media failure is treated as a failure of a critical dbspace. See the "Disk Drive Issues" section of Chapter 2 for more information on protecting critical dbspaces.

Failures of mirrored media are not considered a HADR failure condition since the mirroring mechanism in the engine or the RAID controller will handle the error condition. At some later time during a scheduled maintenance period, you can then swap out the media and bring the chunks and dbspaces back on-line.

When working with secondary servers in a failure recovery process, remember that you still need to use the network-protocol connection alias as explained in the Tip prior to Table 9-1.

Restarting HADR After a Scheduled Maintenance Period

The process of restarting HADR after a scheduled maintenance period is very simple. To begin with, when you shut both systems down, do the secondary server first followed by the primary server. If work needs to be done on both servers, bring each one on-line, perform the tasks, then shut it back down. If DRAUTO is set to "reverse_type," when the secondary comes up, it will attempt to transition to becoming the primary server. Force the server into standard mode by executing the "`onmode -d standard`" command. Secondary servers operating in "retain_type" mode will also transition to being the primary server. There is no need to force it into standard mode because it will transition back to its proper mode when it reconnects with the primary server after the maintenance period.

When the maintenance work is completed, if DRAUTO is *not* set to "reverse_type," bring the primary server on-line. Once it is up, bring the secondary server up. With DRAUTO set to "off" or "retain_type," the two servers will automatically resynchronize.

If DRAUTO is set to "reverse_type," the HADR process will need to be restarted on the secondary server. In this situation, bring the secondary server on-line first. Execute the "`onmode -d secondary primary_server`" command. Then bring the primary server on-line. There shouldn't be much, if any, logical recovery required between the servers in either situation.

What recovery work does need to be done as a result of reconnecting servers following a maintenance period will not require restoring from a logical log tape. The primary should be able to send the logical log records over the network to the secondary server.

Recovering from a Physical Failure

If unmirrored disk media failed on the secondary server, you have no choice but to reinitialize the secondary server. Recovery from other failures on the secondary server will depend on how out of synch the two servers are. See my general recommendation at the beginning of this section on what to do in this situation.

Primary Server Failure with DRAUTO = 0 or 1   If there was a media failure on the primary server *or* some other failure occurred, the server mode type was set to "retain_type," and a significant amount of change occurred in the secondary server, you'll have to reinitialize the primary server. In this case, follow these steps:

1. Put the secondary server into quiescent mode.
2. Create a level 0 archive and a logical log archive.
3. Shut the secondary server down.
4. Execute a physical restore on the primary server, respond "no" to any prompts to roll forward logical logs.
5. Bring the primary server instance on-line. The MSGPATH file will contain messages indicating that the physical restore completed without a logical restore.
6. Once the primary server is on-line, restart the HADR process by executing the "`onmode -d primary secondary_server`" command.
7. Restart the secondary server.

At this point, the two servers should reestablish their HADR connection and continue working as before the failure.

If some other failure occurred on the primary server and DRAUTO was set to "off" *or* DRAUTO was set to "retain_type and very little change occurred in the secondary server while the primary server was off-line, bring up the primary server and let the HADR mechanism resynchronize the servers, and, if DRAUTO is set to 1 (one), reset the server modes.

Primary Server Failure with DRAUTO = 2   If DRAUTO is set to "reverse_type," you need to decide whether you want to go through the work of restoring the primary server to actually be the primary server. If you selected this option for DRAUTO, you probably don't care which server is primary or secondary. In this case, if the failure was not media-related, and not too much activity has occurred in the secondary server since the failure occurred, simply bring the primary server back on-line. The two servers will reconnect, the primary server will assume its new role as secondary server, and the logical log records will be transferred from the new primary server to the new secondary server.

If the failure was media-related, you'll need to reinitialize the primary server with a physical restore and possibly a logical restore. You'll then need to activate the HADR mechanism on this server and set it to secondary mode by executing the "`onmode -d secondary primary_server`" command. It will come up, connect to the new primary server, receive a transfer of any new logs, and continue operating in its new mode.

Remember to start and maintain the logical log archiving process on the new primary server, rather than on the new secondary server, whenever there is a change in server mode. This is particularly important if the transfer of log information occurs in asynchronous mode (DRINTERVAL >= 0). This will minimize the risk of losing transaction information should the new primary server fail prior to flushing its replication buffer.

If you decide that the location of the primary server is important, the process of switching the servers back is a bit of a pain. You'll need to do the following:

1. Shut the new primary server down to quiescent mode.
2. Create a level 0 archive. If the servers are some distance apart, two archives will be required.
3. Shut the new primary server down.
4. Reinitialize the original primary server by executing a physical restore. Do not restore any logical logs.
5. Bring the original primary server on-line. The MSGPATH file will contain messages that the physical restore completed but the logical restore did not occur.
6. With the original primary server on-line, start the HADR mechanism and set the server back to primary mode by executing the "`onmode -d primary secondary_server`" command.
7. Reinitialize the secondary server by executing a physical restore from the archive created in step 2.

8. Start the HADR mechanism on this server and set it to secondary mode by executing the "`onmode -d secondary primary_server`" command.

The two servers should reestablish the HADR connection and begin working as before the failure.

Recovering from a Logical Failure

Recovery of the secondary server when DRAUTO is set to "off" is similar to the recovery process following a physical failure of the secondary. If a significant amount of work has occurred on the primary server, it might be easier to reinitialize the secondary server than to endure a long logical recovery process.

In this case, shut the secondary server down prior to the restoring the network connection. Otherwise, when the network comes back up the two servers will automatically reconnect, the primary will transfer its logs, and the recovery process will commence. Understand, this is not a bad thing, it just could take a long time to complete depending on the amount of work that needs to be rolled forward.

When DRAUTO is set to "retain_type" or "reverse_type," the key factors to consider in the recovery process are:

- What the applications did when the failure occurred
- How critical it is to preserve any work that might be done on the secondary server during the failure condition

Care must be exercised before restoring the network connection if the applications were written to automatically reconnect to the secondary server should the primary become unavailable. As explained earlier in this section, if both servers are on-line when the network connection is reestablished, each will assert to the other server that it is the primary server. If the applications used by some users reconfigured themselves to use the secondary server because they could not communicate with the primary server, there is a high probability that changes occurred on each server which, in theory, should be reflected back on the other server.

Ultimately, the decision is yours whether the value of those changes is great enough to justify either reprocessing the work on the primary server that was performed on the secondary server during the failure condition, or extracting out the changes from the secondary server's logical logs with the `onlog` utility. While the `onlog` utility itself is easy to use, reading and understanding its output can be quite a challenge. If you elect to read the logs, please refer to the *OnLine Administrator's Guide* that accompanied your distribution of the software for a complete description of how to interpret the header and action codes in the log records. Depending on the number of tables that were affected during the failure condition, the `onlog` utility can be run with flags that extract only one table's information. You can also look at just one user's activity as well.

Whether or not you elect to recreate the data, the secondary server will need to be reinitialized to recover from a logical failure. As a result, it should be shut down prior to reestablishing the network connection. Once the network connection is in place, reinitialize the secondary server by executing a physical restore from an archive created on the primary server. Restart the HADR mechanism by executing the "`onmode -d secondary primary_instance`" command.

HADR and Applications

From an application perspective, the only difference between a primary and a secondary instance is that one is read-only. A smart programmer will use that to the benefit of the application, depending on the log transfer mode used.

Provided the secondary instance is relatively easy to get to, from a network perspective (and it should be anyway), applications could be written such that updates and modifications occur at the primary instance. When a report function is triggered however, the application should close the primary instance and open the secondary instance to gather the data for the report. This could be accomplished through hard coding the instance names into the application, or, preferably, changing the environment in which the application operates.

Obviously, if asynchronous transfer mode is being used with a long DRINTERVAL setting, the data on the secondary server might not be an exact duplicate of the primary's data at any moment in time. This might or might not be important for the report. For example, if the date range for the report covers up to yesterday, using the data on the secondary server for the report will be okay. Changing report functions in applications to gather data from the secondary server will reduce the overall processing load on the primary server, freeing it to process new changes to the data.

In the event of a HADR failure, if the secondary server assumes the role of primary server, simply change the environment variables that control the instance to which the application points and restart the application to continue processing work. Earlier in this chapter, I referred you to another book published by Informix Press where you can get more information on coding an application to do this automatically if it determines that an instance is unavailable.

Summary

High-Availability Data Replication (HADR) is a relatively uncomplicated mechanism to provide fail-over protection for your critical instances. While the configuration requirements and the initialization and restoration process requires meticulous attention, once it is up and running, HADR is relatively maintenance free.

You should understand how the HADR mechanism actually replicates data between instances. You should have a clear understanding of the configuration requirements and the sequence of steps required to initialize HADR. You should understand what the different log transfer modes are, and the impact the timeout and transfer interval configuration parameters can have on the restoration process after a HADR failure condition. You should also have an idea of how you can leverage the existence of the replicated instance in your application environment to reduce the processing overhead on the primary server as well as provide for fail-over coverage.

When implementing HADR, keep the following points in mind:
- HADR should only be used in environments with a highly stable, relatively uncluttered network connection between the servers.
- The servers need to be almost identical with respect to hardware, O/S, and OnLine Dynamic Server release level.

- Synchronous transfer mode should be used to ensure the moment-in-time accuracy of the data stored on the secondary server.
- To eliminate data resynchronization problems when recovering from a network failure condition, the server mode (DRAUTO) should be set to "off."
- In many cases, recovery from a physical or logical failure will require reinitializing of the primary or secondary server. In situations where a physical recovery is not absolutely required, you should consider if the length of time required to execute a logical recovery will be significantly longer than reinitializing and act accordingly.

Coming Up

The saying goes that "Into every life, some rain must fall." Regardless of your prowess at creating or tuning an OnLine Dynamic Server instance, at some moment in time a combination of internal conditions or, more likely, an external condition will occur that will cause the instance to crash. In the next chapter, we'll look at the mechanisms OnLine Dynamic Server uses to maintain the operating integrity of the instance and the data it contains. We'll also look into the mechanism employed to verify the integrity of the instance when it is restarted following a crash and the technical support resources Informix can provide to you.

Chapter 10

Recovering from a Crash

- *What mechanisms does the engine use to prevent crashes?*
- *What does the engine do when restarting after a crash?*
- *What options does Informix Technical Support provide and how can they help?*
- *What should the OnLine or database administrator do after a crash?*

Regardless of your attempts to the contrary, at some moment in time you will be faced with an instance that shuts down abnormally. Perhaps the instance was killed when the physical server failed, or some idiot with root privileges killed an `oninit` process. Perhaps it was the internal "sanity checking" mechanisms of the engine that detected a potential error serious enough to warrant an immediate shutdown. In any case, it's important to know how the engine responds to these conditions and what it does when trying to restart an instance after a crash. This chapter will review all of the more important engine mechanisms designed to prevent corruption from occurring in either the instance structures or the data stored on disk.

By the end of the chapter you should understand the logical and physical mechanisms OnLine Dynamic Server uses to maintain data and operating integrity. You should understand the logical and physical recovery process the engine follows in every instance start-up. You should understand what resources Informix Technical Support can provide to you on an ongoing basis as well as in a crash situation. Finally, you should understand what responsibilities you have in verifying the integrity of the instance and the data it contains after a crash situation, as well as on an ongoing basis.

How Does the Engine Protect Itself?

The OnLine Dynamic Server engine, as you would expect, has a number of mechanisms built into its kernel to protect the logical and physical integrity of the instances it manages and the data they contain. To one degree or another, all have been covered in this book. Let's briefly review what these mechanisms are.

Physical Mechanisms

There are five major mechanisms in OnLine Dynamic Server oriented toward protecting the physical integrity of the system. The first is the archive and restoration system. Some would argue that this does nothing to prevent problems from occurring, and to that extent they are correct. I choose to include it in this discussion because it permits you to recover the system after a catastrophic media failure. This recovery can be a complete physical and logical restore, a physical restore only, dbspace-specific, or moment-in-time-oriented.

The archive and restore mechanism can and should be used to archive the logical changes to the data as recorded in the logical logs. These archives of the logical logs can be used to roll forward changes to the data in a recovery situation, as will be discussed later in this chapter.

This book has primarily been focused on the use of the `ontape` utility as the archive and restoration utility of choice, although Informix does have another archiving utility called `onarchive`. A new API called `onbar` is due to be released shortly which will enhance the granularity of the archiving process and transfer to third-party vendors the burden of media management and automatic scheduling. Refer to Chapter 6, Archiving and Restoring, for more information on this mechanism and why I choose to use the `ontape` utility.

Another mechanism is the ability to mirror disks. The mirroring mechanism provides both a physical and logical benefit to the instance. First, it provides instantaneous fail-over protection of the physical media in the event of a disk crash or other abnormal disk behavior. If the engine receives a disk failure error code, it will automatically take the disk off-line. It will automatically convert the mirror from being a read-only device to the active, updatable device. When the disk is replaced or the symbolic link is changed to point to another chunk of disk space, and mirroring is restarted on that chunk, the mirroring mechanism will automatically resynchronize the primary and mirror copies. Once back in synch, the new primary will assume the role of being the updatable device, and the mirror will resume its original function.

The other benefit derived from the mirroring mechanism comes from the instance's ability to use the mirrored dbspaces to enhance query performance. If parallelism is turned on for the instance, the engine will use the mirror dbspaces along with the primary dbspaces for query processing. This can free up the primary dbspaces to handle actual data manipulation. Obviously, these changes will be made to the mirror dbspaces, but with less of an I/O load directed at them with queries executing against the mirrored copies as well, the primary dbspaces can effect their changes quicker. See Chapter 2, Preparing for Initialization, for more information on disk mirroring.

The third physical mechanism is row-level locking. Depending on the query environment the application sets, or specific SQL statements made, the instance will allocate locks from the lock cache to rows of data. These locks remain in place until released by the application, and are used to prevent data from being altered by a second application while the first application needs information out of that row. Not all database actions require rows to be locked, although actions such as updates or deletes do require locks. Certain types of queries, such as "`for update`" cursors, require locking; others do not. See Chapter 5, Building a Database Environment, for more information about locking modes and isolation levels.

The fourth mechanism was discussed in the previous chapter—High-Availability Data Replication (HADR). While this does not prevent problems from occurring within an instance or even a physical server, HADR does protect the ability to access data in the event of a physical or network failure. By transferring logical log records of changes made to databases in a "logged" mode, a secondary database instance on another physical server can be created and maintained as an exact copy of the original instance. In the event of a failure, the surviving server can be configured to assume the role of the primary, or "updatable," server, allowing applications to continue processing work.

The last physical mechanism I will cover at this time is internal assertion checks. This is a hybrid of logical and physical checks made periodically on a number of conditions within the instance. I call them "system sanity checks." During these checks, existing values of certain key components in shared memory and on disk are evaluated against standards coded into the engine logic for the types of operations actively being processed in the instance. If there is a discrepancy, error messages are written out to the MSGPATH file and, if serious enough, the instance is shut down after dumping the core files requested during instance initialization.

Assertion errors of any degree should always be cause for action on your part. An abnormal processing condition, as explained in the error message itself, exists within the instance and must be rectified immediately. Some actions you can take to isolate and then correct data-related errors that could cause assertion failures will be covered later in this chapter. See Chapter 3, Initializing an OnLine Dynamic Server Instance, for more information on configuring core dump parameters.

Logical Mechanisms

The logical mechanisms OnLine Dynamic Server uses are designed to protect the integrity of the data within a transaction, but not necessarily to prevent failures from occurring. These mechanisms include columnar and index-based constraints. These types of constraints are used to ensure that data entered, modified, or deleted meet predefined conditions set up by the database administrator.

At a columnar level, the conditions are either a range of acceptable values, such as "`greater than 0 and less than 10`" or "`greater than or equal to 5 times the value of column xyz`," or, in the case of a "`not null`" constraint, that the column has to contain a value.

Index-based constraints enforce relationships between data elements. This type of constraint is used to ensure the uniqueness of rows within a single table or the parent-child relationship of rows in multiple tables. See Chapter 5, Building a Database Environment, for more information on creating constraints.

Another logical mechanism is the combination of triggers and stored procedures. Stored procedures are data-oriented instructions that are stored in, and executed by, the OnLine Dynamic Server engine. Because stored procedures are stored in precompiled and pre-optimized form in the system catalog tables of a database, a stored procedure is database- and instance-specific in its orientation. This does not mean, however, that a stored procedure cannot execute commands that affect rows in another database. The table name just has to be correctly identified, as explained in the "Introduction to Distributed Transactions" section of Chapter 11, Distributed Transactions.

Stored procedures can be used to eliminate duplication of effort when coding applications or to enforce consistency in actions executed against the database. For example, complex queries or queries that require specialized manipulation of the data, such as

```
select column_1, (2 * (column_2 / (column_9 * 4.5)))
    from table where . .
```

can be written and stored in the database and used like program functions. All applications which need to perform that query simply call the stored procedure and receive back the results.

Users benefit from implementing stored procedures in a data processing environment because they know they have the correct internal calculations occurring in the application's query. Using the previous example, should the business conditions require the calculation to change, modifying the copy in the database ensures that all applications are instantly updated rather than having to find and modify each application where the query is used.

Similarly, if certain data manipulation routines should occur to data stored in the database because of other database actions, the code for the routine can be written once, stored in the database, and automatically executed by all applications rather than having to modify each application to insert the routine.

Triggers, as the name implies, become active and execute their code because their "triggering action" occurs. Most of the time, a trigger calls a stored procedure that proceeds to do whatever work it has written in it.

Triggers can be placed on tables or columns so that if data is inserted into or deleted from the table, or modifications are made to a specific column within the table, the trigger executes. For example, a trigger could be placed on a table such that any time a row is inserted into the table, a row is entered into another table with aggregates of some of the columns of the row inserted into the first table. For more information on using triggers and stored procedures, please refer to *Informix Stored Procedure Programming* by Michael Gonzales, also published by Informix Press.

The combination of constraints, triggers, and stored procedures enable you to enforce what are called "business rules." These rules are derived from the specific business you are in and include, as previously shown, the ability to specify acceptable values within data elements, uniqueness of data, and relationships between various data elements.

Business logic, such as how to calculate adjusted gross sales, is considered part of the "business rules" as well. These queries, automated actions, and relationship checking can be built into the database and executed from within the instance. The end result of placing and enforcing "business rules" in the database is smaller, easier-to-maintain applications.

The third logical mechanism is query isolation levels. An isolation level determines the degree to which your queried data can be affected by other database actions that require the same data. Enforced by the use of shared or exclusive locks, the isolation level of a query can be used to prevent other applications from updating or even reading data you requested for your application session. The careful use of isolation levels in applications can enhance the security and integrity of the database as well as have an impact on the overall throughput and performance of the instance. For more information on isolation levels, see the "Concurrency and Isolation Levels" section of Chapter 5.

The last logical mechanism I will cover is transaction logging. Databases in "logged" mode record changes made to data in the physical and logical logs. While these two logs are physical entities, the function they perform is purely logical in nature. The two sets of logs work in concert to record images of data prior to change, as well as the changes that occurred to the data and the commands issued to make changes. These logs are what allow the engine to reverse a series of changes made to data that have to successfully complete as a single unit of work should one of the changes fail. These logs are so critical to the operation of the instance that if an engine assertion check indicates that a problem could exist with either log structure, the instance will be shut down immediately.

Many of these physical and logical mechanisms are used whenever an instance is brought from an off-line mode through the start-up procedure to being fully active. The fact that the instance crashed beforehand only means some of these mechanisms will have to do more work. In the next section, we'll look at what Informix calls the "fast recovery" process and what the engine does when restarting an instance following a crash.

The Fast Recovery Process

Although it doesn't happen very often in OnLine Dynamic Server, you are now faced with a situation where one of your instances has died unexpectedly. Perhaps there are messages in the MSGPATH file which indicate what the failure condition was that caused the instance to shut down. Perhaps the server itself suffered some sort of hardware failure. Regardless of the reasons behind the failure, you've got to turn the instance back on, but your stomach starts to churn as questions begin to roll around in your head. What is going to happen inside the instance as it restarts? What sort of protection is there so that data will not be corrupted? Will the instance automatically correct whatever the problem was that caused it to fail? Will the instance even come back on-line?

Because of the wide range of possible conditions that might affect an OnLine Dynamic Server instance and cause it to fail, it's impossible to say categorically what will or will not happen to an instance being restarted after a failure. There are, however, some general statements that can be made. The rest depends on what happens when the engine executes what is called the "fast recovery" process.

First of all, let me say that for as long as I have been using OnLine Dynamic Server, I have only run into one or two situations where, apart from server hardware problems or application problems, an instance went down unexpectedly. These situations resulted from known bugs in the engine with the PDQ mechanism, and workarounds were easily devised. The server, if properly maintained, is remarkably stable and getting even better with each new release.

You should rest assured that unless there is media failure or unprotected disks, data within the instance is guaranteed to be "good" up to, and including, the moment in time the last checkpoint occurred. Exactly what a checkpoint is and how it works will be explained shortly. As you will understand later in this chapter, depending on the logging mode employed for databases in the instance, this "known good" period can be extended closer to the moment of failure than just the last checkpoint.

The engine does have some limited capacity to repair or avoid problems that might cause an instance to fail, but on the whole, unless there was some sort of hardware failure on the server that affected the instance, there will be work required on your part to restart an instance following a failure. What that work will be depends on what caused the instance to fail. It might be as simple as retuning shared memory or tweaking PDQ parameters. It could require dropping a dbspace, recreating it, and restoring the dbspace from tape.

If the engine crashes an instance, it will usually enter a reason why the instance was shut down in the MSGPATH file. Depending on the error, or your experience in dealing with the engine, you can either work on the problem yourself or call Informix's technical support department for assistance. The technical support services Informix provides will be covered later in this chapter.

The primary mechanism OnLine Dynamic Server uses when restarting an instance is called "fast recovery." Before I can explain what the fast recovery process is, and how it operates, it is important that you understand what a checkpoint is.

What Is a Checkpoint?

When checkpoints occur, modified data in the instance's shared memory is written to disk. At the completion of a checkpoint, the database is said to be in a "consistent" state. Every change is guaranteed to be successfully stored to disk, and there are no committed data changes left in shared memory buffers.

A checkpoint occurs at more or less regular intervals whenever there are active user threads in the instance. There are several factors that can cause a checkpoint to occur:

- An amount of time equal to CKPTINTVL seconds elapses without a checkpoint occurring.
- 75 percent of the physical log becomes full.
- An "`onmode -c`" command is executed by the OnLine administrator forcing a checkpoint to occur.
- Certain database or instance administrative commands, such as dropping a chunk or changing the size or location of the physical log, are issued.

The checkpoint process itself is not too complicated, as shown in Table 10-1.

At the end of the checkpoint, the logical and physical log buffers are empty, as is the physical log itself. Needless to say, the checkpoint process is considered a critical event within the instance. If it is interrupted, the instance will immediately shut down.

Under normal circumstances, when an instance is brought from an on-line mode to a quiescent or off-line mode, a checkpoint occurs. The checkpoint occurs regardless of the shutdown command issued to the instance; this includes the "`onmode -ky`" or "instant die" command. A checkpoint occurs to make sure all committed transactions are written to disk and the database is in a consistent state, with all the shared memory buffers flushed and the physical log cleared out.

If the instance were to die unexpectedly, there would most likely be information left in the physical log that didn't get flushed out to the logical logs as described in Table 10-1. How much data will be in the physical log depends on the database logging modes employed within the instance.

In the "Logging Modes" section of Chapter 5, I explained the logging modes OnLine Dynamic Server supports. These modes can be divided into two general categories, nonlogged and logged. The nonlogged mode database writes very little information into the logical logs, just DDL statements such as "`create table`" or "`drop index`." Logged mode databases, on the other hand, write out most DML statements and the changes to rows affected by the command as well as DDL statements into the logical logs.

Table 10-1 The checkpoint process.

Action	Additional Description
Some user threads are suspended from accessing the database.	Threads whose state indicate that they could alter data (i.e., "`for update`" cursors) are suspended from accessing or processing data in the instance for the duration of the checkpoint.
A checkpoint timestamp is issued.	
The physical log buffer is flushed to the physical log on disk.	Before images of data that has been changed are written from the active physical log buffer in shared memory to the physical log on disk. There are two physical log buffers in the instance's shared memory. When the flush is completed, the other buffer becomes the active buffer.
Modified data from the buffer pool is written to disk.	New or modified data is written from the buffer pool in the resident portion of shared memory out to the appropriate tables on disk. This occurs as a chunk write—the most effective of the three write types.
A checkpoint message is prepared and stored in the logical log buffers.	
The physical log is written into the logical log buffer.	All of the before images stored in the physical log are written into the active logical log buffer in shared memory.
The logical log buffer is written to the logical log itself on disk.	There are three logical log buffers. When the active buffer has finished writing to disk, one of the other logical log buffers becomes active.

continued

Action	Additional Description
Checkpoint information is entered in the MSGPATH file; information in the reserved pages of the instance are updated.	A message indicating that a checkpoint occurred and the length of time it took to complete is written to the MSGPATH file. Information such as the checkpoint timestamp, physical log position, active logical log and location, and chunk location is written to the PAGE_1CKPT and PAGE_2CKPT reserved pages in the rootdbs of the instance.
Suspended threads are allowed to continue processing.	

Within the logged modes, the unbuffered and mode ANSI logging modes make little use of the physical and logical log buffers. Every time a transaction is committed, including implicit transactions, the buffers are flushed to the physical log and the active logical log on disk. While there is a performance and throughput hit to support this amount of I/O, there is a corresponding increase in transactional security in the event of a failure. This mode enables you to move the "known good" condition I spoke of earlier closer to the moment of failure than the last checkpoint. Each transaction close puts information into the logs that can be used during the recovery procedure.

Buffered logging mode, as the name implies, uses the logical log and physical log buffers to store data rather than immediately writing to the logs on disk at the close of a transaction. Greater instance throughput can be achieved from using buffered logging but it is a less secure transaction environment because if the instance were to die unexpectedly, transaction information stored in the physical and logical log buffers will be lost. Your business environment and transaction requirements will determine which mode is most appropriate for your instances. Now let's look at how the fast recovery process operates.

What Is the Fast Recovery Process?

Fast recovery is the term given to a series of processes that attempt to verify the physical and logical integrity of the instance and the data it maintains when an instance is stated. There are two general phases of the fast recovery process. The first phase checks for the existence and condition of all the physical devices in the instance. The second phase of the fast recovery process verifies the physical and logical integrity of the data following the last recorded checkpoint. The OnLine Dynamic Server engine always executes a fast recovery whenever an instance is restarted, regardless of the reason the instance was shut down. As you will see in a moment, depending on the condition of one element within the OnLine Dynamic Server instance, the fast recovery process will either continue or be aborted after checking the physical devices.

The First Phase—Verifying the Physical Integrity of the Instance

In the first phase of the fast recovery process, a number of the instance's vps are started including the CPU and AIO vps. Even if KAIO is enabled, at least one AIO vp should be configured during the instance initialization process in order to write information to the logical logs. The fast recovery process reads the $ONCONFIG file for the instance and verifies the existence of, and the permissions on, the initial physical devices. If the ROOTDBS (and its mirror if one exists), TAPEDEV, and LTAPEDEV devices exist and have the correct permissions, the engine attempts to read the reserved pages in the rootdbs. If there is a problem with any of these devices, except for the rootdbs mirror, the fast recovery process will abort completely. A restore from tape will probably be required to restart the instance if the problem is in the rootdbs and it is not mirrored.

As Figure 7-12 in Chapter 7, Monitoring the Instance, illustrated, every physical device used by the instance is listed in the reserved pages in the rootdbs. The engine will check the existence of, and the permissions on, each of those devices. If mirroring is enabled, mirror devices are checked to make sure that they exist and are synchronized with the primary device. If there is a problem with either side of a mirror pair, that side will be declared down and the other side will assume the role of primary device. If both sides have a problem, the ONDBSPACEDOWN configuration parameter will determine what actions are taken.

The physical log is checked as well as each logical log to make sure they are 100 percent intact and functional, and that there is no corruption in any of them. Should any of these logs be unavailable, or corruption is found, the instance start-up will immediately abort. Because of the critical nature of these logs, should this type of condition exist, a restore from tape will be required to restart the instance.

Once all the physical devices have been checked and their general integrity verified, the fast recovery process allocates the instance's shared memory according to the offset set by the SERVERNUM configuration parameter. If that range of memory is already occupied, perhaps with a memory image from before the instance crashed, the fast recovery process will abort completely. You will need to deallocate the memory in that range in order to proceed. Otherwise, each portion of shared memory is allocated the amount of memory set by the various configuration parameters in the $ONCONFIG file, and the instance begins the second phase of the fast recovery process.

The Second Phase—Verifying the Logical Integrity of the Data

In the second phase of the fast recovery process, the physical and logical log records are used to verify that the data in the instance is logically consistent. The work performed in this phase of the fast recovery process is accomplished by a special set of "off-line" recovery threads executing on the various instance vps. The number of these threads spawned was set during instance initialization by the OFF_RECVRY_THREADS configuration parameter on the **Parameters:Initialize:perFormance** onmonitor screen.

By now you should understand that at the completion of a checkpoint, there is a complete synchronization between what is recorded on disk and what existed in memory. Barring corruption in the physical media, Informix guarantees the data to be there on disk in its checkpointed form. As work continues to be processed in the instance following a checkpoint, the logical log and physical log buffers begin to refill with data that will get flushed to the logs on disk when appropriate.

As explained in the "What Is a Checkpoint?" section, the logging mode of the databases in the instance will determine how often these buffer flushes occur. For the purpose of discussion in this chapter, let's assume all the databases in the instance are using unbuffered logging, so the flushes occur at the end of each transaction. This means more transaction data will be written in the physical and logical logs for the period of time between checkpoints. It would be a rare occurrence for an instance to fail so close to the completion of a checkpoint that a transaction of some sort wouldn't have committed (or rolled back) and caused transaction information to be recorded in the physical and logical logs. The existence of transaction information in the physical log controls whether or not the second phase of the fast recovery process is executed, or if it is bypassed and the instance brought to the requested operating mode.

During the verification of the physical devices in the first phase of the fast recovery process, the existence and condition of the physical log is checked. During this procedure, several flags are checked to determine whether or not data has been written to the log that has not passed through a checkpoint procedure. If the physical log is empty, the fast recovery process knows that a checkpoint occurred prior to taking the instance off-line and, as a result, the data in the instance was in a consistent state. The existence of "uncheckpointed" data in the physical log indicates that a checkpoint did not occur, that the instance did not close down gracefully, and, as a result, that the second phase of the fast recovery process needs to be executed.

While there might be complications arising from transactions that span across more than one instance, also known as "distributed transactions," assuming there are no other conditions preventing the second phase from completing, the data verification process consists of the four basic steps shown in Table 10-2.

It is during this phase of the fast recovery process that you'll see what I call the "army of marching dots" if you restart the instance manually from the `onmonitor` utility. As the logical log records are being processed, a period is echoed to the screen. I do not know if this represents the completion of a transaction record or not, but it does let you know something is happening inside the instance.

Table 10-2 The four steps of the data recovery phase of fast recovery.

1. All the before images of data in the physical log are written back to disk. Since the physical log only contains data written to it since the last recorded checkpoint, this will reverse any work that occurred since the checkpoint. It also returns the database back to the last known point of consistency where data was guaranteed to be in a "known good" state.

2. The current logical log is scanned to find the last recorded checkpoint. The timestamp and location of this checkpoint was written into the reserved pages in the rootdbs of the instance as part of the checkpoint process shown in Table 10-1

3. Committed changes to the databases recorded in the logical logs after the last checkpoint are rolled forward in the databases.
   If a commit record is read for a transaction opened prior to the last checkpoint, the recovery process will find the beginning of that transaction in the logical logs and scan through that transaction to make sure all the changes listed in the log exist on disk. Since a logical log cannot be written over if it contains an uncommitted transaction, you are guaranteed that the fast recovery process will be able to find the beginning of the transaction in the logical logs on disk.

4. Open transactions are rolled back, and records documenting that action are written into the logical log if a commit record is not found in the active logical log. This includes transactions opened prior to the last checkpoint. If a commit record cannot be found in the logical log records prior to the failure, the transaction must be rolled back to guarantee the integrity of the transaction regardless of the number of checkpoints that occurred while the transaction was being processed.

Any work done as a result of this phase of the fast recovery process, such as rolling back a transaction, is recorded in the logical log. This is another reason to keep the LTXHWM and LTXEHWM configuration parameters set as I recommended in the "Shared Memory" section of Chapter 1. Depending on the size of an uncommitted transaction that opened prior to the last checkpoint, there could be a lot of rollback records to write into the logical logs. If there is not enough logical log space to record the initial changes plus the rollback messages, instance startup will fail again. In restarting, the fast recovery will again attempt to recommit or roll back transactions, but will encounter the same problem with the logical logs and fail. In this situation, your only safe recourse to get the instance back is to restore from an archive tape.

As I will explain in the next major section of this chapter, the Informix technical support department can dial into your machine and modify parameters within the instance so that the instance will come on-line, but the integrity of any open transaction will be completely compromised. It would then be your responsibility to find, and either rollback or complete, all transactions manually to restore the logical integrity of the instance.

Without a doubt, this would be a tedious and time-consuming process to successfully complete. Because of the recovery work that would be required, I strongly recommend against taking this course of action. Take the "ounce of prevention" and tune your logical log parameters correctly so you don't have to suffer the "pound of cure."

At the successful conclusion of this phase of the fast recovery process, the data in the databases will be in a "known good" state. All committed transactions will have been verified, and all data affected by uncommitted transactions will be restored back to its original condition. The fast recovery process will spawn the remaining vps required for network-based communication and other features within the instance, and transition the instance to the operating mode requested. The fast recovery process will have successfully completed, yielding an operational instance.

There are failure conditions that will require input and direction from the technical support department at Informix to analyze or recover from. The various support options Informix provides to its customers are explained in the next section.

Informix Technical Support Options

Although your degree of experience with the OnLine Dynamic Server product will determine how often this happens, situations will arise that require you to contact Informix's technical support department. Informix, like any other large vendor, has a large telephone technical support service program that literally spans the world. Headquartered in Lenexa, Kansas, there are additional sites in London, Singapore, Australia, Hong Kong, India, Japan, the People's Republic of China, and Thailand, as well as throughout Europe to service Informix customers in those areas of the world. The purpose of this organization is to provide installation assistance, general product support, and advanced product support for all of Informix's products. The staffing sizes of the various support offices around the world vary so not all services are available in each office.

As Informix has grown in the last five or so years, this department has experienced a tremendous amount of change and growth itself. No other organization has experienced as many growing pains as a result of the ever increasing market share Informix has been garnering than this department. Even Informix will admit that for a long period of time, their support organization was not up to the task of dealing with the influx of new customers and their need for accurate information to solve problems with Informix's increasingly more complex software. I think I can honestly say, to their credit, that since 1995 the quality of the service received from the Informix support organization has increased significantly. Unfortunately for them, they generally don't get the recognition they deserve from the user community for the improvements they have made.

In preparation for writing this chapter of the book, I spoke with Mr. Keith Brown, Manager of Technical Support for Informix Software. He mentioned that Informix has launched a number of programs and initiatives internally to increase the quality and accuracy of the support calls handled in the United States as well in the international support centers. Informix's goal is to achieve a similar level of technical skills and customer support at all their locations worldwide. The breadth of these goals range from having the initial support call answered within 60 seconds to the average length of time required to resolve and close support issues. He indicated that their job in supporting customers has been getting easier with the significant improvement in product quality that has been occurring since mid-1995.

When you initially purchase Informix products, you can purchase a support contract from Informix for the software. Pricing for support is usually fixed at some percentage of the list price for the software product being purchased. Generally, this cost falls between 15 to 18 percent of the total user license cost for the toll-free telephone support option. Normally, support contracts are renewed annually, although multiyear contracts can be negotiated through your Informix sales representative. Support can be purchased after the initial product purchase, but there is often an increased cost to doing so. Contact your Informix sales representative for more information about purchasing a support contract following the software purchase.

Informix offers several different levels of support to choose from, as illustrated in Table 10-3. The two basic levels, Assurance and OpenLine, both allow you to receive free upgrades of your software within the same release level. Upgrading to a new release level (for example, from OnLine 5.x to OnLine Dynamic Server version 7.x) would require an upgrade fee based on the number of user licenses for the new version. All the support options offer the ability to access the Informix TechInfo Center on the Informix World Wide Web server, or to receive a CD-ROM on a monthly basis with a compilation of the entire Informix WWW site. Some options also provide a subscription to *TechNotes*, the quarterly technical publication from Informix, free training classes, site visits by support personnel, and an opportunity to take one of the Informix Certified Professional examinations. Please see Appendix A, Other Informix Resources, for more information about the TechNotes publication and other Informix-related publications.

There are several options that can be to added to the OpenLine and Regency support options. These include:

- 24x7 Support—A special account code and after-hours phone number is provided to reach Informix support engineers by phone any time of the day or night, including holidays. This service is for emergency down system recovery only and was expanded in July 1996 with the launch of the "Follow-the-Sun" (FTS) program. The FTS program is explained in greater detail in the "International Support Group" section of this chapter.
- After-Hours Support—Only available if purchased in advance, this option provides extended support coverage for designated periods of time beyond normal business hours. Typically this coverage is used for conversion periods when, for example, a transition is being made from one engine family to another.
- On-Site Account Management—A dedicated, on-site technical support engineer is provided as the first point of contact to resolve problems and consult on database and application design issues.

Table 10–3 General Informix technical support options.

Option Name	General Description
Assurance	Formerly known as "Update Only" support, this option allows you to order maintenance upgrades within the same version level free of charge. For an additional charge, you can purchase a subscription to the TechInfo WWW service and/or the monthly CD-ROM.
OpenLine	Formerly known as "Standard Support," this option gives you the ability to call the Informix Technical Support Center for assistance in solving problems. Depending on the conditions causing the problem or the severity of the problem itself, there are several levels of support engineers that can be brought to bear in resolving the issue. *TechNotes* and TechInfo center access are included with this option. Additional services, such as 24x7 or After-Hours coverage, can be purchased as extensions to this support option. These additional service options were explained earlier in this section.
Regency Services	Regency support is a premium upgrade to the OpenLine support option. It is for those environments needing support case management or a dedicated point of contact for technical support for one or more major, mission-critical applications or environments. There are three levels of Regency support available: • Tier 1—provides support case management. The status of, and problem-solving activity regarding, cases opened with the OpenLine engineers is monitored and reported on regularly. The Regency support representative advocates on your behalf with the support organization to provide the necessary physical environments to replicate error conditions and to bring in whatever resources are required to solve the problem. This support tier is restricted to one environment or project.

continued

Option Name	General Description
	• Tier 2—extends the case management process to multiple environments or projects. In addition, one week of on-site consulting time from Informix's consulting division is provided along with a single seat admission to two regularly scheduled Informix training classes and one free Certified Professional examination.
	• Tier 3—At this level, Regency support representatives only handle two accounts, allowing them to provide more hands-on case management and case resolution support for a large number of environments and projects within the account. Additional training course admissions are included, along with two Certified Professional examinations and two weeks of on-site consulting time from Informix's consulting division. Activity reports on open cases are available as needed in a private, password-protected section of the Informix WWW site.
Enterprise Support	The ultimate in hands-on support, the Enterprise Support option provides a dedicated, on-site support engineer. This individual can act as both a technical lead to maximize the enterprise's use of Informix products in development projects as well as the primary point of contact for all technical support issues. A Support Manager from the Lenexa facility or the closest full-service International Support Center is also assigned to the account to assist in the strategic planning of applications and processes. Their job is to ensure compatibility with and successful implementation of Informix products.

Additional services such as regular engine monitoring, archive and recovery planning, security analysis, and access to the product development organization for problem resolution is included. Options such as 24x7 support, admission to training classes, and Certified Professional examinations are also included with this option. |

The Informix Support Organization

According to Mr. Brown, the Informix technical support organization is divided into three major groups, Front Line, Advanced Support, and International Support. Not all support centers around the world are staffed with a full complement of Front Line and/or Advanced Support engineers. Some support centers provide more specific types of services, and this will affect the number and type of support engineers who work there.

The Front Line Group

The Front Line support group answer the phones in technical support centers around the world. According to Mr. Brown, one of the keys to Informix's success in improving the overall quality of its support organization is the quality of people they have been hiring to fill these positions. "Several years ago," he said, "we couldn't even find people who knew what Informix was. Today we often hire people who not only know what our products are but have used them."

Those hired as Front Line engineers must first take, and pass, classes on the Standard Engine product, general SQL, ESQL, and client/server connectivity issues. If the person will be supporting the OnLine product, they take additional classes on that product.

After completing these courses, the person is then allowed to work on the phones under the direction of a more experienced engineer. Over time an additional four or five more classes must be taken in more specialized areas of the product they are supporting. These classes are intertwined with the practical, hands-on experience gained from talking with customers.

Each Front Line engineer spends about four and a half hours a day on the phone answering calls followed by three and a half hours of research and problem solving on unresolved cases. According to Mr. Brown, most of the cases these engineers handle on a daily basis concern assertion failures and index-related problems.

Front Line engineers have available to them what Informix calls their "KnowledgeBase," a comprehensive history of all support calls and their resolution. This database can be searched intelligently for cases or situations similar to the case the engineer is working on to find bug reports, recommended resolutions, and/or workarounds. If this is not enough, there are standard test machines set up in each support center that mirror about 80 percent of the installed base of Informix products. Other servers, operating system releases, and Informix product releases can be loaded to replicate the problem and solve it if the priority of the call warrants.

According to Mr. Brown, about 70 percent of the support calls logged during the day are resolved that same day. Of the 30 percent that remain unsolved after the first day, most are solved within four working days.

The Advanced Support Group

The Advanced Support group is made up of individuals who, for the most part, have progressed up from the Front Line support group. Individuals in the Advanced Support group have shown a desire to dig into the technology and really learn how to use and fix it. In general practice, the Advanced Support group handles cases that have been passed to them from the Front Line group because of technical difficulty or the political sensitivity surrounding the technology or the customer. Typically, these cases involve long setup times to replicate the physical environment for analysis and resolution of the problem, or are critical to the success of the customer's business.

The Advanced Support group typically deals with chunks being marked down, chunks that were dropped but the instance still indicates they exist, or databases that were dropped but still show up. The more difficult assertion failure cases the Front Line receives are passed on to this level of support for analysis and resolution.

One special team within the Advanced Support group is what I call the "911 team." This group only handles production OnLine instances that have crashed and will not come back up. This group has at its disposal a number of utilities it can use to alter shared memory or reserved page settings to allow the instance to come up.

Because these engineers must dial into the affected machines to execute these utilities and gather information to analyze the cause of the failure, a "DialUp Access and Confidentiality Agreement" must be signed by an officer of the customer's company and returned to Informix. This agreement releases Informix from any liability in accessing the system, and indicates that they will make a best effort to resolve the problem but do not guarantee a resolution to it.

If you did not get a DialUp Access and Confidentiality Agreement when you purchased your maintenance agreement, I would strongly recommend you contact the Informix customer service department and ask for one. Have it signed and return it to Informix to be placed in your support file. In the event you ever need to have an engineer dial into your system to work on a down production instance, having this agreement in place will save you precious time in what will undoubtedly be a stressful situation.

Their use of these utilities does *not* mean the condition that caused the problem to occur in the first place is resolved, just that the instance will come up, allowing you to try to repair any damage done and to verify the logical integrity of the data if transactions were partially aborted.

The International Support Group

The International Support group is a select group of highly technically oriented individuals who function in the role of "training the trainers." Their job is to ensure that the level and quality of support given to customers is consistent across all support centers around the world. The people in this group spend significant amounts of time on site at all the support centers around the world, training the staff there on Informix's products and the logistical processes used to support customers.

In July 1996, this group participated in the launch of the "Follow-the-Sun" (FTS) support program. FTS is a worldwide extension to the 24x7 support option available to OpenLine and higher support options.

Previous to the FTS program, 24x7 customers calling for support on an after-hours down system situation had to wait for an after-hours support engineer to be contacted by beeper before receiving support with their problem. With FTS, these support calls are automatically routed to Advanced Support engineers in the Lenexa, London, or Singapore support centers, depending on the local time of day and who can immediately begin working on the problem. In my opinion, the FTS program is a significant improvement in Informix's efforts to support enterprise-wide, mission-critical applications for small or large customers.

How You Can Help Informix's Technical Support Group

If you've ever had someone call you to say that they're having problems with an application, or accessing an instance, you know how frustrating it can be trying to resolve the problem—particularly if the person doesn't know what's wrong other than that it just doesn't seem to work! I hope, in some small measure, that experiences such as these will enable you to have some empathy for those working in the Front Line support group.

All the Front Line support group does, all day long, is listen to people complain about products or features that don't work or appear not to be working. Sometimes those calling are not too polite or considerate when talking with these engineers. So what does this have to do with you and your calls to the Informix support group? According to Mr. Brown, there are several things you can do that will help the support group help you better:

- Plan for failures. Realize that no software product is without some sort of a bug or error in its logic that will manifest itself somehow at some time.
- Gather information. Knowing what was going on in the instance or with the application is as important as what the symptoms of the failure are. In OnLine Dynamic Server versions 7.12 and earlier, the $AFDEBUG environment variable had to be set in the root or informix environment prior to its starting the instance. With OnLine Dynamic Server versions 7.13 and later, this can be set on the fly to stall the instance rather than have it crash. If a failure condition occurs and the instance is stalled, you can run stack traces and other diagnostic utilities to see what is happening in the instance as well as the O/S.
- Enable the shared memory dump configuration parameters that are appropriate for your version of the O/S. Make sure the file system the files will be dumped into is large enough to hold the files. Remember that some dumps will include a complete copy of the instance's shared memory—whatever size it is configured to be. This information might be needed for more detailed analytical study by support engineers. Without these dumps, the conditions causing the failure to occur may not be found.

- Be prepared to experience the failure again as the technical support group works with you to analyze the failure conditions and causes.

- Be kind to those on the phone. The old analogy about using honey or vinegar to attract the bee certainly applies here. How would you want to be treated if the situation were reversed and someone was calling you?

Mr. Brown said that the most important thing a customer can do is be willing to help themselves. Those who are willing to do a little work will, through the process of working with the support group better, understand the product and how it works and learn how to support themselves. In turn, when you do have to call Informix's technical support group, you'll be able to provide them with a clearer analysis of what happened, leading to a quicker resolution of the problem.

Responsibilities of the Administrator Following a Crash

Just as any number of environmental or functional conditions can cause an instance to crash, the work you will be required to perform following a crash will vary. If there was physical failure in the server, that component will need to be replaced. If the failure was network-oriented and High-Availability Data Replication (HADR) was in use, depending on the replication mode, one of the servers might have to be reinitialized. If assertion failures occurred, the place and cause of the failure will guide you toward the work you will need to perform to fix the problem once the instance is back on-line.

The bottom line, as you are well aware, is that you are ultimately responsible for the physical and logical integrity, and security, of your data. The steps you take following a failure need to address those responsibilities. Some of the tasks you might execute could be:

- Create a level 0 archive so you have a copy of the instance to fall back on in the event your efforts to find and resolve data problems lead to unforeseen consequences.

- Have the users review all work they executed five to ten minutes prior to the failure. Make sure the data entered or modified has not changed. Carefully investigate any situation where this is not the case.
- If the problem was caused by an application, assist in redesigning the application, and Q & A the SQL or other commands that interact directly with the instance.
- If the instance is operating without mirroring, set up mirrors on the rootdbs and the dbspace(s) containing the physical and logical logs.
- Check the instance's reserved pages for consistency by executing an "`oncheck -pr`" command. This should be the first step following any type of instance or system failure.
- Check and verify the database management tables, also known as the "system catalogs," for each database in the instance by executing an "`oncheck -cc dbname`" command. If you cannot run this immediately following a failure, it should be run as soon as possible during a quiet or maintenance period to make sure the catalog tables are completely intact. Using the "`-pc`" flag will display the results of the command as it runs.
- Check the instance's use of disk space by executing an "`oncheck -pe`" command. This will ensure that all the free pages within the chunks and dbspaces are properly accounted for and the logical boundaries of each disk chunk within the instance is intact.
- Check the index pages for the affected tables, or better yet the entire instance, by executing an "`oncheck -cI`" command. This is a more intensive check than that done using the lowercase "`i`," and it takes more time to complete, because the data to which the index points is checked and verified. Unless you have an enormous number of indexes or extremely large tables, the time required to run this check following a failure is, in my opinion, worth it. If the command reports back that a problem exists with an index, I recommend dropping and recreating the index rather than letting the `oncheck` utility attempt to fix it. To see the results of the command displayed as it runs, use the "`-pK`" flags instead.
- Depending on the type and severity of the failure, and the size of the databases the instance contains, it might be worthwhile to check the data stored on disk by executing an

"`oncheck -cd`" command. This will scan the non-BLOBspace data pages and check their integrity. Again, depending on the amount of time you have to run integrity checks following a failure, run this check against the most important tables in the affected databases by executing the "`oncheck -cd dbname.tablename`" command. Follow this up with a more intensive check against all tables in all databases in the instance during a maintenance period. If your environment includes BLOBs stored in BLOBpages, and you want to include them in your check, use the capital "D" flag instead of the lower-case "d."

Summary

I realize that very little "hard" information was given in this chapter, as compared to Chapter 3, for example. There are so many physical and logical conditions that could affect an OnLine Dynamic Server instance, and possibly cause it to fail, that it is impossible to design a single, one-size-fits-all scenario for recovering from a crash.

You should, however, understand the various logical and physical mechanisms the OnLine Dynamic Server engine uses to protect against data or general instance corruption. You should understand what a checkpoint is and the work the checkpoint mechanism does. You should also understand what the fast recovery process is, the conditions that trigger the full execution of this process, and what conditions could cause it to fail. You should understand what support services the Informix technical support department offers and how to work with them to achieve a quicker resolution to problems. Finally, you should understand what basic data and instance verification commands should be run following a failure to check the logical and physical integrity of the instance.

When you build your own failure recovery process, keep the following points in mind:

- Regardless of your best efforts, and rare though it will be, instance failures *will* occur.
- The engine has a number of mechanisms built into it that attempt to prevent data corruption. Most of these mecha-

nisms will immediately shut an instance down rather than allow corruption to occur. While the instance will have crashed, damage will have been *avoided* rather than have *occurred*.
- The fast recovery process will, if completed successfully following a failure, ensure that the data in the instance is logically consistent. The only transactions that would be lost are those which were buffered in the instance's physical and logical log shared memory buffers prior to the failure.
- Using the unbuffered logging mode virtually eliminates the possibility of lost transactions in a failure condition, because the physical and logical log buffers are immediately flushed to disk as part of the transaction commit process.
- The Informix technical support department has a number of options you can choose from to help you resolve problems with the software, work with you to avoid problems in the first place, or implement Informix's technology into your environment.
- Be familiar with the basic instance and data verification command flags for the `oncheck` utility. There are several that need to be run following a crash, including "`-pr`," "`-cc`," "`-cd`," and "`-ci`" to verify the integrity of the data or instance structures.

Coming Up

In the next chapter, I'll discuss a database concept called "distributed transactions" and its attendant mechanism, the two-phase commit. I'll also briefly cover the rollback procedure involved in this type of cross-instance communication and the potential problems that can occur should a network or physical server failure occur.

Chapter 11

Distributed Transactions

- *What are distributed transactions?*
- *What is the two-phase commit protocol? How does it differ from the heterogeneous commit protocol?*
- *How does the two-phase commit protocol function?*
- *How does the two-phase commit protocol recover from failures or errors?*
- *What is a heuristic decision and what causes them?*
- *Under what circumstances could a heuristic decision violate the logical integrity of my database?*
- *How do you recover from a heuristic failure?*

As your database environment grows, there will come a time, if you've designed the overall system correctly, that data needed for an application will not be in the database or the instance to which you are connected; you will have to query the data from, or insert, update, or delete data from, another instance, possibly on another physical server. For example, if you have servers in various locations to support the operations of that location, you might have to send data to these instances on a regular basis for the location to function. On a daily basis, pricing information might be sent from the master pricing database tables in the corporate data center to individual store databases to run the local point of sale (POS) system. In this case, you are executing what is called a "distributed transaction" because the databases with which you'll be communicating and the resources that will be used to process the transaction are not on a single server but within a distribution of servers.

This chapter will look at what distributed transactions are, and a mechanism called the "two-phase commit protocol." By the end of the chapter you should understand the phases of the two-phase commit protocol and the communication that takes place between the servers involved in a distributed transaction. You should understand what the presumed-abort mechanism is and its impact in preventing logical data corruption. You should also understand the conditions that can cause a heuristic decision and the impact these can have on the logical integrity of the databases involved in the distributed transaction. Finally, you should clearly understand that distributed transactions should only be used on a highly robust and relatively stress-free network segment. While this was a requirement for the High-Availability Data Replication (HADR) mechanism discussed in Chapter 9, this requirement is more crucial when using distributed transactions. As you will see, the potential side-effects from a network failure on distributed transactions are more severe than with HADR.

Introduction to Distributed Transactions

In the introduction to this chapter, I alluded to what distributed transactions were and how they differed from regular transactions. In a typical transaction environment, all the data required for an application is usually resident within one or more of the databases in the active instance on one physical server. Data residing outside of the current database opened by the application can be queried rather easily by including the database name along with the table name in dotted notation in the body of the SQL query, as shown in Figure 11-1.

```
database region4_sales;
select
    a.strdsls_num,
    b.store_name,
    a.strdsls_dailysales,
    b.store_city,
    b.store_state
from
    store_dsales a,
    master_info_tcp.store b
where
    a.strdsls_num = b.store_num and
    a.strdsls_transdate = "12/24/1996"
order by 1;
```

Figure 11-1 *Querying data from multiple databases within the same instance.*

In this particular retail-oriented example, data that does not change too often is stored in a database called "master_info." The "store" table contains address, management, and other information. On the other hand, daily sales figures and other information are stored in regional-oriented databases. In the example shown in Figure 11-1, the person running the query is interested in getting sales data from stores in Region 4 on Christmas Eve and does so by using the "store_daily_sales" table. Notice that table aliasing was used to reduce the amount of redundant typing of table names in the query.

If data needs to be inserted, deleted, or modified within one or more databases in the same instance, the same database and table notation could be used to communicate with the various tables involved. In this particular case, the actions performed would *not* be considered a distributed transaction even though there is cross-database communication occurring because all the resources required to satisfy the actual transaction are contained in the same instance.

Going back to the example I used in the introduction to this chapter, suppose you had the type of situation shown in Figure 11-2.

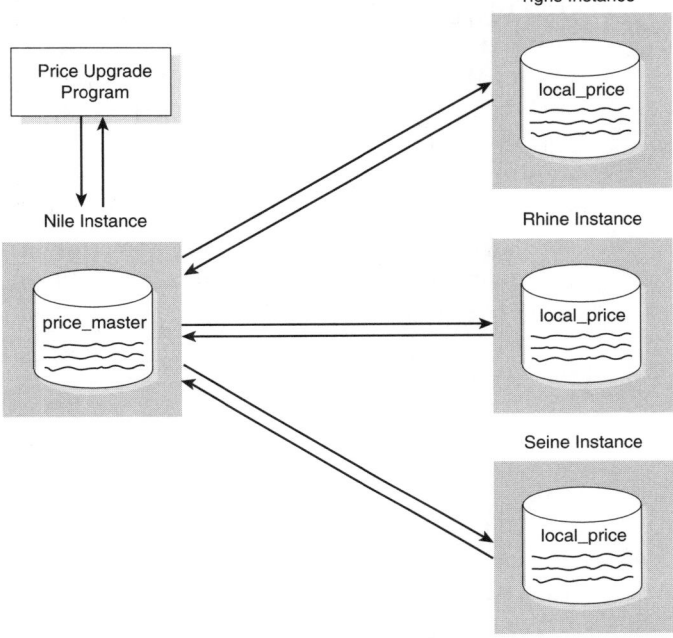

Figure 11-2 *Database instances involved in a distributed transaction*

The "nile" instance in the corporate data center contains a database with a series of tables holding pricing information that needs to be given periodically to databases and tables in the "rhine," "seine," and "tigris" instances. These instances reside on individual servers away from the data center. This update occurs through an application running on the server supporting the "nile" instance, and pushes the data to the other instances. The application used to update the other servers *would* be involved in a distributed transaction because the update process would require resources from more than one database and instance.

> **note**
> *As far as this example, or any other example used in this chapter to discuss distributed transactions is concerned, the individual servers and instances involved in the transaction do not have to be located apart from each other. Whether these servers are co-located or geographically dispersed, the same transaction commit protocol is used to manage the distributed transaction. This transaction commit protocol will be used to manage transactions occurring between two instances residing on the same physical server as well.*

The SQL notation for communicating with a database and table in a remote instance is simply "db_name@instance_name:table_name." For example, at the end of the pricing update application, a single row could be inserted into a table on each of the three remote instances that has an "on insert" trigger created on the table. This trigger would kick off an application on the remote server to process the new pricing information loaded into a holding table earlier by the application running out of the "nile" instance. The 4GL code to accomplish this insert action might look something like that shown in Figure 11-3.

```
    ## NOTE: no error handling code is shown in this example

    ## since pricing changes have to take affect in all stores
    ## simultaneously, make sure that all trigger inserts
    ## occur as a transaction.

begin work

insert into us_stores@seine_tcp:price_trigger values (1)
insert into us_stores@rhine_tcp:price_trigger values (1)
insert into us_stores@tigris_tcp:price_trigger values (1)

commit work
```

***Figure 11-3**   Extract of 4GL code using a global transaction.*

There's obviously no error handling in this example—something you would definitely want to include in a real application. These actions would, however, be handled as a distributed transaction by one of the two commit protocols OnLine Dynamic Server supports. These protocols will be explained in the next section.

As you begin to understand more about distributed transactions and the work involved in recovering from partially aborted network-based transactions, you will understand how crucial it is that distributed transactions only be run over a highly stable, relatively uncluttered network segment. While this was a requirement for HADR, it is much more important with distributed transactions.

I once worked in an environment that had applications using distributed transactions to a number of remote servers and instances connected via a satellite-based network segment. The throughput over this network segment appeared to drop proportionally with the number of network connections established through the dishes. In addition, if the weather was bad in one part of the country, all connections to sites in that area suffered abysmal throughput. If the weather was bad at the satellite hub center, communication was bad to every site.

In an attempt to compensate for what, in my opinion, was an unacceptable network environment, the values of TXTIMEOUT and DEADLOCK_TIMEOUT had to be jacked way up. Even then, there were frequent problems running the applications, and we experienced heuristic decision conditions on a regular basis. These heuristic problems required executing restores or having Informix technical support dial into a server and terminate a global transaction. It was always a pain to deal with, particularly since the application shouldn't have been developed with distributed transactions in the first place based on the network topology.

The ability to use distributed transactions is a nice feature and should not be discouraged if it makes sense for the environment, but they should only be used in situations with a highly reliable network environment.

Distributed Transaction Commit Protocols

Distributed transaction commit protocols serve two important functions: they manage the communication that occurs between the database environments involved in the distributed transaction; and, to a lesser degree, they perform the same type of function as do keys and constraints within an instance.

The SQL language does not support the creation of cross-instance constraints of any kind. If two tables in different instances are logically dependent on each other, any changes affecting the two tables made together have to be managed from a logical perspective by the commit protocol. The changes have to either completely apply to both tables or be completely rolled back.

Obviously, individual changes specifically directed at one table in the pair will not be picked up and enforced by the commit protocol like a key value constraint, but it would evaluate the action against the table on which it was created. So while commit protocols cannot provide full enforcement of data element relationships, they can guarantee the integrity of each distributed transaction it manages.

As of version 7.2, OnLine Dynamic Server supports two different protocols to manage transactions that span multiple instances: heterogeneous commit protocol and two-phase commit protocol. Each will be now explained in greater detail.

The Heterogeneous Commit Protocol

As the name implies, this protocol manages transactions issued from an OnLine Dynamic Server instance against other OnLine Dynamic Server instances and one or more database environments other than OnLine Dynamic Server. The actual communication with non-Informix database environments is managed by the Informix gateway products shown in Table 11-1.

Table 11-1 Non-Informix databases supported by the heterogeneous commit protocol.

Database Servers Supported	Informix Gateway Product Required
IBM DB2, OS/400, SQL/DS	Informix-Enterprise Gateway with DRDA
EDA/SQL	Informix-Enterprise Gateway for EDA/SQL
Any other ODBC interface	Informix-Enterprise Gateway Manager

In order for the heterogeneous commit protocol to manage a distributed transaction, the following conditions must be met:

- The HETERO_COMMIT configuration parameter is turned on. This is a new parameter in versions 7.2 and later of OnLine Dynamic Server that can be set from the **Parameters:SharedMemory** `onmonitor` screen.
- The OnLine Dynamic Server instance that will be managing the transactions must be at version 7.2 or later.
- At least one non-Informix database environment must be affected by the transaction.
- The non-Informix database environment can communicate with the Informix servers through the appropriate gateway product.

I have not used the heterogeneous commit protocol, so I cannot make any further comment on it. Please refer to the documentation that accompanied your distribution of OnLine Dynamic Server and the gateway software for more information about this commit protocol.

The Two-Phase Commit Protocol

The two-phase protocol is used when the distributed transaction only affects OnLine Dynamic Server instances. In accordance with the two functions the distributed transaction protocols are supposed to fulfill, this protocol works to ensure that all instances involved in the distributed transaction get the same type of instruction—either to commit or roll back the changes made locally—and to make sure each instance successfully followed the instruction. I will focus on this protocol for the balance of the chapter and use a series of case studies to illustrate how it works as well as how the protocol responds to failure conditions.

There are several key words and technological mechanisms with which you must be familiar before going through the case studies. These will be explained in the next section.

Terminology and Technology

Just as HADR has key words or phrases specific to that mechanism, so does the two-phase commit protocol. Some of the key words you need to be familiar with are:

- Coordinator—The instance connection that initiates a distributed transaction out of one of its databases, then manages the transaction.
- Global transaction—The proper name for a distributed transaction. A global transaction is a transaction that affects several instances and is under the control of a coordinator.
- Participant—Any other instance involved in the global transaction and having work to accomplish as part of the transaction.
- Independent action—An action that occurs outside of the two-phase commit protocol but affects the work of the protocol. The action might or might not have an impact on the actions of the protocol, and the impact might or might not be in opposition to the work being accomplished by the protocol. Possible side-effects of independent actions include the successful commit or rollback of a global transaction, an error condition (transaction ended prematurely at the coordinator), or a heuristic decision (transaction aborted at participant but not at the coordinator).

Some of the technology and parameters associated with the two-phase commit protocol are:

- DEADLOCK_TIMEOUT—The amount of time a portion of a global transaction will wait for resources from its instance before declaring an error condition. This configuration parameter can be set from the **Parameters:SharedMemory** onmonitor screen.
- TXTIMEOUT—The amount of time a participant instance will wait for instructions from the coordinator after it sends a message to the coordinator. When TXTIMEOUT seconds have passed, the participant will spawn another communication thread and attempt to contact the coordinator to determine what action it should take.
- Heuristic decision—An analysis and recovery process that usually results in a partially executed transaction and logically inconsistent databases. A formal definition of the word "heuristic" indicates that it is a progressive problem-solving technique where, at each stage of the process, the most appropriate choice is made based on the conditions that exist at that stage.

- Protocol messages—A special set of messages that pass between the coordinator and participant instances and drive the actions taken to complete the entire global transaction. There are two sets of messages, one for the coordinator and the other for the participants. They are:

    —Coordinator (includes the global transaction id and instruction): "`prepare to commit`," "`commit`," "`rollback`"

    —Participant (includes the global transaction id): "`can commit`," "`cannot commit`," "`committed`," "`rolled back`"

- Presumed-abort optimization—The underlying communication algorithm to the two-phase commit protocol. In this algorithm, if the coordinator rolls back a global transaction, it sends the "`rollback`" message to all the participant instances, then deletes all information about the transaction from its shared memory. If a participant, due to a TXTIME-OUT condition, queries the coordinator about the transaction, the lack of information in shared memory indicates that a rollback condition occurred, and the participant will roll back its portion. A committed transaction will remain in shared memory on the coordinator until all participants reply with the final status of their portion of the transaction.

    This algorithm is used because it reduces the amount of traffic between coordinator and participant instances. Rollback conditions, for example, do not require status messages to be returned from the participants. In addition, in the event of a perceived failure, the default action of this algorithm is to roll back rather than to commit transactions.

As you might guess from the name of the protocol, there are actually two separate phases, each with its own set of tasks that the coordinator must accomplish for a global transaction to complete successfully. Be aware that a completed rollback is just as successful as a committed transaction as far as the two-phase commit protocol is concerned. Each end result was handled correctly by the protocol and left all databases in a logically consistent state. The two phases, and the activity that occurs in each phase, are shown in Table 11-2.

Table 11-2 The two phases of the two-phase commit protocol.

Phase Name	Actions Taken
Precommit	1. The coordinator directs the participants to "prepare to commit." 2. The participants apply their portions of the global transaction, then reply back to the coordinator whether they "can commit" or "cannot commit." 3. The coordinator reviews the responses from the participants and decides whether to send a "commit" or "rollback" message. Obviously, if a participant "cannot commit," the global transaction is rolled back.
Postdecision	1. The coordinator writes a global transaction commit or rollback into its logical logs and instructs each participant to "commit" or "rollback." 2. If a "commit" message is received by a participant instance, that instance commits its portion of the global transaction, records the commit in its logical logs, and returns a "committed" message to the coordinator. If the participant received a "rollback" message, its portion of the transaction is rolled back and logged in its logical logs. No message is returned to the coordinator in accordance with the Presumed-abort optimization algorithm. 3. If the coordinator issued a "commit" message to the participants in step #1 of the postdecision phase, the coordinator pauses until it receives an acknowledgment message back from each participant instance. When all are received, the postdecision phase completes by closing the global transaction.

There is an automatic recovery mechanism in this protocol that handles short network failures rather gracefully. From the individual instance's perspective, a network interruption would make it appear as though the other instances had suffered a failure. When TXTIMEOUT seconds elapsed, each participant instance would spawn another communication thread to connect to the coordinator, while the coordinator would spawn a thread to communicate with each participant.

When the network connection was reestablished, the threads would all connect. If the participant instances did not find any information about the transaction in the coordinator's shared memory, it would assume a rollback had occurred and roll back its own portion of the transaction. If transaction information is in the coordinator's shared memory, the participant threads go to sleep and wait for the coordinator's thread to connect to the participant instance and relay instructions.

Case Study #1—Successful Commit

In this, the first of several case studies illustrating how the two-phase commit protocol works, we'll look at what happens when a global transaction commits successfully. For a global transaction in all of these case studies, I'll use the application logic shown in Figure 11-3.

When the application running against the "nile" instance reaches this point in the code, it records in its logical logs that it is beginning a global transaction. Then the following steps occur:

1. The "nile" instance sends the data insert instructions to the "tigris," "rhine," and "seine" instances.

2. With the insert instructions sent, the precommit phase of the two-phase protocol begins and the "nile" instance, acting as the coordinator, sends a `prepare to commit` message to the three participant instances.

3. Each of the three participant instances begins a local transaction and inserts the row into the "price_trigger" table. Each participant instance determines the status of the insert and, since it was successful, reports back to the "nile" instance that it `can commit.`

4. Since all participants reported back "`can commit`," the "nile" instance completes the precommit phase by deciding to issue a "`commit`" message to the three participants.
5. The "nile" instance begins the postdecision phase by recording the commit decision in its logical logs and issuing the "`commit`" message to the three participant instances.
6. Upon receiving the "`commit`" message from the "nile" instance, the "seine," "rhine," and "tigris" instances each commits its own local transaction to complete its portion of the global transaction and records the commit in its own logical logs. They send a "`committed`" message back to the "nile" instance.
7. The "nile" instance receives "`committed`" acknowledgments back from all three participant instances. It ends the postdecision phase by ending the global transaction and removing all information about the transaction from the instance's shared memory.

Case Study #2—Coordinator Failure

With this case study, I'll begin to explain the automatic recovery mechanism that is part of the two-phase commit protocol. In this case study, we'll look at what happens if the coordinator instance fails during the processing of a global transaction while in each of the two phases of the protocol.

Failure in the Precommit Phase

If the "nile" instance were to crash, or the physical server supporting it were to experience a failure that affected the "nile" instance while the transaction was in the precommit phase, the actions taken as a result of the presumed-abort mechanism would depend on where in the phase the failure occurred and what instruction was given to the participating instances.

If the instance crashed *after* sending the insert instructions to the participant instances but *before* the coordinator decided to "`commit`" or "`rollback`," the fast recovery process that would execute when the "nile" instance came back on-line would find the open global transaction information in the logical logs. It would see that the transaction was never completed prior to the crash, so the fast recovery process would roll the transaction back.

Meanwhile, depending on the amount of time that has elapsed since the participant instances replied back to the coordinator and have now been waiting for instructions, the participants would have spawned an additional communication thread to query the "nile" instance to see what action they should take. When the "nile" instance came back on-line, the communication threads from the participant instances would not find any information in "nile's" shared memory about the transaction, so each participant instance would roll back their own portion of the global transaction. The databases remain logically consistent.

Failure in the Postdecision Phase

If the "nile" instance went down *after* issuing a "`commit`" command at the beginning of the postdecision phase, when the fast recovery process executed on the instance, it would see the commit action recorded in the logical logs, but it would not see the close of the global transaction that occurs once all the participants have reported back with the status of their portion of the transaction. The "nile" instance would spawn a communication thread and poll each of the participants for information on their portion of the transaction.

At this point, three things could happen:

1. As the presumed-abort algorithm allows, if the three participant instances were able to commit their portion of the transaction, the transaction information would have been written to their logical logs and flushed from shared memory. When the "nile" instance contacted them, it would find no information about the transaction in shared memory and would assume that the transaction had successfully completed. The "nile" instance would record the end of the transaction in its logical logs, and the recovery process would complete. The databases remain logically consistent.
2. Once connected to the participant instances, the "nile" instance could receive "`can commit`" status messages if the "`commit`" message was never received by the participant. In

this case, the "nile" instance would resend the "`commit`" message and wait for the acknowledgment to be returned from the instances. When all acknowledgments were received, further action would occur depending on the acknowledgments received. If all participants reported back that they had "`committed`," the transaction would be completed and removed from "nile's" shared memory. The databases would remain logically consistent. If one or more instances returned a "`rolled back`" error message, a heuristic condition would exist. The logical consistency of the databases could be violated.

3. The "nile" instance could not contact one or more participants. In this situation, descriptive messages would be written to its MSGPATH file, and the "nile" instance would continue to attempt to connect to all the instances. This could lead to a heuristic condition where the local transaction in the "nile" instance is terminated but the global transaction is not. As will be explained in case study #4, this could cause the logical logs to fill requiring a full system restore to bring the system back on-line. The logical consistency of the databases could be compromised in this situation.

The last failure situation to consider is when the "nile" instance fails after issuing a "`rollback`" message at the beginning of the postdecision phase. In this situation, when the fast recovery process executes, it would see the rollback message and end the transaction. If the "`rollback`" message was received by the participant instances, each would act on that instruction, and their work would be rolled back.

If the participant instances did not receive the "`rollback`" message, when the "nile" instance came back on-line, the participant instances would attempt to contact the "nile" instance for instructions after TXTIMEOUT seconds had passed. Once contacted, there wouldn't be any information in "nile's" shared memory about the transaction, so the presumed-abort mechanism on each participant instance would assume the transaction was aborted and roll back its portion of the transaction. The logical consistency of the databases would be preserved.

Case Study #3—Participant Failure

In this third case study, the consequences that follow a participant failure are explained. As in the previous case study, where in the entire transaction process the failure occurs has an impact on what happens on the coordinator and during the fast recovery process that occurs on the participant instance. I'll use the "rhine" instance as the participant instance that fails.

Obviously, if the "rhine" instance fails before the application on the "nile" instance sends the initial insert instructions, there is nothing for it to do. The global transaction will automatically roll back and terminate when DEADLOCK_TIMEOUT seconds have elapsed on the "nile" instance and it has not been able to contact the "rhine" instance.

If the "rhine" instance fails after sending either a `can commit` or `cannot commit` message, the fast recovery process will do one of the following:

a. Read the `cannot commit` message in the logical log and roll back the transaction. If the `cannot commit` message was received by the "nile" instance, the global transaction will have rolled back and ended gracefully. If the message was *not* received by the "nile" instance, when the "nile" instance's communication thread connects to the "rhine" instance, it will resend the `prepare to commit` message. The "rhine" instance will attempt to apply the transaction again and return the appropriate message for this attempt. This message will be reviewed along with the others by the "nile" instance for determining whether or not to `commit` the transaction.

b. Read the `can commit` message in the logical logs, reestablish the transaction in the instance, and wait for further instructions from the "nile" instance. If an instruction is not received after TXTIMEOUT seconds, the "rhine" instance will contact the "nile" instance to determine the state of the transaction. The standard presumed-abort mechanism of checking for the status of the transaction in "nile's" shared memory would apply in this situation.

In all situations, the logical consistency of the databases is protected.

What Is an Independent Action?

Before looking at the next two case studies, it is important to understand what an "independent action" is and how it can affect a global transaction. As I mentioned in the "Terminology and Technology" section of this chapter, an independent action is a command or situation directed at and affecting a global transaction, but not issued as part of the two-phase commit protocol. For the most part, these actions do not occur too often unless there is a heavy-handed administrator manually terminating transactions.

The most frequent types of independent actions are the automatic or manual termination of a transaction. For example, the "seine" instance reports back that it "`can commit`" its portion of the transaction. By the time it receives the "`commit`" message back from the "nile" instance, the LTXEHWM parameter has been reached, and its portion of the global transaction is automatically rolled back within the instance. This type of situation is not handled too gracefully by the two-phase commit protocol; in fact, it creates a heuristic condition and will probably require a manual restoration procedure because the changes to the databases will be inconsistently applied across the instances.

Transactions can be manually terminated by executing an "`onmode -z`" or "`onmode -Z`" command. There is a subtle yet significant difference in the actions of these two similar looking flags. The "`-z`" flag terminates and releases resources of a thread executing locally in an instance; however, it does not terminate global transaction structures.

Since the global transaction has not been terminated, a transaction will remain open as far as logical log archiving is concerned. This will prevent logs from being reused once written off to tape. This could lead to a situation where the logical logs completely fill and the instance crashes.

Since there is no log space left for the fast recovery process to record its changes, the fast recovery process will not complete, and the instance will not come back on-line. A restore from archive or the services of the "911" group at Informix technical support will be required to bring the instance back on-line. Of course, once up, all the global transaction information will be missing from the instance's shared memory tables, causing the presumed-abort mechanism to take actions it might not otherwise take if the information was in shared memory. The databases will most certainly be logically inconsistent.

The "-z" flag acts on the shared memory address of a global transaction (found by executing an "onstat -x") on the coordinator and terminates the global transaction by removing all information about it from the instance's shared memory. The "-z" command only works when a transaction is stalled for at least TXTIMEOUT seconds and the transaction is still open. Since this command flushes information out of the instance's shared memory, it too will have an impact on the actions the presumed-abort mechanism takes with respect to this transaction. Once again, the databases will most certainly be logically inconsistent.

warning

Executing either of these commands on any portion of a global transaction, and the coordinator portion during the postdecision phase in specific, is almost guaranteed to cause a failure in transaction integrity, leave the databases logically inconsistent, and require recovering the instances manually to restore their logical integrity. For this reason, a global transaction should not be interrupted if at all possible; you do so at your own risk and peril.

There are very few conditions under which I would consider interrupting a global transaction. One is if some condition is preventing the transaction from closing and the instance's LTXEHWM is about to be reached. Since the transaction is about to be rolled back by the instance and you're going to have a problem anyway, you might as well be in control of what action is taken and when.

The other condition is if the global transaction cannot close because of a failure at one of the participant instances and the instance will not be brought back on-line in an acceptable amount of time. Since the coordinator has no idea if the participant completed the transaction, you have to assume that the failed participant instance did not commit and treat it as though it is logically inconsistent as far as that one transaction is concerned when it comes back on-line.

There is no question that this will be the situation if the participant was waiting for instructions when it failed. When it comes back up, the fast recovery process executing on the participant will spawn a communication thread to the coordinator and, not finding any information about the transaction in the coordinator's shared memory, will roll back its portion of the transaction.

There is one condition where an independent action will *not* cause an inconsistent database situation; if an "`onmode -z`" or "`onmode -Z`" command is issued against the coordinator *after* it has issued a "`commit`" message to the participants and all the participants successfully commit their portion of the transaction.

Case Study #4—Heuristic Rollback Condition

In this, and the case that follows, we'll look at the impact independent actions have on global transactions. In this particular case study, I'll explain what a heuristic rollback is and what causes them.

A heuristic rollback condition is created when a participant instance sends a "`can commit`" message to the coordinator, the coordinator decides to "`commit`" the global transaction, and the participant portion of the transaction is rolled back due to a long transaction condition or an administrator executing an "`onmode -z`" command on the participant thread.

In the "What Is an Independent Action?" section of this chapter I said that even though a transaction might be rolled back on an instance, it might still be considered open as far as the logical log archiving process is concerned. This would prevent the logs from being reused, but not from continuing to fill beyond the LTXE-HWM parameter. This occurs because the rollback message used by the two-phase commit protocol to close a global transaction in an instance is different than the message the engine sends to roll back transactions such as those causing long transactions.

In a long transaction condition where a global transaction is involved, once the decision is made to roll back the long transactions, the engine closes all the offending open transactions by issuing a standard "close" command. The work is rolled back and, as far as the instance is concerned, there is no condition preventing further use of the logical logs—all the instance-specific transactions have been closed.

Because the global transaction "`begin`" statement is not considered instance-specific, it is not considered significant in the LTXE-HWM calculations resulting in transaction rollbacks. It is significant to the logical log archiving process, however. If the appropriate global transaction "close" message is not logged in the logical logs for an instance, the transaction is still considered open, and the log cannot be reused. This leads to a situation where other transactions occurring in the instance log their work in the logical logs until they are completely full and the instance crashes.

In a heuristic rollback condition, the following steps would occur in a participant instance such as "seine":

1. The "seine" instance, in response to the instruction from the "nile" instance, responds back with a "`can commit`" message. The "nile" instance issues a "`commit`" message.
2. The transaction is aborted on the "seine" instance, either from an `onmode` command issued manually or because of a long transaction condition in the instance. The "seine" instance responds back to the "nile" instance with an error after logging the rollback in its logical logs.

What happens next depends on whether

   a. The other two participant instances return errors as well, or
   b. At least one instance, if not both, returns a "`committed`" message.

In the first scenario, if the other two instances are unable to commit their portions of the transaction as well, the following steps occur:

1. Each participant logs the error condition in their own logical logs and reports the error back to the "nile" instance.
2. Since all three instances reported errors, the "nile" instance will write its own heuristic rollback message to its logical logs.
3. The "nile" instance will terminate the global transaction and instruct the three participant instances to close the transaction as well.
4. The three participant instances will close the global transaction correctly, freeing the logical logs to be reused.
5. A "`-699`" error message is returned to the application.

The databases remain logically consistent.

Case Study #4—Heuristic Rollback Condition

In the second scenario, you have a situation in which at least one of the two remaining instances was able to commit its portion of the transaction and remove the transaction from its shared memory, effectively preventing any type of rollback. In this situation, the following steps occur:

1. The "nile" instance receives back a combination of "`committed`" and "`rolled back`" messages from the participant instances. This is logged in both the logical logs as well as the MSGPATH file. Each participant that was unable to commit the transaction is individually listed in the MSGPATH file.
2. The "nile" instance instructs the participant instances that could not commit their portion of the transaction to close the transaction.
3. These participant instances close the transaction, freeing the logical logs for reuse.
4. The "nile" instance writes an "`end transaction`" message into its logical logs, terminates the transaction, and removes all information about it from its shared memory.
5. The "nile" instance sends a "`-698`" SQL error back to the application.

In this scenario, the databases are not logically consistent and would require a manual recovery process.

Case Study #5—Heuristic End Transaction Condition

A heuristic "end transaction" only occurs when an administrator executes an "`onmode -z`" command. Because all information about the transaction is removed from the instance's shared memory, this affects the actions the presumed-abort algorithm will take. As a result, the administrator who issued the command is responsible for ensuring the logical consistency of the data following the close of the transaction.

The "`-z`" flag to the `onmode` utility was only intended to be used if network communication was lost between the coordinator and participant instances or if the coordinator has failed, leaving open global transactions on participant instances, and the coordinator will not be back on-line quick enough to prevent the logical logs from filling on the participant instance.

If the network is up and the "`onmode -z`" command is issued against the "tigris" instance, for example, during the postdecision phase, the transaction will be closed in the "tigris" instance and all information about the transaction removed from shared memory. If this occurred prior to "tigris" reporting back "`committed`" or "`rolled back`," the "nile" instance will contact the "tigris" instance to determine the state of the transaction and, finding nothing in shared memory, assume "tigris'" portion of the transaction was committed. Assuming the other instances also reported back that they had "`committed`," the transaction would be considered completely committed. However, the transaction would be inconsistently applied, with only the administrator being aware of what and where the problem was. This administrator should follow through and bring the databases back into synchronization as far as the transaction is concerned.

Recovering from a Heuristic Failure

So what do you do if you think (or know) you're facing a heuristic failure condition? First determine if, in fact, a heuristic condition did occur and if the transaction was inconsistently applied. Remember that a heuristic rollback can, under the proper conditions, leave the databases logically consistent.

Check the MSGPATH file on the coordinator instance for any error messages and/or a list of instances that experienced a heuristic end transaction condition. If a heuristic failure occurred, this will give you a good idea of where to start the second step.

If a heuristic failure did occur, the next step is to determine which instances had problems applying the transaction, and the value and impact this missing or incorrect data will have to the environment. You might determine that the steps involved in correcting the problem are not worth the time and effort that would be required.

If the application was not coded such that if it received a global transaction error, it writes out to an error file the line number it was on when the error was received as well as the data that was being worked on at that moment in time, you will have to use the `onlog` utility to parse the logical logs on each of the instances involved in the transaction to find the elements of the global transaction that failed, and the parts that were applied and those that weren't. See the *OnLine Administrator's Guide* that accompanied your distribution of the software for more information on using the `onlog` utility.

Once you've found all the elements of the transaction, the third and final step is to completely recreate the transaction and either apply the changes to the instances that could not apply them or reverse the changes made to the other instances. All in all, it is not a fun process, and should be avoided if at all possible.

Summary

In this chapter, I covered all the important aspects of using global transactions and how OnLine Dynamic Server's two-phase commit protocol manages a distributed transaction. I also covered the recovery process this protocol follows in the event of an error condition and the circumstances that might leave a collection of databases in an inconsistent state as far as a single transaction is concerned.

You should understand what the two phases are in the two-phase commit protocol and what occurs in each phase. You should understand the messaging process that occurs between coordinator and participant servers and how the presumed-abort algorithm affects actions that the recovery mechanism in the two-phase protocol executes. You should understand how a global transaction is committed successfully, some of the conditions that can cause a global transaction to fail, and whether or not the failure will affect the integrity of the databases as far as the transaction is concerned. Finally you should understand what a heuristic condition is, what causes it, the effects resulting from heuristic rollback or end transaction, and how to manually recover from the condition.

When using global transactions, keep the following points in mind:

- Only use global transactions in a networked environment that is stable and has a large amount of uncluttered band-

width. You do not want messages between the servers to be corrupted or not get through.
- Code any applications using global transactions to write out to its error log the data being manipulated as well as line number information in the event of a global transaction error. This will make the recovery process easier to complete. The application should check for error codes "-699," "-698," and "-719"—the global transaction-specific error codes.
- NEVER interrupt a global transaction by using an "onmode -z" or "onmode -Z" command unless one or more of the instances are about to crash because there is no more logical log space available, or one of the instances in the transaction fails and will not be brought back on-line in a short amount of time.

Coming Up

In the media that accompanies this book, there are a number of homegrown and borrowed utilities I have found useful to accomplish OnLine or database administration tasks. In the next chapter I briefly explain each one of the utilities on the media and, for the most part, list its source code. Understand that I am by no means an accomplished shell script programmer, so do not assume that what I have included is the "end-all" of OnLine Dynamic Server end-user-created utilities.

Of particular interest to you should be those utilities that use the sysmaster database with or without querying the active database as well. Use these utilities as an introduction and guide to what you can do with this new SMI interface.

Chapter 12

Scripts to Help Get the Job Done

- *How can I get a concise report of the dbspaces a table was created in?*
- *Is there any way to easily remove index and constraint creation statements from a dbschema file?*
- *How can instance archives be created without giving out the root or informix password?*
- *How can I manage the size of the MSGPATH file?*

The purpose of this chapter is to provide you with some utilities or scripts that will make monitoring your instances or administering your databases easier. In the "Command Line Utilities" section of Chapter 7, Monitoring the Instance, I covered the "onstat" and "oncheck" utilities. In the "Sysmaster Database and the SMI Interface" section of Chapter 3, Initializing an OnLine Dynamic Server Instance, I introduced the sysmaster database and the SMI interface. Each has its purpose and scope. They are quite powerful in their own right to monitor and administer an instance or monitor a database environment. Most of the instance monitoring scripts in this chapter use, and sometimes combine, these three tools to generate their output.

On the accompanying media, there are a series of directories containing the scripts and files discussed in this chapter. Utilities that would be of use to an OnLine administrator are in the "ol_tools" directory while scripts and utilities that a DBA would use are in the "dba_tools" directory. In the "acrobat" directory are the two table sizing worksheets mentioned in the "Calculating Table Sizes" section of Chapter 2, Preparing for Initialization and explained in Appendix B. The "html" directory contains two subdirectories. One contains the most recent version of the Informix FAQ (frequently asked question list) while the other contains articles gleaned from two past issues of the *TechNotes* publication. As I mentioned in "Informix Technical Support Options" section of Chapter 10, Recovering From a Crash and in Appendix A, *TechNotes* is a quarterly technical publication from Informix. The articles I have included on this disc originally appeared in Volume 4 (1994) and Volume 5 (1995). While a bit old, the information they contain is still of value to OnLine Dynamic Server administrators. These articles are used by permission from Informix and I would like to thank Angela Sanchez for working with me to procure them. Many of these articles also appear in the Informix Press book *Evolution of the High Performance Database* published in 1977.

Most of the material on the disc is in plain ASCII however some of the utilities contain multiple files. These were concatenated together using the UNIX "shar" utility and can be identified by the ".shr" file extension. To extract these shar files, copy them into a directory (preferably empty) then type "sh filename.shr" and press return. Once extracted, you can read the READ_ME file or other information that comes with the utility or execute the "make" command to compile the utility. The only exception to this is the dbpriv program but I will explain what is required in that section of this chapter.

I was required to provide this material in a DOS file format for this disc. Unfortunately that means many of the individual utility or script file names on the disc have been truncated to conform to the oh-so-generous DOS file name format. While the shar file archives are not affected by this, you will need to extend the names of most of the OLA and DBA tools and utilities once they are copied over to your UNIX system.

The scripts included on this disc are ones I use in my own database environments. Some of the scripts I wrote from scratch; others I've modified or completely rewritten after being inspired by work done by others. For those scripts I've borrowed or modified, I've tried to give credit where credit is due. I would like to thank Joe Lumbley for letting me publish material created by modifying scripts he included in his Informix Press book, *The Informix Database Administrators Survival Guide*. I also need to recognize Valentin Carciu and Jack Parker as the original authors of the `strip_index` sed script and the `dbdiff2` program, respectively. Lester Knutsen compiled a special full featured demo version of his `dbpriv` program for this disc while Kerry Sainsbury allowed me to use his `misql` utility as well as the Informix FAQ which he maintains. Gavin Nour let me use his `upd_stat.4gl` 4GL and/or NewEra program for generating an "`update statistics`" SQL command file and Jonathan Leffler provided the Informix product `uninstal.shr` utility. Finally, Tim Schaefer allowed me to publish a copy of his `html_ec.shar` and `systabs.shr` utilities from his extensive library of tools. As you read through this chapter, I hope you'll find something of value that you can use either as-is, or for inspiration to create a better utility.

You should be aware that an extensive library of publicly available software and utilities can be found at the International Informix Users Group (IIUG) WWW and ftp servers. The library includes utilities that would be of interest to OnLine administrators as well as application developers. They can be downloaded for free by anyone interested in using them. In addition to the software library on the IIUG server, there is a comprehensive history of all posts to the Usenet discussion group `comp.databases.informix`, the Informix FAQ (frequently asked questions list) maintained by Kerry Sainsbury, and other articles and documentation that would be of interest to Informix users. The IIUG web server can be found at `http://www.iiug.org`, while ftp services are available through `ftp.iiug.org`.

Archiving Scripts

In this collection of scripts, there are three scripts that are archive-oriented. The first, archive_db, enables an operator to create level 0 ontape archives of several instances automatically if properly installed. The second script, chk_archiving, checks to see if an ontape UNIX process exists. This would indicate whether or not an archive or restore procedure was occurring on the server. The third script, do_archive, is simply a wrapper around the ontape command and archives the current instance at whatever archive level is entered.

archive_db

This script resulted from a need to hand off the archiving of several instances on a server to the computer room operations staff. I did not want to teach them the nuances of the ontape utility, or give them access to the UNIX command line or Informix-level general access. The operating environment was such that creating a level 0 archive of each instance every night was achievable in terms of tape capacity and the time required to create the archives.

I created a no-password userid whose principal group was "informix." I modified the /etc/passwd file for this userid to call this script rather than invoking a shell, as usually happens during the login procedure. This prevents the operators from gaining shell access by aborting out the shell script. Should they try, they are automatically logged out since there is no shell specified for their userid.

To archive the instances, the operator simply logs in as the given userid and the script takes over. Obviously, if different archive levels were required, additional logic (such as in the do_archive script) would need to be added to the script in order to read in the archive level and pass the parameter to the ontape utility.

This type of script could just as easily be converted into a 4GL or ESQL program and run with parameters stored in a database table that determine the instances to archive and/or the archive levels at which the archive should be created. A string could be built into the application with the appropriate ontape syntax and flags, then executed with the "run" keyword. The program would have to be run by a userid that was a member of group "informix" or "root" in order to work, but it could be invoked at login in the manner described above.

A listing of the archive_db source code is shown in Figure 12-1.

```
#!/usr/bin/ksh
#
# archive_db
#
# written by CARLTON DOE
# @(#)archive_db1.1 10:17:43 11/11/96
#
# This script will create level 0 archives of any instance properly entered.
# It can be run by an operator logging in with a specific userid that
# belongs to group "informix." To prepare for this, edit the /etc/passwd
# file to call this script rather than a shell. The "exit 0" command
# at the end of the script will terminate the script as well as the user
# session.

# This script assumes that $INFORMIXDIR is the same for all instances to
# be archived. If this is not the case, set the $INFORMIXDIR as appropriate
# using the same type of syntax to set the $INFORMIXSERVER or $ONCONFIG
# environment variables

clear

# archive the columbia instance
print '\n\n\n'
print '\tThis script archives the Informix database instance'
print '\n'
print '\tThe first instance is COLUMBIA. '
print '\n'
print -n '\tInsert the correct tape for this instance and press ENTER to con-
tinue '
read rkey
print '\n'

export INFORMIXSERVER=columbia
export ONCONFIG=onconfig.col

ontape -s -L 0
# Now do kern

print '\n\n\n'
print '\tWhen the tape finishes rewinding, eject it and insert'
print '\tthe tape for the KERN instance.'
print '\n'
print -n '\tPress ENTER to continue '
read rkey

export INFORMIXSERVER=kern
export ONCONFIG=onconfig.ker

ontape -s -L 0
```
continued

Figure 12-1 *The source code for the* `archive_db` *utility.*

```
# Now do styx

print '\n\n\n'
print '\tWhen the tape finishes rewinding, eject it and insert'
print '\tthe tape for the STYX instance.'
print '\n'
print -n '\tPress ENTER to continue '
read rkey

export INFORMIXSERVER=styx
export ONCONFIG=onconfig.sty

ontape -s -L 0

# In my case, certain instance archives are rotated off-site on a daily
# basis. the styx instance is not, there is just a series of tapes that are
# used during the course of a week. This message reminds the operators of
# the procedure to follow.
print '\n\n'
print '\tThe archive process is now complete. Eject the tape and place'
print '\tall the tapes (except for the STYX tape) in the turtle.'
print '\n'
print '\t THANK YOU!'

exit 0
```

Figure 12-1 *continued*

Obviously, you would need to modify this script to include your instance names as well as the appropriate $INFORMIXDIR, $INFORMIXSERVER, and $ONCONFIG information.

chk_archiving

This script was originally written by Joe Lumbley for his book and was called "archiving." I renamed it and modified the script a little to make it OnLine Dynamic Server compatible and slightly more user friendly.

The script just checks to see if an `ontape` process exists on the server. Because the archive-related information `ontape` generates is stored in the rootdbs overhead pages rather than in the SMI tables, there is practically nothing that can be gleaned from, or about, the process while it is in action. If you want to monitor the progress of an archive to see when it terminates, you either have to watch the monitor from which the archive is running or, if at another terminal, run the "onstat -u" command in repeat mode (e.g., "onstat -u -r *numsecs*| grep *archive_session_id*") or this script occasionally.

Figure 12-2 contains the source code for the chk_archiving script.

```
#!/bin/ksh

# chk_archiving originally written by JOE LUMBLEY
# modified and enhanced by CARLTON DOE for OnLine DSA
#
# Rather than scanning for archive activity via onstat -u, this script
# tells you if an archive is currently running. It does NOT indicate
# which instance of the engine is running the archive however.
#
# @(#)chk_archiving1.1 09:58:06 08/01/96
#


if ps -efa | grep "ontape -s" | grep -v grep > /dev/null
then
  echo ""
  echo YES, an archive is running
else
  echo ""
  echo NO archive is in progress
fi
echo ""
```

Figure 12-2   *The* chk_archiving *script source code.*

do_archive

The concept upon which this script was written was derived from a script Joe Lumbley included in his book. I heavily modified his idea to make it OnLine Dynamic Server compatible and more user friendly.

The script creates an ontape archive of the active instance at whatever level the user enters. Again, this script will only work if the userid that invokes it is a member of the "informix" or "root" groups. It can be installed to run automatically, as described in the "archive_db" section of this chapter.

Figure 12-3 contains the source code for this script.

```ksh
#!/bin/ksh

# do_archive originally written by JOE LUMBLEY
# renamed and modified by CARLTON DOE for OnLine DSA
#
# prompts user for archive level to run then executes the archive
#
# @(#)do_archive1.2 16:28:37 11/07/96
#

let arclev=9

until test $arclev -eq 0 || test $arclev -eq 1 || test $arclev -eq 2 ; do
   clear
   echo ""
   echo "Beginning Ontape archive process. "
   echo "You must be user INFORMIX or ROOT to continue. "
   echo ""
   echo "Archive will use device: "
   cat $INFORMIXDIR/etc/$ONCONFIG| grep TAPEDEV | grep -v LTAPEDEV \
     | awk '{print $2}'
   echo ""
   echo "What level do you want to run [0, 1, 2]? \c"
   read arclev

done

echo ""
date
$INFORMIXDIR/bin/ontape -s -L $arclev
```

Figure 12-3   *The* do_archive *script source code.*

Automating Administrative Tasks

As I mentioned in the "Starting and Stopping OnLine Dynamic Server Automatically" section of Chapter 4, Basic Administrative Tasks, I'm basically a lazy person. I try to off-load as many repetitive or general maintenance tasks as possible to the computer system for automatic execution. This includes having to remember to stop or restart an instance when rebooting a server or taking care of instance log maintenance. I've included three scripts in this section that do these tasks for me.

Starting and Stopping the Instance

I created two scripts, `stop_online` and `start_online`, to accomplish these tasks automatically for me when a physical server is shut down or rebooted. These scripts need to be included in the rc0.d and rc2.d directories, as explained in Chapter 4.

Figure 12-4 contains the source code for the `stop_online` script. Figure 12-5 contains the `start_online` source code.

In both of these scripts, you need to enter your own $INFORMIXDIR, $INFORMIXSERVER, and $ONCONFIG values, as well as the correct instance name in the echo statements for your environment.

```
##
## script to stop the Informix OnLine instances on shutdown of the server.
## this should be placed in the rc0.d directory, and numbered appropriately
## for best results.
##
## written by CARLTON DOE
## @(#)stop_online1.1  13:15:17  11/21/96


export INFORMIXDIR=
export PATH=$INFORMIXDIR/bin:$PATH

echo "Shutting down OnLine instances"

echo "Stopping instance_name"
export ONCONFIG=
export INFORMIXSERVER=
onmode -ky

## Repeat previous 4 lines as necessary for the instances on the machine. if
## necessary, also change the $INFORMIXDIR environment variable. Remember to
## re-export the $PATH statement.

echo "OnLine instances stopped"
```

Figure 12–4   *The* `stop_online` *script source code.*

```
##
## start_online
##
## Script to start the Informix OnLine instances when the server boots. This
## should be placed in the rc2.d directory and numbered appropriately
##
## written by CARLTON DOE
## @(#)start_online1.1 13:15:18 11/21/96

export INFORMIXDIR=
export PATH=$INFORMIXDIR/bin:$PATH

echo "About to start OnLine instances"


echo "Starting instance_name" ## change instance_name to a valid instance
export ONCONFIG=
export INFORMIXSERVER=
oninit


## Repeat previous 4 lines as necessary for the instances on the machine. if
## necessary, also change the $INFORMIXDIR environment variable. Remember to
## re-export the $PATH statement.

echo "OnLine instances started"
```

Figure 12-5 *The* `start_online` *script.*

Instance Log Maintenance

Figure 12-6 contains the source code for the `move_logs` script. This script handles instance log maintenance by copying and purging the MSGPATH file.

I set this script up to run on a weekly basis through the root crontab. I have a subdirectory under $INFORMIXDIR called "old_logs" where copies of all the instance's MSGPATH files are kept. Each week, when the script executes, the oldest copy is replaced by the succeeding week's file. Then the current week's worth of information is copied out, after which the MSGPATH file is erased so that a new week's worth of information can be entered. I only keep two weeks worth of old logs, but that could be expanded by adding copy levels to the overall process.

```
#!/usr/bin/ksh
#
# move_log
#
# created by CARLTON DOE
#
# sccsid: @(#)move_logs1.2 14:41:29 12/03/96
#
# This moves the OnLine Dynamic Server message log into a rolling archive
# then clears it out. This script should be executed on the average once a
# week to keep the file to a manageable size.
#
# The files used in this example are:
# $INFORMIXDIR/columbia.prod.log -- current log
# $INFORMIXDIR/old_logs/columbia.old -- 1 week old
# $INFORMIXDIR/old_logs/columbia.older -- 2 week old

# step 1
export INFORMIXDIR=

# step 2
cp $INFORMIXDIR/old_logs/columbia.old \
 $INFORMIXDIR/old_logs/columbia.older

# step 3
cp $INFORMIXDIR/columbia.prod.log \
 $INFORMIXDIR/old_logs/columbia.old

# step 4
cat /dev/null > $INFORMIXDIR/columbia.prod.log


## Copy and repeat steps 2 through 4 for each instance on the server. If the
## $INFORMIXDIR environment variable needs to change, include step #1
```

Figure 12-6 The move_log *script.*

Monitoring the Instance

The five scripts covered in this section enable you to look at dbspace capacity, disk chunk status, a comprehensive activity listing for a user, and control checkpoint frequency.

checkon

This script uses a combination of UNIX and OnLine commands to display a comprehensive list of processes and threads an individual user has running on a server. This script was originally written by Joe Lumbley for his book, but I have modified it to make it OnLine Dynamic Server compatible.

When run, you need to enter the name of the user you want to "`checkon`". The script returns a listing of the user's UNIX processes as well as the output of an "`onstat -u`" command that's been "`greped`" to include just those threads for the userid.

Underneath the "flags" section of the `onstat` command, there is a legend for each flag position with all the possible values that particular flag could have.

Figure 12-7 contains the source code for this script.

chk_chunks

This script queries through the SMI interface and returns a list of disk chunks in the active instance that could have a problem. These chunks are either completely off-line, in a recovery state after being initialized, or in an inconsistent state due to an assertion failure.

If you have a large number of chunks in an instance, the output of this script should be easier to manage than that resulting from an "`onstat -d`" command. This script only reports exceptions, not every chunk in the instance.

Figure 12-8 contains a source code listing for this script.

chk_dbspaces

This script lists all the dbspaces in the active instance and calculates usage statistics for each one. The script uses the instance page size in calculations and was created with a 2 KB page size as the default. This can easily be changed if your port of the product uses a 4 KB page size. Be aware that unlike Informix utilities, the size values reported by this script are in MB rather than pages.

Figure 12-9 contains a source code listing of the `chk_dbspaces` script.

```
#!/bin/ksh
# checkon originally written by JOE LUMBLEY
# modified and enhanced by CARLTON DOE for OnLine DSA
#
# prints out the Unix processes as well as the OnLine threads the entered
# username has running
# @(#)checkon          1.2 16:32:32 11/07/96
#

usage()
{
echo ""
echo "usage: checkon [username]"
echo ""
}


## Main functional piece
if test $# -eq 0
  then
   usage
   exit 0
fi

echo Listing all UNIX processes for $1
echo " "
ps -fu $1
echo " "
echo " "
echo Looking at INFORMIX threads for $1
echo " "
echo "\
address flags pid user tty wait tout locks nreads nwrites"
$INFORMIXDIR/bin/onstat -u | grep $1 | grep -v grep
echo "  ^^^^^^^ "
echo "  |||||||"
echo "POSTION 1234567"
echo ""
echo "1 WAITING ON: B(uffer) Y(waiting for condition) C(heckpoint) L(ock) "
echo "              S(latch) X(rollback) G(log write) S(mutex) T(ransaction)"
echo "2 * (transaction active during I/O failure) "
echo "3 TRANSACTIONS: B(egin work) C(ommitting) R(ollback)
echo "               H(euristic rollback)"
echo "               A(rchive)"
echo "4 THREAD: P(rimary thread)"
echo "5 STATUS: R(eading) X(thread in critical section)"
echo "7 PROCESS: B(btree cleaner thread) M(Onmonitor) D(aemon) "
echo "            C(awaiting cleanup) F(Page cleaner thread)"
```

Figure 12-7 *The* checkon *script source code.*

```
#!/bin/ksh

# chk_chunks
# written by CARLTON DOE for OnLine DSA
#
# prints out a list of chunks for the active instance which are either
# off-line, in an inconsistent state, or are in recovery mode
#
# @(#)chk_chunks1.2 16:45:05 08/06/96
#

echo ""
echo "Checking for chunks in the $INFORMIXSERVER instance which are either"
echo "down, inconsistent or in recovery mode"
echo ""

dbaccess sysmaster - <<!EOF

select chknum Chunk_Num, " is off-line!" Message
 from syschunks
 where is_offline <> 0 or mis_offline <> 0;

select chknum Chunk_Num, " is in recovery mode!" Message
 from syschunks
 where is_recovering <> 0 or mis_recovering <> 0;

select chknum Chunk_Num, " is in an inconsistent state!" Message
 from syschunks
 where is_inconsistent <> 0 ;
!EOF
```

Figure 12–8 The chk_chunks *script.*

chk_ckpoint

This script was originally written by Joe Lumbley for his book. It lists the time and duration of the last five checkpoints that have occurred in the active instance by "greping" through the MSG-PATH file for the instance.

It is important to do this from time to time to check on the amount of time it takes a checkpoint to complete. Since all end-user-oriented activity is paused during a checkpoint, the checkpoint "duration" should be as short as possible. If you begin to see that checkpoints are taking longer to complete, you will need to determine why.

The source code for this script is shown in Figure 12-10.

```
#!/bin/ksh

# chk_dbspaces
# written by CARLTON DOE for OnLine DSA
#
# prints out a list of the dbspaces for the active instance
# as well as their size and usage statistics
#
# NOTE: if your system is using a page size other than 2 KB, change the
# first line of this script
#
# @(#)chk_dbspaces1.2 16:47:58 08/06/96
#

let pagesize=2

echo ""
echo "Calculating dbspace usage for the $INFORMIXSERVER instance "
echo "Using a $pagesize KB page size!"
echo ""

dbaccess sysmaster - <<!EOF

select syschktab.dbsnum, name, sum(chksize) * $pagesize total_size,
  sum(nfree) * $pagesize amt_free,
  trunc((sum(nfree) / sum(chksize)) * 100 ,2) percent_free
  from syschktab, sysdbstab
  where syschktab.dbsnum = sysdbstab.dbsnum
  group by 1,2
  order by 1;

!EOF
```

Figure 12-9 *The source code for the* chk_dbspaces *script.*

```
#!/bin/csh

# chk_ckpoint originally written by JOE LUMBLEY
# modified by CARLTON DOE for DSA
#
# lists last 5 checkpoints made within the instance
#
# @(#)chk_ckpoint1.1 09:58:07 08/01/96
#

$INFORMIXDIR/bin/onstat -
echo Current time is: `date`
grep Checkpoint `grep MSGPATH ${INFORMIXDIR}/etc/${ONCONFIG} \
  | awk '{print $2}' ` | tail -5
```

Figure 12-10 *The* chk_ckpoint *script.*

control_chkpt_intervals

Also based on a script originally written by Joe Lumbley, this script allows you to force checkpoints to occur every X seconds, as entered. Figure 12-11 contains a listing of the code for this script.

chk_logging

This script is a little weak; it could easily fall apart on a system supporting multiple residency because it is not instance specific.

```ksh
#!/bin/ksh
# control_chkpt_intervals
#
# originally written by JOE LUMBLEY
# modified by CARLTON DOE for OnLine DSA
#
# forces checkpoints to occur every X seconds, as entered, until interrupted
#
# @(#)control_chkpt_intervals1.1 16:07:06 11/12/96
#

usage()
{
echo ""
echo "usage: control_chkpt_intervals [# of seconds for chkpt interval]"
echo ""
}


## Main processing function
if test $# -eq 0
 then
 usage
 exit 0
fi


while true
do
 onmode -c
 sleep $1
done
```

Figure 12-11 *The source code for the* `control_chkpt_intervals`

The script allows you to quickly see if any of the instances are still archiving their logical logs out to tape.

Originally written by Joe Lumbley for his book, the script returns the LTAPEDEV device for the active instance and checks to see if continuous logical log archiving is occurring. Since it's searching for the `ontape` command, and you cannot tell which instance a particular `ontape` command is running against, the implied result of this command could be erroneous.

On a server supporting a single instance, the result returned by the script would be valid. It is for this reason that the script is included.

Figure 12-12 contains the source code for the `chk_logging` script.

```ksh
#!/bin/ksh
#
# chk_logging
# originally written by JOE LUMBLEY
# modified and enhanced by CARLTON DOE for OnLine DSA
#
# This script tells you what the logical log archive device for the active
# instance is. It also attempts to indicate whether or not the
# instance is continuously writing logs out to the device by checking
# for the existence of a ontape -c process. There is no guarantee
# in a server supporting multiple residency that the active instance
# is the one to which the ontape command is attached.
#
# @(#)chk_logging1.2 15:36:49 12/03/96
#

echo ""
echo "The logical log archive device for the" $INFORMIXSERVER "instance is:"
cat $INFORMIXDIR/etc/$ONCONFIG| grep LTAPEDEV | awk '{print $ 2}'
echo ""

if ps -efa | grep "ontape -c" | grep -v grep > /dev/null
then
 echo "Continuous logging IS occurring"
else
 echo "Continuous logging IS NOT occurring"
fi
echo ""
```

Figure 12-12 The `chk_logging` script.

Database Monitoring and Schema Modification

The scripts and utilities included in this section of the chapter are the most exciting to me. Perhaps it is because they eliminate quite a bit of the drudgery involved with certain aspects of database administration.

The six scripts included here create DDL statements to synchronize two databases, remove index and constraint creation statements from a dbschema and paste them into another file, generate a report on table sizes and dbspace location, and show how much log space is being used to record transaction information in the logical logs.

chk_table_size

This script queries the sysmaster database for table size information. When executed, the first and next extent size from the table creation statement is returned as well as the total size of the table, the amount of space used, number of table extents, number of rows, and the percentage of space still free. The size information is reported back in MB and uses a 2 KB page size when making its calculations. The page size value can easily be changed in the script if your port of the engine uses a 4 KB page.

When the script is invoked, you are prompted for a database name. This database must exist within the active instance of the engine. Following this prompt, you are asked to enter a table name. You can either enter the name of a specific table within that database or press return to have the script return information for all the tables in the database.

Figure 12-13 contains the source code for the `chk_table_size` script.

where_are_tables

This is a great little utility if I do say so myself. It should be noted that Lester Knutsen, a member of the IIUG Board of Directors, was instrumental in helping me craft the base SQL statement for this script.

```
#!/bin/ksh

# chk_table_size
# written by CARLTON DOE for OnLine DSA
#
# prints out table size statistics for either a single table or all
# tables in a database
#
# NOTE: if your system is using a page size other than 2 KB, change the
# first line of this script
#
# @(#)chk_table_size1.3  09:51:41  08/23/96
#

let pagesize=2

function do_single
{
dbaccess sysmaster - <<!EOF

select tabname tab_name,
 sum(fextsiz) * $pagesize first_ext_kb,
 sum(nextsiz) * $pagesize next_ext_kb,
 sum(nptotal) * $pagesize totsize_kb,
 sum(npused) * $pagesize used_kb,
 sum(nextns) num_extents,
 sum(nrows) num_rows,
 sum (unused1) percent_free
 from sysptnhdr, systabnames
 where dbsname = "$db_name" and
 tabname = "$tab_name" and
 systabnames.partnum = sysptnhdr.partnum
 group by 1;

!EOF
}

function do_all
{
dbaccess sysmaster - <<!EOF
```

continued

Figure 12-13 *The source code for the* `chk_table_size` *script.*

```
      select systabnames.tabname tab_name,
        sum(fextsiz) * $pagesize first_ext_kb,
        sum(nextsiz) * $pagesize next_ext_kb,
        sum(nptotal) * $pagesize totsize_kb,
        sum(sysptnhdr.npused) * $pagesize used_kb,
        sum(nextns) num_extents,
        sum(sysptnhdr.nrows) num_rows,
        sum(unused1) percent_free
      from sysptnhdr, systabnames, $db_name:systables
      where dbsname = "$db_name" and
      systabnames.partnum = sysptnhdr.partnum and
      $db_name:systables.tabname = systabnames.tabname and
      $db_name:systables.tabid >= 100
      group by 1;

      !EOF
      }


      ## the main processing function
      echo ""
      echo "Checking table statistics. NOTE--I'm using a $pagesize KB page size"
      echo ""
      echo "Please enter the database name: \c"
      read db_name
      db_name=${db_name:?"Missing database name"}
      echo ""
      echo "Enter the table name or all [all]: \c"
      read tab_name
      tab_name=${tab_name:=all}

      if [[ $tab_name = "all" ]]; then
       do_all
      else
       do_single
      fi
```

Figure 12–13 *continued*

Depending on the parameters entered, it will return the dbspace location, total space allocated, and the amount of space used for either a single table or all tables in the target database. The script handles fragmented as well as nonfragmented tables and sorts the results in dbspace order.

When invoked, the script will notify you that its calculations are based on a 2 KB page size. As with the other scripts I've included, this can easily be modified if your port of the engine uses a 4 KB page size. You are prompted for the name of a target database. This database must exist within the active instance.

Following this prompt, another prompt asks for the name of a table. You can either enter a table name to get information on that particular table or press return to have the script gather information on all the tables within the database.

If you choose to get information about all the tables in the database, information about any fragmented tables will appear at the bottom of the report away from the nonfragmented tables.

Figure 12-14 contains the syntax for this script.

find_db_names

This script is based on one Joe Lumbley wrote for his book. I modified it to use the new SMI interface.

When invoked, the script generates a list of all the databases in the active instance as well as the database owner, creation date, and logging mode flags for all three modes. As is standard when looking at these type of flags, "0" is false and "1" is true.

Figure 12-15 contains the code for this script.

transaction_size

This SMI query reports back the amount of logical log space being used to record a user's current transaction as well as the largest amount of logical log space used to record any transaction for that same user's session. The values returned are in KB.

The source code for the script is listed in Figure 12-16.

strip_index

If you follow the advice I gave in the "Fragmenting Constraints" section of Chapter 5, Building a Database Environment, when creating index-based constraints on a table, *always* create an index first with the appropriate conditions and columns, then "promote" the index to be a constraint. Using this method enables you to fragment your constraints, a feature not currently supported by the "`alter table add constraint`" command.

```
#!/bin/ksh

# where_are_tables
# written by CARLTON DOE for OnLine DSA
#
# the sql syntax for this germinated from some ideas LESTER KNUTSEN
# sent me.
#
# this will either print out the dbspace(s) a single table is in or a list
# of all dbspaces and the tables in them
#
# NOTE: if your system is using a page size other than 2 KB, change the
# first line of this script
#
# @(#)where_are_tables1.2 15:37:18 08/06/96
#

let pagesize=2

function do_single
{
dbaccess sysmaster - <<!EOF
select systabnames.tabname table_name,
 dbinfo( "DBSPACE" , systabnames.partnum ) dbspace,
 (nptotal * $pagesize) allocated_space,
 ((nptotal - sysptnhdr.npused) * $pagesize) free_space
from systabnames, "$db_name":systables, sysptnhdr
where "$db_name":systables.partnum = sysptnhdr.partnum and
 "$db_name":systables.partnum = systabnames.partnum and
 "$db_name":systables.tabname = "$tab_name" and
 tabtype = "T"
group by 1,2,3,4;

 {now get fragmentation info if the table is fragmented}

select systabnames.tabname fragmented_table,
 dbinfo( "DBSPACE" , systabnames.partnum ) dbspace,
 sum(nptotal * $pagesize) allocated_space,
 sum((nptotal - sysptnhdr.npused) * $pagesize) free_space
 from systabnames, "$db_name":systables, sysptnhdr
 where systabnames.tabname = "$db_name":systables.tabname and
 systabnames.partnum = sysptnhdr.partnum and
 "$db_name":systables.partnum = 0 and
 "$db_name":systables.tabname = "$tab_name" and
 tabtype = "T"
group by 1,2
order by 1,2;
!EOF
}
```
continued

Figure 12-14 *Syntax for the* where_are_tables *script.*

```
function do_all
{
dbaccess sysmaster - <<!EOF
select systabnames.tabname table_name,
 dbinfo( "DBSPACE" , systabnames.partnum ) dbspace,
 (nptotal * $pagesize) allocated_space,
 ((nptotal - sysptnhdr.npused) * $pagesize) free_space
from systabnames, "$db_name":systables, sysptnhdr
where "$db_name":systables.partnum = sysptnhdr.partnum and
 "$db_name":systables.partnum = systabnames.partnum and
 tabid > 99 and tabtype = "T"
group by 1,2,3,4
order by 2,1;

{now get information on any fragmented tables in the database}

select systabnames.tabname fragmented_table,
 dbinfo( "DBSPACE" , systabnames.partnum ) dbspace,
 sum(nptotal * $pagesize) allocated_space,
 sum((nptotal - sysptnhdr.npused) * $pagesize) free_space
from systabnames, "$db_name":systables, sysptnhdr
where systabnames.tabname = "$db_name":systables.tabname
 and systabnames.partnum = sysptnhdr.partnum
 and "$db_name":systables.partnum = 0
group by 1,2
order by 1,2;
!EOF
}


## the main processing function
echo ""
echo "Finding tables. NOTE--I'm using a $pagesize KB page size"
echo ""
echo "Please enter the database name: \c"
read db_name
db_name=${db_name:?"Missing database name"}
echo ""
echo "Enter the table name or all [all]: \c"
read tab_name
tab_name=${tab_name:=all}

if [[ $tab_name = "all" ]]; then
 do_all
else
 do_single
fi
```

Figure 12-14 *continued*

```
#!/bin/ksh

#find_db_names originally written by JOE LUMBLEY
# modified by CARLTON DOE for OnLine DSA
#
# prints a list of database names and owners as well as creation date
# and whether or not logging has been activated for the active instance
#
# @(#)find_db_names1.1  09:58:53 08/01/96
#

echo ""
echo "One moment, scanning for database names in the $INFORMIXSERVER
instance"

dbaccess sysmaster - <<XYZ!
select name Database_name, owner Owner, created Created,
 is_logging Unbuffered_Log, is_buff_log Buffered_Log, is_ansi Ansi
 from sysdatabases
 order by 1;
XYZ!
```

Figure 12-15 The find_db_names *script.*

When moving or recreating a database, however, you'll want to get rid of all the index and constraint creation statements from the dbschema file so you can load data into unindexed tables. Since I'm not a very proficient shell programmer, this process, for me anyway, always required a lot of cat and grep statements. I followed this with a microscopic review of the resulting files to make sure I had all the parts of the index or constraint creation statements loaded into my index creation file and removed from the table schema file.

Not long ago I happened upon a sed script written by Valentin Carciu that took a dbschema file, copied the "create index" statements into another file, then removed these statements from the original dbschema file. With his permission, I added some additional functionality to the script to strip out constraint creation statements as well. I also tweaked the user interface and changed the final output file names to be a little more intuitive.

The script requires a schema file name (*filename*) when invoked and produces two files when finished. The "*filename*_schm.sql" file contains the original dbschema without any index or index-based constraint creation statements. The "*filename*_idx.sql" file con-

```
#!/bin/ksh

# transaction_size
# written by CARLTON DOE for OnLine DSA
#
# This will print out the amount of logical log space being
# used by the current transaction, as well as the largest amount of log
# space used for any transaction, for the given session id. The values
# returned are in KB
#
# @(#)transaction_size1.1  10:36:44  12/16/96
#

echo ""
echo "Finding the transaction size in KB"
echo ""
echo "Please enter the session id: \c"
read sess_id
sess_id=${sess_id:?"Missing session id number"}
echo ""
dbaccess sysmaster - <<!EOF
select logspused current_tran_size, maxlogsp largest_tran_size
from syssesprof
where sid = $sess_id;
!EOF
```

Figure 12–16 *The source code for* transaction_size *script.*

tains the index and index-based constraint creation statements. The original dbschema file is left intact for security's sake.

There is one unpleasant side-effect of this script that you need to be aware of. Because the sed *syntax is executing pattern matching commands, if any of the table names in the schema end in "index" (e.g., tab_index), the syntax for creating that table will be copied into the index output file and removed from the schema file.*

To make sure this does not occur, simply execute an fgrep *command against the index output file as follows:*

```
fgrep -l "create table" filename_idx.sql
```

If "filename_idx.sql" is returned, a table creation statement was copied into the index file. Edit the "filename_idx.sql" file, remove the table creation statement, and put it back in the table creation file. All the table header information for the table used by the dbimport utility will still be there in the table creation file, so it will be easy to find out where to place the table creation statement.

When using the `dbimport` utility, it is particularly important that the tables be created and imported in the same order in which they were exported if the data was exported to tape. The `dbimport` utility simply streams through the data tape in conjunction with the import SQL file. If the table being created in the SQL file, and subsequently loaded with data, is not the same table next up on the tape, the import will immediately abort.

Figure 12-17 contains the source code for this utility. I warn you in advance that I do not make any claim to being a `sed` programmer. If there is a more efficient way to complete the task than what is written, I would appreciate the feedback.

dbdiff2.shr

I found this utility, written by Jack Parker, several years ago and have used it from time to time ever since. It is invaluable if you are in an environment where multiple copies of the same database are spread across several instances (or in the same instance but named differently, for that matter) for development, test, and production purposes.

This program compares the schema of two databases and creates a file containing the SQL DDL statements that would have to be run to synchronize one of the databases with the other. The program does *not* synchronize the data between the two databases, just the schemas. As Jack freely admits in the READ.ME file, there are schema conditions that are not properly supported, but on the whole it's an excellent program.

The `dbdiff2` program is distributed as a self-extracting shar file. To extract its several components, simply type "`sh dbdiff2.shr`" and press return. It is a 4GL application and requires a full-development C-compiler version of Informix-4GL to compile and run.

`Dbdiff2` can only be run against databases in the active instance. While this might, at first glance, appear to be a problem if the databases to be compared are in separate instances, there is a way to handle this: you just run the program separately against the databases in the two instances. Against the first database, use the "`-s1`" flag; against the second, use the "`-s2`" flag. Using the "`-s1`" flag in this manner will create a series of flat files to be used when comparing against the second database. These flat files will be read in by the program when invoked with the "-s2" flag to generate the SQL statements needed to synchronize the schema of the second database with the first database.

```ksh
#!/bin/ksh
#
# strip_index
#
# Created by Valentin Carciu val@garpac.com
# Modified by Carlton Doe
# @(#)strip_index.sh1.3 15:15:43 12/04/96
#
# original notes by creator:
# This script takes a *.sql created by dbexport and takes out all
# "create index" statements and puts them in an *.sql.idx file to be
# renamed to *.sql and to be used with dbaccess (or isql) after the tables
# have been loaded.
#
# Comments by Carlton
# This script has been reworked to strip out "add constraint" commands as
# well. While the original logic of the program is still intact, I
# introduced a couple of intermediary files to hold the output from striping
# the indexes. These intermediary files were then used to create the
# final output files. I'm not sed literate in the least so if you can
# improve upon this script, please send me e-mail at dbaresrc@xmission.com

# Usage: strip_index.sh <filename>
usage()
{
echo ""
echo "usage: strip_index.sh [filename]"
echo ""
}

## Main function
if test $# -eq 0
 then
  usage
  exit 0
fi

input=$1
index_output="$1_idx.sql"
index_temp="$1_idx_tmp"
schema_temp="$1_tmp"
schema_output="$1_schm.sql"
temp1="temp1"
temp2="temp2"
```

continued

Figure 12–17 *The source code for the* `strip_index sed` *script.*

```
## start by finding the index statements and clear those out
echo ""
echo "Parsing out the index statements"

sed -e "/create.*index.*;$/w $index_output" \
 -e "/create.*index.*;$/d" $input > $temp1

sed -e "/create.*index/w /tmp/X$$A" $temp1 > /dev/null
while test `wc -l /tmp/X$$A | awk '{print $1}'` -gt 0
do
 sed -e "/create.*index/N" \
 -e "s/\n/ /" \
 -e "/create.*index.*;$/w $temp2" \
 -e "/create.*index.*;$/d" $temp1 > $schema_temp
 cat $temp2 >> $index_output
 rm $temp2
 cat $schema_temp > $temp1
 sed -e "/create.*index/w /tmp/X$$A" $temp1 > /dev/null
done

cat $temp1 > $schema_temp
rm $temp1
rm /tmp/X$$A

## now find "alter table add constraint" statements and clean those out
echo ""
echo "Parsing out the add constraint statements"

sed -e "/alter.table.*add.constraint.*;$/w $index_temp" \
 -e "/alter.table.*add.constraint.*;$/d" $schema_temp > $temp1

sed -e "/alter.table.*add.constraint/w /tmp/X$$A" $temp1 > /dev/null
while test `wc -l /tmp/X$$A | awk '{print $1}'` -gt 0
do
 sed -e "/alter.table.*add.constraint/N" \
 -e "s/\n/ /" \
 -e "/alter.table.*add.constraint.*;$/w $temp2" \
 -e "/alter.table.*add.constraint.*;$/d" $temp1 > $schema_output
 cat $temp2 >> $index_output
 rm $temp2
 cat $schema_output > $temp1
 sed -e "/alter.table.*add.constraint/w /tmp/X$$A" $temp1 > /dev/null
done

cat $index_temp >> $index_output

rm $index_temp
rm $schema_temp
rm $temp1
rm /tmp/X$$A

echo ""
echo "Done!"
```

Figure 12–17   continiued

For example,

```
dbdiff2 -s1 -od ar_system_dev -all
```

will create a series of files capturing almost all the SQL DDL information about the `ar_system_dev` database. These files are actually unloads of the system catalog tables that store information about the tables, columns, indexes, and so on in the target database. Obviously, if the second database is on another server, these files must be transferred to the other server before rerunning the `dbdiff2` program with the "-s2" flag.

Once the files have been moved to the target server, or the active instance has been changed on the same server, executing

```
dbdiff2 -s2 -nd ar_system_test -o dev_to_test.sql
```

will create a file called "dev_to_test.sql" in the working directory containing the SQL DDL statements that would need to be executed against the `ar_system_test` database for it to resemble the `ar_system_dev` database. The system catalog tables created in the "-s1" step and used by the "-s2" step will be erased at the end of program execution.

If both databases to be compared are in the same instance, you would not need to use the "-s" flags, simply the "-od" and "-nd" flags. The database used in conjunction with the "-od" flag is considered the "old" or "model" database that you want the "-nd" database to become like. For example, executing

```
dbdiff2 -od ar_system_dev -nd ar_system_test -o
    devtotest_strp.sql -t str_purchase
```

would compare the `str_purchase` table in the `ar_system_test` database to the table of the same name in the `ar_system_dev` database. A file called "devtotest_strp.sql" would be created with the SQL DDL statements to synchronize the test database version of the table to the development database version.

The syntax for the `dbdiff2` program is too lengthy to include here as I have done with the other utilities. Instead, Figure 12-18 contains the READ.ME file that accompanies the software. It shows all the valid flags for the application and explains what they do.

```
Enclosed is dbdiff2.4gl and a Makefile to compile it.

dbdiff2 generates SQL to bring one version (-nd) of a database in line with
another (-od). Please be careful with the SQL generated. This program has
been tested - but not exhaustively. Don't run the SQL blind - look at it and
check it first. This pgm is placed in the public domain without any warranty
whatsoever. If you use it and it trashes your database - then you should be
more careful - but it is not my problem.

The purpose in offering this code is to allow y'all to find the bugs for me.
So be sure to let me know what goes wrong eh?

By now you have unpacked the file (or you can read the directions about
20 lines up on how to do that). To compile dbdiff2 type 'make all'. This
should compile dbdiff2 as well as two forms w_log.frm and server.frm.
--------------------------------------------------------------------------
Syntax is listed at the start of the source and explained at the end of this
file - or can be obtained by using a 'dbdiff2 -?'.

In case you don't notice - it outputs to /tmp/mod_db.sql. This can be
changed with a -o switch.

If EITHER of the engines you are working with are SE then use the "-db SE"
switch.

dbdiff2 does not currently resolve columns that are out of order. The only
way I can think of doing that without losing data is to unload the table,
drop, recreate it properly and reload. I am working on a rebuild option to
generate SQL to do that.

In the index portion there is no gaurantee in what order I'll get the indi-
ces. I can't think of a way to sort to resolve this... If I need to CLUSTER
an index, and a different index is CLUSTERED on the target engine then there
is no gaurantee that the code will NOT CLUSTER the old index before CLUSTER-
ing the new index. This would result in a runtime error for the SQL code.
Accordingly I generate a warning - a comment in the SQL code identifying
both indices and a message on the tube.

There may be some things that SE doesn't support ('WITH NO LOG'?), please
let me know.
--------------------------------------------------------------------------
                                                                continued
```

Figure 12–18 The dbdiff2 READ.ME file.

```
Future (prioritized):

Permissions (authority tables)( in process - haven't done columns yet )
Rebuild table option when column order is hosed.
Full Support for ANSI mode
Form driven option

Syntax:

dbdiff2 [-db SE|OL] engine type - SE or Online (Online=default)

    If either of the two engines is an SE engine then use -db SE
    since it will not support the online specific code.

 -od old database name

    This is the database you are using as the model.

 -nd new database name

    This is the database you are generating code to alter.

 [-o] output file name (default = /tmp/mod_db.sql)

    Self explanatory.

 [-a] Authority tables (permissions)

    Will generate code to bring table permissions in line
    with the '-od' database. (In the future this switch will
    also correct column level permissions as applicable).

 [-u] Users

    Will generate code to bring user permissions in line
    with the '-od' database.

 [-s1] Only do segment 1

    Only unload the files from -od. This option is meant for those
    who cannot connect to two databases within the code.

 [-s2] Only do segment 2

    Proceed with generation of code. This presumes that dbdiff2
    has already been run with the -s1 switch.
```
continued

Figure 12–18 *continued*

```
[-dbg] debug mode on

    Currently dbdiff2 is quiet unless it runs into a synonym
    which points to another server - in which case it will
    ask you if you wish the new database to point to a different
    server. -dbg displays status messages as the program rolls along.

[-t] table name specification

    Like it sounds. -t table will generate code for ONE TABLE
    ONLY - where applicable. It may also be used as a wildcard,
    e.g.:
        -t 'prefix*'
          or
             -t '*suffix'
[-c] process constraints. (Default is no)

    will generate code to support constraints

[-trg] process triggers. (Default is no)

    will generate code to support triggers

[-spl] process stored procedures. (Default is no)

    will generate code to support stored procedures

[-q] Quiet mode - no messages

[-svr filename] identifies a file of servers. This is in case your
    first database uses a different set of servers for synonyms
    than the second database (our case). Format of the file is:

    server1|server2

    and means change all references to server1 to server2. Up
    to 20 different servers are supported, each on their own line.
    Feel free to change the code to handle more (max_servers and
    DEFINE servers ARRAY [20]). The default file name is
    "dbd.servers". Upon completion of the program any new
    server changes required are written out to this file. So
    running the program once will log all server swaps you
    normally do and then use those forever after.
```

continued

Figure 12–18   continued

```
[-lg] Turn on logging (default is dbdiff2.log). Status messages
      are written to this logfile.

 [-lgf filename] identifies a file to use instead of dbdiff2.log.
      Also turns on logging.
 [-all] the same as -c -dbg -a -u -spl -trg.

[?] usage

    Generate a brief explanatory message.

Final:

    Only two switches are required -od and -nd. Although the following
    are legal:

        dbdiff2 -od database -s1

    and

        dbdiff2 -nd database -s2
```

Figure 12-18 continued

As this book was going to print, Jack wrote me and said he was about to release a newer version of this utility. This version addresses some of the new functionality in the 7.2 release of OnLine Dynamic Server. This version, and all others he might release in the future, can be found in the software archives maintained on the IIUG server.

Miscellaneous

The scripts and programs included here are more database or instance administrative in nature. All but one were contributed by friends and associates who I recognized at the beginning of this chapter. The programs included in this section will create data dictionaries, build "update statistics" command files, uninstall Informix products, help you manage table privileges, and give you a dbaccess-like utility that also allows you to create forms eliminating the need to buy I-SQL to get that piece of functionality.

datadctnry.4gl

I wrote this quick and dirty 4GL program to create the skeleton of a data dictionary file that could be imported into a word processing program to add comments and so on. The source code for this program is too long to include here but the program is fairly easy to run. When invoked, enter the name of the database in the active instance for which you would like a data dictionary report generated. A file called *"dbname_dict"* will be created in the current working directory with the report. The application will loop around and ask for another database name. If no other reports are needed, press "return" sending a null value to exit the program

The program is intelligent enough to correctly resolve date, datetime, decimal, money, and the various character, variable-character, and NLS data types. Rudimentary instructions on how to run the program are available as well.

dbpriv.uue

This is a full-featured evaluation copy of a program written by Lester Knutsen and is available for purchase from his company, Advanced DataTools Corporation. This program allows you to manage database, table, and user permissions within your instances. Like everything Lester does, it is a top-notch program.

`Dbpriv` requires the RDS version of 4GL to run. It is distributed as a UNIX `tar` file and has been uuencoded in order to survive transferring to the DOS-based disc. To extract this program, copy the `dbpriv.uue` file to a directory and decode it back to its tar format by typing "uudecode dbpriv.uue." A file called "dbpriv.tar" will be created that can be extracted by typing "`tar -xvf dbpriv.tar`." A "scripts" and a "dbpriv" directory will be created and populated with files. I strongly recommend you read the README.TXT file in the dbpriv directory to understand how to proceed from this point and the functionality of the program.

While the evaluation copy of this program was compiled to expire some time in the future, if by the time you purchase this book and attempt to use this program, that date has passed, you can contact Lester via e-mail at lester@access.digex.net or by phone at 703.256.0267 to arrange for a new copy. You can also arrange to purchase this program through these same channels.

html_ec.shr and systabs.shr

Both of these utilities were written by Tim Schaefer and are part of his extensive, quality library of Informix tools and utilities. Tim publishes the Informix-oriented web-zine called "INX-UTIL" as well. Tim can be contacted at tschaefe@mindspring.com. His web-zine can be viewed at http://www.mindspring.com/~tschaefe.

`Html_ec.shr` creates a data dictionary-type file in html that can be viewed with any web browser. It requires the compiled version of 4GL and is distributed in a shar format. Extract the files as previously explained then type "`make -f html_ec.mk`" to compile the program.

I have to admit I have not explored the `systabs` program in great detail but what I've seen I really like. `Systabs` enables you to look at database system tables as well as regular tables in an I-SQL type of interface. It is OnLine Dynamic Server compliant, it will allow you to look at the SMI tables and it also has some limited reporting functionality. This program is distributed as a UNIX `shar` file too and once extracted it can be compiled for use with either the RDS or compiled versions of 4GL. To compile for RDS, type "`make -f systabs.mk rds`"; type "`make -f systabs.mk all`" to use the compiled version of 4GL.

The Informix FAQ and misql.shr

Kerry Sainsbury has, for a number of years, been the principal driving force behind not only the creation but the ongoing maintenance of the Informix FAQ (frequently ask question list). Intended to answer basic and more advanced questions that occur with some regularity in the `comp.databases.informix` Usenet discussion forum, this list should be mandatory reading for those new to Informix products. It includes information on engine and application tools as well as resources to find more in-depth information. Many of the OnLine engine-oriented topics precede the full release of OnLine Dynamic Server as we now know it but that does not diminish the FAQs' value in any way.

The version included here is in html and is distributed as a UNIX `shar` file. During the creation of the `shar` archive, the html tags were interpreted as non-ASCII character sets so the files were uuencoded as part of the process. Simply extracting the `shar` file will decode the individual files back into html for browsing. The top page is called, appropriately enough, "`informix.htm`." As the FAQ continues to evolve, the most current versions will be available at a number of sites including the IIUG web server.

`Misql` was also written by Kerry and is intended to supplement the `dbaccess` utility provided by Informix. For many DBAs, `dbaccess` is all they need to administer the databases in their systems. From time to time though, the ability to create a SQL form would be nice. This functionality is only available in the Informix SQL development product requiring the purchase of another piece of software that only provides one or two extra pieces of functionality beyond `dbaccess`. `Misql` gives you the ability to create and run full function I-SQL-like forms as well as the basic `dbaccess` query functionality.

Once the `shar` file has been extracted, type "`make`" to create executables that can be used with either the RDS or compiled versions of 4GL. When executing either versions, you must pass a valid database name for the active instance as an input parameter to avoid a run-time error.

For more information about the FAQ or the `misql` utility, Kerry can be reached at kerry@kcbbs.gen.nz.

uninstall.shr

I have to admit I have never used this utility because I have never needed to remove a part of the Informix product set or do selective installs. These questions do get asked from time to time on the `comp.databases.informix` Usenet group so Jonathan Leffler wrote the utilities included in this `shar` file. Jonathan wrote the following to explain what these five utilities do:

```
ixcreate
  -- install Informix software from pre-existing
     installation
ixremove
  -- uninstall unnecessary files from existing INFOR-
     MIXDIR
cpinfxdir
  -- create sub-directories where necessary and sym-
     links where possible
mkinfxdir
  -- create INFORMIXDIR using ixcreate and separate
     directories for Tools and Engines.
mkixcpio
  -- recreate cpio file corresponding to selected
     Informix product(s)

Be careful to ensure that you have the necessary
backups in place before doing anything -- these
tools are powerful enough to let you wreck your sys-
tem if abused. Also beware that ixcreate does not
create symlinks into system directories; specifi-
cally, it does not place symlinks in /usr/lib point-
ing to the Informix shared libraries, which can be a
problem for 6.00 and later OnLine systems. You can
fix the link up manually like I do.
```

These utilities are to be used at your own risk. There is no support of any kind implied or offered by the author, his employer, or me for having included them on the disc.

upd_stat.4gl

This 4GL program was written by Gavin Nour and can be compiled and used with either version of 4GL or NewEra, Informix's graphical application development product. Once compiled and executed, it creates a SQL command file containing commands to properly update statistics within the target database. See the "Update Statistics and Data Distributions" section of Chapter 8, Enhancing Performance, for more information on the SQL "update statistics" command.

The program sets up columns heading indexes to be updated "high" and other columns to be updated at other levels or to refresh data distributions. Of course you will want to review the output generated to make sure it matches your needs, particularly if you follow an optimization procedure other than the standard recommended by Informix and others.

The program can take two input parameters although neither are required:

- –d *dbname* The database against which the report should be created
- –o *output_file* The pathed location and name for the generated report.

The defaults for these parameters are the sysmaster database and /tmp/upd_stat.sql. Gavin can be contacted at nourg@selectsoftware.com.au.

Appendix A

Other Informix Resources

There are a number of resources you can turn to in order to learn more about Informix's products, or for assistance in solving problems that occur from time to time. While many of these resources existed only in hard-copy form once, the rapid increase of the general public's use of Internet technology has driven many of these resources to being Internet-accessible, perhaps exclusively based there.

This is not to say that there haven't been Internet-based resources available in the past. Thanks in large part to the efforts of Walt Hultgren at Emory University in Atlanta, Georgia, Informix was the first vendor to have its own database-vendor-specific Usenet newsgroup. The resulting `comp.databases.informix` newsgroup, created in the early 1990s, has become one of the most important Internet-based channels users have to exchange information about their experiences with Informix products and get help to solve a problem or answer a question.

There are also other places to look to for information. In this appendix, I'll briefly introduce some of the more popular and timely products and services focused toward the Informix community.

Publications

There are a growing number of trade journals and other publications oriented to users of Informix's products. With the growth of general public access to the Internet, some of the latest efforts are World Wide Web-based.

Some of these publications require that you have a valid product support contract with Informix. See the "Informix Technical Support Options" section of Chapter 10, Recovering from a Crash, for more information on the support options Informix provides.

Hard-Copy and Web-Based Publications

Several Informix publications are available in both hard-copy and WWW formats. These include *TechNotes*, *CS Times*, and technical White Papers.

TechNotes is a technically oriented journal published quarterly by Informix. Available to Informix customers with a current OpenLine or higher support contract, this journal regularly features articles of interest to both application developers and database and OnLine administrators. Recently published articles have included a discussion of how the OnLine Dynamic Server optimizer processes queries and how you can improve the quality of your SQL statements, building a web-based document management system, designing data warehouse database systems, object-oriented development, a technical introduction to Illustra's ORDBMS technology, using solid-state cache to eliminate disk I/O bottlenecks, and NewEra application partitioning.

If you have a current OpenLine or higher support contract with Informix and are not receiving your copy of *TechNotes*, contact the customer service department at Informix and ask to have your name included on the subscription list to receive the hard-copy version.

You can, however, access the current and all prior issues of *TechNotes* from the TechInfo section of Informix's WWW site. Access to this portion of Informix's site is password-protected and will require that you contact Informix's customer service department to arrange for access to the TechInfo center.

Angela Sanchez, the editor of *TechNotes*, is always interested in receiving proposals for articles to be included in *TechNotes* . If you have a technically oriented article you would like to submit for her consideration, contact her via e-mail at `angelas@informix.com` or by fax at 415.926.6626. She asks that you include a general description of your intended article, and the relevance of your subject to the use of Informix products or services.

A number of Internet-based addresses and URLs (uniform resource locator) will be used in this appendix. Because of the highly dynamic nature of the Internet and Internet-based resources, some changes in addresses or URLs will occur over time. While the addresses and URLs listed here were accurate as of the date of publication, you may have to do some searching to find their replacements if these change.

Informix periodically publishes technical White Papers that explain their technology or how to use their products more effectively. While these White Papers can be ordered through your local Informix sales office or from the Informix customer service department, point your web browser to

```
http://www.informix.com/informix/corpinfo/zines/
    whiteidx.htm
```

for an up-to-date hypertext list of available White Papers.

CS Times is a quarterly publication from Informix's technical support department. Available to anyone interested in the Informix support organization, this publication is intended to keep you informed of the continuing changes and refinements there. A hard-copy subscription can be ordered through Informix's customer service department. You can also read it from the Informix web site by pointing your browser to

```
http://www.informix.com/informix/corpinfo/zines/
    cstmsidx.htm
```

Informix Times is a quarterly sales- and marketing-oriented publication. This publication is available to anyone interested in a broadbrush overview of Informix's products,
with interviews with customers and other general information about Informix. Again, a hard-copy subscription can be ordered through Informix's customer support department, or you can read the current issue and many of the past issues from Informix's WWW site. Point your browser to:

```
http://www.informix.com/informix/corpinfo/zines/
    tinesidx.htm
```

Web-Based-Only Publications

While perhaps not considered publications in the strictest technical sense, there are a number of WWW sites that contain information, utilities, and tips on using Informix's products.

First among these is the site maintained by the International Informix Users Group (IIUG). The IIUG site contains a searchable archive of the `comp.database.informix` Usenet group, a collection of end-user-contributed tools and utilities, and information about Informix user groups located all over the world. You can contact the IIUG by pointing your browser to

```
http://www.iiug.org
```

While any list of web-based sites is almost sure to be out of date by the time it is published, there is one other WWW site worth mentioning here. Tim Schaefer has started a service called INX_UTIL that looks promising. You can access it by pointing your web browser to

```
http://www.mindspring.com/~tschaefe
```

To find more WWW or other Internet-based Informix resources, you can use the popular Alta Vista search engine provided by Digital Equipment Corporation. You can enter various Informix-related keywords and search the resources stored on the Internet. To get to this search engine, point your browser to

```
http://www.altavista.digital.com
```

Miscellaneous Publications

There have not been many third-party publications focused on Informix products as yet.

Prentice Hall and Informix Software have a joint publishing agreement for potential authors (such as yours truly) to write books about understanding and using Informix products.

As I mentioned in the preface to this book, writing a book is an arduous process—particularly if all you've ever written is the odd term paper in college, computer programs, and e-mail letters to friends and colleagues. There is, however, a sense of satisfaction and accomplishment when the writing and publication process is completed. There are very few who take the time, and put in the effort, to complete a project as large as a book. I have a much greater appreciation for those who have done it, and particularly for those who have written for Informix Press.

If you would like more information about Prentice Hall/Informix Press books, point your browser to

```
http://www.prenhall.com/~informix
```

If you would like more information about submitting a book proposal to Informix Press, contact Mark Taub at Prentice Hall (`markt@prenhall.com`) or Sandy Emerson (`semerson@informix.com`) with Informix Software. General guidelines for submitting proposals, the required writing style, and other prepublication information can be found at

```
http://www.prenhall.com/author_guide/
```

Other good sources of information in printed form are newsletters published by local Informix user groups. As I explain in the next section, there are over 40 Informix user groups located throughout the world. Many of these produce either a quarterly or semi-annual newsletter filled almost exclusively with technical articles.

If you do not have an Informix user group in your area, you can locate the one closest to you through the IIUG WWW site. If this group does not publish a newsletter, they should be able to direct you to the groups that do. Some groups even store electronic copies of their newsletters in the ftp section of the IIUG WWW server which can be downloaded via anonymous ftp.

International and Local User Groups

Local Informix user groups have existed in locations throughout the world for a number of years. Organized to meet the differing needs of Informix users in an area, no two local Informix user groups are completely identical. They do, however, share a common goal of providing to their members greater access to information about Informix's products, and the opportunity to draw on the wisdom and experience of others in the geographic area to solve problems or learn how to more effectively use any given Informix product.

There are currently over 40 local user groups in close to a dozen different countries that meet on a regular basis. Many of the larger groups sponsor full-day training seminars where experts in various technologies teach sessions of various lengths. Third-party vendors with products that are Informix-oriented participate in vendor exhibits. Meals are sometimes provided, around which members have a chance to share experiences and ideas. As I mentioned earlier in this appendix, many user groups publish technical newsletters for the benefit of their members as well as nonmembers who pay for a subscription.

Smaller user groups typically meet and bring in Informix Systems Engineers or third-party vendors to provide a hands-on demonstration of their products or services. Often, the group will meet in a local restaurant's meeting room, have the technical presentation, then close with a participant-paid meal. This gives the group's members a chance to network and share ideas.

As you would expect, groups outside of the United States incorporate the various elements of their culture into their group's activities. For example, the Munich, Germany group regularly provides a "stommtisch" for its members. This is largely a social gathering of the group's members to eat and enjoy local "beverages," but quite a bit of work occurs in these meetings. I recently became aware of plans by the group in Belgium to hold a meeting in the chateau of a winery in a particularly scenic part of that country. This group is also trying to arrange group travel plans to the Informix Worldwide User Conference as a service to its members.

The bottom line of all this is that if there is an Informix user group in your area, you would be well served to join it and participate in the programs and opportunities it provides.

International Informix Users Group

In 1995, a group of individuals who were themselves, heads of local Informix user groups formally organized the International Informix Users Group (IIUG). The goals and objectives of the IIUG were simple, yet at the same time somewhat ambitious. They were to

- Promote the growth of local and regional Informix user groups.
- Provide to the user community a unified and coherent voice with which to advise and influence Informix on key issues.

- Foster the development of individual Informix users.
- Coordinate the collection and distribution of user-contributed software or technical resources.
- Provide access to a user group organization to those individuals in areas of the world not served by a local or regional Informix user group.

That same year, Informix began to realize the strategic importance of user groups in providing support and encouragement to individual users of their products and as an avenue to communicate with them as well as to get feedback on what was important to them. In response to this realization, Informix created the Informix User Group Program and hired staff to support the efforts of the IIUG and local user groups.

Since that time, the local Informix user group community has continued to grow. New groups are being formed each year with the support and encouragement of the local Informix office and the IIUG. These groups, like the IIUG, are not puppets of the Informix marketing department. Hard questions are often asked and difficult issues discussed in meetings with representatives from Informix's management or product development teams. At the same time, there is a chance for user group members to get a more detailed look at various technologies, how to implement them, and build a network of peers.

The IIUG has continued to grow and expand in its role. In 1995, the IIUG began to provide many of the Internet-based services I have already mentioned in this appendix. The IIUG computer holds the world's largest public collection of Informix-oriented resources as well as information about all the Informix user groups around the world. Many of these local groups have established their own WWW homepages on the IIUG server to get information out to their members and publicize upcoming events.

In 1996, the Informix User Group Leadership Council (IUGLC) was formed as an advisory body to the IIUG. This Council's membership includes the leaders of all the local and regional Informix user groups. The IUGLC advises and directs the IIUG's efforts on issues that affect local and regional user groups.

The IIUG in 1997 will continue building on its advocacy program launched at the end of 1996. Members of the IIUG Board of Directors are working with several senior-level managers in an effort to refine and enhance several product initiatives. In addition, there is some work being done with a regional manager to develop the first user group organization in that manager's part of the world. Finally, the IIUG will be sponsoring a technical track at the 1997 Informix Worldwide User Conference in addition to its other activities at the conference.

For more information about the IIUG or local user groups, you can contact the IIUG at

```
http://www.iiug.org
```

 by e-mail at `info@iiug.org`
 by phone at 888.234.IIUG (toll-free)
 by fax at 415.926.1199

The mailing address for the IIUG is
International Informix Users Group
4100 Bohannon Drive, M/S 4300-2
Menlo Park, CA 94025 USA

Christine Shannon, the Informix User Group Liaison can be reached by e-mail at `usergrp@informix.com` or through the IIUG contact phone and fax numbers.

The Informix Worldwide User Conference

No discussion of Informix resources would be complete without including the Informix Worldwide User Conference (IWUC). Held annually during the month of July, this four-day/three-night conference brings together users from all over the world in all types of industries.

The conference has grown significantly over the past several years as Informix's market share has grown. In 1996, there were 3807 attendees from 1212 companies and 61 countries. The people who attend this conference are hard-core database or engine administrators and application developers who use Informix's products. In fact, reviewing the demographics of those attending the 1996 conference, attendees indicated that they were database or system administrators by an almost 2 to 1 margin over the next closest job function. They were almost evenly divided among the manufacturing, telecommunications, financial/banking, retail, government, and distribution industries. Most came from companies with revenues greater than US $50M.

The conference is planned and run by Informix staff (Mary Castellone and Heather Gysler, at the time of this publication) and includes the general activities listed in Table A-1.

Table A-1

Conference Day	Activities
Day 1	• Tutorials—a series of half- to full-day by-admission-only technical training classes on the most current Informix products. Admission to these tutorials is included in the conference price if you register early enough. • Opening Reception—open to all.
Day 2	• Opening Session—featuring Phil White, Informix's President and CEO. Mr. White reviews the past year and what the next year has to offer. • General Sessions—a multitrack series of technical and marketing-oriented sessions are held throughout the day. • Exhibit Hall Opens—Informix and other vendors show off their products in the central exhibition area. • Birds of a Feather Sessions—hour-long open sessions after the general sessions close for the day. These meetings focus on specific technical features or implementations of technology. Past BoF session topics include class libraries and DataBlade modules, success stories from OnLine XPS customers, CDR R & D roundtable, using GLS, managing dynamically driven web sites, and archive and restore designs for large database environments. The IIUG holds its annual open meeting during a BoF session. The general business of the organization is conducted, and the election of members to serve on the Board of Directors is held.

continued

Conference Day	Activities
	• Private Receptions—held in the evening after the general conference and exhibit hall closes, there are geographic, lines of business, and corporate receptions to allow attendees with similar interests or backgrounds to meet. Admittance is by invitation only to many of these receptions. The 1996 Conference featured everything from a cruise aboard a yacht, a concert featuring Peter Cetera, to a night at SCTV. The Informix User Group Program has its reception for those involved with user groups around the world. The fact that sushi is served has become a tradition among the receptions.
Day 3	• Keynote Address or Plenary Session—a person of some technical or business stature addresses the conference.
	• General Sessions—additional sessions in a multitrack setting.
	• Exhibit Hall—more time to look at products and gather goodies to take home to the kids.
	• BoF sessions—more focused meetings on specific technologies.
	• Conference Party —those in the know say that the conference party Informix throws is the best in the industry. All I know is that there is a lot of fun to be had with your friends and colleagues.
Day 4	• General Sessions—more track sessions
	• Exhibit Hall closes

Alhough a lot of fun things happen at the IWUC, the bottom line is that reading publications and attending user group meetings will take you a long way to becoming proficient with Informix's products—but there's still more. You cannot stay completely current on what Informix has to offer today, get a perspective of what can be accomplished with the technology that currently exists, or understand where the technology is going without attending the IWUC and hearing it directly from the people doing the work. Every organization that uses Informix's products should send at least one representative a year to the conference.

Using the Internet to Access Informix-Oriented Resources

The rest of this appendix is based on an article I wrote in 1995 for the Informix User News, *the forerunner to the* IIUG News, *the annual publication of the International Informix Users Group. Since that time, the original article has been reprinted by several local Informix user groups in their newsletters as well as by Informix in their* TechNotes *technical publication.*

I am including it here in case you are not yet connected to the Internet and would like a brief primer on the utilities you can use to get Internet-based information. I have expanded several sections and brought many elements of this article current from when it was originally written. I have also added a section on where to look for Informix-oriented information.

In the last few years much has been written about the Internet, some of it actually focused on the positive aspects of the network. In using the Internet, I have found that, like anything else, there is a lot of junk out there, but there is a tremendous amount of useful information as well. A growing number of Informix users are finding that some of the benefits of a traditional user group can be obtained electronically via the Internet especially if they are in an area not served by an Informix user group. There are several worldwide forums that allow you to get technical advice, share a programming trick, or hear the latest Informix-related news, all without leaving your terminal or workstation. This article is intended to help you use the basic tools of the Internet to access those computers which contain Informix related information.

The main suite of utilities you'll be using to access Internet-based resources are a Usenet newsgroup reader, a World Wide Web (WWW) browser such as the Netscape Navigator, a command-line or a graphical anonymous ftp client, a command-line or graphical electronic mail program such as Eudora, a telnet client, and a search service client to access a worldwide service called "archie." While I'll briefly explain what the services are that are accessed through these utilities later in this article, to find out more about these and other services and tools, go to your local bookstore and get one or more well written books on the Internet. O'Reilly and Associates, publishers of the Nutshell series, have a number of excellent publications on the Internet and how to use the tools associated with its services.

Accessing the Internet

There are two basic access methods to use the Internet, an on-line service or an Internet Service Provider (ISP).

On-Line Services

On-line services, such as CompuServe, AOL, or Prodigy, allow you to access the Internet through their computer systems. When you connect to a service such as CompuServe, you are not connecting to the Internet. Instead, you are connecting to a series of computers that the on-line service owns and maintains. These computers have the programs, services, and specialized content the service advertises as reasons to use their service.

Up until about two or three years ago, these services were islands unto themselves. Their programs didn't communicate with anyone else other than those who paid the service money for advertising and to publish content. Now all the on-line services offer some level of Internet access although, consistent with their desire to maintain control over the access process, they dictate the tools and utilities you can use to find and use Internet services. Pricing for Internet access used to be a surcharge, but that has been changing recently as well. All these on-line services now have fairly extensive help files to explain how to use the Internet-based applications. In addition, they also discuss the proper etiquette that should be used when using the various Internet-based facilities. For those with little technical training or intuition, or a desire for the private content any given on-line service may provide, an on-line service is an easy, though somewhat limiting, option for gaining Internet access.

Internet Service Providers (ISPs)

In my opinion, a far better method to access the Internet is to use an ISP. While many ISPs are working at making the connection process easier for nontechnical people, using an ISP does require some degree of technical competence and a willingness to work out problems for yourself. In return, you have much greater freedom in using Internet services.

An ISP is similar to an on-line service in that it maintains computer systems, but these systems are directly connected to the Internet and exist simply to provide Internet access to the subscriber. An ISP does not offer private content like an on-line service, where charges can accrue by the minute or hour of access time. Instead, an ISP offers clear, unaltered access to the Internet. Unlike on-line services, ISPs support a wide range of connectivity options. You can connect to an ISP using almost any type of operating system provided it runs a TCP/IP network stack. Many ISPs allow some amount of disk storage on their systems as well as web publishing services.

Most ISPs provide a starter collection of graphical tools you can load on your own computer that allow you to point-and-click your way around the Internet. You are, however, free to use any other tool you want provided you respect the license and fee requirements. If you can set up a PPP, SLIP, or CSLIP-based connection to the ISP, you can use a mixture of graphic or command-line utilities—either loaded on your own computer or on another remote computer, depending on your needs and abilities.

Understanding Internet Addresses

At first glance, the computer address may seem confusing, but the address tells you a great deal about how to access the computer and where to find the information you need once you are there. For example, in the address of http://www.informix.com/, the "http://" means you need to use a WWW browser to connect to the computer. In the computer name of "www.informix.com," the "www" preface means the computer will most likely respond to queries to use its services in a hypertext-based format, so you'll be able to point-and-click your way around with the browser.

In the address of "`ftp.xyz.com/pub/informix/my_neat_stuff`," you'll need to use "anonymous ftp" to log in to a computer called "`ftp.xyz.com`." Once logged in, the information will be found in the "`/pub/informix/my_neat_stuff`" directory. While most computer systems administrators follow this format to identify their computers, you will see names that have neither "www" nor "ftp" at the beginning. In this case, try using a WWW browser first, then "anonymous ftp."

Internet Information Services

For the balance of this article, I will discuss what some of the various Internet-based services, such as Usenet news groups, the World Wide Web, and "anonymous ftp," are and how to access them.

Usenet News

"Usenet" is the name given to a software program running on thousands of computer systems worldwide that allows them to act as one large distributed bulletin board system. Through a Usenet news reader, you can read and post messages to a newsgroup whose subject matter is specifically oriented to the topic of your message. These messages are first posted to the local computer system, while background software distributes the messages to other news sites, which in turn forward them to other sites.

A "newsgroup" is analogous to a discussion forum on on-line service. At last count there were about 16000 newsgroups, so, as you can imagine, there is a newsgroup on almost any topic or subject you might care to think of.

There is a newsgroup specifically oriented to Informix-related issues. It is known as `comp.databases.informix`, or c.d.i. for short. C.d.i was started in early 1990, I believe, and its charter specifies that it is for technically oriented discussions about the use and support of Informix software and related products. Acceptable topics of discussion include all of Informix's product line and services plus third-party products related to Informix. There are a number of recruiters and contract agencies that post messages about open positions as well. There has been a lot of discussion on whether or not to allow this to continue. Ultimately it will, because people like to know what's happening in the job market, and many of those posting job opportunities wouldn't stop even if asked to.

Anyone, including end users, vendors, and employees of Informix software, can participate in the discussions that occur in c.d.i. The newsgroup is unmoderated, which means no one screens the messages for content, so everyone is solely responsible for what they say. All contributions are welcome, as long as they emphasize substantive information.

The World Wide Web (WWW)

Of all the services available on the Internet, the most talked about right now is the WWW. From a simple-to-use graphical browser such as Netscape Navigator or Mosaic, you can point-and-click through a series of "hypertext" links to find information.

Hypertext links are no more difficult to use or understand than those in the help section of any Windows/Macintosh/X-Window application. In these help sections, words or phrases are highlighted in a different color. If you click on the word or phrase, you go to that section and read about whatever was highlighted.

With the WWW, this access method has been expanded in that these links can be to files on another computer somewhere else on the Internet. In WWW-oriented documents you have the ability to display graphic images as well as text, and to make both hypertext links. "Surfing the web" is perhaps the best way of exploring the various and sundry topics the Internet encompasses. Be forewarned, however, that tremendous amounts of time can be lost aimlessly wandering around if you are not focused in your search.

Anonymous ftp

"Anonymous ftp" is, in my opinion, one of the greatest tools available on the Internet. FTP (short for file transfer protocol) enables you to log in to a computer and copy files from that computer to your own. Primarily a command-line utility, there are graphical ftp clients for Macintosh and Windows environments.

The service takes its name from the login id used to access the remote computer. When prompted by the computer for a name, you enter "`anonymous`." Your own personal e-mail address is used as a password. Once logged in, you have a restricted ability to move around the directories of the remote computer and look at the file names there. However, you cannot see the contents of the files unless you copy them back to your own computer. This is accomplished using the "`get`" command. Help for any of the `ftp` commands, or `ftp` itself, is available by typing the word "`help`" while in an `ftp` session if you have command-line access in your operating system and invoked `ftp` from there. There should be a "help" button available on the graphical utilities that you can click on if you need help using it.

If you've never used "anonymous ftp," Figure A-1 contains a quick primer from Walt Hultgren of the International Informix Users Group, in the form of a sample session on the `mathcs.emory.edu` computer system. Comments are indicated by the use of { }. Lines where you type something are marked with "<<<"and what you type is in boldface. This is a command-line example, but the concepts apply to using "anonymous ftp" through a graphical utility.

If you do not have a graphical `ftp` client, you can use your WWW browser utility to accomplish the same thing, although it is not, in my experience, as efficient or reliable when you compare it to command-line or even an `ftp` graphical client. See your browser's help section for more information on using the browser to `ftp` files.

Electronic Mail

Electronic mail, as its name implies, is the ability to exchange written messages with others. There are so many tools, both command-line and graphical, to send and receive e-mail, I could not attempt to explain how to use them all. E-mail can do more than just send messages to friends and colleagues; you can use e-mail to retrieve files from ftp servers, among other things.

E-Mail Lists There is now only one global Informix-oriented mailing list. A mailing list is, in many ways, like a Usenet newsgroup. The topic is tightly focused, can be moderated or unmoderated, and can extend worldwide. Unlike a Usenet newsgroup, which you can access by simply directing your newsreader toward

```
% ftp mathcs.emory.edu          {or: ftp 128.140.2.1}           <<<
Connected to mathcs.emory.edu.
220 emory FTP server (SunOS 4.1) ready.
Name (mathcs.emory.edu:walt): anonymous                         <<<
331 Guest login ok, send ident as password.
Password: walt@rmy.emory.edu    {use your e-mail address here}  <<<
230 Guest login ok, access restrictions apply.
ftp> cd pub/informix                                            <<<
250 CWD command successful.
ftp> get README                                                 <<<
200 PORT command successful.
226 ASCII Transfer complete.
{once copied to your system, you could read the contents of the file then
     continue on}
ftp> get ls-lR                                                  <<<
200 PORT command successful.
226 ASCII Transfer complete.
     .
     .     {repeat this step for each file you want}
     .
ftp> quit                                                       <<<
221 Goodbye.
%
```

Figure A–1   *An example of an "anonymous ftp" session.*

it, you must subscribe to an e-mail list. Most e-mail lists are free of charge, but some are not. Unlike Usenet newsgroups, there isn't a central control, more or less, for the creation of mailing lists. This means that there could be an unlimited number of mailing lists on any topic that might interest you. The last distinction between a mailing list and a Usenet newsgroup is that your message to a mailing list goes to wherever the mailing list is being run from, then is distributed directly to mailing list subscribers.

informix-list   The main Informix mail list is called "`informix-list`" and is currently based on the `rmy.emory.edu` computer system, located at Emory University in Atlanta, Georgia. In the near future, the list will most likely migrate to the IIUG server.

`Informix-list` carries technically oriented discussions related to the use and support of Informix software and related third-party offerings. `Informix-list` is gatewayed with the Informix-oriented Usenet newsgroup as well. Messages posted to `informix-list` are posted to c.d.i for worldwide distribution. Messages originally posted to c.d.i. are routed to the mailing list so that those without Usenet access can still participate in the larger worldwide discussion.

Membership in the list is open to anyone, including end users, vendors, and employees of Informix software. There is no subscription or registration fee. The list is unmoderated, so subscribers are solely responsible for its content. All contributions are welcome, as long as they emphasize substantive information.

To subscribe to `informix-list`, send e-mail to `informix-list-request@rmy.emory.edu` with the following information:

1. The e-mail address or alias to be added to the list
2. Your name (not just your login ID)
3. Organization or company name
4. Postal address
5. Voice phone number

Telnet

`Telnet` is used for logging into other computers on the Internet. `Telnet` is most often used to gain access to public service computers holding information such as library card catalogs and other kinds of databases as well as search tools like "`archie`." Most computers allowing general public `telnet` sessions require that you use specific login ids and passwords in order to get in. This information should be included with the basic information you received about the services offered from the computer or displayed to you when you connect your `telnet` session to the computer. Once you successfully `telnet` into the computer, the programs you run will execute on that computer, not your local computer.

Archie

`Archie` is a software program running on some Internet servers which helps you find files that exist on other publicly accessible computers. There are a number of `archie` sites around the world—`archie.rutgers.edu`, `archie.au`, `archie.funet.fi`, and `archie.wide.ap.jp` to name just a few. Once logged in to `archie` (via `telnet`), you can ask the program to find file names that contain keywords of your choosing or to suggest files whose description of contents contain keywords of your choice. `Archie` will return the computer name and location of the file(s) matching your search criteria. If you use a graphical-based archie tool such as X-Archie to connect to `archie` services, you can click on the reference returned and you will be logged on to the referenced computer via "anonymous ftp" and be able to download the file directly to your computer.

Where to Find Informix-Oriented Information

So how do you apply all these tools and gather information about using Informix products? The `comp.databases.informix` Usenet newsgroup is a great place to start.

Informix has a WWW site with a tremendous amount of product, and some technical, information. To get to it, simply point your web browser to `http://www.informix.com`.

The most comprehensive noncommercial site for Informix-oriented information is run by the International Informix Users Group (IIUG). The site contains a complete, searchable archive of the `comp.databases.informix` Usenet group, a full listing of local Informix user group organizations around the world, a collection of noncommercial software and utilities to make your job easier, links to other Informix-oriented technical information, as well as information about the activities of the IIUG. To access their services, point your web browser to `http://www.iiug.org`. "Anonymous ftp" service is available at `ftp.iiug.org`.

You can also use any of the more extensive Internet search engines, such as Digital's Alta Vista engine, to search for Informix-related information. To access their engine, point your browser to `http://www.altavista.digital.com`.

If you are new to the Internet or have never used it, I hope this has helped take some of the mystery out of using the tools available to you. The files you can access, the tools, and the people you'll come in contact with using them can be a tremendous source of support and problem-solving ideas as you work in the Informix environment.

Appendix

B

Table Sizing Worksheets

On the media accompanying this book, there are two Adobe Acrobat files. Both are worksheets to help you size tables being stored within OnLine instances. The first file, `5x_work.pdf`, is for OnLine versions 5.x and earlier. It is provided simply as a reference point for comparison against what is required to properly size a table being stored in an OnLine Dynamic Server instance. The second file, `dsa_work.pdf`, contains the table sizing worksheet for tables being stored in OnLine Dynamic Server instances.

   I will briefly walk through the steps involved in properly sizing a table for each version of the engine. I'll start with the worksheet for OnLine version 5.x, then cover the worksheet for OnLine Dynamic Server. The 5.x worksheet assumes the page size for the port of the engine is 2 KB. If you're using this version of the engine, and the page size of your port is different, simply adjust the page-specific calculations as needed.

   Since this worksheet is included only for reference purposes, additional information such as determining row size when the table contains one or more BLOB columns is not included. It is, however, very similar to the process described in Notes 1 and 2 on the General Notes page of the OnLine Dynamic Server Table Sizing worksheet.

The process of properly calculating the size of a table in the OnLine Dynamic Server engine can be a little complicated, even with the worksheet provided. You can, however, generate a very rough approximation of the storage requirements for a table by using the Version 5.x worksheet.

Using the Table Sizing Worksheet for OnLine Versions 5.x and Earlier

There are two parts to this worksheet, the calculation of the table's initial extent and that of its next extent size.

Initial Extent Size

Add up the column sizes for each column used in every index for the table in question. To this total, add 8 bytes for each index on the table. If you have a column of type "varchar," use the average length of the varchar column when summing the column sizes. Enter the total on line 101.

On line 102, calculate the 25 percent overhead for indexes by multiplying line 101 by 1.25.

On line 103, enter the number of rows you anticipate this table will need to hold about six months from now. If, between now and then, you anticipate the table will need to hold a larger number of rows because of periodic rather than constant data purges, use that number of rows.

Calculate the amount of disk space that will be required to store the indexes by multiplying the anticipated number of rows in the table (line 103), by the amount of disk space required to index one row (line 102). Divide this number by 1024 to get the answer in KB; enter it on line 104.

On line 105, calculate the size of one data row by summing up the size of each column in the table, then adding 4 bytes for row overhead. If you have a column of type "varchar," use the average length of the varchar column when summing column lengths.

Calculate the number of data rows that will fit on one data page by dividing the usable size of a data page (2020 bytes out of 2048) by the size of a data row (line 105). Round the result down to the next largest whole number. In the event that the result exceeds 255, use 255 because no more than 255 rows can be stored on a single data page. Enter the result on line 106.

On line 107, calculate the amount of disk space required, in KB, to store the anticipated number of rows. Divide the anticipated number of rows (line 103) by the number of rows per data page (line 106). This interim result should be rounded up to the next whole number. It represents the number of data pages that will be needed to store the rows. Multiply this result by 2 to generate the storage size in KBs.

To arrive at the initial extent size needed for the table, simply add the amount of space required for indexes (line 104) to the amount needed to store the data (line 107).

Next Extent Size

To generate the "next extent" size, which allocates an amount of disk space to allow for table growth over a given amount of time, follow the same type of process.

On line 201, multiply the projected number of rows to be added to the table for the desired time period by the amount of space required to index one row (line 102). Divide the result by 1024 to generate a result in KB.

On line 202, calculate the amount of space required to store the data itself by dividing the projected number of rows to be added by the number of rows that can fit on a data page (line 106). Multiply the answer by 2 to get the result in KB.

The next extent size is calculated by adding the anticipated storage space required for indexes and data, then dividing the result by 7. This yields a slightly larger next extent size than Informix recommends, but it gives you a little more room to work with when dealing with a table that is growing faster than you had originally anticipated. This size helps reduce the total number of table extents allocated to the table as it approaches the total number of anticipated rows stored.

Using the Table Sizing Worksheet for OnLine Dynamic Server

This worksheet is divided into two sections. The first section covers the steps to calculate the amount of space required to store data in the table. The second section covers the steps to calculate the storage requirements for any nonfragmented indexes.

As explained in the "Calculating Table Sizes" section of Chapter 2, Preparing for Initialization, this worksheet only works for nonfragmented tables. The data portion of this worksheet will work for tables with indexes that have been fragmented or partitioned into other dbspaces, provided that the table itself remains unfragmented. A completely different approach is required for sizing tables that are fragmented, as explained in that chapter.

Section 1—Calculating the Data Portion

On line 1, calculate the usable storage space on a data page for your port of the engine by subtracting 28 bytes from the page size. In a 2 KB port, the result will be the same as in the version 5.x worksheet—2020 bytes.

Calculate the total length of one row in the table by summing all the column lengths. If the table contains one or more BLOB columns, see Note 1 on the last page of this worksheet. If you have a column of type "varchar," use the average length of the varchar column. Enter the result on line 2.

On line 3, enter the anticipated number of rows the table will need to store approximately six months from now. If, between now and then, you anticipate the table will need to hold a larger number of rows because of periodic rather than constant data purges, use that number of rows.

At this point, if the length of an individual row is *less than* the usable size of the data page, proceed to the next two lines on the worksheet, labeled steps 4 and 5 and explained in the next section, to complete the storage calculation for the data portion. If the row length is *greater than* the size of the data page, you need to calculate the number of "home" and "remainder" pages that will be required to store the data. This is explained in the section labeled "Row Length Greater than Page Size."

Row Length **Smaller** than Page Size

On line 4, calculate the number of rows that will fit on an individual data page by adding an additional 4 bytes for overhead to the row length, then dividing the usable page size by this new row size value. Round the result down to the nearest whole number. Because no more than 255 rows can be stored on any given data page, this value should not exceed 255.

On line 5, calculate the amount of disk space required to store the rows by dividing the anticipated number of rows by the number of rows that will fit on an individual data page. Round this result up to the nearest whole number, then multiply it by 2 (or 4 for a 4 KB port) to get the amount in KBs.

If you are storing BLOBs "in table" rather than in a separate BLOBspace, you also have to include the amount of space required to store the BLOBs with the space required to store the descriptor information and other standard data type columns. At a minimum, this will add 2 KB per BLOB per row to the data storage requirements for the table. The procedure to follow in calculating the space required to store BLOBs is explained in Note 2 on the last page of the worksheet.

Row Length **Greater** than Page Size

If your calculations indicate that the row length for the table in question is *greater than* the usable space on a data page (line 2 > line 1), the OnLine Dynamic Server engine will create what are called "home" and "remainder" pages for the table within the instances dbspaces. Any given row of the table will initially fill a "home" page. The remaining portion will be grouped together with other remaining portions of other rows on a series of "remainder" pages.

In order to properly size a table with this type of row length, you have to calculate the number of home and remainder pages that will be required. To begin, the number of home pages will be equal to the anticipated number of rows in the table. Enter this value on line 4A.

Remainder pages do not carry as much overhead as regular data pages, so the usable storage on a remainder page is slightly greater. This is important when calculating how many remainder pages will be required to store the rest of the row. First, calculate the amount of additional remainder information to store by taking the length of the data row (line 2) and subtracting from it the value of the usable data page size *plus* 8 bytes. Enter this value on line 4B.

If this value (line 4B) is *greater than* the usable size of a remainder page, then the row will not only fill a full home page, but will also fill a complete remainder page and still have more data to store on a second remainder page. In this case, you need to calculate how many full remainder pages the table will have as well as the number of partial remainder pages. If the value entered on line 4B is *less than* the usable space of a remainder page, only the calculations concerning partial remainder pages need to be done. Those calculations, which start on line 4D, are explained in the "Remainder Portion Less than the Remainder Page Size" section.

Remainder Portion **Greater** than the Remainder Page Size

To calculate the number of full remainder pages that will be required, divide the additional remainder amount (line 4B) by the usable storage space of a data page *minus* an additional 8 bytes for overhead to point to the next remainder page.

Round the result down to the previous whole number, then multiply it by the anticipated number of rows for the table (line 3). Enter this value on line 4C and proceed to calculate the amount of partially filled remainder pages, as explained in the next section.

Remainder Portion **Less** than the Remainder Page Size

To calculate the amount of space needed by partial remainder pages, divide the row length (line 2) by the usable storage space on a data page *minus* an additional 8 bytes. Add 4 bytes to the *remainder* of this calculation. Enter the new value of the remainder on line 4D.

Now calculate a usage ratio by dividing the value calculated on line 4D by the usable storage space of a data page. Enter the result on line 4E.

Depending on the value entered on line 4E, calculating the number of partial remainder pages will vary. Based on the value of line 4E, use the appropriate equation to calculate a value for line 4F.

The total amount of disk space required to store the data for the table in question will be the sum of:

- The number of home pages
- The number of the full remainder pages, if any
- The number of partial remainder pages

The resulting sum will be multiplied by 2 or 4 depending on the PAGESIZE of your port of the engine. Of course, "in table" storage of BLOBs will have an impact on this size as well. To calculate the amount of space required to store the BLOBs, see Note 2 on the last page of the worksheet.

Section 2—Calculating the Index Portion

Calculating the amount of space required to store indexes is only necessary when the indexes themselves are not fragmented, or partitioned off, into dbspaces other than where the table is to be created. If the index itself is fragmented, the engine will calculate the amount of disk space to allocate for the index when creating the index fragments in the requested dbspaces. The fragment size is calculated based on the length of the keys in the index and the initial extent size of the table.

In contrast to this, the overall storage requirements of an index created "in table" is affected by two conditions: the relative uniqueness of the data in the index, and whether or not the table itself is fragmented. Unlike earlier versions of the OnLine engine, where index sizing was accomplished by lumping all the indexes together, when calculating the sizes of indexes in OnLine

Dynamic Server instances you must calculate the size of each index individually.

To begin this process, sum up the size of each key in the index and add 4 bytes to this total. Enter this value on line 201.

Next, determine how "unique" the index is. If the index itself is unique or supports a unique constraint or primary key, let line 202 equal 1 (one). Otherwise, calculate a ratio by dividing the number of unique index entries by the number of rows in the table (line 3). If the table has not been created yet and, as a result, you do not have any data loaded in it to check for unique occurrences of the index key values, use an estimate of the number of unique index entries. Enter this value on line 202.

The size of an individual index entry in the index pages will vary depending on whether or not the table itself is fragmented (but the index does not have its own fragmentation scheme or is partitioned into another dbspace than that which stores the data portion of the table). Use the correct calculation to determine the value for line 203 based on the fragmentation state of the table.

From this point, the rest of the calculations to determine the number of branch and leaf nodes are relatively easy to figure out. Simply follow the instructions for Lines 204 through 207 as printed on the worksheet itself.

If you elected to set the FILLFACTOR parameter when the instance was initialized, or use a "fillfactor" keyword and a value when creating the index, calculate a value for line 208.

Adding the value calculated for line 207 or line 208, to the value calculated for line 5 of the data portion will give you the total amount of disk space required to store the table with its indexes for the anticipated number of rows.

Appendix C

An Interview with Gary Kelley

In January, 1997, I had the opportunity to talk with Gary Kelley, the architect of the OnLine Dynamic Server product. Originally planned as an opportunity to gather some basic background information to be used in the first chapter of this book, the interview quickly became much richer. Gary gave me permission to print an edited version of our conversation as an appendix so that I could share with you some of what he said.

In this conversation, Gary talks about his background and how it prepared him for creating the OnLine Dynamic Server product. He discusses the opportunities and architectural problems other database companies have with their database engines and how they had a chance to use the technology that makes OnLine Dynamic Server what it is today. He also talks about the successes and failures the OnLine Dynamic Server product has had from an architectural perspective, no-knobs database systems, and, in general terms, what the future holds for the product. It was a candid, open, and very insightful conversation. I would like to thank him again for taking the time to speak, at length, with me.

One thing I think I should make perfectly clear—while Gary makes reference to general technology that *might* appear in a particular release, his comments should not be construed as an official statement on the condition of that particular release. As is the case in all software development projects, the difficulty involved in creating, debugging, and testing the code, along with competitive forces and demands of end users could, and will, have an impact on the development process. He shared these, and other thoughts that cannot be included here, simply as indicators of the prevailing development mind-set at the time of the interview. It will almost certainly change over time.

Carlton: First of all, if you wouldn't mind, I know very little about your professional experience. I know that you came to Informix to create Dynamic Server but I don't know when that was, what you were involved in before that had an impact or influenced what you did with Dynamic Server. If you wouldn't mind just sharing with me a little bit about what your professional experience has been.

Gary: This is one of those cases where my background uniquely, just through luck, timing and situations, gave me a set of experiences that came together real nicely. I'm not saying I'm a genius or anything, but I just had the luck and opportunity to be in the database business from 1976 basically through now, which has been sort of the entire evolution of it, well, other than VSAM.

I first started out working at Data General on AOS. AOS was not a standard operating system by any stretch of the imagination, or a modern one, but it had multithreading in it. It had a built-in record oriented file system. It had many features that UNIX and NT have just come up with recently, and that was in the late 70s.

Then I went to Tandem. Tandem, at this point in time, is sort of declining because of their proprietary hardware and software. That has been their main revenue-producing business, but for 15 years or so they were the leader in databases in terms of technology. What they did is take a bunch of standard HP machines—because they're an HP spinoff—HP-like machines, glued them together in a cluster-like bus environment, and built nonstop fault-tolerant computers out of them. And they built an operating system and a database. I worked there with a fellow named Jim Gray that you might have heard of.

Carlton: Yes. I was told I ought to ask you about a "smoking hairy golf ball" or something along those lines.

Gary: That's Jim Gray's design for—Jim Gray in database academic circles is the number one sort of guy. In any event, he and I worked on an object-oriented database system, an extensible system back in the early 80s. At Tandem they were doing fault-tolerant computing, scalable databases in a message-oriented system, and object-oriented stuff in the early 80s. I was fortunate enough to be there in part of that.

Then I went to Synapse, which was a start-up. Synapse's bent was to take the same sort of scalable architecture that Tandem had, and put it on a shared-memory multiprocessor. There's advantages to that. So again, we built the whole operating system and database from scratch, built in a transaction monitor, and we had an object-oriented paradigm, or component system let's say, that was very similar to what Microsoft is doing.

That start-up failed. It ran out of money and I went to 3-Com [with] a group of people, friends, [that] I've worked with at three, maybe four companies now. At 3-Com David Vascovich was there. He's the head of database development at Microsoft.

David was there with a vision to create kind of a Microsoft-like component architecture at 3-Com. [David] started up an independent business unit and I worked for him. I developed a kind of a Sybase-like database system there, a prototype. Then we found out that 3-Com really wanted to make transceivers and we left.

So, as you see, my background has got some operating system, some loosely coupled fault-tolerant systems work, some shared-memory multiprocessor work and all of that was done in the context of start-up companies and kind of the first time it was done [situation]. So that's where I just was lucky and got a lot of good training. Working at 3-Com gave me the microprocessor experience, so I've kind of worked on all types of machines.

Then I got burned out on Bay Area. I got sick of Silicon Valley, said, "I'm moving to Oregon."

I came up and worked for an Intel/Siemens joint venture that turned into a company called Vine, which was a multiprocessor, fault-tolerant, object-oriented database machine. I knew the whole project was going to fail two weeks after I joined the company, but it still was good experience for me. They just had no marketing, and Intel doesn't know how to sell systems, but, you know, Siemens spent $175 million on this project.

Carlton: Yeah.

Gary: So, I stayed there for a while and then I joined Sequent.

Now at that time, Sequent had the same type of machine as Synapse—a shared-memory multiprocessor. Sequent, Pyramid, and one other company, I forget the name of it, they died— Encore, they didn't die but they got consumed. They were the only people that really had shared-memory multiprocessors. We can divert and talk about why they're good or interesting, but what Sequent was trying to do was get out of a niche which they had for shared-memory multiprocessing in the educational and scientific market and move into the commercial market.

The problem with moving into the high-end commercial market is that Oracle, Ingres, Informix, and Unify, who were the UNIX players at that time, didn't really know how to do it and they really didn't feel it was their market. They were working on Sun workstations and they were just happy doing that. So at Sequent my job was to create a group of people to start joint ventures with the four database companies I mentioned to add parallelism to their products, to help them scale and get better price performance than the mainframe.

Carlton: Okay.

Gary: As a result of those efforts, and their individual efforts with each company, we started the TPC wars. The first one that was done was with Ingres called the Turbo Bullet or something, no, the Silver Bullet. Then we went to Oracle, did the Belmont Stakes, and then we went to Informix and did the Turbo Trials or something like that. That fueled this continual battle that the companies have been in ever since. That competition indirectly fueled their whole companies to think higher-end, faster and all of that.

As a result of that [work], I tried to start a joint venture with each of the companies and one of them was Informix. First we had tried Ingres, because Ingres had a bigger market share at that time. We were developing with Ingres and doing good. Then Ingres got bought by ASK and they canceled the project.

So we had some code, [a] multithreading library, and some people. We went over to Informix and said, "Do you want to do this?" They said, "Fine" but they didn't have anyone to lead it. Informix' founder, [their] technical founder Roy Harrington, was kind of ready to retire because he was rich.

Carlton: [laughter]

Gary: So, I said "I'll quit Sequent and work for Informix and manage this joint venture in Portland." The joint venture essentially turned into DSA.

The first week I was here, we wrote a five-year plan. It's been seven years now, but I think we'll get it all done in another year. That five-year plan included versions 6, 7, and 8 and many of the aspects of extensibility. And this was all developed from sort of an amalgamation of the good aspects of the Tandem and Synapse, and to a lesser extent, the other company's products as well.

So, does that help you at all?

Carlton: Yes. So then you came on board at Informix what, around 1990 or so? 1991?

Gary: '90.

Carlton: Okay. So back then it was the Turbo engine, correct?

Gary: Yeah.

There's one more piece on background that you might find interesting. At Synapse we developed a unique logging and recovery scheme. When Synapse went bankrupt, many of the concepts of that logging and recovery scheme I took with me to 3-Com. Now at 3-Com we bought from Informix their C-ISAM record manager and we started adding all these logging recovery and parallelism concepts to it.

Carlton: Um-hmm.

Gary: And in doing so, I developed a relationship with Roger Sippl and Roy Harrington who were the founders of Informix. I understood the Informix code a little bit because C-ISAM grew into Turbo.

Carlton: Right.

Gary: So what happened there [was that] the ideas that I was implementing in 3-Com were also being implemented by Roy at Informix because we worked together. Turbo's logging [and] recovery scheme basically came from Synapse, [and] 3-Com through me working with Roy.

Carlton: Interesting.

Gary: And so that was Turbo. Turbo was really C-ISAM turned into a modern system with up-to-date transaction processing, logging [and] recovery, and the algorithms are all from Synapse and that happened by this circuitous route. It also gave me half of the relationships that gave the people at Informix some trust in me. The other half is a guy named Raiser McKiley, who was someone I worked with at Ingres [and] who went to Informix to head their server division.

So because of my Ingres project and the 3-Com project, I knew everybody. So anyway, that's how I got all that together. Since then, Roy, Roger, and Raiser are all in different places, but that's how we got it started.

Carlton: That's interesting.

Gary: Myself, and a guy named Dave Clay from Sequent, started this office. We just got the Turbo source code dumped in our laps and we said we could multithread it in six months and we did. And that was hell.

Carlton: I'm sure it was.

Gary: Not to say that just Dave and I did it—we hired aggressively and there were five or six other people that came on board real quickly. But Dave and I were sort of the people who got stuck doing most of the work in the beginning.

Later on, a fellow named Bob Gerber [who] was the leader of the Gamma project, a University of Wisconsin query processing multiprocessor machine, [joined us]. They developed the best algorithms that exist even today for doing data warehousing query processing. Bob was the leader there and he was the leader of the DEC RDB-Star project in Colorado Springs that was canceled. So Bob was sort of part of the second wave. He was really instrumental in making DSA the world leader. So we got an influence of Tandem, Gamma, Synapse, and everything in here.

Carlton: So you approached Informix and said, "Do you want to take your Turbo project and multithread it?" and they said, "Okay, sure, but we can't handle it."

Gary: Yeah, I said more than multithreaded, I said, "multithreaded and implement PDQ"—what we called in those days Parallel Database Query.

Carlton: Okay.

Gary: Which is parallel scans, joins, and all the things that people use in data warehousing now.

Carlton: From my perspective, it was my impression that when you came on board, or at least when Informix decided that they were going to create Dynamic Server, they basically said, "Okay, Turbo was a good first attempt, but let's start over from scratch. Throw everything away and build it from the ground up." It almost appears as though what you did is take the Turbo base and just start adding functionality to it. Is that correct?

Gary: Well, when something becomes incremental additions versus [a] rewrite is a subjective measure. We did have a five-year plan, so we didn't just hack.

Carlton: And I didn't mean to imply that you did.

Gary: We did a lot of strategic long-term work. The basic logging and recovery and index code has grown in an incremental manner. But the whole way that we manipulate memory and threads, the way we execute queries and optimize queries, that was sort of started over from scratch.

Carlton: Okay.

Gary: And if you remember what C-ISAM was, it was just really a record manager running in a UNIX process. So that code still is kind of there running in a thread. That might be too technical to understand the difference, but it's not a lie to say that we had a clean sheet of paper and a five-year plan to work from, but we didn't throw away code that we could utilize.

Carlton: I can appreciate that. Who was it that actually drove the design objectives for this engine? Was it you and your team or did it come from the product managers down in Menlo Park? I'm sure that there was some synergy of ideas but did the product managers in Menlo give you a blank slate and say, "Go for it, let's build something. Let's build a better mouse trap" or. . .?

Gary: I would say that the product management for this product, the initiation of it all came from Sequent product management and myself. Sequent, and I was one of the representatives of Sequent, went around proselytizing this type of development. In one day, we'd go to all four companies begging them to do it. [We would] say it was wonderful, show them university prototypes with a fellow named Goetz Graefe who's now up in Microsoft [and who] worked with us at producing prototypes.

We really drummed up the ideas. The person at Informix who was supportive of these ideas, and helped bring them in, was Tim Shetler in product management. The rest of the company didn't understand what it was. Tim was the only person in Menlo Park who understood what we were trying to do and supported it. Phil White backed it too, but it wasn't his initiative because he's a financial and sales guy. Not really a technical guy, so Tim was instrumental down there.

Mike Stonebraker, actually at Ingres [now at Informix], was the guy who helped get it started there.

Carlton: I assume that Oracle and Sybase probably looked but didn't think that your ideas had much value; they wanted to pursue their own path. Would that be an accurate statement to make?

Gary: No, each one's a little [different]. With Sybase, yes. With Oracle, no. Sequent was very insignificant in terms of revenue for Oracle when we first met them. Sequent and Oracle developed a very strong relationship for a few years, partly as a result of us helping prototype things. But their development staff wanted to do more of it themselves. They wanted to do it in a different way.

The architecture you see on the street now is really the result of work that started a couple of years ago, maybe even three years ago for some of it. Bottom line is that at that time, Oracle was very VMS oriented and they developed their parallel system around the DEC VMS world which was VAX clusters. That hardware and software architecture led them to a different approach then what we did with SMPs. Because of that approach, and a number of other things they started, they've never had the chance to rehaul their architecture from the bottom up.

Ingres was all for it. Mike Stonebraker was all for it, but then ASK bought them and it died.

Informix, same thing.

Sybase, way too soon. They came out of the gate really understanding how to do servers well. They did two or three innovations that got them on the map [and] got Microsoft's attention. But after they got in bed with Microsoft, they determined that their strategy is that database server was not a place to differentiate. [They decided] that it was going to be commoditized, and for the bulk of the market it wasn't interesting. I think they're right but I think they were like six or seven years early.

And so they did nothing to their server, and all of their tools [that] they've built around gateway products and separate servers [are] linked together with messages because that was, in their view, what they were trying to push as standards by leveraging their Microsoft relationship.

So they let their server languish and then they bought this thing called Navigation Server from AT&T which was sort of an add-on product to try and glue a multiple of their things together and it's been a disaster for them. So, Sybase is kind of out of the picture because they didn't put the proper investment in at the right time. And it's kind of ironic because their initial product differentiation was multithreading and stored procedures, which were performance features.

Carlton: When you, Tim, and the rest of your design team sat down and were working out what we now call Dynamic Server was going to be, I'm sure that there were a series of trade-offs that you had to make, either in design goals or in implementations. Could you give me some flavor of what those trade-offs might have been and what factors you used to drive your decisions one way or another as you considered each of the trade-offs?

Gary: Well, one of the major trade-offs that we decided early on was to basically do a threaded subsystem. That was one of the first discussions that we had. Because in some sense, why not just use operating system threads or UNIX processes and have operating system ways to do communication and dataflow between cooperating components? We decided that we could leverage the threading package we had developed for Ingres. We had rights to it at Sequent to give it to Informix.

There were a lot of reasons why it turned out to be a winner. Over the last six or seven years, threading packages that have come from operating system vendors have been different. None of them have come close to the Informix starting package in terms of scalability, robustness, and supportability because their design center is so much different than ours. That was a key decision and allowed us to have our own operating system.

That [decision] has been the reason for much of our success in systems, especially systems with a lot of users on small machines. It also gave us a good foundation to build parallel query processing from that was architecture independent.

So that was one decision that was key in the very first part of the project. The other one was that we had to come out with incremental bursts of technology every, let's say every nine months, which gave us like a six-month development cycle. I don't believe in projects that are five miles [and] five years long. They just don't work.

That shaped the way we designed versions 6, 7 and 8. We kind of did right to left scheduling based on "let's get incremental pieces of technology out there" to make the market understand that we're delivering on our promise, to gain credibility, and also give our customers little bits of this at a time.

Version 6 we decided was going to be simply multithreaded and have a new backup and restore system that had the features that mainframe people wanted. That was a tough decision and probably wouldn't make it today through our marketing department because it's not one you get a lot of glamour for. You don't get a lot of press for having incremental backups and being able to back up and restore one disk even if your database spans ten disks. We put a lot of effort into that, which our customers really appreciate, but we really get no credit for in the press.

Carlton: Right.

Gary: In the multithreading aspects of it, we only had one parallel SQL operation, which was adding an index. A lot of people liked that but it wasn't really a big bang for your buck. The real big benefit that people got was the fact that each user had a thread instead of a UNIX process on the server machine. That allowed people to run, on a given machine, maybe four or five times the number of users. The number of times is dependent on how heavy the server part of the application is.

So that was version 6. We designed [it] around those three goals: parallel index build, getting more users by virtue of the thread system on a given piece of hardware, and a new archive system.

The next key decision was whether we worked on clusters, or MPPs—cluster/MPPs—they're really kind of the same thing, or SMP hardware. And this is where we took a different approach than Oracle and Ingres really.

Ingres and Oracle in the old days were the VMS companies, and Unify and Informix were the UNIX companies. And Sybase later [was] a UNIX [company]. Because of their focus on DEC and VMS, and at that time Digital did not have SMPs—they were going with VAX clusters, those companies went with cluster approaches first and stayed away from a threading model. Informix focused on SMP machines first. So we came out with something that worked on these 4-way and 8-way SMP's which are now the predominant machine in the UNIX market.

What did we do for an SMP machine? We implemented the first version of PDQ. And that included explicitly fragmented tables, which are necessary to get parallelism and to manage large databases. This is another thing we get very little credit for, but they're absolutely necessary to manage multigigabyte databases.

We did it along the lines of what Tandem had done. Oracle still doesn't have them. They're not putting them in 'til version 8. The other aspect is PDQ, [where] we did parallel selects and parallel joins. We have many slide shows that describe that technology. The concepts like exchange, vertical, and horizontal parallelism.

Basically in that release, we wrote a lot of [the] query execution sub-system.

Carlton: And that's what, version 7?

Gary: That's version 7.

Carlton: Okay.

Gary: And it turns out that work is kind of a neverending job. There's all kinds of variants that are still going in every release for different types of queries that we didn't parallelize in the first release, but we got the bread and butter queries [in] the first release.

Version 8 is going out in multiple releases now. You know there's three or four releases that define version 8. [It] was designed to add two things; two large high-level things. One was "let's take this query technology and move it to clusters." So now we're moving to the cluster market, but not the VAX cluster market, which is very specialized hardware and software, the generic cluster market. [This] means you can plug any two boxes together, with any communication mechanism, and not have shared disks or anything fancy, and you can build yourself a larger machine. You can take 20 Dell workstations, plug them together with Ethernet, and we'll build a 20-processor database for you. We're taking the version 7 type parallel technology and moving it into loosely coupled environments. And very generic loosely coupled environments.

The second thing is once you move to loosely coupled environments, you have the opportunity to add hardware fault tolerance like Tandem did. Fail-over—if one node goes down, the other node takes over the devices and the user generally doesn't even know it happened. So fault tolerance and loosely coupled machines is version 8. And along with that, of course, there's a million other types of queries that we're handling better.

Another trend that is kind of 8+, which we really hadn't focused on until more recently, so this is sort of a new thing, is the Red Brick technology type. Bitmapped indexes and [the] handling of more complex queries than SQL databases had done in the past. And so that's new technology that's going out in our 8.2 product. So those are the major trends other than extensibility.

Carlton: It's my understanding that some of that Red Brick technology, in terms of indexing, is also supposed to come down into the 7.x DSA product,—tableless indexes, and so forth. Is that correct?

Gary: I'm not following that aspect of it. They may or may not backport all kinds of features. I don't keep abreast of that.

Carlton: When you were designing DSA, did you plan to someday accommodate nonstandard data types? I'm not saying Illustra-type technology, but did you consider that at all when you were designing the database and did that just happen to make the merge between Illustra and the DSA engine that much easier to accomplish?

Gary: Yeah, in our five-year plan that we did the first week I was here, we had [what] we called abstract data types [at] that time. Support for nonstandard access methods was on the charter.

We didn't really do much about it until a year before the Illustra purchase. At that time, we had a group up here, and in Menlo Park, both working on doing exactly what Illustra did. Stonebraker's approach was identical to ours and that's one of the things that made our executives like Illustra. "You know there's some synergy there", so buying Illustra simply bought 30 or 40 programmers that had done that part of it before. They came in and accelerated the process.

In his address to the opening session of the 1996 Informix Worldwide User Conference, and at other times, Phil White spoke about the number of potential or existing clients that had been asking for a product that was as scalable and robust as the OnLine Dynamic Server engine but had the ability to extend to new or different data types. Phil approached Mr. Stonebraker with an offer to purchase their technology that was refused.

This led to the effort Gary mentioned—to build what Phil called an "Illustra-killer." After the year's work mentioned by Gary, the timeline to continue developing the technology was too long to continue funding it, so Phil approached Mr. Stonebraker again and closed the deal.

Carlton: Hindsight is always 20/20. As you look at the DSA engine now, what in your opinion has been successful in the engine? What do you wish would have worked better, and are there any surprises, things that either worked out better than you had anticipated or didn't work out as well as you had hoped?

Gary: Let's take those things one at a time.

We tried a couple of times acquiring technology, loosely integrating it, and that basically failed. We tried buying an initial version of a data replication project and we did buy the `Onarchive` tool. Both of those things were—even though we got a product out of one of them—from my point of view, they were both a failure. The underlying system support was okay but the tool was terrible.

Buying kernel technology and trying to glue it in is a mistake, and that's what killed Sybase. Fortunately for Informix, we only tried that with sort of ancillary things.

With Illustra we really didn't buy code, we bought people, and they reimplemented probably 75 percent of what they did in the context of our engine. They utilized some of the code because, when you think of an abstract type manager, a database engine is already set up for multiple types like integer, char, date, and so it's already set up for a multiple of those. To generalize that is done in a somewhat isolated manner. It doesn't scatter throughout the code a lot. We had to do that for [the] Asian language [and the] European language.

So type management was already encapsulated in a clean subsystem so that most of the Illustra work in high-level extensibility types could go on without rippling through the engine. The low-level blades, like access methods and all that, we had already started that work and so that went kind of smoothly.

Anyway, the high-level answer is there are certain things that belong in the kernel for performance reasons. You can't buy those. The attempts that we made at buying them failed. So that was a failure.

I think some of the things that worked out better than we thought was this whole PDQ exchange paradigm, which is a dataflow mechanism. We've leveraged that. On the white board it looked like it was a great design choice to kind of encapsulate all dataflow between threads or processes in a library and then just make that library fast as hell. I really had nagging doubts in my mind that we were going to get that big of a bang out of it. [I thought] just using UNIX or something would have been as good, but we have made huge features, in short amounts of time, run fast by exchange optimizations. So that concept of encapsulating dataflow was a winner, bigger than what I thought it would be.

Probably the biggest, in terms of hindsight, [and] we knew we were doing this at the time, but the biggest challenge as we move forward now is that there's so many different types of queries and data types that the query optimizer that we have needs a—not the execution engine or the basic access methods—but the optimizer itself, is getting difficult to add new features to and to prove correct. So I guess if I had infinite resources and time I would have liked to have done a more major overhaul of the optimizer. But because we could get good functionality out, in a short period of time without doing that, we chose not to. So that's sort of a regret, but it was a good business decision.

Carlton: Do you see that overhaul happening in the future in, let's say, the 8.x product?

Gary: We're starting to do a little of it in the 8.x product, but I think a more major overhaul should be done in sort of 9.x, or not 9.x because that's really I-US, [version]10.x.

Carlton: I haven't heard anything beyond 8.

Gary: I-US started with version 7 and grew from that. So that's version 9. So I-US project version 9 and XPS are on separate code streams and development streams right now. The biggest challenge for the company now is bringing those two code streams together, and we don't want to do any major, major overhauls of the optimizer until that happens.

Carlton: Do you see that in the future, the standard database environment that companies will be running will be a combination of standard and nonstandard data types, or do you see that there will still be a significant need for an engine that is specifically tuned to handle your normal standardized data types for data warehousing purposes or just day-to-day OLTP, type environments?

Gary: Data type is kind of an overloaded term. I think a lot of people focus on high-level language issues around data types—like being able to create C++ objects and lay them down in the database transparent layer without [what] they call the "impedance mis-match" between programming languages and databases. I think that's really insignificant and will continue to be insignificant.

I think the more significant aspect is that people will be putting word processing documents, video clips, and the types of objects that people currently have scattered on desktop machines into the same database subsystem that they have their commercial data processing in. They will search and categorize those things using text search. That leads me to believe that the most important part of I-US, from my perspective, is to have a good text-search engine and a good large objects storage capability.

I think everybody will be doing that. Companies like Sarros and Documentum are building products to organize documents around that model.

The next thing that will happen is there's still three-quarters of the world's data still on paper on shelves and folders. And all that's going to start coming in, in different image forms and text forms. And that's all going to come into the system. So I think that's where the multibillion-dollar quick growth is—in new data types brought into database machines.

All of this embedded methods, being able to twirl polygons, do geospatial, that's interesting but I don't think it's nearly the same magnitude as the basic commercial types.

Carlton: It's good for the flash factor, but the bread and butter is going to be the document. As far as the life span for the OnLine Dynamic Server product is concerned, do you see it continuing up into, I guess, the merge that will occur in the 10.x space?

Gary: Yeah, I see that it will continue on. Once version 10 exists, and we have an extensible system that runs on SMPs, loosely coupled platforms, and unies all in one product, I think there is little to do in the kernel other than make it easier to use, more robust, and more highly available. That means features like hot spare replacement support, installation without bringing the system down, on-line in-place reorganization. Those types of features.

Version 10 will probably be a merger of all this stuff with a little bit of that robustness added in, and then version 11 we'll probably just be making it more robust, more available in terms of on-line in-place administrative operations, and easier to use. Then we're kind of done with the kernel because I don't see any new types of hardware architectures on the horizon. We'll still need an army of people to maintain it and make it better, but from an architectural perspective, we've got the right, major components in place.

So maybe what we can do [then] is take some of the ones that are difficult to change now, like the optimizer, and rewrite it. That helps the product be more maintainable and more extendible, from an internal perspective.

We [also] have to think about the world three, four years from now when Microsoft components will be a bigger player [with] NT. Microsoft SQL-Server will take over some percentage of the UNIX moderate-sized database market, probably a significant chunk. Informix will be well positioned at the higher end [and] be able to differentiate because of the extensibility features.

Carlton: There is the Dynamic Workgroup server, and there's also a single user version called Personal Online that works in the NT space. Do you see the same development emphasis going into those products as the UNIX versions? I mean is it fair to say that within the next couple of years that DSA on NT and DSA on UNIX—as long as that is a separate product and not absorbed into I-US—that those two product families will achieve some sort of parity?

Gary: Anything that's released on different platforms, by definition, isn't equal. Because the instant you release, there's a feature that goes in one or the other versions. But almost immediately the NT versions, both of them, will be at parity with our [UNIX] ODS.

ODS and I-US with the next release will be at parity. And NT also. On the other stream which is XPS, XPS and NT will be at parity in a couple of months.

That's one of the side-effects we got of building our own threading system, and using it, is that the NT group really doesn't have to make changes to most of the server to be successful. All they have to do is port at the threading library. That's for the kernel product. They have to do a lot of things for system administration differently, and installation and performance tuning is different, but the basic engine does not have operating system calls in it except in one library, which is our meta operating system.

That made one group from IBM [able to port] version 7 to OS/2 in a few days and they'd never seen the engine before.

The point I'm trying to make is there's no significant difference in the engine kernel between the NT version and any of the other versions. Any differences are kind of artificial because they have to release on a different schedule, or something like that.

Personal Online is just the same code with initial buffer sizes and numbers of this and that tuned down. So there's not significant development in that either.

That was our design goal at the beginning—to have a system that would grow as the need grows. We wouldn't have one system if you had a huge footprint, and another one that had a small footprint by definition. We'd have a system that started off small and as you added more threads or more data, the overhead would grow incrementally.

Carlton: Just one or two more questions. One of the big marketing things that I'm starting to hear now, at least from our sales rep, is that there is a concerted effort to turn the database environment into a no-knobs type of an environment from a tunable or an administrative—not necessarily a completely no-knobs in administrative, but to significantly reduce the amount of knobs that can be tweaked within the database engine. From your perspective, is that something that's achievable, or even desirable, and is there any sort of development effort underway to make that happen? I know in the NT space there's very little that can be done tuning-wise; you just install it and it goes.

Gary: I think that this is an area that we've been slow to move on, but there's sort of three parts to the problem. One of which is all these silly parameters that we have in our configuration file. All of those can be [completely] automated for most systems—even for large systems, with two or three high-level questions. That's being done in both our XPS administrative tool and in the NT administrative tool. So that is achievable, being worked on, and quite simple actually. It's because the underlying system is self-tuning as I mentioned before, it kind of grows as the need grows. So that's one part, the configuration file.

The second part is the physical design of your database. How do you want to break up your database across disks on a system? That's a problem that no one has solved anywhere well. Tandem and Terradata both made attempts at solving half of the problem that were reasonable. But it's a very fascinating problem that I would like to see us make a lot of progress on, and that's one of my future goals.

For example, Terradata, if you've got a terabyte database, they have one option which is kind of nice. It's no knobs, but you spread all your data across all your disks. Each table gets spread evenly across all disks that you've got. That's nice because there's no knobs, but it's not optimal. If you want to look for all the John Does, or let's say if you want to look for a range of names between M and Q, you have to search all the disks.

Carlton: Right, round-robin fragmentation.

Gary: You either use hashing, which is a little better than round-robin because they can find unique values looking at one disk, but [for] a range they have to search all disks. So, Terradata's achieved that and we now have that hashed mechanism.

I think it's nice for a lot of customers, but I think the range partitioning still adds enough value so that we need that knob there. But in order to make that knob easy to use, we need some tools to ask very high-level, simple, questions—or measure performance on a running system to try and automate the choices, or give some choices to the customer, by using tools.

So, that's the second part of it which is your data layout of a terabyte of data across disks. There's some problems to be solved there. On the other hand, there are some Terradata-like techniques for hashing which can be run with no knobs that will work for a lot of customers.

Carlton: From my perspective being a database administrator, I like the feel of being in control—that I can go in and say, "I want two CPU vps or three CPU vps;" to have that level of control over how the engine as a whole operates. The idea of just putting in the tape, hitting "install" and the thing just goes out and goes, well. . .

Gary: I think that a customer should not know what a vp or thread is and that if we need more, the database administrator should answer one question, "How much of the machine, in terms of memory and processors, do you want the database application to consume at what parts of the day?" We don't do that much yet, but we sort of do a little of that.

So you see what I'm saying, the database administrator can answer that type of question, to know how important one application is over another. It shouldn't even be the database server, it should be the database application. Like you might say that a test application group should have access to a lot of memory and a lot of processors in the evening but during the day they only have one. This is an area that I think we need to grow in dramatically—resource management and control. But I think it can be done at a much higher level than having somebody say, "I want to add a vp to this server." I think it should be "I want accounts payable to use 50 percent of the hardware on this machine," and if the users aren't getting the response time they need, I want to go in and say, "Now they should use 75 percent of the resources on the machine."

It's not just processors, it's memory, it's the priority of tasks coming into the system, it's too complex to have people turning five or six knobs, so it's got to be done at high-level. Which is what percentage of the machine, which application, and which times of the day? But I agree with you halfway, but just a little different implementation.

Carlton: One last question. Is there anything in the engine that you really would have like to have done, besides the optimizer? Is there anything that you wish you would have built into the engine that's not there now?

Gary: I guess, yeah, there are a few things and they will go into the engine eventually. The support for some of the features that STG, which is a company Informix purchased, they have precomputed aggregates and sort of multidimensional cubes and things. Support for that should be put into the engine eventually. Since access to that type of technology is mainly through tools right now, and mainly through one tool. It really doesn't matter too much right now, but in the future, access to that type of technology should be available to any query. So that's one thing that we haven't done yet.

One of our biggest wins was putting data replication into the server. There was a lot of pressure for us to use third-party products that depended on triggers, external processes, and subsystems to do that and [it was] incredibly inefficient. I think as distributed computing continues to gain momentum, distribution of copies of data will be as big a part of the performance of a server as anything else. The fact that we've built it into our threading subsystem differentiates us from Oracle and Sybase.

Carlton: Now are you talking about CDR or High-Availability Data Replication?

Gary: CDR. HADR isn't strategic in the network computing sense, it's just a high-availability option for two nodes.

Carlton: Okay. So you're saying that the product such as the Praxis OmniReplicator.

Gary: Right. The Sybase data replication things are extremely inefficient, not scalable and having that technology in the control of other companies who don't have the same performance, scalability, and robustness goals as us, would be a disaster. Now we have a relationship with Praxis for gateways to IBM and all that, and I think that's fine, but for high-volume use we gotta do it in-house. And we did it in-house. That was a win.

Carlton: Well, thank you for taking the time to speak with me.

Gary: I'd like to recognize half a dozen of the key people that were pivotal in making this thing successful.

Carlton: Certainly.
   Gary:
   There's Dave Clay from Sequent. He brought in all the parallel SMP experience that we had developed while working with other database companies. He has just been the lead get-it-done person, compromiser, wheeler-dealer. He's been on the project since day one.
   Then there's Bob Gerber who is the, in my opinion, the world's best query execution expert and totally dedicated to this project. He came from the Gamma project at the University of Wisconsin. Without both of those, without the three of us being a team, this thing wouldn't have happened. There were a lot of other wonderful, great people on this project, but the three of us com-

plemented each other's strengths and weaknesses and really made this happen.

A lot of other people came in and made huge contributions [to the engine's technology] too.

Also, a special note should go to people who influenced our early design [who] were outside of the company. Goetz Graefe-he was a Portland State University here and also part of the Gamma project. And David Dewitt, who was the guy who started all this parallelism stuff off and gave me the idea in the first place. He's professor at the University of Wisconsin.

Carlton: Is there anything else that you'd like to add or that you think would be important for people to know and understand about the engine, where it came from or where it's headed?

Gary: Oh, nothing that I can think of as a wise 30-second sound byte, but I'll think about it. I mean there's certainly a lot of things I could say, and maybe a good spokesman for—as I think about extensibility and dealing with the world of Microsoft and how it's evolving, there's a whole other hour we could spend, but it's less formed than history and would take more thought for me to just babble about it.

Carlton: Well, good. Again, thank you very much.

Index

Symbols

$INFORMIXDIR/release directory 46
.netrc file 56
.rhosts 292
/dev/null 188, 191
/etc/hosts 55
/etc/hosts.equiv 56, 292
/etc/passwd 55
/etc/rc0.d 136
/etc/rc2.d 136
/etc/services 48, 52, 229
    examples 58
    port number, defined by service class 59
    port number, requirements 53
/sbin 136
~/.rhosts 56

Numerics

4GL cursors 271
4GL functions
    fglgetret 166
    fglgets 166

A

AFF_NPROCS
    See configuration parameters AFF_NPROCS

AFF_SPROC
    See configuration parameters AFF_SPROC
alarm programs 97, 229
ALARMPROGRAM
    See configuration parameters ALARMPROGRAM
ANSI compliance 140
archive_db 363
archiving 309
    focused approach 183
    impact of BLOBs 189
    impact on instance activity 184
    information 219
    levels 185
    logical logs 187, 303
    OLAP, recommendations 186
    OLTP, recommendations 185
    strategies 46
    strategy 182
    tape device issues 189
    to /dev/null 188, 191
    to disk 192
    understanding the process 193
    whole-istic approach 184
assertion checks 311, 332
assertion failures 97

B

big buffer pool 13

BLOB
    affecting TCP/IP communication buffer size 57
    BINARY, defined 19
    defined 18
    impact on the archiving process 189
    reading and writing through shared memory 14
    replication under HADR 291
    TEXT, defined 19
    verifying existance 227
BLOBpage 120
    sizing 121
BLOBspace
    adding a chunk 122
    adding mirroring 125
    archived early 194
    differences compared to dbspaces 120
    dropping 124
    dropping a chunk 123
    dropping mirroring 126
    managing 114
    not replicated under HADR 291
Btree cleaners 210
buffer cache
    logical log 12
    physical log 12
buffer pool 12, 317
BUFFERS See configuration parameters

BUFFERS
bufwaits 91
business rules 6
    enforcing through triggers and stored procedures 157

C

cascade delete 159
checkon 135, 371
checkpoint 315
    affect on HADR 285
    conditions causing to occur 129, 316
    controlling frequency of 375
    defined 22
    during archives 194
    forcing to occur 68, 110
    interval between 90
    monitoring 373
    required before BLOBspace activation 68
    updating time stamps 195
chk_archiving 365
chk_chunks 208, 371
chk_ckpoint 373
chk_dbspaces 371
chk_logging 375
chk_table_size 377
chunk
    adding to a dbspace 122
    being dropped from dbspace 123
    changing status of 126
    cooked
        defined 19
        enlarged to size at initialization 72
        for dbspaces 41, 45
        for temporary dbspaces 79
        permissions required for use 74, 126
        to be used as mirror 125
    defined 17
    mirror, information 216
    primary, information 216
    raw

        defined 19
chunk write 317
CKPTINTVL
    See configuration parameters CKPTINTVL
CLEANERS
    See configuration parameters CLEANERS
concurrency 168
configuration parameters
    AFF_NPROCS 87
    AFF_SPROC 87
    ALARMPROGRAM 97
    BUFFERS 12, 82, 89, 212
    CKPTINTVL 90, 129, 316
    CLEANERS 80, 89
    CONSOLE 96
    DATASKIP 44, 100
        effect on queries 127
    DBSERVERALIASES 78, 289
    DBSERVERNAME 77, 289
    DBSPACETEMP 78, 117
    DEADLOCK_TIMEOUT 79, 341, 344, 351
    DRAUTO 94, 282, 286, 287, 298
    DRINTERVAL 93, 284, 287, 303
    DRLOSTFOUND 95
    DRTIMEOUT 94, 286
    DS_MAX_QUERIES 99, 272
    DS_MAX_SCANS 272
    DS_TOTAL_MEMORY 99, 272
    DUMPCNT 97
    DUMPCORE 97
    DUMPDIR 97, 98
    DUMPGCORE 97
    DUMPSHMEM 97
    FILLFACTOR 85
    HETERO_COMMIT 343
    LBU_PRESERVE 83
    LOCKS 81
        shared memory used for each 82
    LOGBUFF 81
    LOGFILES 76

    LOGSIZE 76, 131
    LOGSMAX 76, 81, 130
    LRU_MAX_DIRTY 89, 212
    LRU_MIN_DIRTY 90
    LRUS 12, 89
    LTAPEBLK 73
    LTAPEDEV 73, 184, 319
    LTAPESIZE 73, 193, 196
    LTXEHWM 84, 133, 322, 352
    LTXHWM 84, 133, 322
    MAX_PDQPRIORITY 99, 262, 271, 273
    MIRROR 72, 75
    MIRROROFFSET 75
    MIRRORPATH 72, 75
    MSGPATH 62, 96, 187, 369
    MULTIPROCESSOR 86, 88, 89, 255
    NETTYPE 91, 255
    NOAGE 88
    NUMAIOVPS 87, 256
    NUMCPUVPS 87
    OFF_RECVRY_THREADS 89, 320
    ON_RECVRY_THREADS 89
    ONDBSPACEDOWN 82, 320
    OPTCOMPIND 100, 269
    PAGE_SIZE 85
    PDQPRIORITY 98
    PHYSBUFF 81
    PHYSFILE 75
    RA_PAGES 90
    RA_THRESHOLD 91
    RESIDENT 12, 62, 79
    ROOTNAME 72, 73
    ROOTOFFSET 74
    ROOTPATH 74
    ROOTSIZE 72, 74
    SERVERNUM 77, 320
    SHEMTOTAL 85
    SHMADD 13, 80, 85
    SHMMAX 45
    SHMTOTAL 13, 100
    SHMVIRTSIZE 13, 80, 211
    SINGLE_CPU_VP 88, 39, 255
    STACKSIZE 80
    STAGEBLOB 73

TAPEBLK 72
TAPEDEV 72, 184, 192, 319
TAPESIZE 73
TXTIMEOUT 83, 341, 344, 351
USE_OS_TIME 88
USER_THREADS 91
connect SQL statement
    See SQL statement
        connect
connection options 53
    buffer size 56
    keep-alive 54, 57
    security 54
connection protocol 15, 92
connections, controlling 91
CONSOLE
    See configuration
        parameters
        CONSOLE
constraints 158, 312
    check 158
    enforces business rules 158
    fragmenting index-based 161
    function compared to indexes 160
    index-based 158
    mode
        deferred 160
        immediate 161
    object modes See violations and diagnostics
    upgrading an index 161
    vs indexes 158
context switch 248
control_chkpt_intervals 375
cooked chunks See chunk cooked
cooked files See chunk cooked
crash recovery
    responsibilities of the administrator 332
critical section
    checkpoint 316
    defined 134

D

D/B Cockpit 57
    See also oncockpit
da-RA 91
data page See page
database
    becoming 'su'
        See SQL statement set session authorization
    checking
        data and index integrity 227, 321, 322
        tables 222
    creating 142
        dbaccess 142
        dbimport 142
        SQL statements 143
    data dictionary 393, 394
    finding all in an instance 380
    managing priviledges
        See roles
    mode ANSI 170
    monitoring 213
    populating 162
        dbimport 162, 384
        dbload 164
        flat files through 4GL 166
        load 163
        onload 165
        onpload 165
    privilege maintenance 393
    reconciling tables and indexes 385
    renaming See SQL statement rename database
    viewing table and index information 394
database connection
    verification process 55
database consistency, defined 22
database design issues
    factors affecting 26
    general 25
    guide to creating the physical model 27
    third party software 27

database logging modes
    See logging modes
datadctnry.4gl 393
DATASKIP
    See configuration
        parameters
        DATASKIP
datetime 88
dbaccess
    ability to create forms 395
    database
        create 142
        log 142
    to create a database with SQL statements 143
    to create/alter tables 144
dbdiff2.shr 385
DBEDIT See environment variables $DBEDIT
dbexport 162
dbimport 111, 142, 162
    manipulating load table flag 163
dbload 164
dbpriv.uue 393
dbschema 162, 258
DBSERVERALIASES
    See configuration
        parameters
        DBSERVERALIASES
DBSERVERNAME
    See configuration
        parameters
        DBSERVERNAME
dbspace 28
    adding a chunk 122
    adding mirroring 125
    creating 118
        Informix's recommendations 44
    defined 17
    design issues 43
    dropping 124
    dropping a chunk 123
    dropping mirroring 126
    failure in 82
    finding tables created in 377
    information 216
    managing 114

mirroring 119
sizing 44
temporary 74, 78, 116
  activating 119
DBSPACETEMP
  See environment variables
    $DBSPACETEMP
DEADLOCK_TIMEOUT
  See configuration
    parameters
      DEADLOCK_TIMEOUT
Digital Alpha 8400 38
disk drive issues 32
distributed transactions 79,
  83, 321
  See global transactions
DMA 15, 20
DNS 55
do_archive 366
DRAUTO
  See configuration
    parameters
      DRAUTO
DRINTERVAL
  See configuration
    parameters
      DRINTERVAL
DRLOSTFOUND
  See configuration
    parameters
      DRLOSTFOUND
DRTIMEOUT
  See configuration
    parameters
      DRTIMEOUT
DS_MAX_QUERIES
  See configuration
    parameters
      DS_MAX_QUERIES
DS_TOTAL_MEMORY
  See configuration
    parameters
      DS_TOTAL_MEMORY
DSS See OLAP
DUMPCNT
  See configuration
    parameters
      DUMPCNT
DUMPCORE
  See configuration

parameters
  DUMPCORE
DUMPDIR
  See configuration
    parameters
      DUMPDIR
DUMPGCORE
  See configuration
    parameters
      DUMPGCORE
DUMPSHMEM
  See configuration
    parameters
      DUMPSHMEM
dynamic index joins 268

E

engine
  defined 16
Enterprise Command Center
  229
environment variables
  $AFDEBUG 331
  $DATASKIP 145
  $DBCENTURY 61
  $DBDATE 61
  $DBEDIT 61
  $DBMONEY 61
  $DBPATH 298
  $DBSPACETEMP 79, 117
  $DBUPSPACE 260
  $INFORMIXDIR 59, 61
    location of 59, 60
  $INFORMIXSERVER 60, 77,
    282, 298
    affect on sysmaster data-
      base 60
  $INFORMIXSQLHOSTS 49,
    60, 61
  $ONCONFIG 60, 62
  $ONCONFIGLOCATION 48
  $OPTCOMPIND 263, 267,
    269
  $PATH 60
  $PDQPRIORITY 262, 271,
    274
  $PSORT_DBTEMP 79
  required 59

extent
  defined 20
extent size
  initial 29, 30
  next 29, 30, 31
  of indexes 30

F

FAQ 394
fast recovery 84, 102, 108,
  135, 314
  failure 322
  logical integrity phase 320
    controlled by physical log
      321
  physical integrity phase 319
FILLFACTOR
  See configuration
    parameters
      FILLFACTOR
filtering
  See violations and
    diagnostics
find_db_names 380
foreign keys
  See keys
fragmentation 262
  alter fragment
    adding a fragment 153
    attaching tables 155
    detaching a fragment
      156
    dropping a fragment 154
    modify fragmentation ex-
      pression 153
    to defragment a table 153
    to fragment table 152
  altering
    double disk condition 152
  attaching tables 154
  benefits of 30
  by expression 30, 32, 147
    effect on data 30
    evaluating the expression
      149
    hash expressions 149
    verify expression 153
  creating differently sized
    fragments 146

DATASKIP 100
detaching fragments 155
  inherited attributes 156
dropping fragments 154
fragment growth 146
index 145
  in table 30
  partitioned 30, 32, 151
  round-robin 147
  sizing 32, 151
indexes
  partitioned 222
of index-based constraints 161
of indexes, defined 30
of tables, defined 30
remainder attribute 150
round-robin 30, 146
  adding a fragment 153
table 145
to create history tables 155

G

global transactions
  commit protocols 341
    heterogeneous commit protocol 342
    two-phase commit protocol 343
  defined 337
  See also two-phase commit protocol
  terminology
  syntax for SQL statements 340

H

HADR 93, 281, 311
  behavior of primary server 293
  behavior of the secondary server 94, 282, 287
  BLOBs 291
  changing database logging modes 291
  checkpoint activity 285
  configuring

Informix software 289
network 291
server and software 289
step by step approach 292
databases that are replicated 290
failure conditions 286, 300
failure recovery
  affected by DRAUTO 298
  general recommendations 300
  logical failures 304
  logical logs 303
  physical media failure 301
  primary failure, DRAUTO=0,1 302
  primary server, DRAUTO=2 302
  redirecting applications 298, 299
  restarting after maintenance 301
  step by step process 300
  switching servers 303
  impact on applications 305
  integrity of transactions 283, 285
keyword definitions 282
log transfer modes
  asynchronous 284
  synchronous 283
replication buffer 283, 284
replication modes 93
secondary server mode
  off 298
  retain_type 299
  reverse_type 299
hash index 78
hash joins 101, 264, 268
heuristic condition 341, 344, 350
  recovery from 357
hostname 52
html_ec.shr 394
Hultgren, Walt 398

I

I/O balancing 43, 207

idx-RA 91
IIUG 401, 417
  goals and services 404
  software library at 362, 392
independent action 352
  See also two-phase commit protocol
  terminology
index fragmentation
  See fragmentation
indexes 158
  cluster mode 227
  deleting index for constraint 161, 162
  function compared to constraints 160
  hash 268
  object modes
    See violations and diagnostics
  recommendations on dropping and recreating 261
  to enhance query performance 159
  upgrading to a constraint 161, 222
  verifying integrity 227
  vs constraints 158
Informix products
  partial installation or removal 395
Informix publications
  TechNotes 361
Informix Technical Support 95, 323
  CS Times 401
  DialUp Access and Confidentiality Agreement 329
  Follow-the-Sun 330
  goals 324
  groups
    Advanced Support 329
    911 Team 329, 352
    Front Line 328
    International Support 330
  helping them solve your problem 331

KnowledgeBase 328
support options 325
TechInfo Center 325, 400
Informix Worldwide Users
   Conference See IWUC
INFORMIXDIR See environment
   variables
   $INFORMIXDIR
informix-list
   See Internet-oriented
      programs and services
      electronic mail
INFORMIXSERVER See
   environment variables
   $INFORMIXSERVER
INFORMIXSQLHOSTS See
   environment variables
   $INFORMIXSQLHOSTS
initializing an instance 67
   building the sysmaster
      database 102
   data replication 93
   devices 71
   diagnostics 95
   PDQ 98
   shared memory 76
   step by step 70
   vps and performance 86
instance
   checking
      fast recovery 321
      page usage 225
      reserved pages 216
      tables 220
   configuration information
      216
   coordinator
      See two-phase commit
         protocol
         terminology
   creation information 216
   defined 16
   monitoring 201
      dbspaces 233
      disks and chunks 207
      general 211
      graphical utilities 228
      logical logs 235
      SQL statement 234
      user threads 205, 234

participant
   See two-phase commit
      protocol
      terminology
   reserved pages 216, 319
instance connection methods
   14, 78
instance modes 107
   changing 108
   determining 107
   off-line 108
   on-line 109
   quiescent 108, 128
   read only 109
   recovery 89, 108
   shutdown 109
   starting or stopping
      automatically 135
instance name 50
interleaving 28, 226
   table extents, defined 20
International Informix Users
   Group
   See IIUG
Internet-oriented programs
   and services 409
   accessing the Internet 410
   anonymous ftp 413
   archie 416
   electronic mail 414
   telnet 416
   understanding Internet
      addresses 411
   usenet 412
      comp.databases.infor-
         mix 398, 412
   World Wide Web 413
IPC 14
isolation levels 168, 313
   committed read 171
   cursor stability 170, 271
   default 171
   dirty read 171
   repeatable read 101, 170,
      269
IWUC 406
   general schedule of activities
      407
ixda-RA 91

J

JABOD 32

K

KAIO 88, 208
keep-alive
   See connection options
      keep-alive
kernel tuning See tuning
   kernel
keys 158
   foreign 162
   primary 162
killing a thread 134

L

LBU_PRESERVE
   See configuration
      parameters
      LBU_PRESERVE
listen thread 15
ln
   See symbolic links
      creating
lock types
   exclusive 169
   promotable 169
   shared 169, 170
LOCKS
   See configuration
      parameters
      LOCKS
locks
   duration held 169
   row level 310
LOGBUFF
   See configuration
      parameters
      LOGBUFF
LOGFILES
   See configuration
      parameters
      LOGFILES
logging modes 111, 139, 316
   affect on HADR 284
   changing 70, 291

changing between logged
    and unlogged modes 112
changing between logged
    modes 112
criteria for selecting a mode
    141
differences between logged
    and unlogged 141
mode
    buffered 318
    buffered logging 140, 187
    mode ANSI 140, 318
    no logging 140, 316
    unbuffered logging 140,
        187, 318
select statements 140
selecting from dbaccess 142
utilities to change modes
    112, 196
what happens if change is
    interrupted 113
why are they changed? 111
logical integrity
    protecting 311
logical logs
    activating for use 131
    archiving 187
    archiving modes 196
    buffers 316
    check to see if being
        archived 375
    defined 18
    dropping 131
    exclusive access to 84
    I/O handled by vps 255
    information 216
    inital number to create 76
    initial size 76
    maximum number 81
    monitoring 235
    moving or resizing 130
    open global transactions
        354
    proper sizing 133
    protecting 33
    reserving last free 83
    transfer modes under HADR
        See HADR
            log transfer modes

logs 6
    creating, moving, and
        resizing 127
LOGSIZE
    See configuration
        parameters
        LOGSIZE
LOGSMAX
    See configuration
        parameters
        LOGSMAX
long transactions
    See transaction
        long
LRU queues 12, 89, 90, 91, 212
LRU write 89, 213
LRU_MAX_DIRTY
    See configuration
        parameters
        LRU_MAX_DIRTY
LRU_MIN_DIRTY
    See configuration
        parameters
        LRU_MIN_DIRTY
LRUS See configuration
    parameters
    LRUS
LTAPEBLK
    See configuration
        parameters
        LTAPEBLK
LTAPEDEV
    See configuration
        parameters
        LTAPEDEV
LTAPESIZE
    See configuration
        parameters
        LTAPESIZE
LTXEHWM
    See configuration
        parameters
        LTXEHWM
LTXHWM
    See configuration
        parameters
        LTXHWM

M

MAX_PDQPRIORITY
    See configuration
        parameters
        MAX_PDQPRIORITY
memory pools 13
MGM 271
    gates 274
    parameters
        DS_MAX_QUERIES 272
        DS_MAX_SCANS 272
        DS_TOTAL_MEMORY 272
        MAX_PDQPRIORITY 273
MIRROR
    See configuration
        parameters
        MIRROR
mirroring 32, 43
    adding 125
    dropping 126
    establishing size of mirror 75
    problems during fast
        recovery 319
    software based 34
    using OnLine DSA utilities
        33, 39, 72, 310
        advantages 33
        disadvantages 33
MIRROROFFSET
    See configuration
        parameters
        MIRROROFFSET
MIRRORPATH
    See configuration
        parameters
        MIRRORPATH
misql.shr 395
modes, operational
    See instance modes
monitoring a database See
    database
        monitoring
monitoring an instance See
    instance
        monitoring
move_logs 96, 369
moving a database system 40
MSGPATH
    See configuration

parameters
    MSGPATH
multiple residency 49, 61, 375
MULTIPROCESSOR
    See configuration
        parameters
        MULTIPROCESSOR

N

nested-loop joins 263, 267
NETTYPE
    See configuration
        parameters
        NETTYPE
nettype word 50, 91
network service name 52, 59
    uniqueness 52
NewEra 396
NOAGE
    See configuration
        parameters
        NOAGE
NUMAIOVPS
    See configuration
        parameters
        NUMAIOVPS
NUMCPUVPS
    See configuration
        parameters
        NUMCPUVPS

O

OFF_RECVRY_THREADS
    See configuration
        parameters
        OFF_RECVRY_THREADS
off-line mode
    See instance modes
offset 74
    advantages to using 114
    disadvantages to using 115
OLAP 32, 188
    archiving
        recommendations 186
    defined 21
    using PDQ 270
OLTP 32

archiving
    recommendations 185
    defined 21
    recommendations for
        $OPTCOMPIND 268
ON_RECVRY_THREADS
    See configuration
        parameters
        ON_RECVRY_THREADS
onarchive 83, 103, 181, 220, 282
onbar 46, 182, 190
oncheck 10, 103
    -c 213
        c, 333
        D 227
        d 227, 333
        I 227, 333
        i 227
    -p 213
        c, 333
        D 227
        d 227
        e 126, 226, 333
        r 129, 195, 216, 333
        T 222
        t 222
    syntax tree 213
    what it verifies 201
oncockpit 81, 115, 228, 229
    dashboard display 232
    dbspaces display 233
    physical log display 236
    session-based metrics 229
    sessions display 234
    severity codes 230
    shared memory display 236
    syntax tree 232
onconfig file 48, 67, 216, 256, 274
ONCONFIG See environment
    variables
    $ONCONFIG
onconfig.std 48
ONCONFIGLOCATION See
    environment variables
    $ONCONFIGLOCATION
ondblog 112, 196
    to change logging modes 112

ONDBSPACEDOWN
    See configuration
        parameters
        ONDBSPACEDOWN
oninit 109
    -i 67, 110
    -p 109
    -s 109
onipcshm 52
OnLine Dynamic Server
    architectural model 8
        disk component 15
        process component 9, 249
        shared memory component 11
    what is it 5
on-line mode
    See instance modes
ONLINE_7.x 46, 79, 88
ONLINEDOC_7.x 46
OnLine-Optical 73, 80
onload 165
onlog 305, 358
onmode
    -a 110
    -c 110, 121, 316
    -D 274
    -F 80
    -k 110
    -ky 316
    -M 274
    -m 110
    -p 254, 256
    -Q 274
    -S 274
    -s 110
    to add vps 254
    to an immediate shutdown 110
    to an orderly shutdown 110
    to change MGM parameters 274
    to drop vps 256
    to force a checkpoint 110
    to kill a thread 110
    to on-line from quiescent 110
    to quiescentfrom on-line 110

-u 110, 134
-Z 134, 352, 356
-z 110, 134, 352
onmonitor 47, 49, 67
   end user access to 68
   ring menus 68
      dbspaces
         add_chunk 122
         create 119
         dataskip 127
         drop 124
         info 75
         mirror 125
         status 126
      force-ckpt 68
      logical_logs
         databases 112
      logical-logs 70
      mode
         add-proc 254
         drop-proc 256
      parameters
         add_log 130
         data replication 93
         diagnostics 95
         drop_log 132
         initialize 71
         PDQ 98
         performance 320
         physical-log 128
         shared_memory 76, 343
         vp and performance 86
onparams
   -a 130
   -d 131
   -p 128
   to add a logical log 130
   to drop a logical log 131
   to move or resize physical log 128
onperf 115, 228, 238
   graph options 239
   metric selection details screen 240
   metrics selection screen 240
   tools
      disk activity graph 242
      query component display 242, 270
      top-level graph 239

onpload 165
onprobe 57, 228, 229
   lifespan 231
   syntax tree 230
onspaces 114
   -a 122
   -b 120
   -c 119
   -D 126
   -d 124
   -f 125, 127
   -m 125
   -O 126
   -r 126
   to add a chunk 122
   to add a mirror 125
   to change DATASKIP 127
   to change status of chunks 126
   to create BLOBspace 120
   to create dbspaces 119
   to drop a chunk 124
   to drop a dbspace/BLOBspace 124
   to drop mirroring 126
onstat 10, 103, 244
   - 108
   analyzing memory dumps 97
   -C 210
   -D 208
   -d 75, 115, 208, 233, 371
   -F 90
   -g
      glo 213, 250
      iof 208
      ioq 253
      mgm 274
      seg 80, 211
      ses 135, 206
      sql 207
   -i 204
   interactive mode 204
   -k 81
   -l 81, 129, 131, 235
   -p 81, 82, 91
      B 122
   -R 212
   -r 205
   resetting values to zero 208
   -rz 205

   syntax tree 202
   to monitor MGM parameters 274
   -u 205, 270, 366
   what it monitors 201
   -x 353
   -z 208
ontape 46, 112, 181, 195, 219
   -a 121, 188, 196
   archive levels 185
   -c 188, 196
   -f 198
   handling EOT conditions 73
   new functionality 46
   -r 198
   -s 196
   tape rewinds 193
   to archive logical logs 188
   to change logging modes 112
onunload 183
OPTCOMPIND
   See configuration parameters OPTCOMPIND

P

page
   defined 16
page cleaning 89
page size
   See configuration parameters PAGE_SIZE
PAGE_1CKPT 318
PAGE_2CKPT 318
parallel processing 7
parallel scans 99
PATH
   See environment variables $PATH
PDQ 270
   See as well MGM
   statements not executed in parallel 271
PDQPRIORITY
   See configuration parameters PDQPRIORITY

PHYSBUFF
    See configuration
        parameters
        PHYSBUFF
PHYSFILE
    See configuration
        parameters
        PHYSFILE
physical integrity
    protecting 309
physical log 81
    buffers 316, 317
    controlling fast recovery 321
    defined 18
    I/O handled by vps 255
    intial size 76
    moving or resizing 128
    protecting 33
    role during archives 195
    sizing 75
presumed-abort algorithm 356
presumed-abort algorithm See
    also two-phase commit
    protocol
    technology
primary keys
    See keys
privileges
    maintaining for databases
        and users 393
process
    oninit 250
    sqlturbo 249
process affinity 87
PSORT_DBTEMP
    See environment variables
        $PSORT_DBTEMP
Publications
    other
        INX_UTIL 402
publications
    Informix
        CS Times 401
        Informix Times 401
        TechNotes 325, 399
        White Papers 400
    other
        IIUG News 409
        Informix Press 402

Q

quantum 272, 274
query optimizer 100, 148,
    159, 256, 263
    factors affecting 263
quiescent mode
    See instance modes

R

RA_PAGES
    See configuration
        parameters
        RA_PAGES
RA_THRESHOLD
    See configuration
        parameters
        RA_THRESHOLD
RAID 32
    level 0 35, 39
    level 0 + 1 37
    level 1 36, 39
    levels 5 and 6 37, 39
    software based 38, 75
        disadvantages 38
RA-pgsused 91
raw chunk See chunk
    raw
referential integrity 158
replication buffer 12
    See HADR
        replication buffer
reserved pages, instance See
    instance
    reserved pages
RESIDENT See configuration
    parameters
    RESIDENT
restore 197
    cold 197
    warm 46, 89, 184, 197, 282
roles 174
rootdbs 118, 318, 319
    defined 18
    protecting 33
ROOTNAME
    See configuration parameters
        ROOTNAME

ROOTOFFSET
    See configuration
        parameters
        ROOTOFFSET
ROOTPATH
    See configuration
        parameters
        ROOTPATH
ROOTSIZE
    See configuration
        parameters
        ROOTSIZE
rowid 30
RSAM 15
rules, ability to set 313

S

scalability 9
server alias
    See configuration
        parameters
        DBSERVERALIASES
SERVERNUM
    See configuration
        parameters
        SERVERNUM
shared memory 11
    allocated during fast
        recovery 320
    dynamic allocation 11, 13
    impact of PDQ queries 270
    maximum allocated 85
    monitoring 211, 236
    portions
        message 14
        resident 12, 82, 283
        virtual 13, 80, 85, 211
    quantums 272
SHMADD See configuration
    parameters
    SHMADD
SHMMAX
    See configuration
        parameters
        SHMMAX
SHMTOTAL See configuration
    parameters
    SHMTOTAL

SHMVIRTSIZE See
    configuration parameters
    SHMVIRTSIZE
shut-down mode
    See instance modes
SINGLE_CPU_VP
    See configuration
        parameters
        SINGLE_CPU_VP
SMI interface 103, 243
sort-merge joins 268
spin locks 86
SPL 157
SQL statement
    ! 68
    load table 163
    alter fragment 146
        adding a fragment 153
        attaching tables 155
        detaching a fragment
            156
        dropping a fragment 154
        modify fragmentation expression 153
        to defragment a table 153
        to fragment table 152
    alter table 153, 161, 380
    attach 154
    cluster 227
    connect 54
    create index 383
    deferred mode 160
    global transaction syntax
        340
    init 154
    load 163
    mod 149
    on delete cascade 159
    rename database 175
    select into temp 140
    set 174
        constraints deferred 161
        explain on 242, 264, 268
        isolation 171
        log 112, 140
        pdqpriority 272
        session authorization 175
    start violations table 172
    stop violations 174
    unload 183

update statistics
    syntax tree 257
    utility to generate script
        396
    with error 174
    with no log 117, 140
    without error 174
sqlhosts file 49, 61, 78, 92,
    229, 292
    configuration examples 57
    creating a universal file 57
STACKSIZE
    See configuration parameters
    STACKSIZE
STAGEBLOB
    See configuration
        parameters
        STAGEBLOB
start_online 136, 368
stop_online 136, 368
Stored Procedure Language
    See SPL
stored procedures 157, 312
strip_index 162, 163, 380
symbolic links
    creating 41
    importance of using 39, 290
sysmaster database 60, 74,
    102, 103, 220, 244
    creating stored procedures
        103
    using in select statements
        104
systabs.shr 394
system tables 12

T

table
    finding location of 377
table fragmentation See
    fragmentation
table placement, trial and error
    43
table size
    calculating 28
        OnLine 5.x 29, 419
        OnLine Dynamic Server
            29, 421

checking existing 377
    effected by fragmentation
        30
    with "by expression"
        fragmentation 31
    with round-robin
        fragmentation 31
tables
    creating
        dbaccess 144
        dbimport 144
tape devices 189
    ability to rewind 193
    affected by onbar 192
    remote 191
tape parameters
    changing 70
TAPEBLK
    See configuration
        parameters
        TAPEBLK
TAPEDEV
    See configuration
        parameters
        TAPEDEV
TAPESIZE
    See configuration
        parameters
        TAPESIZE
tbcheck 201
tbstat 201
temporary tables 109, 265
third party software See
    database design issues
    third party software
thread
    ability to service user
        connections 93
    in-line 92
    listen 91
    poll 91, 250
    suspended during
        checkpoint 317
thread stacks 13
time stamp 193
    updated during checkpoints
        195
transaction 111, 314
    committed 318

committed, defined 22
defined 21
long 152
   affect on global transactions 354
rolled back 84, 134, 322, 354
rolled back, defined 22
roll-forward 89, 322
transaction_size 236, 380
triggers 157, 313
trusted host communication 292
tuning
   checkpoints 90, 129
   impact of SQL statements 266
   kernel 45, 62
   logical logs 133
   misc. 86
   read and write cache 82, 291
   semaphores 45
   shared memory 79
   TCP/IP communication buffer 56
   update statistics 263
      confidence value 260
      data distributions 258, 261
      data resolutions 259, 260
      high 259, 262
      improving performance of 99
      low 257, 262
      medium 260, 262
      modes 259
      recommendations 261
      syntax tree 257
   vps 252
two-phase commit protocol
   case study
      coordinator failure 348
      heuristic end transaction 356
      heuristic rollback 354
      participant failure 351
      successful commit 347
   phase descriptions 345
   recovery from heuristic condition 357
   recovery from network failure 346
   technology 344
   terminology 343
TXTIMEOUT
   See configuration parameters TXTIMEOUT

U

uninstall.shr 395
UNIX commands
   dd 192
   kill -9 134
   ln
      See symbolic links
   ps -ef 250
   sar 254
   shar 361
   top 254
   touch 126, 192
untrusted client connection 56
upd_stat.4gl 396
update statistics
   See tuning update statistics
USE_OS_TIME
   See configuration parameters USE_OS_TIME
users groups 403
   See also IIUG

V

violations and diagnostics 172
virtual processors See vps
volume managers See RAID software based
vps 9, 45, 248
   adding 254
   ADM 250
   ADT 250
   AIO 13, 87, 208, 250, 253, 255, 319
   classes 250
   CPU 87, 92, 250, 255, 256, 270, 319
      binding to processor 87
   displaying information about 213
   dropping 256
   LIO 250, 255
   monitoring and tuning 252
      guidelines 252
   MSC 250
   NET 92
   OPT 250
   PIO 250, 255
   SHM 250
   SOC 250
   TLI 250
   to support HADR 290

W

where_are_tables 124, 226, 377
Windows NT 37

LICENSE AGREEMENT AND LIMITED WARRANTY

READ THE FOLLOWING TERMS AND CONDITIONS CAREFULLY BEFORE OPENING THIS CD-ROM PACKAGE. THIS LEGAL DOCUMENT IS AN AGREEMENT BETWEEN YOU AND PRENTICE-HALL, INC. (THE "COMPANY"). BY OPENING THIS SEALED MEDIA PACKAGE, YOU ARE AGREEING TO BE BOUND BY THESE TERMS AND CONDITIONS. IF YOU DO NOT AGREE WITH THESE TERMS AND CONDITIONS, DO NOT OPEN THE CD-ROM PACKAGE. PROMPTLY RETURN THE UNOPENED CD-ROM PACKAGE AND ALL ACCOMPANYING ITEMS TO THE PLACE YOU OBTAINED THEM FOR A FULL REFUND OF ANY SUMS YOU HAVE PAID.

1. **GRANT OF LICENSE:** In consideration of your payment of the license fee, which is part of the price you paid for this product, and your agreement to abide by the terms and conditions of this Agreement, the Company grants to you a nonexclusive right to use and display the copy of the enclosed software program (hereinafter the "SOFTWARE") on a single computer (i.e., with a single CPU) at a single location so long as you comply with the terms of this Agreement. The Company reserves all rights not expressly granted to you under this Agreement.

2. **OWNERSHIP OF SOFTWARE:** You own only the magnetic or physical media (the enclosed cd-roms) on which the SOFTWARE is recorded or fixed, but the Company retains all the rights, title, and ownership to the SOFTWARE recorded on the original media copy(ies) and all subsequent copies of the SOFTWARE, regardless of the form or media on which the original or other copies may exist. This license is not a sale of the original SOFTWARE or any copy to you.

3. **COPY RESTRICTIONS:** This SOFTWARE and the accompanying printed materials and user manual (the "Documentation") are the subject of copyright. You may not copy the Documentation or the SOFTWARE, except that you may make a single copy of the SOFTWARE for backup or archival purposes only. You may be held legally responsible for any copying or copyright infringement which is caused or encouraged by your failure to abide by the terms of this restriction.

4. **USE RESTRICTIONS:** You may not network the SOFTWARE or otherwise use it on more than one computer or computer terminal at the same time. You may physically transfer the SOFTWARE from one computer to another provided that the SOFTWARE is used on only one computer at a time. You may not distribute copies of the SOFTWARE or Documentation to others. You may not reverse engineer, disassemble, decompile, modify, adapt, translate, or create derivative works based on the SOFTWARE or the Documentation without the prior written consent of the Company.

5. **TRANSFER RESTRICTIONS:** The enclosed SOFTWARE is licensed only to you and may not be transferred to any one else without the prior written consent of the Company. Any unauthorized transfer of the SOFTWARE shall result in the immediate termination of this Agreement.

6. **TERMINATION:** This license is effective until terminated. This license will terminate automatically without notice from the Company and become null and void if you fail to comply with any provisions or limitations of this license. Upon termination, you shall destroy the Documentation and all copies of the SOFTWARE. All provisions of this Agreement as to warranties, limitation of liability, remedies or damages, and our ownership rights shall survive termination.

7. **MISCELLANEOUS:** This Agreement shall be construed in accordance with the laws of the United States of America and the State of New York and shall benefit the Company, its affiliates, and assignees.

8. **LIMITED WARRANTY AND DISCLAIMER OF WARRANTY:** The Company warrants that the SOFTWARE, when properly used in accordance with the Documentation, will operate in substantial conformity with the description of the SOFTWARE set forth in the Documentation. The Company does not warrant that the SOFTWARE will meet your requirements or that the operation of the SOFTWARE will be

uninterrupted or error-free. The Company warrants that the media on which the SOFTWARE is delivered shall be free from defects in materials and workmanship under normal use for a period of thirty (30) days from the date of your purchase. Your only remedy and the Company's only obligation under these limited warranties is, at the Company's option, return of the warranted item for a refund of any amounts paid by you or replacement of the item. Any replacement of SOFTWARE or media under the warranties shall not extend the original warranty period. The limited warranty set forth above shall not apply to any SOFTWARE which the Company determines in good faith has been subject to misuse, neglect, improper installation, repair, alteration, or damage by you. EXCEPT FOR THE EXPRESSED WARRANTIES SET FORTH ABOVE, THE COMPANY DISCLAIMS ALL WARRANTIES, EXPRESS OR IMPLIED, INCLUDING WITHOUT LIMITATION, THE IMPLIED WARRANTIES OF MERCHANTABILITY AND FITNESS FOR A PARTICULAR PURPOSE. EXCEPT FOR THE EXPRESS WARRANTY SET FORTH ABOVE, THE COMPANY DOES NOT WARRANT, GUARANTEE, OR MAKE ANY REPRESENTATION REGARDING THE USE OR THE RESULTS OF THE USE OF THE SOFTWARE IN TERMS OF ITS CORRECTNESS, ACCURACY, RELIABILITY, CURRENTNESS, OR OTHERWISE.

IN NO EVENT, SHALL THE COMPANY OR ITS EMPLOYEES, AGENTS, SUPPLIERS, OR CONTRACTORS BE LIABLE FOR ANY INCIDENTAL, INDIRECT, SPECIAL, OR CONSEQUENTIAL DAMAGES ARISING OUT OF OR IN CONNECTION WITH THE LICENSE GRANTED UNDER THIS AGREEMENT, OR FOR LOSS OF USE, LOSS OF DATA, LOSS OF INCOME OR PROFIT, OR OTHER LOSSES, SUSTAINED AS A RESULT OF INJURY TO ANY PERSON, OR LOSS OF OR DAMAGE TO PROPERTY, OR CLAIMS OF THIRD PARTIES, EVEN IF THE COMPANY OR AN AUTHORIZED REPRESENTATIVE OF THE COMPANY HAS BEEN ADVISED OF THE POSSIBILITY OF SUCH DAMAGES. IN NO EVENT SHALL LIABILITY OF THE COMPANY FOR DAMAGES WITH RESPECT TO THE SOFTWARE EXCEED THE AMOUNTS ACTUALLY PAID BY YOU, IF ANY, FOR THE SOFTWARE.

SOME JURISDICTIONS DO NOT ALLOW THE LIMITATION OF IMPLIED WARRANTIES OR LIABILITY FOR INCIDENTAL, INDIRECT, SPECIAL, OR CONSEQUENTIAL DAMAGES, SO THE ABOVE LIMITATIONS MAY NOT ALWAYS APPLY. THE WARRANTIES IN THIS AGREEMENT GIVE YOU SPECIFIC LEGAL RIGHTS AND YOU MAY ALSO HAVE OTHER RIGHTS WHICH VARY IN ACCORDANCE WITH LOCAL LAW.

ACKNOWLEDGMENT

YOU ACKNOWLEDGE THAT YOU HAVE READ THIS AGREEMENT, UNDERSTAND IT, AND AGREE TO BE BOUND BY ITS TERMS AND CONDITIONS. YOU ALSO AGREE THAT THIS AGREEMENT IS THE COMPLETE AND EXCLUSIVE STATEMENT OF THE AGREEMENT BETWEEN YOU AND THE COMPANY AND SUPERSEDES ALL PROPOSALS OR PRIOR AGREEMENTS, ORAL, OR WRITTEN, AND ANY OTHER COMMUNICATIONS BETWEEN YOU AND THE COMPANY OR ANY REPRESENTATIVE OF THE COMPANY RELATING TO THE SUBJECT MATTER OF THIS AGREEMENT.

Should you have any questions concerning this Agreement or if you wish to contact the Company for any reason, please contact in writing at the address below or call the at the telephone number provided.

PTR Customer Service
Prentice Hall PTR
One Lake Street
Upper Saddle River, New Jersey 07458

Telephone: 201-236-7105

REAL Books by REAL Authors for REAL Professionals

FROM PRENTICE HALL PTR

NEW!
INFORMIX-OnLine Dynamic Server Handbook
Carlton Doe

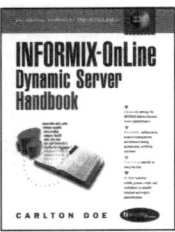

Hands-on information that will help INFORMIX-OnLine Dynamic Server administrators get their job done as effectively as possible. This book transforms the dry technical details of Informix documentation into practical, hands-on techniques and ideas for effective administration. It serves the needs of both DBAs and administrators responsible for multiple database environments. This book covers the entire process of starting up and running an INFORMIX-OnLine Dynamic Server database environment, including preparing for initialization; initializing an OnLine Dynamic Server instance; building a database environment; archiving and restoring; monitoring and optimization. It reviews issues related to high availability and distributed transaction environments. There is cogent, careful coverage of how to recover from a crash. The accompanying CD-ROM's extensive library of scripts can save you hundreds of hours by automating many essential administration tasks.

1997, 496pp., paper, 0-13-605296-7
A Book/CD-ROM Package

Informix Performance Tuning, Second Edition
Elizabeth Suto

Maximize the performance of your INFORMIX-OnLine System. This insider's guide to Informix performance has been completely updated to reflect all recent releases of INFORMIX-OnLine, INFORMIX-OnLine Dynamic Server and INFORMIX XMP. No matter which release you're running, this book will walk you through all the performance-related issues you need to understand, including: query optimization, database design, disk layout, memory utilization, and processor usage.

1997, 192 pp., cloth, 0-13-239237-2

NEW!
JDBC Developer's Resource
Art Taylor

JDBC allows developers to create Java applications which fully leverage their existing corporate database resources. This book is the first comprehensive tutorial and reference for learning and using JDBC. The author begins by introducing the JDBC standard and its relationship to ODBC; then shows how JDBC can be used to enable a wide variety of applications. It shows how JDBC provides for enhanced security, through techniques such as trusted applets. There is detailed coverage of Java database access application design, including both two-tiered and three-tiered applications. Techniques for using JDBC are also covered. An extensive tutorial section walks developers through every step of developing three sample applications, demonstrating most of the techniques developers will need, including how to implement multithreading support, register drivers, and execute SQL statements. The book also contains listings of every JDBC class method, with usage examples and tips. All code appears on the accompanying CD-ROM — along with the exciting new Mojo rapid application development environment for Java, and JDBC/ODBC drivers from Visigenic — everything a developer needs to build database-enabled Java applications.

1997, 752pp., paper, 0-13-842352-0
A Book/CD-ROM Package

Informix Stored Procedure Programming
Michael L. Gonzales

Informix stored procedures, which can be used to dramatically improve the performance of SQL code, tighten security, reduce maintenance of permissions, and maximize data integrity, are often difficult to understand. This book offers numerous examples and illustrations that show how stored procedures can be used to optimize code while improving security and data integrity. Also included is a comprehensive SPL syntax reference, as well as more than 20 stored procedures that can be used or adapted as needed.

1996, 200 pp., paper, 0-13-206723-4

INFORMIX Press

Evolution of the High Performance Database
Informix Software

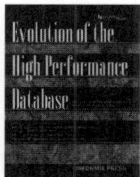
Industry technologists preview tomorrow's high-performance database solutions. Evolution of the High Performance Database is an up-to-the-minute guide to the most exciting trends in database technology, and how they'll impact you and your organization. In this book, the industry's premier technologists walk you through today's most revolutionary database developments: Databases on the Web, Data Warehousing, and Object Relational DBMSs.

1997, 432 pp., cloth, 0-13-594730-8

Optimizing Informix Applications
Robert Schneider

Developers and administrators can now improve Informix application and systems performance and increase productivity and system quality with this new title. The book offers detailed tips and shows how to set up an optimization test environment, indexing strategies, and using the Informix optimizer effectively. Also offers a variety of real-world case studies.

1995, 300 pp., paper, 0-13-149238-1

INFORMIX-New Era:
A Guide for Application Developers
Art Taylor and Tony Lacy-Thompson
1996, 300 pp., Paper, 0-13-209248-4

The Informix Database Administrator's Survival Guide
Joe Lumbley • 1995, 320pp., Paper, 0-13-124314-4

Programming INFORMIX-SQL/4GL:
A Step-By-Step Approach
Cathy Kipp • 1995, 500pp., Paper, 0-13-149394-9

Advanced INFORMIX-4GL Programming
Art Taylor • 1995, 400pp., Paper, 0-13-301318-9

ALSO AVAILABLE:
Selected Documentation from Informix Software, Inc.

▲ INFORMIX-4GL By Example
▲ Informix Guide to SQL: Reference
▲ Informix Guide to SQL: Tutorial

 These and all Prentice Hall PTR titles are available at local Magnet Stores throughout the world. To locate the store nearest you, visit us at: **http://www.prenhall.com**

PRENTICE HALL PTR WORLDWIDE ORDERING INFORMATION

DIRECT FROM THE PUBLISHER (USA)

Single Copy Sales
Visa, Master Card, American Express, Checks, Money or Orders only

Tel: 515-284-6761
Fax: 515-284-2607
Toll-Free: 800-288-4745

Government Agencies
Prentice Hall
Customer Service
Toll-Free: 800-922-0579

College Professors
Desk or Review Copies
Toll-Free: 800-526-0485

Corporate Accounts
Quantity, Bulk Orders totaling 10 or more books. Purchase orders only — No credit cards.

Tel: 201-236-7156
Fax: 201-236-7141
Toll-Free: 800-382-3419

INTERNATIONAL INQUIRIES

Canada
Prentice Hall Canada, Inc.
Tel: 416-293-3621
Toll-Free: 800-263-6051 (Outside Toronto)
Fax: 416-299-2529
     416-293-5646

UK, Europe, and Africa
Simon & Schuster Int'l, Ltd.
Tel: 881900
Fax: 882277
Country Code: 441
Area/City Code: 442

Asia
Simon & Schuster (Asia) PTE., Ltd.
Tel: 278-9611

Fax: 378-0370 / 476-4688
Country Code: 65
Area/City Code: None

Australia/New Zealand
Prentice Hall of Australia, PTY, Ltd.
Tel: 939-1333
Fax: 939-6826
Country Code: 61
Area/City Code: 2

India
Prentice Hall of India, Private, Ltd.
Tel: 332-9078 / 332-2779
Fax: 371-7179
Country Code: 91
Area/City Code: 11

Latin America, Mexico, the Caribbean, Japan
Plus all other countries not mentioned above. International Customer Service, Old Tappan, NJ USA
Tel: 201-767-4900

Latin America/Mexico
Tel: 201-767-4991

Caribbean
Tel: 201-767-4992

Japan
Tel: 201-767-4990

All Others
Fax: 201-767-5625

plug into
Prentice Hall PTR Online!

Thank you for purchasing this Prentice Hall PTR book. As a professional, we know that having information about the latest technology at your fingertips is essential. Keep up-to-date about Prentice Hall PTR on the World Wide Web.

Visit the Prentice Hall PTR Web page at
http://www.prenhall.com/divisions/ptr/
and get the latest information about:

- New Books, Software & Features of the Month
- New Book and Series Home Pages
- Stores that Sell Our Books
- Author Events and Trade Shows

join prentice hall ptr's new internet mailing lists!

Each month, subscribers to our mailing lists receive two e-mail messages highlighting recent releases, author events, new content on the Prentice Hall PTR web site, and where to meet us at professional meetings. Join one, a few, *or all* of our mailing lists in targeted subject areas in Computers and Engineering.

Visit the Mailroom at http://www.prenhall.com/mail_lists/
to subscribe to our mailing lists in...

COMPUTER SCIENCE:	ENGINEERING:
Programming and Methodologies	Electrical Engineering
Communications	Chemical and Environmental Engineering
Operating Systems	Mechanical and Civil Engineering
Database Technologies	Industrial Engineering and Quality

get connected with prentice hall ptr online!